W9-AMQ-758

UNDERSTANDING THE JOURNEY

A PARENT'S GUIDE TO DIPG

EDITED BY
RUTH I. HOFFMAN, MPH

UNDERSTANDING THE JOURNEY: A PARENT'S GUIDE TO DIPG

Edited by Ruth I. Hoffman, MPH
Copyright © 2012 by American Childhood Cancer Organization® (ACCO)
Printed in the United States of America

Published by American Childhood Cancer Organization®

Cover and Interior Design: Ruth I. Hoffman MPH

Interior Layout: Ruth I. Hoffman, MPH, Devon Harp

Printing History: May 2012

ISBN 978-0-9854593-0-7

Library of Congress Control Number: 2012908135

The American Childhood Cancer Organization's® name and logo are registered trademarks of the national office of the American Childhood Cancer Organization®. Visit us on the web at: http://www.acco.org.

This book is written to provide information about childhood cancer and should not be used as an alternative to receiving professional advice. Every effort has been made to ensure that the information in this book is accurate at the time of printing, however, there is no guarantee that the information will remain current over time. Always seek the advice of a trained professional.

With the support of

Dedicated to all of the children who have battled or will battle DIPG, and to Andrew Smith—for the impact you left on my life.

"It is only in the darkness, we can see the brightest stars."
Martin Luther King Jr.

Table of Contents

Part IV. Research

Part V. End of Life Decisions

Part VI. Appendices

Preface

The American Childhood Cancer Organization's (ACCO) mission is to provide information and support for children and adolescents with cancer and their families; to provide grassroots leadership through advocacy and awareness; and to support research leading to a cure for all children diagnosed with this life-threatening disease.

Since ACCO's founding in 1970, clinical research has increased the five-year survival rate of childhood cancer in the U.S. to approximately 80 percent. This improvement in survival brings hope to tens of thousands of families whose children are treated for cancer each year. In spite of the progress, however, too many families still endure the loss of their precious son or daughter to cancer. In the U.S. cancer continues to be the primary cause of death by disease in childhood. As a result, families whose children are currently fighting this disease need access to information to help them with the many treatment decisions they must make; and there is an acute need for an increase in pediatric oncology research funding that will lead to the development of new treatments for children diagnosed with cancer in the future.

Among the many devastating childhood cancers, children who are diagnosed with diffuse intrinsic pontine glioma (DIPG) desperately need access to new treatments. Regarded as *the* most aggressive of all pediatric brain tumors, all of these children face a dismal prognosis. Currently, radiation therapy offers a short reprieve from a ravaging disease. The tragedy of this disease is best expressed in the following words from one parent's writing about her precious daughter.

> "Imagine that you had a cherubic, mischievous, energetic and moody two year old with flashing blue eyes, a brilliant smile and curly red hair. Imagine that each morning she got you up at 5:15 a.m. by standing up in her crib and shouting, "Maaamaaa, I'm awaaaake! Maaamaaa, where are you?" Imagine if when you went into her room she threw both her arms up towards you in a great big hug and chattered her way into the living room, telling you she wanted Cheerios for breakfast…with banana…and milk…and can we paint now…and watch Caillou. Imagine if when you tried to get her dressed

in the morning, she ran away from you laughing, no matter how exasperated you got. Imagine if she insisted on picking out her own clothes, and you let her, rather than fight about it. Imagine if she could sing the entire theme song to "Golden Girls," could go down the slide on her own, could pee on the potty, catch a ball, dance and chase her friends. Imagine when you step off the subway after work and walk into her daycare room, all the kids turn to look at who has entered the room, and when she sees you she flashes the most brilliant smile and comes running with her arms up, saying "Mama! Mama! Mama!" Imagine if no matter how many times she had a tantrum and demanded things from you and exhausted you, she ended each night with a snuggle and a kiss and you breathed in the smell of her curls and felt warm happiness all over. Imagine if you could never love anything as much as you loved your first born child, your dream come true, your daughter.

Now imagine it is 9 months later. Imagine she is lying next to you in your bed. She can't walk. She can't use her arms or hands. She can't hold her head up. She can't see the television. She can't tell you she loves you. She can't hug you. She is lying in the bed sound asleep, but coughing on her own saliva, which she is starting to choke on because she can barely swallow. Imagine she was dying and there was nothing you could do to change it. Imagine if you knew that one day soon you would never get to see her again. Never see her smile, feel her hand slip into yours, kiss her warm cheek, feel her sigh into your chest.

That is the simple reality of what we are living with. And it's hard. No matter how many good things happen to us, no matter how much we believe in a bright future for ourselves and a time of healing, we are being tortured. No matter how well or easily we manage to get through the days, to talk with our friends, to laugh and joke and even fight sometimes, we are broken inside. It's a very strange way to live. We need to not focus only on what we are losing, but on all we have gained, but despair creeps in nonetheless.

What is keeping us moving forward right now, even when our hearts are completely broken, is watching how our daughter has chosen to live her short life. How she treats each day as a new adventure; pushes herself both physically and mentally to ensure that she accomplishes what she wants on that particular day. Sometimes it's something big—painting with her mouth and visiting the pigs at the farm. And sometimes it's just being able to mouth the words "ice cream," and then napping most of the day. But she is always true to herself, and even though things are hard for her, she ignores the barriers of DIPG and chooses to forge her own path. Most importantly, she believes that when life gives you a hundred reasons to cry, you need to find a thousand reasons to smile…And in my own smiles, I have become familiar with the bittersweet taste of getting to parent my precious daughter—the best experience in the world, but like a spring day that is much, much, too short."

As this parent so eloquently states, having a child diagnosed with DIPG is the most difficult journey that any parent will ever endure. This book was written to help parents understand that journey so that they are better equipped to make decisions regarding their child's diagnosis, treatment, entry into clinical trials, palliative care and quality of life during this critical time. It was also written to provide hope for a future when children diagnosed with DIPG will be cured of their disease and able to live long and healthy lives.

The Contributors

In November 2009, I was introduced to Andrew Smith—a magical young boy who was battling DIPG. He was hospitalized at the National Institutes of Health (NIH) in Bethesda, Maryland, where he and his family were making a decision regarding his participation in a clinical trial. It was Thanksgiving, and through Andrew's determination to communicate and the communication skills of his parents with the "yes/no" questioning technique, we learned that the hospital menu did not include pumpkin pie—a "must have" item during the holiday season. We also learned that Andrew (who was a "foodie") would love not just a piece of pumpkin pie, but an entire pie! I was blessed with making that for Andrew, and also blessed with his life and the personal introduction to DIPG.

Around the same time, Loice Swisher—a friend and fellow childhood cancer advocate—informed me of the need for a book that parents could turn to that would assist them with their understanding of the disease and the treatment decisions they needed to make on behalf of their children. We worked up a draft of potential chapters and authors and thus began the "journey" of this book. Our hope was to provide essential information from the diagnosis of DIPG through to the end of life. Clinicians and scientists who were researching and/or treating children with DIPG were asked to volunteer their time and expertise in the writing of this much needed resource. Every expert who was asked agreed to participate—each contributing a chapter that detailed their DIPG research and/or their clinical specialty.

To add a perspective from the 'trenches,' each chapter (with the exception of the research chapters), is followed by personal stories written by parents. These sections entitled "Parent Perspectives" illustrate the despair and the hope that accompany the DIPG experience. As with all hardships, those individuals who have endured life's burdens become experts in their personal journeys. Like the professionals who are researching and treating our nation's children with brainstem glioma, parents of children with DIPG also became experts in knowing how to provide the best of care for their children.

I am deeply indebted to the following professionals who gave of their time and expertise to author comprehensive chapters for this book. My deepest gratitude is extended to: Violette Renard Recinos, MD, George I. Jallo, MD, Eric H. Raabe, MD, PhD, Kenneth Cohen, MD, MBA, Sven Hochheimer, MD, Javad Nazarian, PhD, Suresh N. Magge, MD, Jonathan Finlay, MD, Girish Dhall, MD, John Grimm, MD, Stefan Bluml, PhD, Adam Cohen, MS, MD, Howard Colman, MD, PhD, Michael H. Handler, MD, Arthur Liu, MD, PhD, Roger J. Packer, MD, David N. Korones, MD, Eric Bouffet, MD, Ute Bartels, MD, Deborah Lafond, DNP, PNP-BC, CPON, CHPPN, David Brownstone, MSW, RSW, Caelyn Kaise, MHSc, SLP (C), Reg. CASLPO, Ceilidh Eaton Russell, CCLS, MSc (candidate), Patricia Baxter, MD, Susan Blaney, MD, Mark W. Kieran, MD, PhD, Oren J. Becher, MD, Michelle Monje, MD, PhD, Zhiping Zhou, MD, PhD, Mark M. Souweidane, MD, Christopher Moertel, MD, Cynthia Hawkins, MD, PhD, Angela Punnett, MD, FRCPC, Justin N. Baker, MD, FAAP, AAHPM, Adam J. Tyson, MD, Javier R. Kane, MD, Tammy I. Kang, MD, MSCE, and Chris Feudtner, MD, PhD, MPH.

My thanks would not be complete without expressing my deepest appreciation to all of the parents who took their time to write and share their children's personal stories. There are 164 writings by parents in this book. These stories give credibility and passion to the book and emphasize why the book is so critically needed. These stories also serve as a reminder that these are the precious lives of children who just want to grow up.

The words "Thank you," cannot adequately express my gratitude for the time that Sandy Smith spent pulling together the parent stories. Sandy is a woman who has turned her own grief, from losing her son to DIPG, into generously giving of herself to help DIPG families navigate their journeys. She makes herself available—whether it's to assist a family as they are starting down this path, or to facilitate tissue donation at the end of life. She makes herself available as a trusted patient navigator and friend. As a result of working together on this book, I too am proud to be able to call Sandy a very dear friend. I also want to personally thank Kim Spady, Jonathan Agin and Nettie Boivin for the time they spent reviewing parent stories, providing personal insight into the DIPG journey, and for answering my emails day or night during the final production phase of this book. Your generosity of time and wisdom are appreciated more than you will ever know.

My heartfelt appreciation is extended to Dr. Andrew von Eschenbach for the thoughtful and compassionate words that he provided for the back cover copy of this book. I am forever grateful for his commitment to childhood cancer research and the role that he played during his term as Director of the NCI to provide funding for TARGET—an initiative that utilizes genomic technologies to identify therapeutic targets in childhood cancers (http://target.cancer.gov). His belief that increasing efforts to target and control cancer by modulating and altering the behavior of the disease on a molecular level directly resulted in the funding of this innovative childhood cancer research project.

I am personally grateful to Dr. Peter Adamson, Chair of the Children's Oncology Group, for also contributing to the back cover copy text of this book. Dr. Adamson's dedication to children with cancer as a clinician, and his strong leadership as chair of the world's largest pediatric oncology clinical trial research group, is inspirational.

Finally, I wish to thank Ryan and Maria Reilly for sharing the picture of their precious son Liam which graces the cover of this book. Liam responded to radiation and was given the "gift of a honeymoon period." His "bucket list" during that brief time included visiting the special place where this photo was taken. By sharing Liam in this way, Ryan and Maria have personalized the disease for many, and are building awareness of DIPG as a result. Thanks as well to Marie-Dominique Verdier of Sand Point Photography for her help with enhancing and cropping the photo for the book cover. My sincere gratitude is also extended to ACCO board member Nicole Roman for suggesting the title of the book as a result of her daughter Sophia's childhood cancer journey.

Book Composition

This book is written for both parents of children diagnosed with DIPG, as well as health care providers. Chapters are written independently so parents and providers are encouraged to read those chapters that most directly apply to a child's current medical needs. For example, parents with a newly diagnosed child might want to start with chapter 10: The Use of Steroids in Patients with DIPG. Others might want to read the book from start to finish.

The book is divided into six major sections. **Part I: Understanding the Diagnosis** provides an overview of diffuse intrinsic pontine glioma including the diagnosis and typical history, pontine anatomy and function, and DIPG imaging.

Part II: Treatment outlines treatment related issues including clinical trial design, surgery, radiation, radiosensitizers to treat DIPG, chemotherapy and biologics, as well as the use of steroids.

Part III: Other Care Issues identifies additional treatment concerns including caring for your child at home, and provides information to assist with communication when a child can no longer speak.

Part IV: Research provides an overview of the hurdles to DIPG research, as well as the hope found through genomic and proteomic techniques, animal model research, neural stem cell research, convection-enhanced delivery, and vaccine treatment strategies for DIPG.

Part V: End of Life Decisions addresses the difficult questions that families face as they come to the end of life stage. These include autopsy tissue donation, organ and tissue donation, as well as integrating palliative care while making difficult decisions. The book concludes with a letter of hope written by two physicians to families of children with DIPG.

Finally, there are four useful appendices at the end of the book.

- **Appendix A** includes a sample medications form.

- **Appendix B** provides a glossary of medical and research terms used throughout the book.

- **Appendix C** lists a sampling of resources—books, websites, listservs, and organizations that assist families of children with DIPG.

- **Appendix D** is a compilation of journal articles that provides further reading opportunities for those wishing to dig deeper into a specific topic.

Acknowledgements

This book would not have been possible without financial support. I am indebted to **Mr. and Mrs. A. James Clark, and Courtney Clark Pastrick of the Clark**

Charitable Foundation for their generous donation that made the printing of this book possible. Their commitment to making a difference in the lives of children is inspirational. They are true heroes to children with cancer.

My heartfelt thanks to **Joseph E. Robert, Jr.** and **The Team Julian Foundation**, founded by his family in loving memory of courageous Julian B. Boivin, for their financial support to cover additional expenses related to the distribution of the book to families.

Finally, I am deeply grateful to **Christine Martin** for her financial support from the **Just One More Day Foundation**, which she started to honor the memory of her daughter Alicia. Through her generosity, parents of children diagnosed with DIPG will have access to information that will provide them with an understanding of this difficult journey and assist them with the decisions they must make.

I come away from this book with a renewed burden for our nation's children with cancer and their families. It is not good enough that 80 percent of America's children with cancer survive. It is not acceptable that children diagnosed with DIPG don't grow up to live out their dreams. We must never tire of the need to increase awareness of the impact of childhood cancer in the United States. As parents of children with cancer, and their advocates, we must continue to let our voices be heard. We must continue to knock on politicians' doors and insist that research for childhood cancer receive priority funding. We must continue to do our part to raise funds to build programs that help children being treated for cancer today, as well as research funds that will help children diagnosed with cancer tomorrow. We must continue to work together in the belief that doing so is the only way to make a difference, and doing less is simply not good enough.

Ruth I. Hoffman, MPH
Executive Director, Editor
American Childhood Cancer Organization

"If there ever comes a day when we can't be together, keep me in your heart, I'll stay there forever."
Winnie the Pooh

Chapter 1

Brain Tumors 101

Violette Renard Recinos, MD
George I. Jallo, MD

Brain tumors are the most common solid tumor found in the pediatric population. Each year, approximately 3,400 children are diagnosed with a primary tumor of the central nervous system (CNS)—comprising the brain and spinal cord. While all primary brain tumors arise from cells originating in the brain, these CNS tumors can differ significantly with regards to location, cell origin and pathology, clinical manifestations, prognosis, and treatment options. Some of these tumors may exhibit a slow benign (noncancerous) growth pattern, while others are more aggressive and classified as malignant or cancerous. Due to the sensitive, important structures of the CNS, even a benign tumor may cause significant clinical symptoms if located in or near critical brain or spine structures. Similarly, surgical access to these so-called "benign" brain tumors can be limited or dangerous, making the tumor inoperable and thus the potential to act as a more malignant lesion over time.

Advances in imaging with computed tomography (CT) and magnetic resolution imaging (MRI) allow clinicians to better visualize the mass and determine key characteristics that may help differentiate one tumor from another. By evaluating the tumor size and shape, identifying its location and effect on adjacent structures, and examining patterns of contrast enhancement (a substance that enhances the contrast of body structures on medical imaging), clinicians may be able to diagnose the tumor with imaging alone. Sometimes further studies, such as blood work or cerebrospinal fluid (CSF) analysis by lumbar puncture—also called a spinal tap—can also help with the diagnosis. When feasible, direct histological evaluation by either biopsy or tumor resection is the gold standard in diagnosing the specific tumor type. Often, however, the imaging, together with clinical presentation and a laboratory workup, can help clinicians formulate the best suitable treatment option for the patient.

Treatment of brain tumors can vary widely

Dr. Recinos is a Pediatric Neurosurgeon at the Cleveland Clinic Foundation, Cleveland, OH.

and may include close clinical observation with interval imaging, surgical resection, chemotherapy, radiation, or a combination of these modalities. The exact combination of therapies will depend upon the expected behavior of the tumor, and clinicians will need to carefully weigh the risks and benefits of the treatments. Pediatric tumors and their treatment differ from their adult counterparts, especially as long-term effects from chemotherapy and radiation have a greater impact on the developing CNS of a child.

Epidemiology of Brain Tumors

Brain tumors are the leading cause of cancer death in the pediatric population. They are the second most common malignancy in children behind leukemia, and the most common solid tumor found in the pediatric population. According to the 2009 statistical report of the Central Brain Tumor Registry of the United States, 7% of all reported brain tumors are found in patients younger than 20 years of age. The overall incidence of brain tumors found in the age group comprising 0–19 year olds is 4.58 per 100,000 individuals. Overall, there is a slight male predominance in pediatric brain tumors, however, depending on the individual histology, certain tumor subtypes are found more frequently in females. Brain tumors are also more common in whites than blacks. The age distribution varies depending upon the specific tumor, with certain tumors such as pilocytic astrocytomas, malignant gliomas, and medulloblastomas more common in the younger pediatric population of 0–14 year olds, while germ cell tumors are more common in 15–19 year old age group.

The majority of pediatric tumors are located in the cerebral hemispheres, mainly within the frontal, parietal, temporal, or occipital lobes, overall making up 24% of brain tumors. Sixteen percent of tumors are found in the cerebellum, 12% in the brainstem, 6% within the ventricles, 11.6% in the pituitary, and 3.2% in the pineal region. The remaining less common sites include the meninges, the cranial nerves, the spinal cord, and other brain areas.

Brain Tumor Histology and Classification

There are more than 120 different classifications of tumors, most of which are classified by the cell type from which they arise. A better understanding of this classification system can be gained through a brief review of the cells that comprise the central nervous system and its coverings.

As a very general overview, the majority

Dr. Jallo is a Professor of Neurosurgery, Oncology, and Pediatrics at the Johns Hopkins Children's Center, Baltimore, MD.

of CNS cells can be divided into two groups: neurons, which are cells that send and receive electrochemical stimulation to and from the brain and spinal cord, and glial cells, the cells that support neurons. There are many different types of neurons found throughout the brain which carry a variety of signals depending on their function and location. Unlike many other cells in the body, neurons, do not regenerate after damage, although there have been notable exceptions to this rule. Glial cells are far more plentiful than neurons, making up about 90% of brain cells. These cells are further specialized to provide specific functions to support the neuronal tissue. Some glial cells function to provide structural or nutritional support, while others help to insulate the neurons, provide defense against pathogens, and clean up cellular debris. The most common glial cells are astrocytes, oligodendrocytes, Schwann cells, microglia, and ependymal cells. Covering the brain and spinal cord is a membrane called the meninges, comprised of meningothelial cells. Tumors may arise from any of these subtypes and thus be named according to their cells of origin. Hence, the terms astrocytoma, oligodendroglioma, ependymoma, etc. may sound familiar. You may frequently hear of tumors referred to as gliomas, or glial tumors. These are generally referring to tumors arising from astrocytes as these are most commonly the cell of origin.

The World Health Organization (WHO) has categorized gliomas into four classifications based on tumor aggressiveness and malignancy. WHO grade I tumors are low-grade lesions that are non-infiltrating and have well-defined borders. These tumors can be cured if in a location amenable to surgical resection. They are slow growing and may remain inactive, even if they are not completely excised. Examples of WHO grade I tumors include pilocytic astrocytomas and pleomorphic xanthoastrocytomas. WHO grade II tumors are more infiltrative. These tumors tend to invade normal tissue, making complete surgical resection more challenging than WHO grade I lesions, especially if the tumors are located in critical brain structures. These tumors tend to be slower growing than the higher-grade lesions, but they may evolve into WHO grade III or IV lesions over time. Examples of WHO grade II lesions are oligodendrogliomas and low-grade astrocytomas. WHO grade III tumors are known as anaplastic astrocytomas. They are considered malignant because they are infiltrating, fast growing, and often require treatment with surgical resection, chemotherapy, and radiation. Grade IV lesions, also known as glioblastoma multiforme (GBM), are even more aggressive than anaplastic astrocytomas and may grow so rapidly that they outgrow their blood supply and cause tumor necrosis. GBMs are malignant lesions with poor prognosis regardless of the treatment (e.g., surgery, radiation, and chemotherapy).

Another cell type to note is the "embryonal" cell. In development, the neurons and glial cells are thought to derive from a common progenitor cell that differentiates at different stages depending on certain genetic signaling and other local factors. Several tumors in the pediatric population have features that resemble this more primitive "embryonal" cell. These tumors can be very undifferentiated or they can contain certain features that place them into a more specific category depending on cytoarchitecture or immunohistochemical staining. Included in this group are tumors such as medulloblastomas, primitive neuroectodermal tumors (PNET), and atypical teratoid/rhabdoid tumors (ATRT).

Germ cell tumors are another group of tumors requiring special note. As with embryonic tumors, germ cell tumors arise from cells that are not commonly found in the adult brain. These tumors originate from cells in the developing embryo's yolk sac endoderm that migrate throughout the embryo. They frequently are found in the pineal and suprasellar/pituitary region, as well as the third ventricle and posterior fossa. Germinomas are the most common germ cell tumors in the pediatric population.

Classification of Brainstem Gliomas

Overall, the most common brain tumors found in the pediatric population are pilocytic astrocytomas, malignant gliomas, and medulloblastomas. Within the glioma category, brainstem gliomas constitute 10–20% of all pediatric CNS tumors. We will narrow the scope of our discussion to brainstem gliomas, as they tend to present a unique and challenging tumor with its own classification scheme that provides a framework to predict growth patterns, surgical resectability, and overall prognosis.

Many classification schemes have been devised to categorize brainstem tumors based on imaging and tumor characteristics. All of these systems categorize tumors based on diffuse or focal imaging characteristics. Several more complex classification systems further divide the tumors based on location, growth pattern, and presence of hydrocephalus or hemorrhage. All of these characteristics can be determined with a high-quality MRI image [Table 1].

1986	Diffuse
	Focal
	Circumscribed mass less than 2 cm, no edema
	Cervicomedullary

1991	Location
	Midbrain, pons, medulla
	Focality
	Diffuse or focal
	Direction and extent of tumor growth
	Degree of brainstem enlargement
	Exophytic growth
	Hemorrhage or necrosis
	Evidence of hydrocephalus
1996	Focal
	Midbrain, pons (dorsal exophytic pontine glioma), medulla
	Diffuse

Table 1: Classification Schemes for Brainstem Tumors

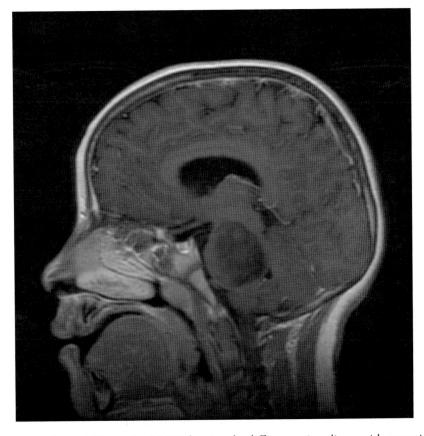

Figure 1a: Sagittal T1-weighted MRI showing the diffuse pontine glioma with expansion of the pons.

One of the main characteristics determined on imaging is the degree of focality; in other words, is the tumor diffuse and infiltrating or does it have a clearer demarcation of margin? Diffuse gliomas make up 58–75% of all brainstem tumors and are the most common tumor found in this location. On MRI imaging they have indistinct margins and are characterized by diffuse infiltration and swelling of the brainstem [Fig. 1 a, b, c]. These tumors are usually located within the pons, however they may also extend into other areas of the brainstem. These tumors have variable contrast enhancement and tend to be high-grade lesions. The usual histopathology is typically a malignant fibrillary astrocytoma, WHO grade III or IV.

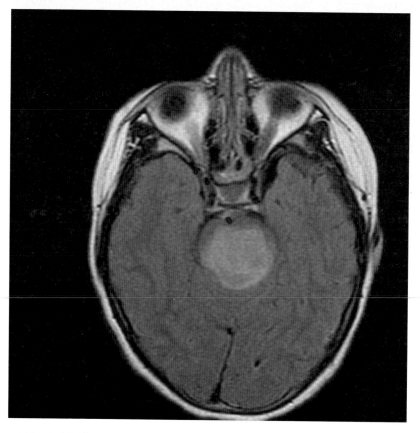

Figure 1b: Axial Flair MRI sequence showing the pontine glioma, which involves the entire pons.

Focal tumors have more clearly defined margins and, when in the brainstem, are usually found in the midbrain, pons, or medulla [Fig. 2]. They usually are not infiltrating and are not associated with swelling of adjacent structures, also known as edema. These focal tumors are often benign on histology and

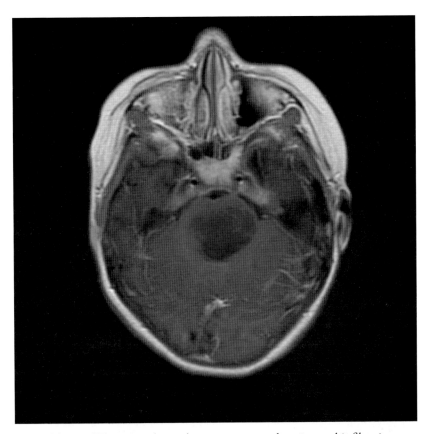

Figure 1c: The axial T1 image shows the noncontrast enhancing and infiltrative tumor.

graded as WHO grade I or II, although cases of more aggressive tumors have been reported.

In addition to degree of focality, some classification schemes also consider whether the tumor is primarily inside the brainstem, which is defined as intrinsic, or if it resides mostly outside the brainstem, which is defined as exophytic. Exophytic brainstem gliomas arise from the subependymal glial tissue and the majority of the tumor is located in the fourth ventricle. These are usually well-defined tumors that are almost always low-grade gliomas.

Location of brainstem tumors is also a consideration when classifying them. For example, cervicomedullary tumors, found where the lower part of the brainstem connects to the top of the cervical spinal cord, tend to be slow growing and focal lesions and thus are considered benign low-grade astrocytomas. However, more aggressive cervicomedullary tumors, which are more infiltrative and grow up into the brainstem, have been found in this location.

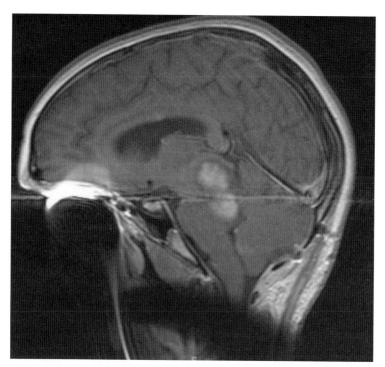

Figure 2a

Figure 2b

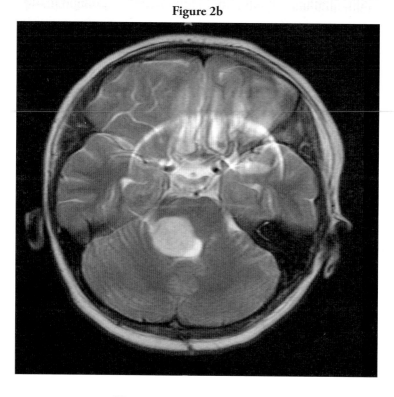

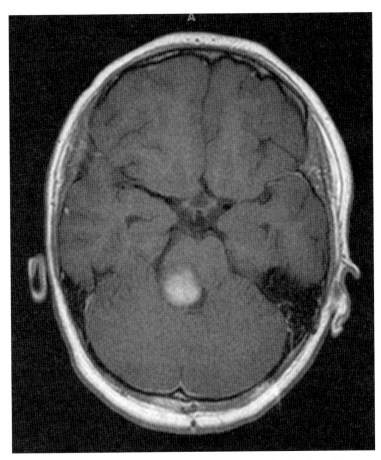

Figure 2a: Sagittal T1-weighted MRI with contrast shows a focal enhancing tumor in the pons and midbrain. **Figure 2b:** T2 weighted axial image shows the focal noninfiltrative or diffuse nature of the tumor. **Figure 2c:** T1 weighted axial image shows a focal tumor, which is not invading the pons or brainstem; this is a benign juvenile pilocytic astrocytoma.

Using these classification schemes—combining degree of focality (i.e. diffuse or well delineated), intrinsic or exophytic, and tumor location—health care providers can formulate a differential diagnosis and establish a reasonable treatment plan. Characteristics that may help further classify the tumor include direction and extent of tumor growth, degree of brainstem enlargement, hemorrhage or necrosis, and evidence of hydrocephalus.

Another simpler classification scheme divides brainstem tumors into typical and atypical brainstem gliomas. The term typical brainstem gliomas is synonymous with the term diffuse intrinsic pontine gliomas (DIPG). As mentioned earlier, these tumors are diffuse and infiltrative, located in the pons but potentially extending into other areas of the brainstem. Surgery or biopsy of these lesions is not usually recommended at this time, unless the diagnosis is in question.

Atypical gliomas include the focal lesions which are well circumscribed. They may be contained in the brainstem or may grow out in cysts or outside of the brainstem. Unlike typical brainstem gliomas, the atypical gliomas tend to arise from the midbrain (the top of the brainstem) or the medulla. These atypical tumors tend to be lower grade lesions which may be amenable to some degree of surgical resection or biopsy.

The majority of brainstem tumors are diffuse pontine gliomas that are mainly high grade on histological examination and have poor prognosis. In this book, we will review the current treatment strategies, role for surgery, radiation and chemotherapy, and future directions in the treatment of this disease.

Parent Perspectives

Our world splintered into millions of pieces on Sunday, February 1st, when Bryce at age 13 was sitting in church with us and he turned to look at me. His eye turned in toward the center. Then it went back. I almost wasn't sure that I had seen it happen. Then, later in the day, Bryce had a hockey game, and came off the ice to tell us that he could see two hockey nets, not just one, and that "he had shot at the wrong one and missed." We knew something was wrong, and on Monday, we called for an appointment with our family doctor. He had us in to see an eye specialist by that afternoon. On February 10th, Bryce had a CAT scan, which didn't show anything. Luckily, the specialist was persistent, and he ordered an MRI. He told us that at 13, an eye turning in was not "normal" if he didn't have it at birth.

And so, Bryce's journey began. On Feb. 26th, Bryce went for an MRI where we were whisked out of the waiting room by a radiologist and sent to Bryce's pediatrician, who told us about the growth—a diffuse intrinsic pontine glioma, which is a tumor located completely inside the brainstem. He told us that treatment would involve going to Children's Hospital, and that he wanted us there that night. We were floored. I don't remember much, but I remember looking at Bryce's face, and his eyes filling with tears. He didn't say much. None of us did, I think we were in shock. We went home and packed a bag, and of course, family started pouring into our house as we were preparing to leave. I was crying, and he just looked at me and said, "It's just cancer, mom. It will be fine."

Blood was drawn and another series of neurological tests were performed. Ellie was incredibly brave for the scan and held very still as the machine whirled around her head. I remember being outside her room trying to find water and hearing the emergency room doctor being paged by a doctor we know through the girls' school. My stomach jumped to my throat. An IV was administered and an MRI was ordered. Ellie was very scared as she felt fine and did not understand what was going on and why she needed all these tests. She was exhausted.

My husband stayed with Ellie while my father, Ellie's pediatrician and I met with the neurosurgeon in a private area to view the scan. I really had no clue what I was looking at but a child's head. I looked around at the three doctors and watched my father and our pediatrician find chairs. Their faces said it all. Ellie's golf ball size inoperable tumor was situated in the pons of her brain stem and had grown to the point where it was sitting on nerves that obviously affected her left side.

We spent the next three nights in the hospital medicating, testing and meeting an army of staff to try and assist us in navigating through this whole new world. We heard the words diffuse intrinsic pontine glioma... can you please write that out? We were told surgery was not an option nor was biopsy. We were devastated and heartbroken and my husband and I challenged each other every moment of every day to keep our spirits high, in order to be strong for Ellie.

The diagnosis came quick after a trip to Children's Hospital's emergency room. We were in a complete haze. I knew I needed to get a second opinion and didn't know how to go about it and unbelievably I felt sheepish about asking for the copies of the results—even though I did.

The second opinions came slow but we knew we had to act fast for any treatment. We weren't given much hope but were told that radiation would be the only thing that would relieve her symptoms and buy her some time; maybe a year or two.

There was no chemo that anyone had any confidence in but we could always try one that is well tolerated by some other kids. We did the exhausting process of radiation and they said it would get worse before it gets better and it did. After the radiation we thought we saw signs of the honeymoon period. Unfortunately, the honeymoon was held off by an infection of her shunt. After that was cleared we saw a fast improvement and we finally had our old Tatumn back! But that time was soooo quick. By the time the steroids were totally out of her system and her hair started to grow back from the radiation her symptoms subtly started to reappear. Then her journey ended very quickly. It was about 5 1/2 months total from diagnosis.

Lovis first had a CT scan at our local hospital after which we were told about a mass in her cerebellum, most likely to be operable. Because it

was a Saturday night, we had to wait to be transferred to the Children's Hospital where an MRI was done on Sunday night. The wait for the results was terrible. Lovis was completely exhausted, weak and almost could not speak or drink.

On Monday morning at 10:00 a.m. we were shown the scans and were told that Lovis had diffuse intrinsic pontine glioma that presents itself as tiny little spots all over the pons in the brainstem—thus inoperable and sentencing our daughter to death in about 9 months even if we chose to radiate. We fell apart. I remember screaming "No, no" and then turning back to the screen, wanting to know EVERYTHING about this tumor. So one nurse left and printed off more information right away.

We immediately opted for radiation, both my husband and I. But Lovis was too weak for the daily sedation that goes with it since she had just turned three. We were told to wait, try steroids and temozolomide for lack of better agents, aware that the latter would not be a great help. The doctors thought that even one general anesthetic would have been enough to kill Lovis if we had started to radiate right away. If she didn't get better within a few days, stronger and able to be sedated, she might likely die within the next 10 days. That was the diagnosis.

I was diagnosed with breast cancer on a Monday afternoon. Three days later we ended up in the emergency room with my 6 year-old-son Andrew. After a CT scan, a young physician's assistant came to talk with us, and I will never forget her words. "There is a large area of swelling in the brainstem. We suspect a mass." Andrew responded casually, "My mom has a mass!"

When I think of a mass, I think of a ball or an egg or something that can be removed. I remember being told that there were parts of the mass reaching out like fingers into the brain. It was not until eight months after diagnosis that I truly understood the meaning of the word diffuse. We were not dealing with fingers reaching into the brain. We were dealing with cancer cells sprinkled among healthy brain cells in the pons (part of the brainstem). Andrew's neuro-oncologist explained it by using the idea of sand (cancer cells) in grass (healthy brain tissue). I have also heard people use the idea of marbling in steak.

Our oncologist and neurosurgeons we consulted with, told us the hard truth but to the point that my husband and I were so discouraged that we almost did nothing. Because of Connor's age they did not recommend radiation and the evidence of effective chemo was null. We almost felt as if we were dismissed with all of our questions and concerns because of the known outcome with this type of tumor. We did go ahead with the radiation and Connor was great for several months until the tumor didn't follow the "typical course" so we were then sent for a third opinion and subsequently a biopsy.

Six months after the original diagnosis we found out that Connor's pathology report came back with a different tumor type. He had a new diagnosis of a PNET which was some positive news we thought. The only problem was by the time we found this out it had progressed in the brain and into the spinal cord.

We did not know until a few months after diagnosis that a pediatric oncologist is not a specialist in pediatric brain tumors. We were very happy with our son's medical care, but we wish we would have understood earlier the importance of having a pediatric neuro-oncologist involved in the situation. Our level of understanding about our son's brain tumor, possible treatments and related issues changed drastically as soon as we established a relationship with a pediatric neuro-oncologist. Even though this specialist was located in another state, she worked well with our son's local team to manage his medical care. Looking back, that was the best decision we made.

My mom, Bizzie and I headed to the emergency room. When we got there we were taken into a room and told we were going to have to get Bizzie to lie still for a CT scan. Well, when they talked about possibly sedating her, I called my husband. Funny, but back then I could not even think about holding her while she was sedated or undergoing a procedure. That would change. I did get her to stay still for the CT scan by singing Row, Row, Row your Boat to her repeatedly. I remember looking into the booth and seeing the emergency room doctor look at the results. The technician walked us back to the emergency room. They all knew. We did not—yet. My husband was there when I returned. The emergency room doctor came in and spoke

to us, "There is a mass on her brainstem."

I ran out of the room hysterical; but I returned in a minute. I needed to hear this and be there for Bizzie. I remember snippets. She needed an MRI, which meant an IV and sedation. The doctor told us that he suspected that it was a diffuse intrinsic pontine glioma. The MRI would confirm this. She also needed surgery to drain the fluid around her brain caused by the mass. We would be admitted and she would be started on steroids. My husband asked on a scale of 1 to 10 how bad was this? The doc quickly replied, "It's bad."

So Bizzie had her MRI. The anesthesiologist was impressed by Bizzie's strength when she came to. "Wow, she would do great in a bar-fight." She was kicking and hitting. I finally got her to calm down and we settled into room 4 of the PICU. The pediatric neurosurgeon was sent the images from the MRI and came in to talk to us about them. I sent my husband out to talk to her. I stayed with Bizzie. When they came back, he had his poker face on. He explained to me that it was a big tumor, and it could not be removed surgically.

At that point I cut him off and turned to the neurosurgeon. "So, it's inoperable. What now?" She explained that standard treatment was radiation followed by chemo, but that chemo was proven ineffective with these types of tumors. I knew what she was saying. "So, how long?" I asked. "Six to twenty-four months," was her reply.

At that point Bizzie pulled my face back towards the book we were reading. "Momma...READ!" I kissed her sweet little head. "Of course Bizzie, how silly of me to not be paying attention to you."

And that was diagnosis day.

At 3:00 p.m. I received a call from Liam's pediatrician's office. They asked that we come in and that it would be better if we could leave our children with a friend. I begged the woman who called to please tell me what was wrong over the phone. She was very kind, but of course could not. They told us we needed to come as soon as possible. I called my husband who was at work a half hour away. I sat on my bathroom floor with the door locked barely able to tell him he needed to come home, that something was wrong with Liam's scan. It was the longest 30 minutes of my life while I waited for him on our front porch. We drove in silence and my heart pounded. We

sat for only moments in the doctor's waiting room. They brought us into an exam room where Liam's pediatrician gave us the news that they found a lesion on his brain. I looked right at this woman and every part of me thought she had to be to be lying to us and I just couldn't understand why. Before I even realized, I heard myself calling this poor woman a liar and asking her why she would lie about our son like that. She quickly came and took my hand. I apologized after a moment. With great compassion she told us what needed to happen next and that those plans had already been set in motion. We would take Liam to the University Hospital the next day. Our appointment was with a pediatric neuro- oncologist. In those very moments, everything became marked with a new definition of time. Everything was now defined as "before" and "after."

Chapter 2

Typical History of DIPG

Eric H. Raabe, MD, PhD
Kenneth Cohen, MD, MBA

The brainstem is divided into three major areas—midbrain, pons and medulla—and different types of tumors can occur in any of these locations. A glioma is a tumor that arises from a cell in the brain called a glial cell. One type of glioma is called an astrocytoma, which is a tumor that arises from a specific type of glial cell called an astrocyte. The two major types of astrocytomas are pilocytic astrocytomas and diffuse, infiltrating astrocytomas. The term DIPG specifically refers to a diffuse, infiltrating astrocytoma that develops in the pons.

Who is Affected by DIPG?

Each year approximately 200 children in the United States are diagnosed with DIPG. The age range is broad, but the most common age at diagnosis is 7 to 9 years. All races and both sexes are equally affected.

Why do certain children get DIPG?

In short, doctors don't know why. There are no known associations of DIPG with any environmental or infectious agents. Most researchers who study DIPG believe these brain tumors, similar to other tumors affecting children, arise when normal developmental and maturational processes go awry. In this case, developing brain cells accumulate alterations in their DNA that prevent them from properly maturing. These alterations allow the developing brain cells to continue growing, and this growth eventually becomes out of control, leading to cancer. During the process of uncontrolled growth, DIPG cells can gain DNA alterations that allow them to resist the effects of radiation and chemotherapy, making these cancer cells extremely difficult to kill.

Dr. Raabe is an Instructor in the Divison of Pediatric Oncology, and Physician-Scientist at the Sidney Kimmel Comprehensive Cancer Center at Johns Hopkins, Baltimore, MD.

Clinical signs of DIPG

The signs and symptoms of DIPG can start gradually. As described in chapter 3, the pons contains nerve centers that control eye movements, facial movements, swallowing, and speech. As pontine glioma tumors grow, the cancer cells interfere with these centers, causing disruption of their functions. Sometimes parents notice odd eye movements, slurred speech, difficulty swallowing, and trouble maintaining balance, or drooping of one part of their child's face. The pons also contains nerves that run from the brain to the rest of the body. Pontine tumors can press on and interfere with the function of these nerves, leading to weakness in an arm and/or a leg.

Tumors in the brainstem can also cause increased pressure within the skull. The swelling from the tumor can cause increased pressure directly, or it can block the flow of spinal fluid from the skull (where it is made) to the spinal cord (where it is absorbed). Increased pressure can cause patients to complain of persistent headaches and in some patients can lead to nausea and vomiting. These daily signs of increased pressure inside the skull will get worse over time, as the tumor grows.

DIPG Appearance on MRI

A magnetic resonance imaging (MRI) scan is the best non-invasive way to determine the size and properties of brain tumors. DIPGs have a characteristic appearance on an MRI, which other tumors that grow in the pons or other parts of the brainstem do not share. The boundaries of a DIPG are difficult to determine, because the tumor cells invade the surrounding tissue of the pons. A DIPG generally does not have portions of the tumor that push outside of the pons' normal structure. In contrast, a pilocytic astrocytoma, another less-aggressive brainstem tumor, has a more focal appearance, is more likely to have a part that buds out of the normal structure of the brainstem, and will displace rather than invade surrounding brain tissue. The differences between how a pilocytic astroyctoma and a DIPG appear on an MRI are summarized in the following table [Table 1].

> Dr. Cohen is Clinical Director of Pediatric Oncology and Director of Pediatric Neuro-oncology at the Sidney Kimmel Comprehensive Cancer Center at Johns Hopkins, Baltimore, MD.

DIPG	Pilocytic Astrocytoma
Diffuse	Focal
Invasive into surrounding tissue	Displaces surrounding structures and tissue
Diffuse brightness on T2 weighting on MRI; no enhancement on T1 weighted images	Tumor well defined on T1 and T2 weighting MRI
Associated with brainstem swelling	Minimal brainstem swelling
Located centrally in pons with extension to midbrain or brainstem	Located in midbrain and brainstem without extension

Table 1: MRI Characteristics of DIPG Compared with Pilocytic Astrocytoma

Because the MRI appearance of the two most common types of pediatric brainstem tumors, DIPGs and pilocytic astrocytomas, are so different, they can be accurately identified the vast majority of the time by MRI alone. In rare cases where the diagnosis is uncertain based on MRI results, neurosurgeons can perform biopsies to obtain small amounts of tissue for examination under a microscope by pathologists (doctors trained to identify the type of tumor by examining it under a microscope). The biopsy is performed very carefully, but because the pons contains many important neurologic centers, including those that control breathing and swallowing, there can be complications of biopsy, including additional neurologic impairment. For these reasons, biopsy is generally only performed in cases where the diagnosis is not clear from an MRI scan. In the future, some clinical trials may include a biopsy to find out more information about the tumor prior to starting therapy.

Pathologic grading

Pathologists grade a tumor based on its features. The characteristics that pathologists examine include cell growth, cell death, invasion of surrounding normal cells, and the architecture of the tumor itself—this refers to how mature or immature the cells look, among other factors.

Pathologists grade brainstem tumors on a 1 to 4 scale. The lower numbers generally indicate less-aggressive tumors, including pilocytic astrocytomas. The lowest grade consistent with a DIPG is a grade 2 tumor, but many DIPG tumors will be grade 3 or 4 (the most-aggressive, fastest-growing grades).

Clinical Course of DIPG

Once the diagnosis of a DIPG is suspected, anti-inflammatory steroids (such as dexamethasone) are usually started. The steroids can improve symptoms quickly by decreasing the swelling associated with the tumor. Steroids can cause side effects including increased moodiness, agitation, weight gain, increased appetite and high blood pressure and blood sugar. These last two side effects can be controlled with medication, if they become severe.

The only treatment that is routinely recommended for the treatment of all children with a DIPG is x-ray radiation therapy (XRT). XRT can be given either alone or with chemotherapy and usually takes 4 to 6 weeks to complete. Side effects during radiation can include mild nausea and fatigue.

Many chemotherapeutic drugs have been tried for DIPG, with studies looking at the use of chemotherapy before XRT, during XRT, immediately following XRT, and at the time of tumor progression. The results have been disappointing, with no drug(s) to date improving survival. While pediatric oncologists continue to develop new therapies for DIPG, the mainstay of current treatment remains XRT. There are ongoing clinical trials for DIPG, which allow new drugs to be tested in this disease. While there are always risks when enrolling in clinical trials, they are the best way to get your child the most promising new medications and to make sure the pediatric oncology community learns all it can about what therapies work best for DIPG.

Most DIPG tumors in the beginning respond to a combination of radiation and steroids. The child's neurologic deficits will very often decrease and may disappear completely. Over the course of weeks to months, the steroids can be decreased and then stopped in many cases. The child can often return to school, take special trips, and almost return to normal life. During this time, the child has regular MRI scans to measure the regression of the tumor and monitor if the tumor is coming back.

In almost all cases, after about 6 to 12 months, the DIPG tumor starts to grow again. Sometimes the neurologic symptoms are the same as when the child was first diagnosed with DIPG. Sometimes new nerves and systems are affected. The child will often begin to show neurologic symptoms even if the MRI scan of the tumor appears largely unchanged.

Once the tumor has started to grow again, no further treatment has been shown to improve survival. When children start to have neurologic symptoms, they are often restarted on steroids. This treatment can sometimes improve symptoms for a short time. However, the tumor will continue to grow, and even if the steroid doses are increased, the child's symptoms will continue to worsen. Eventually the tumor grows until it affects nerve centers that are important for swallowing, breathing, and controlling heartbeat.

If the tumor is blocking the flow of cerebrospinal fluid (CSF), some parents—in discussion with the doctors—may decide to have a neurosurgeon place a VP-shunt to help with pressure symptoms. A VP-shunt is a flexible plastic tube that bypasses the blockage in the brainstem and allows the CSF fluid to pass out of the skull. Neurosurgeons place the shunt into the fluid cistern in the brain, and then pass it out of the skull, under the skin, and to the abdomen, where the CSF is absorbed. This procedure can improve some of the headache and nausea symptoms of increased intracranial pressure, and it can extend the life of children with DIPG; it does not, however, change the ultimate outcome.

Only very few children are long-term survivors of DIPG. Because biopsies are not performed on these children with typical appearing DIPGs, it is unclear whether or not they actually had DIPG to start with, or in fact had a different tumor or condition that looked like a DIPG on the MRI. There is no one treatment that these children received that set them apart from the vast majority (more than 95 percent) of children who die from DIPG. Pediatric oncologists are actively looking for new treatments and are trying to learn more about DIPG. They hope that by learning more from tumor tissue taken at autopsy from children who die from DIPG they can help children who develop DIPG in the future.

Parent Perspectives

My son Andrew was diagnosed with DIPG following a couple months of not feeling well. Initially we thought he had the same virus as his brother. Perhaps he did, but he did not recover. He was clearly ill—sleeping more than usual, feeling dizzy and unstable. Someone mentioned to us that it was funny to watch him go upstairs. We began to notice that his gait was not right. He looked like he was walking with one foot on the ground and one foot on a curb, but there was no curb. He struggled to control his left hand in a piano lesson, and almost fell leaving the studio that day. When we thought about it, we realized that he had been falling regularly— either from a standing position or while riding his bike. One night I had difficulty rousing him from a nap, and had to hold his hand to help him walk to Children's Church. That same night a nurse in our church noticed that one side of his face was drooping. By the next morning he was clearly feeling worse. He could not climb onto my bed, so he lay on the floor in my bedroom while I called our primary care physician. He vomited, and we settled him on my bed to rest. When we took him to the doctor that afternoon, the physician's assistant sent us to the emergency room. All along they had been thinking it was a virus or a problem with his ears; no one was thinking it was a brain tumor.

We took our daughter in as a healthy looking beautiful child with only a bit of drooling, facial numbness, and a bit of balance concern. All of these symptoms were MINIMAL. If I hadn't insisted on an MRI (the neurologist didn't think it necessary but agreed to do it) we wouldn't have found the tumor when we did. From there it was a whirlwind and you do what you do.

Although it is a blur in some respects, I clearly remember my first thoughts and words when I was told that my grandson, Miguel had a diffuse intrinsic pontine glioma. I remember the room clearly. It was a small room in the PICU area of the hospital. My daughter told me that the doctor said that if we were lucky Miguel would be with us for two years but the average

survival was around eight months and even then much of that time may not be good. I remember saying to my daughter, "two days, two months, two years, whatever it is I'll take it." He was alive at that moment and that was all that mattered.

In retrospect, there were signs something was wrong but they could mostly be attributed to normal things (allergies, eating too much too quickly, tripping over his own growing feet). Over a weekend he began to hold his head to the side (probably compensating for double vision) so a doctor's visit was in order. Perhaps there was something wrong with his vision. At the doctor's office, his pediatrician asked him to lie down and he wouldn't lay flat. I am sure that he also saw something with the tracking in his eyes.

Miguel's pediatrician decided an MRI was in order and scheduled it for that same week. Immediately following the MRI Miguel was admitted to the hospital and placed in the PICU where he stayed for five days while a plan was put in place. His treatment, we were told, would involve radiation to try and shrink the tumor. If it responded well, he would have a "honeymoon period." His tumor was about 6 mm and the response to the radiation was nothing short of amazing. All of his symptoms subsided and he was even able to return to school to finish out the year.

After you've swallowed the words "average survival is less than 1 year," the next phrase you grasp onto with all of your might is "the honeymoon period." Now you don't know for sure what this is yet but you know honeymoons are good so, initially you are pretty happy to hear something that even comes close to positive. As a parent, you find yourself really looking forward to it as somewhat of a light at the end of a dark and unknown tunnel.

In the first few days after diagnosis, things tend to be a blur. As we advance and options change for our kids your road may be slightly different than mine but for the time being it goes something like this. Your relatively normal looking child begins to exhibit symptoms of some sort. Eye issues, balance issues, headache, and nausea, just to name a few. Depending on how you respond, you eventually find yourself in a pediatric oncologist's office where you can feel the air being sucked from your lungs as if you've just had the wind knocked out of you.

I decided to take Bizzie to see our pediatrician because she just seemed—off. She was only two, about to turn three. For the past few months we had noticed that she wasn't developing as quickly as we thought she should be. But, her well visits went fine. She was drooling a little and stumbled from time to time. Then she started to choke on some foods. Finally, I just decided to bring her in for a sick visit. My mom was down for a visit, so I brought her along with me. The pediatrician examined Bizzie. After a few minutes of looking in ears, mouth, etc. she still did not state any specific issue. "I'm not worried about her, but…" She talked about sending her in for a blood test, maybe a CT scan to rule out anything serious. Then she tested Bizzie's reflexes. Now she seemed to change her plan. She said she would be right back—that she wanted to arrange those tests for us.

She left and a minute later someone closed the door to our room. I started to wonder—that seemed odd. When she came back, she let us know that we should go right over to our local Children's emergency room for testing, that there was a doctor there with whom we should connect.

Our Kayla was diagnosed with DIPG on Aug 23rd. It was her first day of kindergarten. She had been drooling, she was seeing double, she was choking sometimes when she ate, and she was getting clumsy. Even a few months prior I had noticed that she couldn't keep her right flip flop on when she walked. So we had an MRI done after our optometrist realized this was more than a case of misaligned eyes and we were told that Kayla had 6 to 9 months to survive if we did the radiation treatment and 10% chance of surviving a year with Temodar—a type of chemotherapy. We were in such disbelief that this could happen to our family but we could clearly see that she was not well. This was a huge turning point in our lives.

Once this bomb was dropped on us, we instantly went into survival mode. We came up with hundreds of questions and searched the internet all day and night trying to understand the disease that we were dealing with.

+ + +

Courtney was diagnosed with DIPG on April 19th. The only symptoms she had prior to her diagnosis were fatigue and she had a period of time where she had dizzy spells about 6 months before her diagnosis. April 14th we noticed her eye turning in, and took her to the eye doctor on the 16th. He sent her to the emergency room where they did a CT scan and told us she had some type of brain tumor but they weren't sure what kind. They sent us home and told us to come back on Monday the 19th for an MRI. That is when we found out she had DIPG and that it had spread to her upper spine. I think we started grieving that day. Not because we didn't hope that she would make it, but because we knew that the odds were greatly against her survival. It felt like we walked into that conference room with a normal life and when we walked out it felt like we had walked into a whole new world—one that would sometimes feel like a bad dream.

Our son Liam was diagnosed with DIPG in April, just days after his sixth birthday. The previous month Liam had what we all thought was a nasty virus. He woke one morning vomiting and continued to do so throughout the day. At one point I had emailed my husband with concerns that this did not seem like typical vomiting. It seemed almost more violent than a normal stomach bug. I remember asking Liam if his neck hurt at all, if anything else hurt at all, trying to ease the nagging feeling that something wasn't right. He ran no fever and the vomiting continued intermittently throughout the day until evening. The following day the vomiting had stopped but he suddenly was running a fever. We decided to call his pediatrician who had us come in. At that time Liam had no other symptoms that were worrisome to us. His doctor thought that he probably had a case of the flu and did a rapid test for strep. That came back positive. In hindsight, that was most likely coincidental and the intense vomiting of the day before was our first real look at the beast we would come to know so well.

Sam's case is a little on the atypical side—first because he was 19 when diagnosed, and second because his tumor extended into the cerebellum from the brainstem. He was fine until January—no hint of anything at all out of the ordinary. On Jan 11th he woke up with a bad sore throat and because his band had a show that weekend we went in to our regular doctor to see if he needed any antibiotics. It wasn't strep but he went ahead and gave him antibiotics because Sam was prone to sinus infections. Two days later he woke up with a horrible earache so back we went to the doctor

who switched his antibiotics. That seemed to do the trick and he felt better enough by the weekend to perform with his band.

The next week he was really, really tired, taking naps in the afternoon which was very unlike him. Towards the end of the week he mentioned the right side of his face was feeling numb. Since it was the same side as the ear infection we assumed the infection had not cleared up and figured if it's not better by Monday we'll go back to the doctor. Over the weekend he mentioned his left leg feeling tingly like it was asleep. That worried me, but I still thought it would be something minor. So we went to the doctor on Monday and he said the ear infection was all cleared up and he had no idea what was causing the facial numbness and leg tingling. He suggested we see a neurologist and get an MRI so we saw the neurologist on Wednesday who also noticed an issue with his right eye and agreed that an MRI was in order. We had that the next day and within half an hour of being home the doctor called and told us there was a mass on his brainstem and we needed to see a neurosurgeon.

The next morning Sam was admitted, and we consulted with the neurosurgeon and the neuroradiologist on Saturday. They explained that Sam had a pontine glioma that was diffuse in nature with tumor extending into the cerebellum making it extremely difficult to control. They never gave us an estimate of time, in fact when we asked they said, "Every case is different." The radiologist was the most upfront, telling Sam that this was a very difficult tumor to beat. Sam asked, "Is it possible to beat it?" and her response after some hesitation was, "Well, it's not impossible."

Chapter 3

Pontine Anatomy and Function

Sven Hochheimer, MD
Javad Nazarian, PhD
Suresh N. Magge, MD

Children who are diagnosed with DIPG often experience varying clinical symptoms. Families are sometimes left wondering why their child exhibits a particular symptom, while another child may not. Additionally, families may feel overwhelmed when trying to decipher their child's MRI, leaving them unsure how to interpret the findings on the MRI as they relate to the clinical signs evident in their child. Understanding pontine anatomy and function can assist with interpreting MRI reports, as well as explain the variable clinical symptoms of children diagnosed with DIPG.

General Overview of the Human Nervous System

The human nervous system is divided into the peripheral and central nervous system (CNS). The peripheral nervous system consists of:

- The somatic nervous system, which is responsible for functions under conscious control such as body movement and reception of external stimuli;

- The autonomic nervous system, which regulates functions under subconscious control, such as blood pressure, heart rate, breathing, and digestion.

The central nervous system is subdivided into the spinal cord and brain, which includes the cerebrum, cerebellum, and brainstem. The brainstem consists of the midbrain, pons, and medulla and serves as a passageway between the brain and spinal cord. Above the pons is the hypothalamus, and to the back sits the 4th ventricle [Fig. 1].

Dr. Hochheimer is a Neurosurgery Resident at Walter Reed National Military Medical Center, Bethesda, MD.

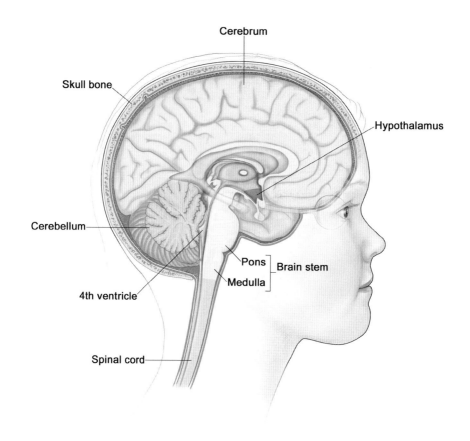

Cerebrum

Skull bone

Hypothalamus

Cerebellum

Pons] Brain stem
Medulla]

4th ventricle

Spinal cord

© 2010 Terese Winslow
U.S. Govt. has certain rights

Figure 1: Basic anatomy of the Central Nervous System

The pons—which means "bridge" in Latin, is an approximately 3.5 cm. long "knob-like" structure that occupies the central portion of the brainstem between the midbrain and the medulla [Fig. 2a]. Any messages descending from the brain or ascending to it must cross this critical "bridge-like" structure. Anatomy and function of the pons will be the focus of this chapter.

Dr. Nazarian is a Molecular Geneticist and Assistant Professor in Integrative Systems Biology and Pediatrics at Children's National Medical Center, and The George Washington University School of Medicine and Health Sciences, Washington, DC.

Dr. Magge is a Pediatric Neurosurgeon and Assistant Professor of Neurosurgery and Pediatrics at Children's National Medical Center, and George Washington University School of Medicine and Health Sciences, Washington, DC.

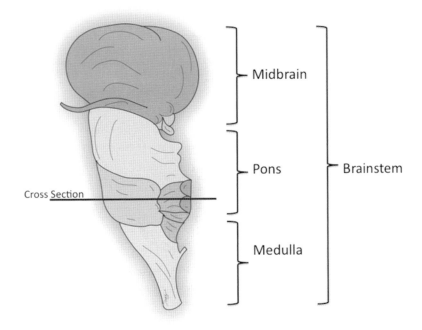

Figure 2a: Schemata of brainstem cross section

Neurons and Tracts

To best understand anatomy, it is important to gain an understanding of the terminology of the system being described—in this case the nervous system. The basic cell of the nervous system is the neuron. Humans have billions of neurons, yet neurons only make up approximately 10 percent of cells in the human brain. The remaining 90 percent of cells are support cells called glia.

Neurons

A neuron is composed of dendrites, a cell body, and an axon. Dendrites receive information for the neuron. The information is then passed through the cell body and on to the axon. The axon then passes the information along to dendrites of other neurons. In this way, a neural message gets passed from one neuron to the next. Axons are covered by myelin, which is produced by glial cells and serves as an insulation that allows rapid signal transmission.

Collections of neurons that serve a particular function are called nuclei. Their axons are bundled into collections of thread-like fibers called tracts. Tracts that carry information from the peripheral nervous system up toward the brain are called ascending tracts, while those that carry signals from the brain to the spinal cord and peripheral nervous system are called descending tracts.

Organization of the pons

The pons consists of a) the basilar pons in the front (ventral portion), and b) the pontine tegmentum in the back (dorsal portion). The basilar pons and the pontine tegmentum contain nuclei and tracts [Fig. 2b]. The basilar pons contains a complex combination of tracts (bundles of axons) and nuclei (collections of cell bodies of neurons). The pontine tegmentum is made up of cranial nerves which serve the head and neck, associated nuclei, the reticular formation (neural network involved in functions including cardiovascular control, pain modulation, sleep and awakening), and tracts (both ascending and descending).

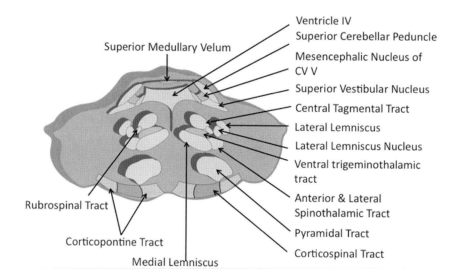

Figure 2b: Cross section of the pons (at the level indicated in Fig. 2a) showing various tracts and nuclei

Ascending tracts of the pons

The major ascending tracts include the dorsal columns, spinothalamic tracts, and spinocerebellar tracts, which are described below.

Dorsal columns: The dorsal columns convey information about position sense (proprioception), vibration, and discriminatory touch. Before reaching the pons, the fibers from these columns cross at the level of the lower medulla to form a structure called the medial lemniscus, which then traverses the pons. Damage to the medial lemnisci, at the level of the pons, results in sensory problems on the opposite side of the body.

Spinothalamic tracts: These tracts convey sensations of pain, temperature, and light touch. The tracts cross shortly after entering the spinal cord and do not change sides as they ascend through the pons. Damage to the spinothalamic tracts, at the level of the pons, results in sensory problems on the opposite side of the body.

Spinocerebellar tracts: These tracts convey subconscious information pertaining to proprioception (position sense) to the cerebellum, the part of the brain concerned primarily with posture, tone, and balance. These tracts travel to the cerebellum via structures called cerebellar peduncles. Also, there are several nuclei within the pons whose axons unite to form one of the cerebellar peduncles which play a role in the function of the cerebellum. Therefore, damage to these tracts result in problems with posture, tone, and balance.

Descending tracts

The most important **descending** tracts of the brainstem include the corticospinal, corticobulbar, and corticopontine fibers, which are described below.

Corticospinal tracts: These tracts are critical for voluntary movement of the body. They originate from the motor areas of the brain and pass through the basilar pons before crossing at the level of the lower medulla on their way to the spinal cord. Damage to the brain or corticospinal tract at the level of the pons results in weakness or paralysis on the opposite side of the body (remember, these tracts cross to the opposite side in the medulla while on the way to the spinal cord).

Corticobulbar and corticopontine tracts: Corticobulbar tracts originate in the brain and control voluntary movement of the muscles of the head and neck. Corticopontine fibers provide a connection between the brain and cerebellum to coordinate and refine movement. These tracts also cross, so damage to corticobulbar fibers result in difficulty moving the opposite side of the face, while lesions of the corticopontine fibers result in lack of coordination of the opposite arm and leg.

Other tracts

Two other important tracts, which convey both ascending and descending information and are prominent in the pontine tegmentum, are the medial longitudinal fasciculus (MLF) and the central tegmental tract (CTT).

MLF: The MLF is important in coordinating eye, head, and neck movements. Damage to this tract results in problems associated with double vision, and difficulty with coordination of head and eye movements.

CTT: The CTT provides an avenue for ascending tracts involved with taste, as well as provides a path for descending tracts to connect the midbrain to the cerebellum.

Cranial Nerves and Nuclei of the Pons

As previously mentioned, a number of nuclei (groups of cells that serve a particular function) reside within the pons. In the basilar pons (front/ventral portion) reside the pontine nuclei, which serve to connect the brain and cerebellum. Lesions here result in difficulty with coordination of the opposite arm and leg. Cranial nerves are the nerves that control functions of the head and neck, and the pontine tegmentum (back/dorsal portion) contains several of these nuclei.

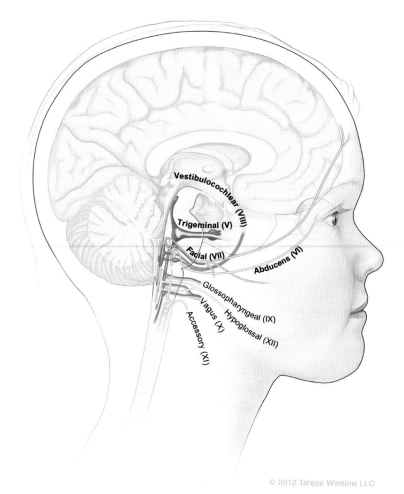

© 2012 Terese Winslow LLC

Figure 3: Schemata of the origin within the brain of the cranial nerves

The lower pons contains cranial nerves (CN) VI and VII [Fig. 3 and 4]. CN VI, known as the abducens nerve, controls a muscle of the eye known as the lateral rectus muscle. This muscle allows the eye to move away from midline toward the temple, a motion known as abduction.

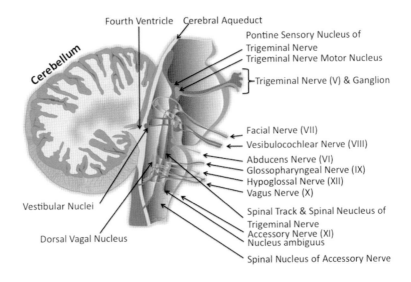

Figure 4: Schemata of the pathways of the cranial nerves

Damage to the nerve results in difficulty abducting the eye on the same side and results in double vision, which is also known as diplopia. The nucleus of the abducens coordinates the lateral rectus muscle of one eye with the medial rectus muscle of the other eye, making it possible to move both eyes to the same side. For this reason, damage to the abducens nucleus results in an inability of both eyes to look toward the side where the tumor is located, rather than the double vision seen in abducens nerve lesions.

CN VII, the facial nerve, also resides in the lower pons. Damage to the facial nerve or its nucleus, results in weakness or paralysis on the same side of the face. Clinically, this manifests as asymmetric facial expressions and can result in difficulty with eating and speaking. Additional important structures that reside in the lower pons include the vestibular nuclei, portions of the spinal trigeminal (the fifth cranial nerve, also called CNV) nucleus and tract, and the superior olivary complex. The vestibular nuclei are involved in balance, so damage here results in dizziness, vertigo, and postural unsteadiness. The spinal trigeminal nucleus and tract mediate pain and temperature sensation from the face. Damage to the spinal CNV nucleus results in sensory disturbances in the face. The superior olivary complex contributes fibers to a structure known as the lateral lemniscus and these structures are involved in hearing. Lesions of the superior olivary complex or lateral lemniscus result in diminished hearing.

The middle portion of the pontine tegmentum is home to three nuclei (called the trigeminal nerve) of CNV—the motor, mesencephalic, and principle sensory nuclei. The motor nucleus controls the muscles that are involved in chewing, while the mesencephalic nucleus is involved with the position sense of these muscles. The principal sensory nucleus is primarily involved with touch sensation from the face. Damage to the motor, mesencephalic, and principle sensory nuclei result in difficulty for the child to coordinate chewing movements, weakness when chewing, as well as facial numbness. The lateral lemniscus that forms in the lower pons, and is involved in hearing continues its ascent through the middle pons. As previously mentioned, damage here results in diminished hearing.

Other Structures Impacting Function

Reticular formation

The reticular formation is a collection of small neural networks that courses through the center of the brainstem, including the midbrain, pons and medulla. It is involved in various functions, including modulation of consciousness, sleep cycles, pain, posture, tone, and balance. Damage to this critical structure can cause sleepiness, coma, and death.

Fourth ventricle

The brain has ventricles or cavities that naturally produce cerebrospinal fluid (CSF). This fluid circulates throughout the brain acting as a cushion to the nervous system. In a normally functioning brain, this fluid circulates and provides nourishment to the nervous system, and it is subsequently reabsorbed into the bloodstream. If the tumor compresses the 4th ventricle, which is located near the pons, cerebral spinal fluid can build up thereby creating abnormally high pressure within the skull. It is essential that the pressure be relieved so that the tissues in the central nervous system aren't damaged and the blood flow throughout the brain can be restored. Failure to do so can result in compromised or lost neurological function. Treatment for this fluid buildup—termed hydrocephalus, and also often referred to as "water on the brain," is most often achieved through the surgical placement of a shunt or an endoscopic third ventriculostomy. As is true with the above mentioned clinical manifestations of DIPG, not all children with DIPG develop hydrocephalus.

Conclusion

An understanding of the anatomy of the pons and the structures it contains provides the framework for deciphering the various neurological deficits that can be seen in patients afflicted with tumors that damage or displace these structures. A number of problems, including weakness, paralysis, numbness, incoordination, hydrocephalus, difficulties with taste, balance, chewing, hearing, vision, and disturbances of consciousness, may occur if these important structures or nearby structures are affected.

Parent Perspectives

Every child has a different journey with DIPG. The tumors don't always grow in the same place, or at the same speed. The brainstem where the tumor grows controls motor functions. The tragedy of DIPG is that it slowly robs the patient of motor functions such as walking, arm movements, speech, sight, eating and breathing while leaving their brain completely intact. That means that children with DIPG are aware of their decline and continue to grow and develop cerebrally in every other way.

For Stella, the first thing to disappear was her ability to walk which left her in August. She has been unable to grasp small objects and do things like feed herself since mid-September. Her eyesight is compromised, but she is still able to see some things although we're not sure how much, as it is difficult to communicate with her. However, Stella's smile remains intact and the fundamental parts of her personality—fearlessness, humor and mischievousness are still completely present.

Wednesday May 5th, Ellie stubbed her left toe while swimming with friends. The next day her tennis coach called because she felt weak and complained she was not seeing the ball right. It was hot and she said she had not taken in enough water so we assumed she was a bit dehydrated. Friday she traveled for the fourth grade field trip for a day of swimming. She had a blast! She spent the weekend with her good friend playing at the beach.

The following Tuesday on the way to tennis practice she complained her left leg and arm felt weak. We attributed her left leg to her toe injury but the arm weakness definitely did not make sense. I called my brother-in-law, a local physician. He ran through a series of neurological tests and definitely noted weakness on her left side. We left for the emergency room where we were met by family and Ellie's pediatrician. A virus was suspected but a CAT scan was ordered as a precaution.

Johnny came bounding toward me juice box in hand, when he started to stumble. His eyes shifted to the left and his head tilted to the left as his gait

fumbled before the fall. He caught himself, but staggered to our meeting place and finally fell right before he got to me. I helped him up, asked him if he was alright, made a mental note to call the doctor, and we finished out a fun afternoon.

That night Johnny had a baseball game and we decided to stop for pizza before the game. While eating his pizza, Johnny was turned around in his chair. Always the squirrely kid, Rob and I both told him to turn around and eat. As he did, he fell out of his chair. We both exchanged concerned glances since this had happened a few times over the last couple of weeks. This was not normal. Johnny was our most coordinated child. He was the one on a skateboard at one, roller skates at one and half, and road a bike with training wheels before his second birthday. Something wasn't right. Again, making a mental note to call the doctor in the morning, we headed to his ball game.

The next morning I called the doctor's office to schedule an appointment. They asked me why I wanted to bring him in and I recalled the incidence from the day before, stating I thought it might be an inner ear issue. Thirty minutes later we were at the doctor's office. The doctor asked me about the symptoms I noticed. I told him about his eyelids only opening halfway, giving him a sleepy look. I also recalled his clumsy balance, his appetite decrease and sleep increase. I had noticed most of these changes within the last couple of weeks, except his eyelids. They had been slightly drooping for around a month. Since I had all the kids with me, I was quite distracted and let the doctor do his assessment without my engagement. I could see Johnny walking up and down the hallway and the physician's assistant shaking her head no, with a concerned look. A few minutes later the doctor came in and said he was going to schedule an MRI because Johnny had failed a neurological assessment, and to not leave until he came back with the time for the MRI. Being unknowledgeable about this, I smiled, agreed and waited. A few minutes later, he came back in to say we had an MRI scheduled at 2:30 that day. The doctor also said to not eat anything since they might want to do sedation. It was starting to sink in. Something was wrong, very wrong. Before I left, I called my husband to fill him in on all the details. I also called our parents for support.

As the days went on Liam seemed to recover to a certain degree from the strep and what we thought was a bug, but never in a way that left us totally

comfortable. We began to notice his eyes were at half-mast at times. We would ask him about it and he promised that he really wasn't doing it on purpose. These symptoms seemed to come and go. He went to school every day and overall seemed ok. However as March turned to April those concerning things we were seeing began to happen more frequently. Liam came home from school one day with some school pictures. He took them out to show me and said, "Look Mom, I don't think I know how to smile anymore." I looked down at his picture and his crooked grin. It was around this time that things began to change at a rapid pace and Liam's health changed daily. We become very concerned. His affect began to be flat and we noticed balance issues. I remember waking up early just to watch him walking to the bathroom to see how his balance seemed when no one was watching. He walked the long hallway bumping into the wall and I remember thinking his walking reminded me of a child with cerebral palsy. By his birthday weekend our concern grew to alarm. At his birthday party he did not look well at all. We had watched in a matter of days the brutal symptoms of his disease come into full view and we voiced our deepest concerns to family.

Brendan was diagnosed at age 6. Two weeks before diagnosis we noticed several things. His eyes were cloudy and unfocused which we mistakenly attributed to conjunctivitis. He had given up napping when he was a toddler but was very tired and he fell asleep in the middle of the afternoon. We thought he may be having a growth spurt or was coming down with something. We noticed he was laughing and talking restlessly in his sleep where previously he had been a very quiet sleeper. He had difficulty swallowing and chewed very slowly where he never ate slowly before. His voice was raspy and he didn't smile anymore. He was experiencing painful urination and was constipated. He was holding books very close and putting his face up close to the computer and we and his teacher thought he needed an eye exam. We finally took him to the doctor when he began falling and saying he was dizzy. We noticed these symptoms for about 2 weeks before his falling really alarmed us. Any of the other symptoms alone could be dismissed as something else but all of it and his falls made it very serious. We were told his tumor was DIPG. It was in the pons and was typical. They wouldn't biopsy it because it could cause harm and possibly death, and it wouldn't change the treatment options available.

He responded well to radiation and was symptom free for 10 months. Upon progression his eyesight became blurry and he told us he was seeing double again. He lost dexterity in his right hand so he began to write with his left until he lost his left side too. He became very clumsy and was falling so we got him a walker with wheels which he loved to zip around on.

He responded well to re-irradiation and was symptom free for another 6 months. Upon his second progression he experienced the same sorts of problems with eyes, first his right side then left, and speech, chewing, swallowing and finally lost neck control and had breathing difficulty. There were no other options which could give him another "honeymoon." He progressed rapidly this time and was gone within 6 weeks of the recurrence of his first symptom of blurry vision.

Looking back after diagnosis on July 29th I can see things that were red flags but not nearly as significant as many children have displayed. At some point near the end of the school year Hope drooled a couple of times and had food on her face at meal times. I remembered these things that first week in August but nothing rang any bells then. I remember her brother coming in the house complaining that she couldn't even ride a bike straight after they had been on a ride on their tandem bike. Again nothing tied together until after her diagnosis.

On July 7th we were watching a little league ball game. Hope sat in a lawn chair between her brother and me. I looked over and saw that she had drooled down her chin and onto her blouse. When I asked her if she realized it she replied, "Mom, how would I feel that? My face has been numb for 6 weeks." You can insert a healthy dose of 12 year old attitude to that statement and then you can imagine my face. As we drove home from the game several things came to light—like while away for a week at a choir camp with her best friend, they developed a signal for when Hope had food on her face. That way she could wipe it off and wouldn't be embarrassed.

Aimee started complaining of headaches in January, noting that they were nothing that Motrin couldn't take care of at first. Then they became more severe in late February early March. Upon a trip to the doctor, without tests being done, it was determined she had migraines and was put on meds for her headaches. Aimee was a cheerleader and had several competitions

between May and August and began losing her balance, started getting hiccups even with just a sip of water. Then she began complaining she couldn't breathe. After several more trips to the doctor's office—again with no tests done, she was given acid reflux medicine, as well as asthma medicine. We were told she was dehydrated and to push the fluids. They also gave her several antibiotics for an inner ear infection. They claimed that was causing the dizziness and loss of balance. Finally, at the end of August she began to vomit and needed to sleep often. She told me that the doctors were crazy, because the only thing wrong with her was that she had a brain tumor. I of course told her she was crazy, because "kids don't get brain tumors." Then she made a bet with me for $10.00 because she said she felt it growing.

September 25th, I took Aimee to see a new doctor; he did several neurological examinations and referred us to a neurologist. The earliest appointment we could get was in October. Upon leaving the office Aimee began to vomit profusely, refused to go back in to see the doctor and just wanted to go home and sleep. She stayed home from school the next day, and slept and vomited off and on all day. Then on Thursday the 27th, Aimee woke up with an extreme headache but still wanted to go to school because it was picture day. Her balance worsened as well. A few days later, we began to ride our bikes and Aimee was swerving all over the road. I joked that she was going to get a DUI for her riding. Upon returning to the house I called the doctor who was not in. His nurse called me a few minutes later and advised me to get her to the emergency room right away—they are expecting you.

Gunner was not himself the whole Thanksgiving holiday. He was pretty lethargic and was complaining of headaches for over a week. He said it was in the back of his head and moved up and forward to the front. We decorated for Christmas and he usually is right in there helping, but most of the time he just laid or slept (which is really unusual for him). He complained of being hot all the time (which again is not his character). He is usually cold. He didn't have a fever at all. He always runs a fever when he is not feeling well. He also began to just stare off into space—a couple of times while in the middle of a conversation with me. Gunner started walking and then sitting down with his head bent down. It made me very uncomfortable to watch him. He just seemed to have no posture anymore. He started playing

with, and twisting his ears. He also started this mouth swishing thing—it sounds like when you are washing your mouth out with mouth wash.

I also think he was hard to understand at times. I really had to listen to what he was saying. Could his speech be getting worse? When I asked Gunner about his headaches he told me that sometimes he has trouble seeing the board at school. When I told him that we could get his eyes checked, he got upset and told me that he was joking. I didn't think he was joking. He just didn't want to go to another doctor appointment. When I tried to calm him down about his headaches and his eyes, he told me that the TV was split in half and that when I walked into the room my upper body was not attached to my legs. He continued to complain of a pain in the back of his head. He also complained about being dizzy, and tingling in his left hand. I took him to counseling, a behavior specialist, occupational therapy, an optometrist, our local doctor, and was given the diagnosis of autism. I felt like we just kept hitting walls and weren't getting the help we knew we needed.

Johnny's tumor is in the pons. It is actually in the back side of the pons close to the cerebellum. The cerebellum controls motor function. The tumor is growing and pressing into the cerebellum which is why he is having difficulty walking and with his balance. The pons controls all his involuntary functions—his heartbeat, his breathing, swallowing, muscle control and many other life giving functions. The pons is like grand central station in the brain. This tumor is taking over those functions and shutting them down.

Julian's heart rate had slipped into the 30's in PICU which led to an emergency midnight flight from Detroit to Memphis. It was one week before Christmas. That morning, I found myself sitting in the basement of a brand new hospital waiting to speak with one of St. Jude's neurosurgeons while Julian was having an MRI. There was intense debate about whether the dangerously low heart rate was the result of tumor progression or continued hydrocephalus. Sleep deprived and practically a shell of myself, our surgeon sat next to me on an exam table and began to draw a diagram of Julian's tumor on the sterile white paper between us.

To my horror, the picture looked like a snake wrapping itself around our beautiful son's control center as if holding his life for ransom. Only there was no bargaining. The site of the tumor controlled his heart rate and respiratory function and through the middle ran the critical basilar artery making it too risky to attempt to surgically debulk. When tears came, I explained that this was the first time anyone had shown me the anatomy of this monster. It was then that the disease earned my respect. It was the most formidable of foes and it held the upper hand. No drugs had any proven effect. So sly, so cunning, it reminded me of an evil serpent almost taunting us with its advantage. It was explained to us that even with intense radiation therapy, we could never kill every single cell. With even two or three microscopic cells left behind, it would come back. And when it did, it would return with a vengeance.

Months after we lost Julian, I read how a DIPG researcher described the deadly glial cell's shape under a microscope as a preschooler's illustration of sunshine. I found it so ironic.

Chapter 4

Imaging DIPG

Jonathan Finlay, MD
Girish Dhall, MD
John Grimm, MD
Stefan Bluml, PhD

The understanding of brainstem tumors, including diffuse infiltrating pontine glioma (DIPG), has advanced considerably over the last few decades largely as a result of advances in imaging technology. Nevertheless, the understanding of brainstem tumors by imaging has always been, and continues to be, limited by the lack of histopathology (microscopic evaluation of tumor tissue) correlating to the imaging characteristics. This is primarily related to the risk involved to the patient through the biopsy of these tumors accompanied by the questionable direct therapeutic benefits for the child.

The development of Magnetic Resonance Imaging (MRI) has significantly improved our understanding of these tumors. MRI allows improved visualization and characterization of brainstem tumors in comparison to Computed Tomography (CT). MRI provides superior imaging of the posterior fossa of the brain in comparison to CT, which is limited secondary to artifacts related to the thick bones of the skull base. Furthermore, in comparison to CT, MRI has superior soft tissue contrast resolution, which aids in characterization of these tumors [Fig. 1a, 1b]. The recent development of advanced imaging techniques including magnetic resonance spectroscopy and magnetic resonance perfusion imaging will continue to improve our understanding of these tumors.

History of the Imaging of "Brainstem Glioma" and the Recognition of DIPG

Historically, tumors in the brainstem were both regarded and treated as a single entity, namely "brainstem glioma." In the early 1990s, as MRI became more widely available and utilized, several attempts

Dr. Jonathan Finlay is Director of the Neural Tumors Program at Children's Hospital Los Angeles, and Professor of Neurology and Neurosurgery at the Keck School of Medicine, University of Southern California, Los Angeles, CA.

were made to characterize brainstem tumors based on MRI criteria. An early classification system based on MRI was established by Dr. A. James Barkovich of the University of California, San Francisco, and several of his North American colleagues. Specifically, tumor characterization was based upon:

- the site of primary involvement in the brainstem;

- the longitudinal and axial extent of the tumor within the brainstem;

- the tumor growth pattern (diffuse or focal);

- the enlargement of the brainstem;

- and the presence or absence of exophytic growth (i.e. growth extending outside the brainstem) enhancement, cysts, hydrocephalus, hemorrhage or necrosis.

Later correlation of such MRI criteria against survival statistics found several imaging characteristics to be significant. The particular segment or region of origin within the brainstem was found to be important. Tumors arising from the midbrain have the best prognosis. Tumors arising from the medulla have an intermediate prognosis. Tumors arising from the pons have the worst prognosis. A diffusely infiltrative appearance of the tumor was also found to have a significantly worse prognosis. A diffusely infiltrative appearance referred to tumors that had ill defined margins and involved more than one half of

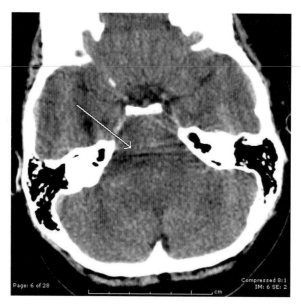

Figure 1a: Axial CT demonstrating poor visualization of the tumor, made worse by artifact from the adjacent thick skull base.

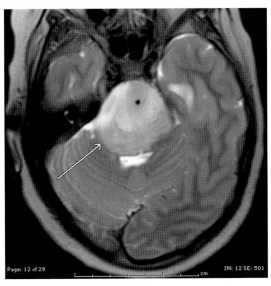

Figure 1b: Axial T2 MRI of the same tumor demonstrates the improved soft tissue contrast resolution, improving visualization and characterization of the tumor.

the brainstem segment of origin, or infiltrated the segments of the brainstem both superior and inferior to the segment of origin (i.e. infiltration of both the midbrain and the medulla if the segment of origin was the pons).

Finally, enlargement of the brainstem by the tumor was found to be negatively related to survival, with a tumor that enlarges the brainstem having a poorer survival [Fig. 2a, 2b].

As a result of these findings, attempts were made to develop new classification systems that better reflected prognosis. Dr. N.J. Fischbein and colleagues of Germany proposed a classification system in which tumors were divided into 6 groups, each having its own prognostic implications. The six groups included: 1) focal midbrain tumors, 2) diffuse midbrain tumors, 3) tectal tumors, 4) focal pontine tumors, 5) diffuse pontine tumors, and 6) cervicomedullary tumors.

It soon became clear that brainstem tumors were a diverse group of tumors with variable prognoses. Accordingly, management of the tumor needed to be tailored to the suspected tumor type. Studies in which biopsies were obtained for larger numbers of patients confirmed this observation. Of note, Dr. Paul Fischer and colleagues working at Stanford School of Medicine found that most brainstem tumors could be divided into two classes: pilocytic astrocytomas (World Health Organization grade I tumor) or fibrillary

Dr. Dhall is an Assistant Professor of Pediatrics in the Department of Hematology/Oncology at Children's Hospital Los Angeles, CA.

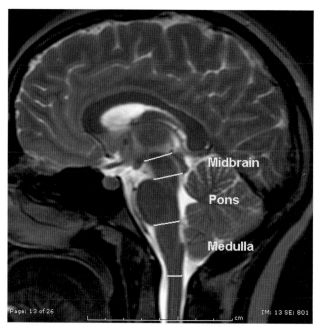

Figure 2a: Sagittal T2 MRI of a normal brainstem demonstrating the normal anatomy of the midbrain, pons and medulla.

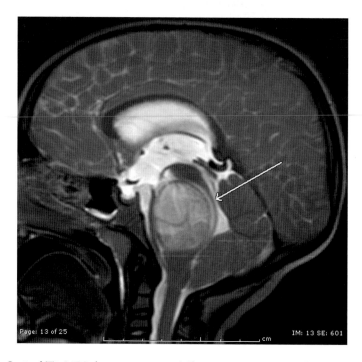

Figure 2b: Sagittal T2 MRI demonstrating a diffuse intrinsic pontine glioma originating from the pons, diffusely infiltrating and enlarging the pons.

astrocytomas. Pilocytic astrocytoma had a favorable prognosis (5 year survival of 95%) and were associated with a location outside of the ventral (anterior) pons and a dorsal (posterior) exophytic growth. Fibrillary astrocytomas had a poorer prognosis (5 year survival of 15%) and were associated with a location in the ventral pons that engulfed the basilar artery [Fig. 3a, 3b].

In addition to these two main tumor types, other tumor types which are less frequently found within the brainstem include: ganglioglioma, primitive neuroectodermal tumor (PNET), atypical teratoid rhabdoid tumor (AT/RT),

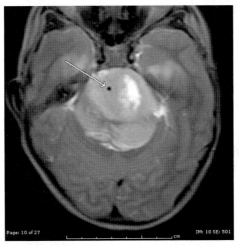

Figure 3a: Axial T2 MRI of a fibrillary astrocytoma (diffuse intrinsic pontine glioma) demonstrating a mass arising from the pons, enlarging the pons and engulfing the basilar artery.

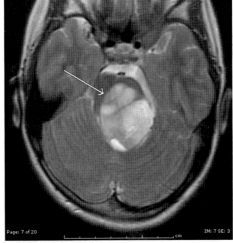

Figure 3b: Axial T2 MRI of a long term survivor of a "brainstem glioma" which is likely not a fibrillary astrocytoma. This image demonstrates more benign features including a focal mass with well-defined margins centered in the dorsal (posterior) pons with a dorsal exophytic growth.

oligodendroglioma, and lymphoma.

Conventional Imaging

It is now generally accepted that there is a distinct subtype of brainstem tumor which can be identified on imaging as a diffuse intrinsic pontine glioma (DIPG). These invariably correspond to fibrillary astrocytomas on pathology and have an extremely poor prognosis, the worst of any type of brainstem tumor. They demonstrate many of the characteristics that have been outlined above. Those characteristics include:

- They generally arise from the pons, more specifically the ventral pons.

- They are diffuse tumors, infiltrating greater than half the transverse diameter of the brainstem segment of origin and having indistinct margins.

- They also tend to expand the segment of the brainstem from which they arise.

- This expansion coupled with the common location in the ventral pons results in the tendency to engulf the basilar artery.

- These masses are generally iso- to hypo-dense (equal to or dark) to normal adjacent brain on CT, hypointense (dark) to normal adjacent brain on T1 weighted MRI, and hyperintense (bright) to normal adjacent brain on T2 weighted MRI.

- These imaging characteristics generally reflect the increased water content of these tumors.

- The presence of enhancement after the administration of contrast, cysts or necrosis, and hemorrhage is variable in these tumors [Fig. 4a, 4b, 4c, 4d]. Necrosis is generally described as areas of relative increased T2 signal and decreased T1 signal within the tumor with peripheral or "ring" enhancement.

These typical findings of DIPG, considered to represent fibrillary astrocytomas, are in contrast to focal tumors of the brainstem, which usually represent tumors of different histopathologies.

Several studies focusing on DIPG have attempted to determine if any conventional MRI characteristics at the time of tumor presentation are helpful in predicting

Dr. Grimm is an Assistant Professor in Pediatric Neuroradiology at Children's Hospital Los Angeles, CA.

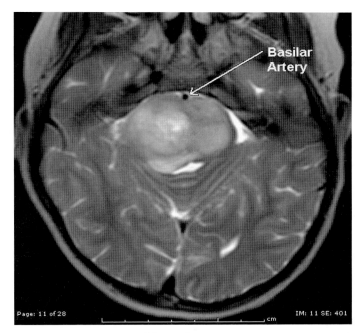

Figure 4a

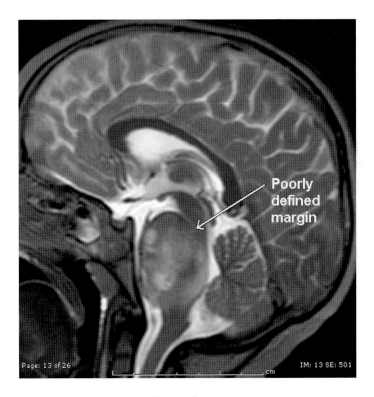

Figure 4b

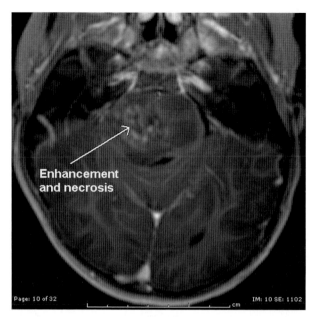

Figure 4c

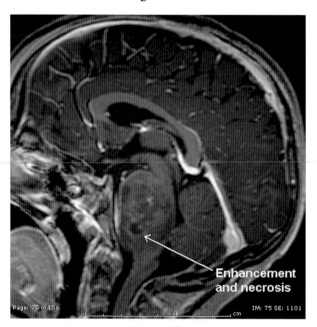

Figure 4d

Figures 4a, 4b, 4c, 4d: Axial T2 (a), sagittal T2 (b), axial T1 post contrast (c) and sagittal T1 postcontrast (d) MRI of a diffuse intrinsic pontine glioma demonstrating a diffusely infiltrating and ill-defined mass of the pons which involves more than half of the pons and enlarges the pons, having mass effect on, but not yet engulfing the basilar artery. It is predominantly hyperintense (bright) on T2 and hypointense (dark) on T1 with small areas of enhancement and possible necrosis.

Chapter 4: Imaging

prognosis. No findings on conventional MRI at tumor presentation have been found to be correlated to response to therapy, progression, or overall survival. Imaging characteristics that have been analyzed include: volume and extent of tumor, signal intensity on T1 and T2 images, appearance of borders, peritumoral edema, exophytic components, encasement of the basilar artery, necrosis or cysts, hemorrhage, gadolinium enhancement, and metastatic disease [Fig. 5a, 5b, 5c].

It is now thought that regardless of the histopathology of the DIPG at the time of diagnosis, even if the tumor is a low grade WHO II astrocytoma at diagnosis, most diffuse intrinsic pontine gliomas will progress to WHO III anaplastic astrocytoma or WHO IV glioblastoma multiforme at the time of

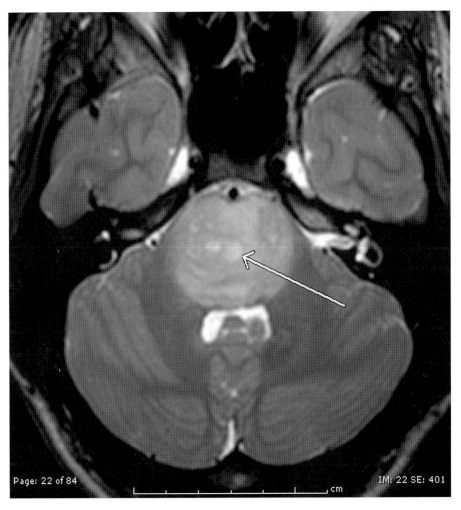

Page: 22 of 84   IM: 22 SE: 401

Figure 5a: More images of diffuse intrinsic pontine gliomas. Axial T2 MRI demonstrates a mass originating from and enlarging the pons. Subtle areas of increased signal intensity (brighter) may represent small areas of necrosis.

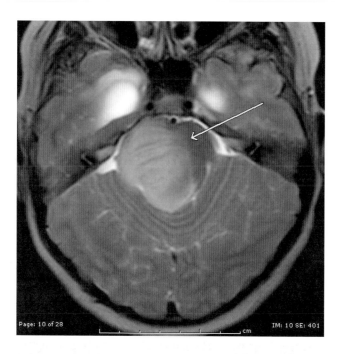

Figure 5b: Axial T2 MRI demonstrating a mass originating from and enlarging the right side of the pons with ill-defined margins.

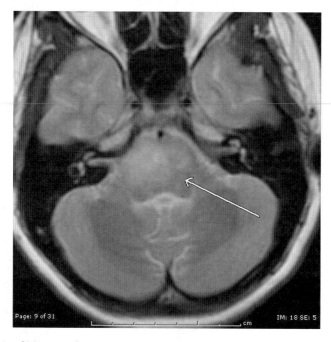

Figure 5c: Axial T2 MRI demonstrating a smaller mass originating from the right side of the pons with ill-defined margins and subtle, if any, enlargement of the pons.

death. Although a small percentage of DIPG will demonstrate areas of necrosis at presentation, almost all will develop areas of necrosis during the course of the disease. There is debate regarding whether the development of necrosis indicates treatment related changes (i.e. radiation necrosis), or reflects the natural malignant degeneration of low grade tumors (WHO II) to high grade tumors (WHO III and IV). Although positron emission tomography (PET) has been used to make this distinction with other brain tumors (see section below on advanced imaging), there has been difficulty in applying this to DIPG. Nevertheless, many consider the development of new areas of enhancement or necrosis a grave prognostic indicator that often precedes death [Fig. 6a, 6b, 6c, 6d].

In addition to developing areas of necrosis, most tumors will continue to infiltrate more portions of the brainstem during the course of the disease. They preferentially grow in a cranial direction through the midbrain into the cerebral peduncles and thalamus, and it is suggested that this finding may also be a poor prognostic indicator.

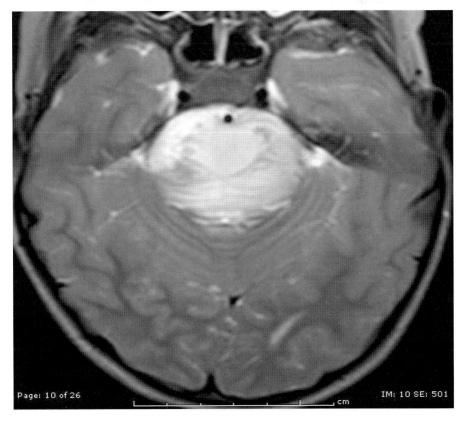

Figure 6a

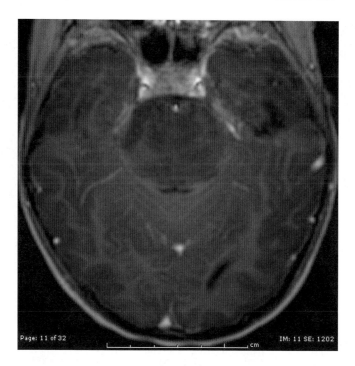

Figure 6b

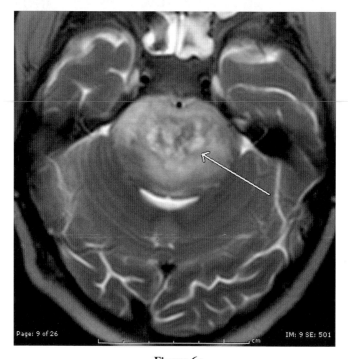

Figure 6c

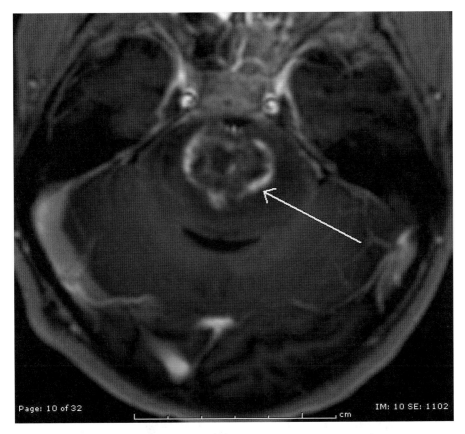

IM: 10 SE: 1102

Figure 6d

Figures 6a, 6b, 6c, 6d: Axial T2 (6a) and axial T1 post contrast (6b) MRI at presentation and axial T2 (6c) and axial T1 postcontrast (d) MRI one and one half months later demonstrating the development of necrosis visualized as an area of peripheral enhancement.

Despite the fact that conventional MRI has not been helpful in the development of prognostic criteria for DIPG at initial presentation, there continues to be a small subset of patients that have an unexpectedly long survival. It is uncertain if the lesions in these patients represent a more benign tumor type other than a fibrillary astrocytoma or even lesions other than tumors, such as inflammatory lesions that mimic DIPG on imaging. Furthermore, perhaps these tumors are less biologically active or are more sensitive to treatment. The advent of new advanced imaging techniques including magnetic resonance spectroscopy and magnetic resonance perfusion imaging may soon improve our understanding of the biology and natural history of DIPG and lesions that mimic them on conventional MRI.

Dr. Bluml is an Associate Professor of Research Radiology at Children's Hospital Los Angeles, CA.

Advanced Imaging

Magnetic resonance spectroscopy

Proton magnetic resonance spectroscopy (MRS) can currently be performed on most standard MRI machines. The interaction of protons with their environment helps to identify and measure various substances within the brain. The most commonly measured substances include:

- choline (Cho, 3.2ppm), related to the synthesis of cell membranes and increased in states of high membrane turnover (example tumor);
- creatine (Cr, 3.0ppm), a reflection of cellular metabolism and generally used as an internal reference;
- N-acetyl aspartate (NAA, 2.0ppm), located primarily in neurons and considered a normal neuronal marker, decreased with neuronal destruction;
- lactate (Lac, 1.3ppm), a product of anaerobic metabolism which is increased with abnormal blood flow, abnormal metabolism or necrosis;
- lipids (Lip, 0.9ppm), a constituent of cell walls which is increased as a product of necrosis and cell membrane destruction.

Theoretically, malignant lesions should demonstrate high Cho to Cr ratios and high Cho to NAA ratios due to the rapid turnover of cell membranes increasing Cho, and the destruction of normal neurons decreasing NAA. Accordingly, Smith and colleagues found that MRS may be helpful to distinguish neoplastic from non-neoplastic lesions in the brainstem, with neoplastic lesions having high Cho and low NAA levels and non-neoplastic lesions having normal to low Cho and low NAA levels. Furthermore, MRS may be helpful to differentiate between different tumor histopathologies when the conventional MRI appearance is uncertain. MRS may be helpful to suggest other histopathologies such as pilocytic astrocytoma or PNET, which can often have characteristic profiles on MRS [Fig. 7a, 7b].

Although no metabolic measures on MRS at tumor presentation have been found to be significantly associated with survival, several studies have reported the changes on MRS over time to help to understand tumor biology. Dr. Laprie and colleagues examined the changes in MRS with radiotherapy. They found that Cho to NAA ratios initially decreased within 2 months following radiotherapy corresponding clinical and conventional imaging responses. Subsequently, Cho to NAA and Cho to Cr ratios were observed to increase at the time of relapse. Furthermore, in some patients, changes in MRS preceded both clinical and MRI deterioration by 2 to 5 months. Similar results were

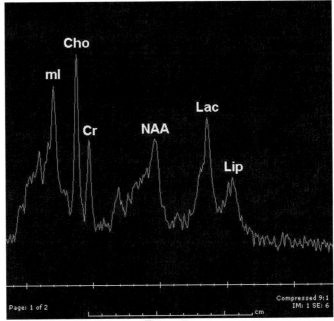

Figure 7a

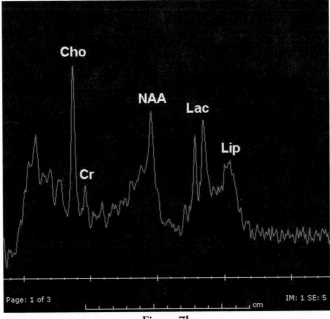

Figure 7b

Figures 7a, 7b: Magnetic resonance spectroscopy comparing diffuse intrinsic pontine glioma (a) to pilocytic astrocytoma (b). MRS of a DIPG demonstrating elevation of myoinositol (mI), choline (Cho), lipid (Lip) and lactate (Lac) with decreased creatine (Cr) and NAA. MRS of a pilocytic astrocytoma demonstrating a high choline to creatine level with a characteristically low absolute creatine level and a relatively preserved NAA.

obtained by Dr. Panigrahy and colleagues who also found that metabolic changes on MRS preceded clinical deterioration. Serial examination of tumors demonstrated increasing levels of Cho and Lipids and decreasing levels of NAA, Cr, and myo-inositol relative to Cho. These changes likely reflect malignant degeneration and possible transformation from low grade to high grade tumor [Fig. 8a, 8b].

Magnetic resonance perfusion

Magnetic resonance perfusion imaging (MRP) has recently been studied in supratentorial gliomas in adults and has been found to be a good predictor of world health organization (WHO) tumor grade, progression free survival, progression and death. MRP of tumors is typically performed using dynamic contrast enhanced perfusion imaging techniques.

MRP techniques rely on the magnetic susceptibility signal loss that intravenous gadolinium produces on T2* sequences during MRI. By measuring the degree of T2* signal loss caused by the gadolinium in blood vessels over time, one can determine the relative volume of blood, or relative cerebral blood volume (rCBV), within a tumor. Similarly, the relative cerebral blood flow (rCBF) and the mean transit time (MTT) can also be measured. These measurements

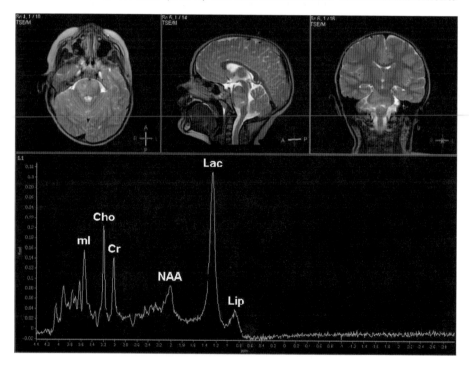

Figure 8a

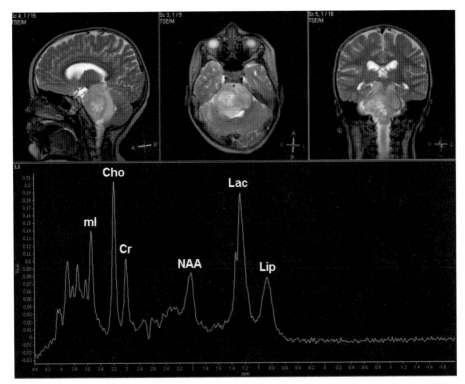

Figures 8a (previous page), 8b (above): Magnetic resonance spectroscopy demonstrating signs of progression with interval increase in choline (Cho) and the choline to creatine (Cr) level over a period of 5 months from 8a to 8b.

are thought to be surrogate markers for blood vessel proliferation within malignant brain tumors—an important feature in the grading of gliomas on histopathology. Accordingly, several studies have shown that gliomas with low rCBV, and theoretically lower tumor blood vessel proliferation, have longer time to progression and gliomas with high rCBV, and theoretically higher tumor blood vessel proliferation, have shorter time to progression. This was found to be true regardless of WHO grade on biopsy. Some studies have even suggested that measurements of rCBV were more predictive of prognosis than histopathology and WHO grade on biopsy. It has been proposed that this finding is most likely the result of either sampling error on biopsy (as tumors are heterogeneous and the portion of the tumor with the highest WHO grade may be missed on biopsy) or variability in consistency of diagnosis among pathologists.

To date, little research has been performed utilizing MRP in the analysis of DIPG. This may be a promising avenue to help stratify patients based on the aggressiveness of their tumors and their prognosis [Fig. 9].

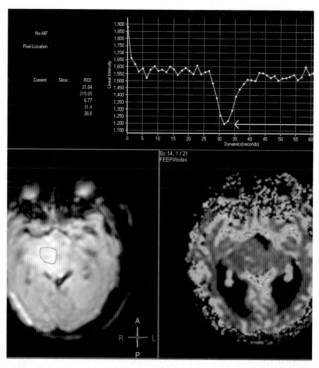

Figure 9: Magnetic resonance perfusion imaging of a diffuse intrinsic pontine glioma measuring relative cerebral blood volume. The graph plots the signal intensity of the tumor over time. The signal intensity decreases when the contrast bolus enters the blood vessels within the tumor.

Positron emission tomography

Positron Emission Tomography in combination with CT (PET/CT) is a tool that helps radiologists understand the metabolic activity of tumors. PET/CT measures the accumulation of tracers in cells that are incorporated into the cells during metabolism. The most commonly used tracer in PET/CT is 2[18F] fluoro-2-deoxy-D-glucose (FDG). FDG is a measure of glucose metabolism, and most tumors have increased glucose metabolism in comparison to normal tissues. A less frequently used and less widely available tracer in brain tumor imaging is 11C-L-methionine (MET), which is involved in amino acid transport, also increased in tumors. MET may be more sensitive for low grade tumors, in comparison to FDG, due to the lower background activity of MET in normal brain.

Several studies focusing on brain tumors have shown that PET/CT can help to separate less aggressive tumors from more aggressive tumors, tumor from radiation necrosis, and tumor from scar tissue. Fewer studies have focused exclusively on brainstem tumors in children. These studies have suggested that

PET/CT may also be helpful in the evaluation of DIPG to differentiate low grade tumors from high grade tumors, with FDG uptake being increased in high grade tumors. Dr. Kwon and colleagues found that only WHO IV glioblastoma multiforme tumors were FDG hypermetabolic ("hot") [Fig. 10a, 10b, 10c].

Furthermore, Dr. Pirotte and colleagues noticed that patients with the highest FDG uptake had shorter survival times. PET/CT has also been found to be useful in planning biopsies. In comparison to utilizing contrast MRI for planning biopsies, PET/CT has a higher diagnostic yield, requiring a fewer number of biopsies. Furthermore, PET/CT guidance yielded an equivalent or higher tumor grade in comparison to MRI guidance. As mentioned previously in the section on perfusion imaging, DIPG are heterogeneous in their histopathology, and PET/CT can help to guide a biopsy to the areas of a tumor with the highest grade. This will help to prevent the under-grading of a tumor with a conventionally guided biopsy. There have only been a few small studies of PET/CT in brainstem tumors and further work is needed to develop this promising technology.

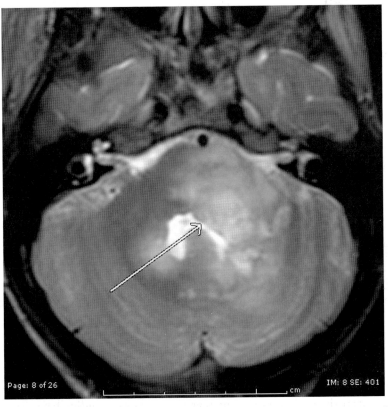

Figure 10a: Axial T2 MRI (a) demonstrating a diffusely infiltrating mass involving the left pons and left cerebellar hemisphere.

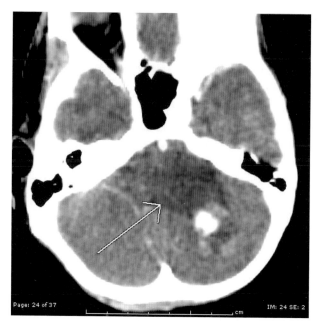

Figure 10b

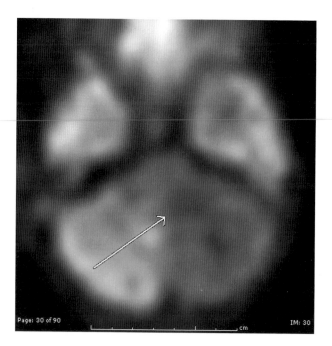

Figure 10c

Figures 10b, 10c: Corresponding axial CT (b) and axial FDG PET (c) demonstrate a hypometabolic (cold) lesion.

Summary

Advances in imaging techniques over the last several decades have improved our understanding of brainstem tumors. It is now generally accepted that there is a specific subtype of brainstem tumor that can be identified on imaging as a diffuse intrinsic pontine glioma (DIPG). This tumor invariably represents a fibrillary astrocytoma on histopathology and has an extremely poor prognosis—the worst of any type of brainstem tumor. On imaging this tumor is typically:

- T2 hyperintense (bright);

- arises from the pons;

- is diffusely infiltrating with ill-defined margins;

- involves more than one half of the pons;

- expands the pons often engulfing the basilar artery.

Despite advances in imaging technology, we have yet to find imaging features that can help to predict prognosis. New imaging techniques, including magnetic resonance spectroscopy (MRS), perfusion imaging and positron emission tomography (PET), may someday help us to better understand the biology of this tumor, and in turn improve the treatment of this tumor.

Parent Perspectives

I think that imaging is important in this diagnosis because it can be very risky to do a biopsy. However I highly recommend sending scans to a few other doctors that deal with this tumor regularly for their opinions. We did try to read and understand the scans and it was difficult and overwhelming often. I would try to print off comparable images from different scans. A few times our doctors did pull up our scans right at the hospital to talk to us about them directly. Our doctors were very kind and spoke to us about our child's prognosis (when it was good and bad) while reviewing the scans with us.

When Tatumn was diagnosed we asked for copies of the MRI scans so we could send them to other centers for second opinions. I felt a little strange about diagnosing her tumor with just an MRI. My personal background taught me the only way to really be sure of cancer is a surgical biopsy. But all of the doctors were in agreement that this was a DIPG and this was how they did it now. To be sure I had them sent to other hospitals and received the same response.

After being home from the hospital a week or so we decided to open one of the discs on our own computer because we were still trying to wrap our head around what was going on in her sweet little head. So we downloaded a program to open the scans on our computer. A lot of the pictures were hard for me to decipher and I was trying so hard to remember what the doctors had explained to me on that overwhelming night.

I found what I call a profile shot. It showed her tumor from the side of her head. I saw that hazy mass and was overtaken by nausea. That picture was so hurtfully powerful and so ugly at the same time. I knew I couldn't look at any more of the pictures and neither could my husband. We never opened them again. When she had her first scan after radiation, the doctors were excited to tell us that there was about a 25% reduction. Since there are so many pictures and angles I couldn't sort through everything I saw. So I asked to see an original diagnosis image and a matching after radiation image from the same perspective. I wanted to see a difference. I don't know why I had to ask that and it wasn't just shown to me that way. Nonetheless our neurosurgeon took the time to try and show me comparative scans—then and now from the same angle. I saw some stuff I didn't like but I also saw the reduction in size in spots and some clean edges of the brainstem where before I saw that diffuse haze. It was very good to refuel my hope.

When her tumor started to progress a month later she was rescanned. I knew it was back. This time they scanned her spine and it had spread there too. I didn't need to see any more scans at that point in time.

Tumor measurements were very important to us following the first few scans. It was six months after diagnosis when we began to realize that measuring a diffuse tumor was not an exact science. The cancer cells are sprinkled among healthy brain cells. So how do you know where to start measuring? It was about this time that we understood the importance of having the same radiologist read and compare scans. One radiologist's measurements may differ substantially from another's. We also realized by this time that DIPG scans need to be read by someone who has a good amount of experience with DIPG. We got a copy of every scan and sent it to Andrew's neuro-oncologist for her opinion.

I feel that the MRIs that Noelia had done were sufficient to get an accurate diagnosis. I personally did not try to read them though. I listened to our doctors explain them to us (usually the day after the scan was done) and I have reviewed the written reports which did not give me any more information I would understand. Our doctors did a great job explaining each scan. They took the time to answer all of our questions and even explain the scans to other family members that had questions in Spanish. My first impressions were mind numbing though, because the doctors we spoke to were very direct in the prognosis of the tumor. They did not try to sugar coat it. I understand that there is no cure. I understand it's inoperable. I understand that there is no reason why. Noelia's tumor was located in the middle of the pons and we could see it very clearly in the scans. We also saw the change in the tumor after radiation. It reduced in size about 50 percent, but obviously it grew back. We did not have any more scans done after the symptoms came back. We knew what was happening.

Fear was written all over Johnny's body, as he faced the unknown of an MRI. An MRI requires the patient to hold very still for at least fifteen minutes. The technician offered two options. Johnny could have sedation but I would not lay on the table with him or he could go without the sedation and I would lie on the table during the MRI. Johnny chose to have me on the table and gave up the sleep medicine. The tech explained everything that was going to happen and about how long it would take.

As he lay down on the table, they put a brace around his head with a mirror on it. Instead of moving his head to see me, he could look in the tilted mirror. It is a small tube that you slide into and when they turn on the machine the magnets bounce around making a horrendous noise. My husband and I were given ear plugs. Johnny had on headphones and was able to listen to the radio. As I lay on the bed, I watched as my seven year old son showed more tenacity than most adults. He lay there with his eyes closed. Periodically he would open them, and look at me. I would smile and he would smile. I would wink and he would smile. I would close my eyes and he would return to closing his eyes. At one point he even fell asleep and I watched as his breathing evened and his chest rose in rhythm. The noise was deafening even with ear plugs in. I didn't find out until later how terrified he was and how much comfort I was to him. The magnets slowed in their bounce, the technician came in and told us he did a great job and we headed toward home.

In the morning, we had an appointment to meet with the doctor. As we entered the doctor's office we were taken to a room with large windows. The room had a wooden porch bench, a computer, a stool and a patient table. We sat down on the wooden bench with the doctor sitting on the stool next to the computer, and the physician's assistant standing on the other side of the monitor. The MRI scan was displayed on the computer. The doctor explained that there was a mass around four centimeters in the middle of the brain called the pons. He gave us a photocopy of a brain and circled the pons. He went on to explain, "This area of the brain controls all the involuntary functions of the body—everything a body does without thinking."

We nodded with partial understanding and amazed disbelief. He turned on the monitor to show us the scan. He showed us exactly where the mass was, outlining the perimeter. The scan was very clear showing to us that Johnny had done a great job holding still. There were multiple frames and angles of the brain and the mass. The doctor asked if we had any questions. We were speechless. It was an unbelievable moment to find out that our son had something in his brain and we would drop life to do anything to fix the problem so he could be healthy again.

We learned that Johnny had a cancer called DIPG. The tumor is inoperable and the cancer is incurable. At the sound of those words, I buried my face in my hands. In the background I heard details about radiation and experimental chemotherapy. The doctor recommended not taking a biopsy or attempting to remove the tumor due to its location, but if we did want to pursue that option there was a hospital in France that was taking biopsy tissue. We both nodded in agreement that this was not a course of action we were interested in pursuing. After answering questions, he briefly discussed the protocols available and we began an eight week treatment plan.

Upon discharge, we were given a CD copy of all of his scans. We went back every eight weeks for a follow up MRI to monitor tumor changes.

We met with Liam's neurosurgeon who showed us the CT scan done the day before. This was our first time seeing the image. I knew almost instinctually that this could very well be our worst case scenario playing out. The doctor pointed out the lesion and then the area around it. Liam's doctor said that area was what we needed to understand better and would with an MRI. His words and direct eye contact struck me. I turned back to the image and couldn't take my eyes off that area.

Later that same day, Liam had his MRI. We were given the news the next morning. We were taken to a small room filled with at least four doctors, a nurse and a social worker. The MRI image was brought up on a screen. It was clear it was in his brainstem. His neurosurgeon told us it was a brainstem glioma that originated in the pons of Liam's brain. It was inoperable. The first words from my mouth were: "How long do we have with him?" Our doctor answered, "Possibly a year but most likely less." As strange as it may sound I felt relief. Based on how quickly Liam's health had declined and how sick he was when we brought him to the hospital I had thought surely he had, at the most, only months. I was trying desperately to squash the terror that we may not be able to even bring him home from this place. A year seemed, in this strange and terrifying new world, like a blessing. It was our first lesson in the gift of perspective that this journey gave to us.

Around November, I began to notice very small changes—changes even Liam's Dad did not sometimes see without me pointing them out. Soon though, he began to notice them as well. Intermittent vomiting returned. Strangely this came with no nausea or warning and once finished did not bother Liam at all. He took to calling it his "party trick." In December and early January we noticed balance issues here and there. He was scanned after the holidays but his scan appeared relatively stable. We did not believe this was the case based on what we were seeing at home and we were blessed to have doctors that listened when we voiced our concern. We were told, "If mom or dad tells us that something is not right, we believe them. That's all we need to hear. We will always treat Liam not his scan." How blessed were we! It was decided to rescan Liam in 4 weeks vs. the two months that was previously the norm. We had learned that sometimes a scan doesn't always reflect how a child is presenting clinically, especially with DIPG. It's that old sand analogy again. Hard to sometimes visualize the subtle changes that are occurring in the brain on a scan but that are clear as day when spending time with the child himself and especially when viewed under the VERY, and by this point, practiced and careful eye of his parents! In four weeks, Liam's scan matched what we were seeing in our every day. Nine months from diagnosis the "honeymoon period" was over and tumor progression had settled in.

Initially our son was given a CT scan of the brain ordered by his local pediatrician. This image only showed the area of necrosis within his tumor and an area of abnormality around that. However, the area of concern around the "lesion" could not be definitively diagnosed without an MRI which was done two days later.

In subsequent images taken, the MRI in general was a good marker for progress. However, later when his symptoms slowly started to re-appear his MRI image did not reflect what we were seeing symptomatically. Thankfully his doctors recognized that it can take the scan image some time before it reflects what a parent may be seeing clinically.

We were very fortunate that the same person sat with us every time to review his scans. This is not always the case and can be problematic at times. It's important to establish continuity of care as much as possible. It's also advisable to have someone (maybe not too many doctors though) review your child's scan who is very experienced in reading scans of DIPG kids.

Chapter 4: Imaging

We were extremely fortunate to have our son's neurosurgeon read and review every one of his scans with us personally while he was recovering from anesthesia. At times the radiologist also called us in if there were any areas she had a particular concern over so that we might be able to discuss them then and not wait. Because this time was taken, we always walked away from each scan with a peace and understanding about what the results said. This practice is not the most common but if possible can do so much to aide in the continuity of care for families. It was a blessing in the midst of so much uncertainty.

We took Gabby to see her pediatrician after she was having problems with her balance and her speech seemed off. The pediatrician didn't seem too concerned with her reflex test as well as her balance, but she wanted to keep getting her tested to ease our minds. We were scheduled for an MRI a week later and in that time we went for blood tests and an eye exam. Over the following weekend Gabby's balance got so bad that she was holding on to furniture to walk. We decided not to wait the extra day for her MRI and took her to the emergency room. She had a CT scan in the emergency room that day and we were told there was some fluid buildup but they were not really impressed by it. She was going to be admitted and they would schedule her MRI for the next day. When we went for the MRI they decided since she would be sedated they would do a lumbar puncture as well. After the MRI while she was in recovery from the sedation they had decided against the lumbar puncture and were sending her back to her room.

That's when we first knew something was wrong. The same doctors we saw in the emergency room came to deliver the news to us that she had a tumor and it was not good. They were assembling a team and they would be back in an hour to discuss it with us. Left in total shock and disbelief, my husband and I waited more like 3 hours to hear from the doctors again. They brought us into a room and showed us her slides from the MRI. They described the tumor as being in the pons of her brainstem and diffuse so they were calling it DIPG, but it was also in several other areas of her brain that made it atypical for this disease. They recommended an additional MRI with contrast, and a biopsy of her cerebellum to be sure we knew what we were dealing with. The additional MRI did not show anything else.

I sat in the balcony for the final performance of a play that Hope was in that summer. I was surprised to see her stumble over a simple dance step but no one else noticed and she didn't miss a beat so I let it go. On Sunday night I was not connecting this to the other symptoms. I would begin to do so by Tuesday. On Monday the neurologist also thought I was crazy. He reiterated our family doctor's diagnosis saying that she had Bell's palsy, that it would take some time, but if I was worried he'd order an MRI to make me feel better. I remember very clearly seeing him backing out of the room smiling, somewhat like I was a crazy over-protective mother, saying he was sure this was nothing. As "luck" would have it there was a cancelation at the MRI suite at our local hospital on Tuesday. We took it thinking it would be great to get this over and done with so we could move on with our summer. On Tuesday, the look on the MRI technician's face—who practically held my hand as he walked us to the door—spoke volumes. He sent us directly back to the neurologist's office who gave us the news that there was a "mass" on the brain.

When Sam was first diagnosed and we were in the hospital the neurosurgeon made a point of showing Sam and my husband the MRI and the tumor and where he was going to remove what he could. I was not there at the time so missed that. Later when we had MRIs done after the radiation and when he was on chemo the neuro-oncologist always showed us the MRIs but he went so fast from view to view. I understood what he was showing us at the time but could never find those views once I got home with the CD. We have all the MRIs on a CD along with the radiologist's reports but there are hundreds of views on the CD for each MRI done and I can't figure out which ones are the ones we looked at in the hospital. It was frustrating at the time and still is a source of frustration that I can't see the images of his tumor on the CD.

Chapter 5

Clinical Trials for DIPG

Adam Cohen, MS, MD
Howard Colman, MD, PhD

Many researchers are working hard to develop new treatments for DIPG. To date, no therapies are available that provide a lasting cure for this disease. As new treatments become more readily available, parents will be given additional opportunities to enroll their children in clinical trials. This chapter is focused on clinical trial design. Parents who are familiar with study design terminology and who have a basic understanding of the purpose of clinical trials are better equipped to make informed treatment decisions. Every child is unique, and treatment decisions are also unique to individual children and families.

What is a Clinical Trial?

A clinical trial is a way to test possible new treatments. Clinical trials are done in cancer to find out:

- whether a treatment is safe;

- whether a treatment has the effects on cancer cells that scientists think it will;

- whether it is effective at shrinking tumors, delaying growth of tumors, or making people live longer.

A clinical trial is a scientific experiment that must follow certain rules to ensure patient safety and that the results are true and not due to chance or bias. A clinical trial may test several different types of experimental treatments including:

- A brand new drug (usually not already FDA approved for other cancers or uses).

- A new combination of drugs (that could include new or existing drugs).

- A new technology.

- An old drug that is being used in a new way or on a new population of patients.

Dr. Cohen is an Assistant Professor in the Division of Oncology, and Department of Internal Medicine at the Huntsman Cancer Institute, Salt Lake City, UT.

There are many types of clinical trials. When participating in a clinical trial, it is important to know:

1. What kind of trial it is.

2. What the purpose of the trial is.

3. What is new and experimental about the trial.

Clinical trials are an essential part of medical research. Without clinical trials, medical knowledge cannot grow and new treatments that may save or improve the lives of future cancer patients would not be identified.

What a Clinical Trial Is and Is Not

Clinical trials must have specific characteristics that qualify them as well-designed scientific experiments. Not every study is a clinical trial. In this section, we give examples of studies that are not clinical trials and give some of the qualities of a good clinical trial.

Clinical trials must study a predetermined group of people, given a predetermined treatment and use statistics to analyze results. "Case reports" or "case series" are reports by physicians giving the results of a specific treatment observed in just a few patients. While potentially useful to other physicians, case reports of one or two patients are not true clinical trials because not enough patients are treated with a specific therapy to know if the results are due to luck, to the treatment given, or to some unknown factor. Because everyone likes a happy ending, examples of patients who seemed to respond to a treatment are much more likely to be published than examples of patients who did not respond to a treatment.

Retrospective series are also not true clinical trials, but generally provide more data and reliability than case reports. Retrospective studies look backward in time to study a group of patients with the same disease. Retrospective series are not clinical trials because the group of people and the treatment were not defined before the treatment was given. Therefore, the results may be biased by the choices both doctors and patients make. For example, healthy people tend to be treated aggressively, and healthy people tend to live longer; but that does not mean that more aggressive treatments make people live longer.

Dr. Colman is an Associate Professor and Director of Medical Neuro-Oncology in the Department of Neurosurgery, at the Huntsman Cancer Institute, University of Utah, Salt Lake City, UT.

A well-designed clinical trial needs to include:

1. A clear research question.

2. A hypothesis.

3. A specifically defined population.

4. A description of the treatment so that everyone in the trial gets treated the same way.

5. A follow-up plan that describes how often the effects of the treatment will be reassessed.

6. A statistical plan that describes how to determine at the end of trial, the answer to the initial question.

A **clear research question** describes the purpose of the clinical trial. Examples of clear questions are:

1. How often do people taking this drug experience severe side effects?

2. How often do tumors shrink when people take this drug?

3. Which drug makes people with a brain tumor live longer?

A clear question prevents misinterpreting unexpected results that could be due to chance.

The **hypothesis** is the researcher's educated guess at the answer to the question. The hypothesis spells out how safe or effective a treatment should be for the trial to be considered a success. The hypothesis also makes it clear how to know if the trial does not succeed, so that unsafe or ineffective treatments are not studied again.

Clinical trials are conducted in **specific, well-defined populations.** The population may be limited by specific diagnoses (cancers), ages, symptom levels, overall health, or other factors. These limitations are called the **inclusion and exclusion criteria.** For example, a clinical trial of brainstem gliomas may allow adults and children, just children under 18, or just children under 12, etc. Most, but not all, clinical trials require participants to have normal liver and kidney function and exclude patients with other major medical problems or multiple cancer types. Limiting the population for clinical trials helps to ensure the scientific validity of the trial. However, clinical trial results may not apply to people outside of these limits. For instance, results from a clinical trial allowing adults with brainstem glioma may not apply to children with diffuse intrinsic pontine glioma if they were excluded from that trial.

A clinical trial must have a treatment plan, follow-up plan, and statistical plan set out before starting the trial. This ensures that everyone in the trial is treated the same way and that the doctors running the trial cannot change things to make the trial results appear better than they actually are. It also potentially limits the treating doctor because tests or treatments may need to be done at specific times that are less flexible than they would be with treatments outside of a clinical trial.

Clinical Trial Phases

Clinical trial phases correspond to the different stages of testing that a drug goes through before approval. For people with brain tumors, the clinical trial phases are phase 0, phase 1, phase 2, or phase 3. The phases are sometimes referred to using the Roman numerals 0, I, II, III.

Phase 0 studies

Phase 0 clinical trials are usually done very early in the testing of a new drug. Phase 0 clinical trials test whether a drug gets into the brain or brain tumor cells and whether it "hits" the expected target. For example, if a new drug is developed to inhibit the growth protein EGFR, a phase 0 study can look at the activity of the EGFR protein in the brain tumor before and after treatment with the new drug. Phase 0 studies usually require surgery to obtain a sample of the tumor after treatment with the drug; however, depending on the specific drug and the expected target, testing of drug effects can sometimes be done on blood samples or other tissues. A common way of doing phase 0 studies is to have someone take a drug for a week before a planned surgery and then use some of the tumor removed during surgery to determine the effects of the drug on the tissue. One important aspect for patients to understand about Phase 0 studies is that they generally are not expected to benefit the individual entering the study. These studies are often done very early in the development of a drug before the optimal dose is determined, and treatment is often continued only for a short period of time. These studies do, however, potentially allow for a better understanding of how a drug works; this, in turn, aids in the planning of further trials. Phase 0 studies are generally not applicable for patients with inoperable tumors, such as diffuse intrinsic pontine gliomas, which some believe cannot be biopsied safely.

Phase 1 studies

Phase 1 clinical trials are done early in the testing of a new drug or new treatment combination to find what doses of a drug are safe to give. Phase 1 clinical trials often also test how long the drug stays in the body and how the body processes and gets rid of the drug. There are sometimes a number of extra tests required in phase 1 studies, such as blood tests, urine tests, EKGs of the heart, etc., that test for toxicity to different organs and to see how long the drug is staying in the body and how it is getting out of the body.

For traditional chemotherapy drugs, phase 1 studies often have the goal of defining what is called the **Maximum Tolerated Dose, or MTD**. The maximum tolerated dose is the dose just below where a high proportion of people have unacceptable side effects from a drug. The maximum tolerated dose is the highest dose that should be used for that drug because higher doses are generally too toxic. Sometimes, particularly for modern drugs that target specific molecules in cancer cells, phase 1 studies do not go all the way to the maximum tolerated dose, but stop at a dose where the drug is expected to completely inhibit the molecule it is targeting. This is called the **Biologically Effective Dose**.

People are enrolled in phase 1 studies as part of a group, which typically is called a **cohort**. Cohorts usually consist of three people but can vary in size from 1 person to many people. Each cohort is given a different dose of the drug being tested. The first cohort gets a very low dose. If the side effects are tolerable, the next cohort gets a higher dose. This continues until too many people in a cohort get intolerable side effects. These intolerable side effects are called **Dose Limiting Toxicities (DLT)**. The highest dose whose cohort did not get intolerable side effects is the **Maximum Tolerated Dose (MTD)**.

Phase 1 trials are a very important step in developing new cancer drugs, and everyone in a phase 1 trial is helping patients in the future. Traditionally Phase 1 studies have not focused on how well a drug works—just the safety and dosage. In most phase 1 studies, once you are in a cohort, the dose of the drug will stay the same for you. Other people who are in other cohorts may get a higher dose of the drug. Therefore, people in the earlier cohorts of a phase 1 study may get a dose of the drug that is below the dose that is thought to be needed to shrink the tumor. For this reason, as well as the fact that most drugs tested in Phase 1 will not go on to demonstrate significant efficacy in future studies, the expectation is that most people in a phase 1 trial are not likely to personally benefit from the treatment being tested. Therefore, phase 1 trials are often most appropriate after patients have failed standard treatments with proven benefit or when there are no proven treatment options available.

However, as drug companies have become more focused on drugs targeting specific proteins and molecular pathways in tumors, the role of Phase 1 testing has started to change. In the case of these drugs, the specific targets are sometimes known before the study. Thus, it is possible in these specific situations to hypothesize that patients whose tumors have that specific molecular target may be more likely to respond to that specific drug. So, in addition to defining the Maximum Tolerated Dose, some more recent Phase 1 studies also include initial measurements of tumor response or drug effects on tumors. This approach has been used successfully by scientists to demonstrate potential efficacy of promising drugs early in their development, which has accelerated the subsequent Phase 2 and 3 studies and FDA approval. It is possible that in the future, patients participating in Phase I trials of targeted drugs may have a higher chance of getting benefit from the treatment in the situation in which the patient and the physicians know that the patient's tumor has that molecular target.

Phase 2 studies

Once the safe dose of a drug is known, phase 2 clinical trials are used to see if the drug is effective against a certain kind of tumor. Phase 2 trials may have many different designs. In some Phase 2 studies, called single arm studies, everyone gets the same drug and dose. In multi-arm or randomized studies, there are several different treatments being tested or compared. Patients may get a specific treatment based on particular criteria of the study, or patients may be randomly assigned to treatment arms. Randomly assigned, also called **randomization**, means that neither you nor your doctor can choose what treatment you get. Such randomization is necessary because otherwise conscious or subconscious biases can influence the results of a trial. For example, if doctors gave everyone with small tumors the new drug and everyone with big tumors the old drug, then the new drug might look better even though it might not be better than the old drug.

The goal of a phase 2 study is to see if a new drug or combination of drugs has some beneficial effect on the tumor or other preferred patient outcomes. However, even though some Phase 2 trials include more than 100 patients, they are generally not large enough to conclusively prove whether people live longer when they take the new drug or to prove absolutely that a new drug helps. Instead, phase 2 trials often look at endpoints other than how long people live that can indicate whether a drug is helpful. These **alternate endpoints** can include:

- **Response rate:** the percent of tumors that shrink a certain amount (usually 25%) with a treatment.

- **Disease control rate:** the percent of tumors that shrink or stay the same size with a treatment. Because of random variation between scans, tumors must grow by at least 20% to 25% to not be considered the same size. Thus, if a tumor grows 10% or shrinks 10% it is considered stable, i.e., the same size.

- **Progression Free Survival (PFS):** the amount of time from the start of treatment until someone either dies or the tumor progresses, which means it grows more than a set amount. PFS is often described as a median, the amount of time until half of people die or have tumor progression. For example, if the median PFS is 6 months, then by 6 months after the start of treatment, half of the patients have either died or had their tumor grow and half of the patients are alive with tumors that are either the same size or smaller.

- **PFS3 or PFS6:** the progression-free survival at 3 months or 6 months respectively, after the start of treatment. This is the percent of people who are alive with tumors that are the same size or smaller at the specified time point.

While it seems intuitive that treatments that shrink tumors or that delay tumor progression will make people live longer, there are occasional cases where this has turned out not to be true. For example, sometimes tumors can grow back faster after a drug stops working or a tumor may appear to shrink on an MRI but the cells are continuing to grow and invade new parts of the brain. Because the study is testing how effective a drug is, patients participating in a phase 2 trial have a higher chance of personally benefiting from taking the drug than in earlier Phase studies. However, trial participants may not benefit if the treatment turns out to be ineffective or if the treatment only works at certain doses or in certain people. Often as part of a phase 2 trial, tests are done on tumor specimens or on blood samples to try to identify which people are more likely to benefit from the drug. A test that can distinguish people who might benefit from a drug and those who will not benefit from a drug is called a **biomarker.**

Phase 3 studies

Phase 3 clinical trials are large trials designed to definitively prove whether or not a treatment really works. Phase 3 clinical trials are done to compare a new treatment to something else, often the treatment that is considered "standard of care" for that disease and situation. This standard treatment may be another older treatment or in some cases may not involve active treatment against the tumor. Phase 3 trials must be randomized; meaning the treatment you receive is decided randomly by a method determined by the study designers, not by you or your doctors. Random means no one can control what treatment you get, as if it is determined by the flip of a coin or the roll of a die. The group you are randomized into is called an arm of the trial. Randomized phase 3 trials are needed because the results of non-randomized trials, such as many phase 2 studies, can be misleading. Non-randomized trials compare their results to what one would expect to happen to the usual patient in that situation. However, non-randomized studies can give a falsely optimistic view of a new drug because:

- People who volunteer for clinical trials are usually healthier and physically stronger than those who do not volunteer. The inclusion criteria for clinical trials, as discussed above, weed out people who have other health problems or are expected to be very sick soon.

- People who can travel to big hospitals for clinical trials tend to have slower growing cancers than people who cannot travel.

- Over time doctors have gotten better at preventing and managing symptoms and side effects, so people may live longer.

- People in clinical trials may see their doctor or be contacted by nurses more often than people not in clinical trials. Therefore, problems can be dealt with early before they become untreatable.

- When doctors and patients think a treatment is working, they are more likely not to see evidence that it is not working.

Although not very common in oncology, when there is no known effective treatment for a particular situation, then it is considered ethical and appropriate to compare a new treatment to giving no anti-tumor treatment. Giving no anti-tumor treatment does not mean "doing nothing." It may be called **Best Supportive Care**, which means treating all of the symptoms of the tumor but not giving anything to fight the tumor. Giving no anti-tumor treatment may also involve a **placebo**. A placebo is used so that neither the person in the study nor their doctors know whether the person is getting the new drug that is being tested. When people and their doctors do not know what treatment someone is receiving, they are said to be **blinded**. Placebos prevent doctors and patients from being subconsciously biased in interpreting MRIs and symptoms by knowing a person's treatment arm. Placebos also prevent people from dropping out of the trial and entering another trial if they are randomly assigned to the arm with no tumor treatment. A placebo will be a pill or infusion that looks and feels identical to the active drug, but it does not have any drug in it. Some people call placebos "sugar pills" because they used to contain sugar instead of drugs.

Many people do not like the idea of getting a placebo or of getting randomized. Rarely is the outcome without treatment so certain or a treatment so good that randomized trials are not needed. Some people like to joke that randomized, placebo-controlled trials are not needed to show that parachutes are helpful if you jump out of an airplane. However, most cancer treatment situations are not that clear cut. Although clinical trials are done when it is believed a new treatment is a good thing, sometimes it turns out that the new treatment is worse than not treating the tumor as there are unexpected additional side effects.

Some phase 3 trials allow people to receive the experimental treatment from the other arm of the trial when the tumor grows. This is called **crossing-over**. For example, a trial may randomize people between receiving drug "A" or a placebo. When the tumors of the people receiving the placebo grow, those people may be able to cross-over to the other arm and receive drug "A". Not all trials allow crossing over. Whether crossing over is permitted or not depends on the purpose of the trial, the resources available for the trial, and regulatory requirements.

Side Effects in Clinical Trials

There is a special vocabulary for talking about side effects in clinical trials. The side effect of a treatment during clinical trials is called an **Adverse Event (AE)**. The National Cancer Institute (NCI) has established a standardized way to measure the seriousness of an adverse event. This is called the **Common Toxicity Criteria for Adverse Events (CTCAE)**. Over the years these criteria have changed, and in 2012 the most current version is version 4. The complete CTCAE can be found at the NCI website: http://ctep.cancer.gov/protocolDevelopment/ electronic_applications/ctc.htm.

Adverse events are graded on a scale from 1 to 5. (Grade 0 refers to not having a symptom or problem, so someone with grade 0 pain has no pain at all.) Grade 1 adverse events are mild and generally not bothersome. Grade 2 events are bothersome and may interfere with doing some activities but are not dangerous. Grade 3 events are serious and interfere with a person's ability to do basic things like eat or get dressed. Grade 3 events may also require medical intervention. Grade 4 events are usually severe enough to require hospitalization. Grade 5 events are fatal.

Most clinical trials and doctors focus on grade 3 or higher events, because those are the most dangerous. Grade 2 events however, can significantly impact the patient's quality of life, even if they are not medically dangerous. For example, a grade 1 headache is mild. A grade 2 headache keeps the patient from doing things like shopping or cooking. A grade 3 headache keeps the patient from getting out of bed even to go to the bathroom.

Consent and Assent

One basic principal of medical ethics is that no person should be included in any sort of experiment without his or her agreement. This agreement is called **consent**. In the past, heinous examples of medical experiments occurred where people were given injections of experimental drugs or even diseases without knowing it. However, since the Nuremburg trials in the 1940s and particularly since the 1970s, experimenting on people without their agreement and consent has been considered unacceptable in the U.S. and the rest of the civilized world.

Informed consent refers to the idea that not only should people know they are in a clinical trial, but that they also must understand what will happen to them during the trial. Informed consent is a process that involves both talking to someone involved in running the trial to learn about the trial and signing a paper, called the consent form, that explains the trial. The process of informed consent should include:

- What is known about the experimental treatment.

- What will happen during the clinical trial, including what medicines will be taken, when and how they will be taken, and what and when tests or procedures will be done.

- What parts of the trial are considered standard, i.e., they would happen even if you are not involved in the trial, and what parts of the trial are experimental. Experimental parts of the trial can be treatments, office visits, tests, etc.

- What the alternative is to being in the trial and what the treatment and testing would be like if you do not participate in the trial.

- Whether there will be any financial costs to participate in the trial.

- Whether the trial is expected to benefit the participants personally or whether it is to benefit patients in the future.

- Whom to contact if you have questions or complaints about the trial.

- What the procedure is to stop participating in the trial.

All clinical trials are overseen by an **Institutional Review Board (IRB)**, which is a group of scientists and non-scientists that ensure that clinical trials are done in an ethical manner. Each university or cancer center has its own institutional review board. The institutional review board approves all aspects of clinical trials, including what is included in a consent form. The consent form should have contact information for the institutional review board in case you ever feel uncomfortable with what is happening in a clinical trial.

Giving informed consent requires that someone has the mental capacity to understand his or her options and to make a rational and consistent choice. Some patients, such as children or people with mental impairments, are thought to need special protection because they may not understand enough to give informed consent. In that case, two things are needed. First, the person's guardian, such as the parent for a child, must give informed consent. Second, if possible, the child or impaired person needs to agree to the trial, which is called giving **assent**. Sometimes this is impossible, for example for young infants or people who cannot communicate. The age at which assent is required will vary from trial to trial, but national groups such as the American Academy of Pediatrics, and the Children's Oncology Group recommend that children 7 years of age or older not be enrolled in clinical trials without their assent. Requiring assent allows a child to say no and to have some control over what happens to his or her body. Not only are uncooperative children difficult to get useful scientific results from, but some children may tire of participating in medical research before parents, who naturally hope for a miracle.

Questions to Ask

If you are considering participating in a clinical trial, here are some questions you may want to ask:

1. What phase is this trial?

2. What do we know right now about the treatment being tested and what is unknown?

3. What is the purpose of the trial?

4. What is the chance that this trial will benefit my child?

5. What would my child's treatment be if he/she does not participate in the trial?

6. Are there extra tests my child would have to undergo if he/she participates in the trial?

7. What will I or my insurance be charged for and what will the trial pay for

during the trial?

8. If my child get sick or is hospitalized during the trial, who will pay for that?

9. Is the trial randomized?

10. Is there a placebo or blinding, or will I know what treatment my child is taking?

11. Who is paying for the clinical trial research? Is it the company producing the drug?

12. Does my child receive any type of financial reimbursement for participating in this trial?

Conclusion

All of the advances that have developed to successfully treat many types of cancers have come from clinical trials. Millions of people are alive today because of people who participated in clinical trials. However, while clinical trials have the potential to benefit the individual patient and future cancer patients, clinical trials are scientific experiments and there are important considerations that need to be understood before patients agree to participate. There are pros and cons to participating in clinical trials. A clinical trial may or may not benefit the patients in the trial. Clinical trials limit the flexibility of doctors and patients because it is necessary to get scientifically valid results. Asking questions of your doctor is the best way to get information about any clinical trial you are considering for your child.

Parent Perspectives

When Caleb's DIPG was diagnosed, he was less than three months from his 4th birthday. His tumor was diagnosed in the Emergency Room after an MRI, and the doctors were crystal clear at the immediate outset that he could not survive this tumor. Even given this clear-cut, seemingly straightforward assessment, we decided that a review of our available options was vital. We were at one of the best Children's Hospitals in the country; however, we thought it beneficial to seek other opinions.

Of course, the first thing one does is usually an Internet search. In 2006, there was considerably less material available for DIPG. Only a few parents had brought their story to the Internet (we found two); there were no DIPG support groups, Facebook pages, parent communities, or the like. The medical literature that was available publicly was clear—long-term survival with DIPG was unlikely. The parent stories we did find also echoed that sentiment, and both children had passed away.

We visited one of the premier cancer centers in the US in Houston, Texas, and found doctors very willing to discuss options with us. They had treatment protocols for DIPG. I recall the discussion with the doctor vividly: he told us that long-term survival was not possible. We asked about extension of life, and he said that this was definitely possible—he could promise a longer life for Caleb. We asked him what the "extension" would likely be and he felt certain that "a few months" was possible.

While we were consulting with him, other children were there. One was vomiting violently from the treatment she had been given. The doctor shared the details of what Caleb's treatment would be, and he described the mouth sores and other side effects the treatment would probably produce. We were not willing to compromise Caleb's quality of life for a few extra months of him being sick from treatment. We wanted what life he had left to be full of living.

Knowing that Caleb's long-term survival was not likely, and that treatments with severe side effects would perhaps extend his life "a few months," we did not want to pursue them. Our doctors at the Children's Hospital provided us with an option: a Phase II clinical drug study at NIH which was testing the effectiveness of a proposed treatment. Side effects were minimal if any. We opted to participate in this study, for two reasons: first, it would provide information to researchers; and second, we did feel like we were doing something to help Caleb. This treatment, in the end, did not help Caleb. But it also did not compromise his quality of life.

Caleb survived about ten months past diagnosis. While the initial few months were challenging with the radiation and Decadron treatments, his quality of life overall was quite good. He struggled off-and-on with some neurological problems which were treated with medications, and his abilities did diminish as the disease progressed. Up until the last few days before his death, he was alert, aware, and until his last week or so, he could participate in activities. He was never sick to his stomach, had just one hospital stay related to the tumor, and was a cheerful little boy.

It's hard to say, now, that we would have done the same thing as more treatments are available and some differing degrees of success have been seen. However, the process would be the same—the compromise to his quality of life, versus an expected benefit. And, in the end, every parent has to weigh that carefully for their child and make their own decisions.

Quality of life was absolutely number one from the first day. We told our doctor that we would NEVER prolong Hope's life without a guarantee that she would have top quality. We even chose some of our clinical trials including lack of hair loss as criteria. It was a balance of feeling like we were doing something to give her a fighting chance (hoping we'd get our honeymoon and more good days) and not putting her through things that were for naught.

Lovis just loves to be home. Coming back from a trip, I can see so much what this means. She really wants to be home. When it comes to trials, yes, we are interested (of course), but then I couldn't think of taking her somewhere far away, by plane, when the only thing I hear from her is "When are we going back home?" I am still stunned by how much travel families do for and with their children to make treatment possible.

I am still not sure what to do. The inner fight we all know: How much am I going to compromise my child's quality of life versus a slight chance of maybe doing something against the tumor with unproven drugs that might have terrible side effects?

The conversations we always had with her doctors stemmed from the need to preserve her quality of life—hence no other meds or trials. They would have provided them to us if we asked, but we both agreed that none of the approaches were a cure. They helped us understand and accept that there were trade-offs—her quality of life versus the need to keep her with us longer. And they leaned very much towards her quality of life.

Emma's case was constantly reviewed. Emma stumped some of the doctors, because she was on no medications at all—no chemo, no trials—just radiation and at the end a small dose of dexamethasone to help her swallow. She survived 16 months. Her doctor said, and I quote, "If we could teach other parents the approach we had in dealing with our daughter we could do so much good. We just don't really know how to describe that approach." I found that interesting to hear, as I don't think we did anything overly different than what other parents have done—but perhaps we did.

We sent Liam's scans to be reviewed by a leading doctor in the DIPG community to get her thoughts and opinions going forward. It was agreed that in fact Liam's tumor had progressed. We also sought the opinion of another doctor well versed in the care of DIPG patients. We wanted opinions of studies and clinical trials that might have benefited Liam. We were told very forthrightly that generally children live six months following the diagnosis of progression and that oftentimes had little to do with what new treatments were tried. This weighed heavily on us. We decided (and were also advised) that what our current hospital could offer Liam for care would be just as effective as anywhere else. We made the very personal decision not to pursue a clinical trial at that time in large part because of Liam's rapidly declining health. We decided to do a combination of two chemo drugs in the hopes that they would keep things relatively "quiet" for as long as possible. Liam by this point was back on higher doses of steroids and they were increased as needed.

During Brendan's symptom-free periods he regained full abilities and appeared healthy. He was always doing some sort of treatment though whether it was off label or clinical trial. His quality of life was very good aside from the expected side effects of the treatments he endured. He wanted to fight so he participated in 2 clinical trials—one before progression and one after. We took our cues from him and as long as he wanted to fight and live we found treatment options for him.

This decision to not try to prolong her life using treatments was not one we took lightly, and we are extremely pleased with the high quality of life we have been able to offer Stella, free of the burdens of invasive medications, side effects, sedation, etc. that a 2-year old would not have understood. Because of this decision, we were able to spend the summer taking Stella to cottages, the zoo, Riverdale Farm, the library and on play-date after play-date instead of being chained to the hospital. In fact, Stella has been home the entire time since her diagnosis which has been wonderful for all of us.

Clinical trials were discussed only as a second option if/when the radiation failed. In hindsight I wish we had gone home and taken a few days to do some research and consider second opinions. We could have become better informed and Sam would have had a few days to enjoy his friends while he was still feeling pretty well. As it turned out Sam never had a "honeymoon" period so if we had gone home to think and research he could have had a few days more of "normalcy."

We knew very little about DIPG at that point yet felt like we had to make critical decisions quickly without the information needed to make informed decisions. I'm still not convinced that the surgery did anything other than cause him to forfeit the honeymoon period. There is no way to know if the surgery did anything to extend his life at that point. Perhaps the radiation would have stopped the tumor in the cerebellum from growing as it did the tumor in the pons (at least temporarily). But our goal at the beginning was to be one of the few to beat the horrible odds and it seemed like surgery would help that goal.

I wish when Sam was diagnosed that someone could have said, "Here is what he has, here is the typical timeline, here is our most up to date information on DIPG, and here are the options including clinical trials. Take it home and then come back in a few days with questions, and to discuss the path to take that would be best for Sam."

At diagnosis there were no choices to be made. If Miguel was going to have a chance to survive he would need weeks of radiation. My daughter (Miguel's mom) spoke with Miguel about his diagnosis and the treatment he was about to receive. Miguel had just turned eight a month before and was a very bright child. There really was not an option of keeping things from him. Miguel's mom always kept him informed, including showing him the scans so that he could see for himself.

At progression, it was different. There were choices to make. How do you know which treatment option to go with when you are given five? My daughter decided that this decision could not be made alone and that Miguel would have the final say. There were four primary caregivers for Miguel: my daughter, her boyfriend, my youngest daughter and myself (Miguel's grandmother). My daughter decided that the best approach would be to analyze and rate each clinical trial individually and then we would come together to assess the results. The top two options were clear and we all agreed that there was one that was probably a better approach for Miguel. Now that there was a choice of two, she presented them to Miguel. It was important that he was aware of the treatment, including how the medication would be delivered into his body, and any side effects that were almost certainly going to occur. The decision was made and the final choice by all, including Miguel, was Nimotuzumab.

Aimee didn't do any clinical trials; she only did radiation, 6 weeks, 5 times each week, with external-beam radiation therapy. ...She was supposed to do some new trial that was gadolinium based. She was not eligible for any trials once she was put on the ventilator....

As parents who knew that radiation was the only thing that had some impact on DIPG, we were ignorantly devoted to the Phase II clinical trial which was causing such horrific side effects. We knew that the fact that a therapy was in Phase II did not mean that it had been effective in Phase I. At the same time, we mistakenly believed that it would not have moved from Phase

I to Phase II if it hadn't shown some promise in the first trial—if children who received the maximum tolerated dose hadn't responded positively.

Had we known that the children who received the treatment in Phase I, even at the maximum dose, did not have a better course than children who received radiation therapy alone, I don't know if we would have made a different choice. In retrospect, I wish we had. If we had had that knowledge and understood that radiosensitizers were not "new" or "novel," as we were told they were, but had been tried in various forms for years, I know we would have been better informed. We would not be living with the feeling of regret compounded by guilt as a result of our ignorance.

We had been in a hospice mindset for a few days when we received a phone call from Andrew's neuro-oncologist letting us know that a clinical trial slot (we had previously planned to do) had opened. She knew that we would most likely choose not to do the trial, but she wanted to allow us to be the ones to make that decision. Andrew surprised us by saying that he wanted to participate, so we made a final trip to NIH. An MRI there confirmed that the tumor had spread throughout the brainstem and to other parts of the brain. He qualified to do the trial, but when he realized all the pills that he would need to swallow, he told us that he did not think he could do it. We were so overwhelmed by the extent of the tumor spread, and by how well he was doing in light of that, that we could not imagine asking him to swallow all those pills. Andrew, age 8, and his neuro-oncologist spent a few moments alone together to talk about the clinical trial and what he wanted to do. That conversation, between our son and the physician he loved and trusted, confirmed in our hearts that he was truly ready to stop treatment. It was clear to all of us that after living life to the fullest for over 25 months in spite of DIPG, he was tired. He made the decision to stop treatment understanding exactly what that meant.

Chapter 6

Surgery: What It Can and Cannot Offer DIPG

Michael H. Handler, MD

The problem with operating on diffuse intrinsic pontine gliomas (DIPGs) is captured immediately by the name itself—they are diffuse, they are intrinsic, and they are in the pons. Tumors elsewhere in the brain tend to grow as a lump that pushes aside more normal brain tissue, but DIPGs do not. Lumps of DIPG cells are generally not large individual masses that a surgeon can try to take out. Instead, the cells making up the tumor project diffusely in fingers that sit widely among other areas of normal brain tissue.

With DIPGs, it isn't possible to separate normal from abnormal tissue when the surgeon looks at it. Thus, an attempt to remove large pieces of tissue to try to control the tumor (and improve the child's outcome by getting enough of the tumor out) is not possible. Instead, attempts to remove abnormal tissue result in pieces of normal brain tissue being removed. Removal of normal tissue can also happen during surgery on other parts of the brain, but in other parts of the brain the nearby normal tissue usually doesn't have as important a function as pons tissue.

The Pons

The pons is a small area of the brain about 3.5 cm. long and 2.5 cm. wide. In it are the brain centers that control sleeping and waking, eye movements, facial movement, and hearing. The major pathways for movement of the arms and legs, and for most of the body's sensations, pass through it in a complex manner (see chapter 3). The cerebellum which sits behind the pons sends fibers from one side of the brain to the other through the pons. The cerebellum controls smooth muscular movements and balance,

Dr. Handler is a Professor and Chairman of Pediatric Neurosurgery at the Children's Hospital Colorado and the University of Colorado School of Medicine, Aurora, CO.

and some of the balance centers of the brain are located in the pons. Additional centers controlling balance are located in the medulla. Thus, the pons is a critical structure that highly influences the entire body's ability to function properly. When the pons is damaged, it can have an extremely wide impact on the body's ability to sustain itself. Any surgeon should be extremely cautious when attempting an operation in this region. Taking small amounts of tissue may be possible without inflicting serious neurologic damage, but taking large amounts of tissue simply is not.

History of DIPG Diagnosis and Imaging

Surgeons' current thinking about DIPG tumors is based on the tumors' history. In the past, surgeons would generally try to remove brain tumors. But that was, and is still, rarely possible in the pons. With tumors in other areas of the body, surgeon's usually try to take a small amount of tissue with a "needle biopsy" to gain a better understanding about the tumor before considering a larger operation. Biopsies, however, were rarely done on brain tumors, because biopsies were much more difficult in the brain than elsewhere in the body. The reason for the difficulty was that it used to be very difficult to know exactly where in the skull, and therefore where in the brain, a needle should go to make a diagnosis. While surgeons used a variety of external landmarks for placing needles in the brain, this technique—called stereotactic biopsy—was not good enough for widespread use. Forty years ago, that began to change. New computerized brain imaging technology suddenly made it possible to see anatomic details in a remarkable way. The technique of stereotactic biopsy became feasible, and surgeons began to use it.

Meanwhile, brain imaging itself became much more precise. In particular, MRI revolutionized surgeons' ability to understand and visualize the location of tumors, particularly in the posterior fossa—the back of the brain where the pons is located. MRI and stereotactic technology were now linked in a constructive way, and surgeons began to try stereotactic biopsy in the pons.

Clinical Study Recommendations for Standard of Care

Pediatric oncologists have long worked collaboratively to try and develop the best new treatments for tumors, in the most efficient way. One such collaborative study, organized through the Children's Cancer Group (the CCG study 9928), looked at patients with diffuse pontine gliomas and proposed new treatments. This study, published in 1993, concluded that when an MRI shows specific characteristic features of changes in the pons, it was sufficient evidence to make a DIPG diagnosis without a biopsy. It also turned out that when a biopsy was taken, the result of the pathology was not helpful in planning a particular treatment strategy and did not appear to alter a child's subsequent outcome. Therefore, the recommendation became that no biopsy should be undertaken in cases that appear to be typical pontine gliomas.

At that time, the risk for harm from a biopsy was not yet well known, because the technology for stereotactic biopsy was still relatively new. But because the benefit from biopsy is so small, the risks were too large for it to be undertaken. Based on this historical data, the accepted standard of care has become that no biopsy need be done for DIPGs.

When the neurosurgeon, oncologist, and radiologist agree that a tumor does not appear to be a typical DIPG it is considered appropriate to proceed with a biopsy. Since the publication of the CCG study, many more publications have documented the safety of stereotactic biopsy in the posterior fossa with relatively little inflicted harm. Thus, the decision to do a biopsy is based on whether the tumor appears enough atypical that a different diagnosis could be considered. In addition, some tumors—in the opinion of the surgeon, oncologist, and radiologist—remain so unusual that an open operation (removal of a flap of the skull and entering the brain tissue with instruments larger than a needle) is more appropriate.

Stereotactic Biopsy

A stereotactic biopsy is based on obtaining a computerized image on which a target (tumor) can be identified; that image can be an MRI or CT scan. Technology is then used to calculate the position of the target in relation to the scan. Several different technologies are available to do that, some using a rigid frame that is attached to the head before the scan, and others that can map the surface of the face and use that as the basis for determining the tumor's position. With the head in a fixed position and the trajectory calculated, a very small hole is made in the skull to allow the needle to pass to the target and obtain the tissue. The tissue is then removed and prepared so as to identify the pathology; other studies may also be done. Stereotactic biopsy has the advantage of a very small incision, a small hole in the bone, and less risk than a larger open operation.

Most studies of stereotactic biopsy have shown relatively little damage as a result and a very low rate of death from the procedure (less than 1%).

Deciding When to Operate

The decision whether or not to operate must be based on the imaging features of the tumor and on whether the treatment is appropriate for the individual child.

The DIPG's location presents a problem (in addition to that of the tumor itself). The brain produces cerebrospinal fluid (CSF), which circulates through a series of spaces in the brain called the ventricles, which include:

- **Lateral ventricles:** One lateral ventricle is found in each cerebral hemisphere, and each lateral ventricle communicates through a small channel (called the foramen of Monro) to the third ventricle.
- **Third ventricle:** The third ventricle sits on the midline at the base of the brain and ends in a channel, called the aqueduct of Silvius that goes to the fourth ventricle.
- **Fourth ventricle:** The fourth ventricle sits behind the pons and medulla, in front of the cerebellum.

CSF goes downstream from the lateral ventricles to the third and fourth, then leaves the fourth ventricle through channels that connect to the space around the brain (the subarachnoid space) where CSF is absorbed into the bloodstream. Because DIPGs sit adjacent to this fluid pathway, as they grow they may at times block the flow of CSF. This blockage causes fluid pressure in the brain to go up and the fluid spaces to enlarge—a condition called hydrocephalus. When the fluid pressure builds up, it can cause headaches, vomiting, mental changes, and even coma. Thus, sometimes children with DIPGs need procedures to control the fluid pressure.

Treating Hydrocephalus

The most common and well-established procedure to treat hydrocephalus is the ventriculoperitoneal shunt (VP shunt). A tube is placed from the outer surface of the head through the skull and brain into a lateral ventricle. The shunt is connected to a device—the valve—which determines how much pressure must build up before CSF starts to flow, and makes sure CSF only flows out of the ventricle and not back in. The valve sits under the skin and connects to a tube that leads to a place in the body where the CSF can be absorbed back into the blood stream (where it would have gone from the brain directly, if it could). The most common end point of shunts is the peritoneal cavity—the belly—but other times shunts go to the chest, through blood vessels to the heart, or even to the gall bladder. Effective shunts have been around for about 50 years, and they save and improve the lives of tens of thousands of kids each year.

Shunts, however, have their own problems. They are foreign to the body, so the body may react to them and block off their flow. They are also mechanical systems that can break or malfunction. The most common way they become a problem is when they become infected. Infections happen between 5 to 14 percent of the times they are implanted. (Neurosurgeons are very focused on how to reduce the rate of these infections.) When a shunt is infected, it has to be removed, and—after a period of time—replaced with a clean system.

Because of the problems with shunts, another way to drain fluid from the ventricles is the endoscopic third ventriculostomy (ETV), which creates an alternative pathway from the third or fourth ventricle when the normal pathway is blocked. Whether the ETV is an option depends on the particular anatomy of a child with hydrocephalus due to a DIPG. This is a matter only the surgeon can assess. (The pons sits behind the area where CSF goes after an ETV. If a DIPG can block the CSF pathway behind it, it can block the pathway in front as well.)

Biopsy of More Routine Tumors: Why or Why Not?

A fundamental ethical dilemma raised by the current standard of care is that when the tumor looks typical on MRI, the recommendation (based on research completed 20 years ago) is that no biopsy should be done. The potential risk for the individual child, as interpreted at that time, could not be balanced by the potential benefit. Since then, two things have changed:

1. Many more patients have undergone safe biopsy of brainstem masses than had done so when that observation was made;

2. The ability to study tumors has been vastly advanced by genomic analysis.

DIPG tumors will not be understood as other pediatric brain tumors are, unless more tissue is obtained for study by contemporary techniques. The cancer community will have to decide the most appropriate course of action with DIPG tumors.

Federal Guidelines for Clinical Research

Federal guidelines for conducting research, particularly in children, stipulate that there must be the potential for benefit for the individual child if he or she is to undergo a procedure with more than a minimal amount of risk. What will be the benefit to undergoing a procedure; will the procedure allow us to better understand the nature of the tumor; and will it benefit a particular child? How should we measure benefit? If the child and his or her family decide that to help advance knowledge is a very significant benefit to that child, is that substantial enough to offset the notion that because "the child's survival won't change," there is no potential benefit? This is the overarching question that has no easy answers.

Parent Perspectives

Our son Caleb, had his DIPG diagnosed at a critical point where his tumor had grown to the point of obstructing cerebrospinal fluid (CSF) circulation between the brain and the spinal cord. The higher ventricular pressure, from the CSF obstruction and resulting hydrocephalus, was visible on the MRI and a syrinx (pocket of fluid) was also evident. Clinically, Caleb was sluggish, limp, couldn't keep his eyes open, and was clearly having problems from the hydrocephalus. So we had an immediate problem which needed to be addressed. His medical team recommended a ventriculoperitoneal (VP) shunt be placed immediately.

We struggled with the decision of what to do. This was "Day 1" for us. The idea of DIPG, shunts, radiation, what we would do to treat Caleb—these things were all questions we faced immediately. The shunt issue, however, seemed to be the most pressing since the hydrocephalus needed to be promptly addressed. We needed time to figure out what to do about the base DIPG diagnosis, and the shunt bought us that time.

Nonetheless, the idea of operating on Caleb's brain was not an attractive one. We assembled his medical team in the room, and the question we put directly to them was, "If this was your son, what would you do?" With zero hesitation the neurosurgeon quickly said, "I'd place the shunt." In hindsight, this was one of the most simple and straightforward procedures performed on Caleb. After the surgery, Caleb was awake and ready to play. His body adjusted to the shunt almost immediately.

Caleb's VP shunt worked well. We never had problems with it. As the tumor progressed, he did have other neurological problems which occasionally brought him to the emergency room—and the very first thing the doctors would do was check the operation of the shunt.

In hindsight, we would do that part of Caleb's treatment the same way again. If his DIPG had been diagnosed at an earlier stage when hydrocephalus was not already a problem, it might have been a different question for us. However, given the point we were at, the shunt was the treatment that bought us the time to treat him with radiation and consider our other options.

Quickly our attention became focused on what we needed to do next to help Liam. Liam's neurosurgeon reviewed with us the most pressing issue at the moment which was the fluid that had accumulated on his brain. We opted for a 3rd Ventriculostomy. Not every child is a candidate for this surgery nor is it performed by every doctor. The significant risk was explained to us. We felt extremely confident in our doctor and felt this would be the best option for Liam going forward.

After this decision was made we walked the long hallway back to Liam's room to give him the news. Not ALL of the news mind you, but a small piece and the next steps that needed to take place. The three of us sat with Liam, told him that his doctor needed to help him feel better and that there was too much fluid in his brain that shouldn't be there and he would need surgery. We explained that he would be asleep and wouldn't feel anything and would wake up and be able to see Mom and Dad right away—which the operating room staff made happen for us. At this point in time, Liam was so sick and weak he barely responded but simply nodded his understanding. Our sweet boy looked every bit of his little six year old self in that hospital bed and our hearts were absolutely broken but also incredibly resolved to do everything we needed to protect and help him on this journey.

As the weeks and then months went on, and with the help of a successful 3rd Ventriculostomy, surgery, effective radiation treatment, and the use of steroids, Liam's symptoms greatly improved. He returned to school and eventually came completely off steroids and became symptom free. His meds and periodic visits to his oncologist were just a minor interruption to the real business of the day—being a kid.

✦ ✦ ✦

Our experience with neurosurgery was brief, I suppose. The neurosurgeon put in Tatumn's shunt at diagnosis since she did have some hydrocephalus. It did relieve the pressure but it was always an uncomfortable question to ask ourselves, "so how long will this thing be in her head?" when we knew the answer wasn't relevant given the prognosis.

After Tatumn's six week run of radiation we started to see signs of the "honeymoon period," and we were reducing her steroids. We saw some light at the

Chapter 6: Surgery

end of the tunnel! Tatumn was using her hands again and was speaking better and we had hopes of her staring to walk again. Well, high fevers set in and she started to be very uncomfortable to move. We had to be slow to move her and she had definite abdominal discomfort. They checked her blood for infection but couldn't find anything. They did an x-ray and didn't see anything either. Our neuro-oncologist wasn't available. It was during Thanksgiving week so the doctors we saw said maybe it was the tumor and her body temperature wasn't being regulated right. But I could sense it was more. So we went on her wish trip and fevers kept spiking. I called her radiation oncologist when we got back and he said to take her in immediately and have her shunt tested for infection. He was right. Tatumn had an infection probably caused by the shunt and since it emptied into her peritoneal area I think that is why she had the discomfort. The shunt was removed and during our 10 day hospital stay on antibiotics (right before Christmas) they monitored her cerebral fluid and said she would be fine without it and they didn't put a new one in. We felt so good to have that gone.

What do I wish I had done differently? I wish I had listened to my intuition more. I knew Tatumn's fevers were more than tumor related. Maybe we would have caught it sooner and her wish trip would have been better.

About a year after diagnosis, our son began to show symptoms of tumor progression. It was at this point that we chose to meet with a pediatric neurosurgeon to explore the possibility of surgical intervention, if necessary, to treat hydrocephalus. We were more interested in an ETV than a shunt because it seemed less invasive to us. The neurosurgeon confirmed what we had heard from others—that surgical intervention to treat hydrocephalus is not recommended for most patients with DIPG. While surgical intervention may prolong life, and even help with quality of life in some ways, it does not stop the tumor from growing and affecting the body in other ways. So it's possible to treat hydrocephalus successfully and prolong the child's suffering.

As I understand it, many of Bizzie's initial symptoms were related to hydrocephalus. We were told that she needed surgery; it was not presented as a choice of having surgery or not, but rather ETV or shunt. This was presented to us along with her diagnosis, so we were at the hospital, in the PICU,

digesting the diagnosis. In fact, the pediatric neurosurgeon was the one who officially diagnosed Bizzie. We were still so shell shocked when we made the decision. We chose the ETV surgery. We did so based on the facts as they were presented to us. My husband also spoke with another neurosurgeon so that we had a second opinion about the surgery. We decided that we should go ahead with the ETV and then consider moving to a large cancer center for treatment. I don't think we understood, though, how important the facility and nursing staff is in recovery.

We were admitted on Friday and Bizzie's surgery was scheduled for Monday. We were given the impression that Bizzie's level of hydrocephalus presented an emergent situation, but that they also wanted the steroids (dexamethasone) to be given a chance to do some work. Of course, it was also Friday. Monday morning came and it was time for Bizzie's surgery. I was sick. I was shaking holding her as the nurses and transport fought over stupid logistics. When I sputtered out a plea for help, the nurse looked at me and said in a testy voice "What? I can't understand a word you say." That memory still sticks with me. I wasn't looking for sympathy, but I really needed some help getting through that moment.

Bizzie refused to take off her princess dress and wear the standard green gown. My husband and I begged and pleaded. Finally, we convinced her that it was a Tinkerbell costume because it was green. I rode down on the bed with Bizzie in my lap. They sedated her and the surgery began. The surgery was successful. She came back up to the PICU for recovery. In the early morning following her surgery, Bizzie was transported by the PICU nurse, the receptionist, and a technician to the MRI area. My husband was with them while I tried to sleep. When they returned, Bizzie had a seizure and they intubated her. The doctors went back and forth as to the cause—low sodium levels, or the monitoring piece near her brain perhaps brushed something in transport. Bizzie remained on the vent for two days. They told us that she would not be able to breathe on her own when they pulled the tube, but she did. She did not talk for several days after that. She just stared. Our PICU neighbor thought that Bizzie had a twin—the girl she saw before the surgery who was making quite a racket in the PICU, and this other girl who did not respond to anything. Bizzie did recover slowly, although she didn't walk again for several months. But that was the worst she was until the day before she died.

Sam's tumor extended into the cerebellum and the neurosurgeon recommended we do surgery to remove what he could from that area. I was under two misconceptions at the beginning—one that the tumor in the cerebellum was a focal rather than diffuse tumor and second that diffuse was more like tentacles. Later I learned that that the cerebellum tumor was also diffuse and that diffuse was more like sporadic tumor cells spread throughout, and not really connected like you would think of a tentacle being. I don't know that either misconception affected our decision to do surgery but I wish I had had a better understanding in the beginning nonetheless.

I know most kids with DIPG never go through surgery like this but perhaps Sam's experience will be informative anyway. The surgery itself lasted 4 to 5 hours and was terrifying to think of him in there where anything could happen. Everything went smoothly though, and he actually recovered well in the first few days. They had "PT, OT, and Speech" evaluate him and it was decided he could handle outpatient rehab as opposed to inpatient. We were so excited to have him come home. At that point he needed a little help walking but otherwise seemed ok. That was on a Wednesday. When he was released I went over the prescriptions he would need at home, specifically asking the resident discharging him if he needed to still be on the steroids and was told that he didn't need them anymore. What a fool I was to accept that answer.

The next few days Sam seemed fine. There was nothing unusual, considering his surgery. Then by Sunday he seemed to be having more trouble walking and was a lot more tired. He'd had a lot of friends visiting so we thought it was from trying to do too much too soon. Monday night he threw up and Tuesday he could barely walk so we headed off to the emergency room where they did an MRI and said the tumor was reacting to the surgery. The neurosurgeon said the area in the cerebellum was fine but that the tumor in the brainstem was causing problems. They bumped up the schedule for radiation and gave him lots of steroids. By now he could not even sit on the side of the bed without help, let alone walk; his right eye was turned inward causing double vision; he had lost his hearing in his right ear; and he had difficulty swallowing. He was released to inpatient rehab for 10 days then home again. He started on the 6 week course of radiation and the Temodar while in rehab. When he came home from rehabilitation he was so much worse physically than when he came home from the surgery. It broke my heart to think that it could have been prevented had he been on steroids at home.

Sam spent the next three months working so hard with his therapists to get better.

By June he was walking with a cane and able to do much more for himself again. He was even on track to get prism glasses for his double vision. He stayed pretty stable from mid-June until mid-August then had problems with his balance. Within a matter of days he could not walk again—this time from the balance issues. So off to the emergency room again where they determined he had a cyst growing in the cavity in the cerebellum where they had removed the tumor before. It was pressing on the fourth ventricle causing his balance problems. So he had another surgery to remove that and came home again— this time with steroids. Unfortunately, the tumor in the brainstem seemed to have been aggravated because he never bounced back from that surgery and in fact on his next MRI there was progression.

In hindsight knowing what I know now I might have pushed for no surgery and just gone with radiation and some other chemo. I think he may have had a longer time until progression and a better quality of life during that time. But there is no way to know. Others think that without the surgery he may have had less time.

Chapter 7

Radiation Therapy

Arthur Liu, MD, PhD

Radiation therapy is the standard treatment for children with diffuse intrinsic pontine gliomas (DIPGs). This type of therapy uses high-energy x-rays, similar to those used in a computed tomography (CT) scanner but at much higher doses. These x-rays deposit energy within the tumor, causing damage to the DNA of cells. The tumor cells are then unable to repair the damage, and ultimately die when the tumor cells try to divide.

The Radiation Therapy Process

Before starting radiation, parents of a child with a DIPG consult with the radiation oncologist to discuss the planned therapy and potential side effects. After this initial consultation, the child undergoes a planning session (also referred to as a simulation). At that time, a mask will be custom-made for the child. The mask allows accurate, consistent positioning of the head for each treatment and helps the child remain still during treatment. The mask is made out of a special type of plastic that becomes moldable when heated in a water bath. After the mask is completed, a special CT scan is performed. This entire process takes approximately 1 hour.

After the planning session, the radiation oncologist uses the CT scan to define the area that corresponds to the tumor and the regions of the brain that should not receive radiation. With the assistance of dosimetrists (who specialize in calculating the dose of radiation to ensure the tumor gets enough radiation) and physicists (who develop and direct quality-control programs for radiation equipment and procedures), a radiation therapy plan is developed to maximally treat the tumor while minimizing the amount of radiation delivered to normal brain tissues and surrounding tissues.

Radiation therapy is then delivered daily, Monday through Friday, for about 6 weeks to a total dose of about 54 Gray (Gy). Smaller daily fractions accumulating to the total dose over weeks is intended to allow normal tissues the chance to repair some radiation-induced

Dr. Liu is the Director of Pediatric Radiation Oncology and Program Director of the Radiation Oncology Residency Program at the University of Colorado, Denver, CO.

DNA damage while still destroying the tumor.

As radiation patients must lie still and alone on a table, some children are too young or too ill to tolerate the radiation treatments while awake. In these cases, the planning session and treatments can be performed under general anesthesia. A commonly used anesthetic agent in radiation therapy is propofol. Propofol is an intravenous anesthetic that allows for rapid induction and recovery, and—most importantly—does not require intubation (insertion of a tube) for protection of the airway. Even with daily use, the risks of complications with propofol are very low. Typically, the child is brought into the room awake, with the parents, and the anesthesia is initiated. After induction of anesthesia, the parents leave the room and the radiation therapy procedures are performed.

Effectiveness of Radiation Therapy

Radiation therapy is an effective palliative treatment that improves symptoms in about 80% of children with DIPGs. The dose of radiation therapy is limited by the tolerance of the surrounding normal brain tissue. However, given the high rate of response, in the 1980's a number of institutions increased the dose of radiation therapy from 54 Gy to greater than 70 Gy and had promising preliminary results. To escalate the dose of radiation delivered, smaller doses per treatment were used (referred to as hyperfractionation). These smaller doses allow greater recovery of normal tissues, and thus a higher total dose can be given. However, a Pediatric Oncology Group randomized trial showed that while the higher dose of radiation was well tolerated by most children, there was unfortunately no difference in survival rates.

Medical professionals have an interest in exploring agents that may be given along with radiation to improve the effects of this therapy; these agents are referred to as radiosensitizers. Some types of chemotherapy, such as carboplatin, can be used as radiosensitizers. Other experimental agents are also being studied. For example, arsenic trioxide given concurrently with radiation therapy is undergoing clinical trials to determine safety and to provide information that can be used for studies of effectiveness.

Possible Complications of Radiation Therapy

A common complication of radiation therapy in children with a DIPG is radiation necrosis—cell death of brain tissue. This may cause swelling and potentially lead to neurologic symptoms such as headache, nausea, vomiting, cranial neuropathies, and ataxia (loss of muscle movement coordination).

Radiation necrosis can be very difficult to distinguish from tumor recurrence by manifesting clinical symptoms or by imaging. Steroids are typically used for the symptomatic treatment of radiation necrosis. However, steroids can also cause side effects, including behavioral issues, insomnia, and weight gain. These steroid-related complications can significantly impact the child's quality of life. The exact mechanism of radiation necrosis is poorly understood, but vascular endothelial growth factor (VEGF) appears to play a role. Bevacizumab is a monoclonal antibody that interferes with VEGF and is being studied as a possible treatment for radiation necrosis.

Technologies for Delivering Radiation Therapy

Many different technologies are used to deliver radiation therapy. The most common radiation therapy machine is a linear accelerator, in which high-energy electrons impact a target to generate high-energy x-rays. There are a number of different manufacturers, but most of the machines only have slight technical differences. Some machines provide the ability to perform a CT scan for localization; these machines include Tomotherapy (TomoTherapy Incorporated, Madison, WI), Trilogy (Varian Medical Systems, Inc., Palo Alto, CA), and Synergy (Elekta, Stockholm, Sweden). The Novalis Tx (BrainLAB, Westchester, IL) uses orthogonal planar x-ray imaging for localization. There is no clinical difference in any of these machines. From a technical standpoint, the Cyberknife (Accuray, Sunnyvale, CA) is the most different from other machines. The Cyberknife mounts a linear accelerator on a robotic arm and is primarily used to treat small tumors throughout the body. Due to the relatively large size of the brainstem tumor in children with DIPGs, Cyberknife is typically not an option.

Proton radiation therapy (PRT) is a form of radiation therapy that has very limited availability. PRT uses protons to deliver therapeutic radiation. Protons differ significantly from the photons used in conventional radiation therapy because they have no mass or charge, compared to protons, which have mass and are positively charged. The mass and charge of protons results in a phenomenon called the Bragg Peak, which results in no energy deposited after a certain depth in tissue depending on the energy of the proton (higher energies go deeper). This technique allows protons to potentially deliver less radiation therapy to normal tissues, with fewer late effects of therapy. Numerous theoretical modeling studies have shown benefit to using proton radiation. For children with DIPGs, the potential benefit of protons is unfortunately minimal. The difference in normal tissue radiated between PRT and current photon radiation therapy techniques is small, and late effects in these children is not yet a significant concern due to the extremely low survival rate in this population.

In summary, radiation therapy is the current standard treatment for children with a DIPG. Radiation therapy improves clinical symptoms in the majority of children, but that improvement is temporary. The most active areas of research are exploring the addition of therapeutic agents to a backbone of standard radiation therapy.

Parent Perspectives

Radiation is the ONLY thing that has proven to help SOME of our kids so we chose to do it. I don't regret it necessarily as we were fighting for our child. The steroids took way more than the radiation did. While our daughter didn't get the "honeymoon period" that many children do, we continued to believe that we would be the recipient of a miracle. She only lost some hair in the back but no one knew it because her hair was long enough to cover the loss. She did not lose her eye lashes.

Andrew's pediatric oncologist called the tumor a pontine glioma. She said that the standard treatment was radiation, and that it could possibly shrink the tumor temporarily. She told us that sometimes people use chemotherapy in an attempt to make the radiation more effective. Andrew started radiation with two chemotherapies, but we quickly chose to stop that part of the treatment. We decided that the possible benefit of the chemotherapies was not worth the definite side effects (nerve pain, nausea, etc.) Radiation alone was the right choice for us. Andrew's tumor did not begin to grow again until a year from diagnosis.

Hope got no "honeymoon." Hope saw no relief from the radiation. We were devastated as her tumor barely shrunk at all. It began to grow almost immediately and had areas of necrosis which caused further harm to our beautiful girl. Hope was courageous. She continued to speak in terms of, "when I get better" and "after treatment." She attended therapy even when it hurt because she knew it was "good for her."

The first time our son had radiation as an outpatient, we arrived at the hospital by 8:00 a.m. The nurse and aide checked him over, hooked him up to I.V. fluids and monitors, and took him down for sedation and radiation at 9:00 a.m. A nurse changed the dressing for his port while he was still sedated. Another nurse monitored his vital signs while he recovered and made sure he was able to drink, eat, and use the restroom. We didn't get

home until noon. I had not expected to be there for the whole morning. The radiation treatment takes moments, but the preparation and recovery take more time.

He began to lose some hair two or three weeks into radiation. It looked like someone had taken clippers and shaved off one to two inches around the outline of his ears. We had his hair cut short so that the hair loss was not as obvious.

We were able to get a second round of radiation. When we first talked to our neuro-oncologist about re-irradiation she said it simply was not an option. A couple of weeks later I spoke to her about the work being done at another treatment center and she was mildly accepting of it; then when I presented her with the ISPNO abstract she began to consider the idea and was willing to look into it further. Bringing concrete information to her definitely helped.

If parents are interested I would suggest starting to talk about re-irradiation early. We had been told radiation was a one-time deal. I found that talking about it each time I saw his doctor was helpful. At first she said, "No way, absolutely not." As time went on and I presented her with more information she became more open. By the time progression happened she knew we wanted re-irradiation and went to bat for us with the radiation oncologist.

The radiation oncologist who did the first round of radiation decided she would not do it so our doctor found another that was willing. The radiation oncologist that did the second round said that the swaying factor was that she knew that we knew it was not a cure. She knew we were looking for a second "honeymoon period" and she felt that was reasonable.

My nephew had an experimental new radiation course that a radiologist was studying. He had just five days of a higher dose of radiation instead of 30 days at a lower level.

I spent days and nights on the computer and on the phone with numerous doctors; we sent Ellie's scans everywhere. We were given the typical radiation/chemo option knowing very well radiation could not be put off

for long. We also learned that jumping into a treatment option may preclude you from others. While with this monster there is no right or wrong we wanted to receive a good feel for all available options. We explored both proton beam radiation and IMRT (intensity-modulated radiation therapy). After consulting with two neuro-oncologists we opted for IMRT and were very happy with this decision.

During Ellie's six week IMRT we were determined to pinpoint what next steps we would take. Ellie tolerated her radiation therapy in very good health. She really did very well. She never had to be sedated and with the exception of fatigue, experienced little side effects. Her determination to gain her strength back and get back to all the activities she sorely missed, served her well.

We met with the radiation oncologist, who explained to us, and to Bryce, about what radiation would be like. Bryce had another MRI to plan his treatment. Then we went home to face our family and friends after being in hospital for 5 days. We were home for one week, and Bryce chose to go to school, to keep things normal as much as possible. I think back on that now, and even that is telling of his character and how Bryce handled all of this.

I remember asking his doctor how long Bryce would have had without treatment, and was given the answer of one month. These radiation treatments would give us time to learn to live with this new reality, and hopefully the treatment would make him feel better because he was already having headaches and dizziness, as well as having difficulties with poor gait.

So, from March 10th to April 23rd, we stayed at Ronald McDonald House from Monday to Friday as Bryce underwent radiation. We made another good decision—to keep our whole family together during treatment. By the end of it, Bryce was 50 pounds heavier from steroids and had lost his hair, but the earlier dizziness and headaches had gone away for the most part.

I have to tell you that when treatment was over, I was scared to death. So what were we supposed to do now, go home to wait for him to die? We were so happy to be going home, and yet terrified, because we knew that at some point, Bryce would lose his battle—the tumor would resume its growth. Bryce deserved to go home and just be 13—not go home to wait for the other shoe to fall.

We chose to do radiation treatment concurrently with Temodar® and the tumor shrank considerably. We stopped chemotherapy after much prayer and used a nutritionist to fully change Kayla's diet. We used many, many alternative therapies and her tumor shrank further. We were incredibly blessed with 4 ½ years of generally symptom-free living for Kayla. She was in piano, ballet, and did well in school. When she was 10, her cancer returned and she died 5 months later on June 18, 2010.

Courtney was admitted to the hospital and started on steroids. We were given the option of the standard chemo/radiation treatment. We considered taking her to a well-known children's hospital or somewhere else for treatment, but decided that since they couldn't offer us anything that would give her a better chance of survival we would stay close to home. We were confident that she would get as good of care at our local children's hospital as she would anywhere else.

She had 6 weeks of radiation and about 5 weeks into it she started having more muscle weakness in her legs. By the time she had completed radiation she was in a wheelchair. Courtney was on Avastin®/Temodar® after she completed radiation. I wish we had just given her the radiation treatments and left off the chemo. The Temodar® wiped out her white blood cell counts and because of this it really affected her quality of life. She had to spend 114 of the 186 days she lived after diagnosis in the hospital. She was taken off the chemo in August because of this.

October 6th we had to take her to the hospital because she had a severe headache. An emergency MRI was done and it showed the tumor was progressing in the spinal area. At this point there was nothing else we could do. She couldn't start on chemo because her white count still had not recovered and she was ineligible for re-irradiation because it had only been 4 months since she had completed her first round. We took her home and planned to cherish the time we had left with her. Three days later she had to be admitted to the hospital because she was having difficulty breathing and severe headaches that we couldn't get under control. She spent her last 22 days of life there and died on October 31, 2010.

After quite some pushing from our side, radiation started and was successful. The doctors still felt uncomfortable sedating her but I remember thinking "If she is going to die because of this tumor right now, we might at least try radiation. I wouldn't blame anyone if the sedation did go wrong." At the same time I was wondering how I was able to think that without losing my mind.

Liam endured the standard six week protocol of radiation along with a bolus not always done at the end of that standard time. We were told radiation was the only thing known for this kind of cancer that truly had the possibility of shrinking the mass. DIPG was much like sand sprinkled in Jello we were told. Radiation was very effective. Liam's tumor shrank considerably.

Stella is not, and has not, received any treatment. Because Stella was barely 2 years old at the time of her diagnosis, the standard treatment of radiation therapy would have entailed 6 weeks of Stella being sedated on a daily basis to receive the therapy. With no guarantee it would work, Stella's young age, and the fact we wanted desperately to enjoy our remaining time with her, we opted for no treatments. She was on steroids for one week post-diagnosis, but we despised the changes we saw in her (huge appetite, tantrums known as "roid-rage," discomfort, etc.) so we took her off immediately with no plans to put her back on.

We did the proton radiation at a facility near where we live. I was told that there would be fewer side effects than regular radiation. Warren started off doing fine. He only lost a small amount of hair, and you really couldn't tell. He was tired but not overly tired. But at the same time he was doing radiation he was also doing physiotherapy, so that played a role in him being tired as well.

Joseph responded well to radiation. Our neuro-oncologist told us that the first post treatment MRI showed remarkable tumor reduction however, his clinical response was poor even after the second MRI showed more reduction in tumor size.

The radiation-oncologist told us to expect fatigue. He slept twenty-two hours a day. After our second visit to the neuro-oncologist after radiation therapy they called it somnolence and increased the dexamethasone which kept him awake twenty-two hours a day and totally changed his personality.

I remember looking at the MRI wanting to find something solid not a white cloudy section. It was never truly explained to me what size a normal pons should be or why my boy did not respond to treatments after evidence of radiological improvement. We had set up second and third opinion appointments but Joe did not make it to them.

I wish I had known that not all DIPGs respond to radiation. I would not have waited for him to improve clinically to do more activities together as a family.

When my 17 year old brother Daniel was diagnosed with DIPG, our family was very overwhelmed. The doctors tried very hard to get my brother to begin radiation immediately and this worried my parents very much. As Daniel's oldest sibling, (and not living at home for many years) I was close enough but not too close to be paralyzed by the fear and pressure from the doctors. I realized that it would be wise to devote a few days to get second opinions, and research all the options and make an educated decision rather than just rush into the radiation. After looking at all the options my brother chose not to proceed with the standard treatment of radiation and/or chemo. Instead we began looking into alternatives including supplements, dietary changes and Chinese medicine. We don't know the future, but the tumor is stable eight months after diagnosis. We hope he will beat the odds, having done something different.

Chapter 8

Radiosensitizers for DIPG

Roger J. Packer, MD

Radiation therapy remains the only effective treatment for brainstem gliomas in children. Because its effectiveness is transient for most patients, attempts to improve the benefits of radiation therapy have been a focus of clinical research. These efforts have included increases in the total dose of radiotherapy delivered, and alterations in the fractionation of radiation received (i.e., times per day radiation is given and the dose at each delivery). These modifications to date have not resulted in improved survival. The use of multiple small doses of radiation per day to allow for a higher total daily dose (called hyperfractionated radiation therapy) resulted in increased toxicity. Radiation damage to the brainstem (called radionecrosis) is associated with increased neurologic deficits.

Radiosensitizers

Radiosensitization is another means to improve the therapeutic balance between efficacy and toxicity of radiation therapy. This research has been explored over the past two decades, and continues to be studied. Radiosensitizers are defined as compounds that, when combined with radiation, achieve greater tumor inactivation than would have been expected from just the additive effects of the two modalities of treatment. The premise that underlies radiosensitization is that the toxicities of the chemical agent used and the radiation do not significantly overlap, thereby not increasing toxicity. Also, the chemical agent chosen should not make the radiation therapy more toxic to the normal brain cells within the region of the brain receiving the radiation. Optimally, the benefits of radiosensitization should allow the tumor site to be exposed to an effectively higher dose of radiation without increased toxicity. In reality, this hoped-for

> Dr. Packer is the Director of the Brain Tumor Institute and Senior Vice-President of Neuroscience and Behavioral Medicine at Children's National Medical Center, and Professor of Neurology and Pediatrics at The George Washington University, Washington, DC.

synergistic effect of radiosensitization is a balance between how much more effective the radiosensitizers make radiation in killing more tumor cells, compared with how much more damaging the treatment will be to normal cells that are exposed to the radiotherapy.

Another basic concept that has been difficult to prove with brainstem gliomas is that increasing the effective dose of radiation therapy actually improves disease control. At best, most radiosensitizers increase the dose intensity of radiotherapy by 20% to 30%, yet it is unclear whether such an increase results in improved long-term disease control.

Types of Radiosensitizers

Hypoxic cell sensitizers

The largest early experience with radiosensitizers was the use of agents that act to sensitize hypoxic cells to radiation therapy. The use of these agents was based on the assumption that a chronic state of tumor hypoxia (when tumor cells exist in an environment low in oxygen) occurs in brainstem gliomas. Using agents that make these hypoxic tumor cells more sensitive to radiation therapy may provide a therapeutic advantage by killing more hypoxic cells and sparing better oxygenated cells (in theory, normal cells) from the damaging effects of radiation. A series of hypoxic cell sensitizers have been utilized for other cancers, but they have not been used in brainstem gliomas due to concerns about toxicity, including enhanced neurologic toxicity, and lack of any clear benefit when used on other types of tumors.

An alternative means to radiosensitize hypoxic cells is to make the tumor less hypoxic—in other words, get more oxygen to the cells. Different methods that have been used to accomplish this include hyperbaric oxygen, the use of red blood cell transfusions, and the delivery of oxygen carrier substances. The combination of nicotinamide and carbogen has been used based on the theory that nicotinamide will decrease the presence of intermittent hypoxia (a deficiency in the amount of oxygen reaching tissues), and the carbogen will re-oxygenate tumor cells. Other approaches have included using drugs such as nitric oxide, which causes vasodilation (widening of the blood vessels), to alter the tumor vasculature.

Non-hypoxic cell sensitizers

Some of the earliest work in non-hypoxic cell sensitizers was the use of cell-cycle-specific radiosensitizers that act independently of the effect of oxygen.

Drugs such as BUDR (bromodeoxyuridine) and IUDR (idoxuridine), which are halogenated pyrimidine analogs, have been tested. It is presumed they would primarily sensitize rapidly proliferating cells, with the drug sensitizing tumor cells to a much greater degree than the normal surrounding cells. For efficacy, these drugs require extended exposure to allow incorporation into the tumor cell's DNA. The use of halogenated pyrimidine analogs has not been shown to be effective in adults with high-grade gliomas, and has not been extensively studied in children.

Gadolinium-texafyrin is a molecule that penetrates well into enhancing regions of the brain. Gadolinium is the primary contrast agent used for magnetic resonance imaging (MRI) studies. Gadolinium-texafyrin is an oxygen-independent radiosensitizer with a low toxicity profile. A phase I dose-limiting toxicity study (see chapter 5) in children with brainstem gliomas demonstrated minimal side effects. A phase 2 study of this drug regimen given on a Monday through Friday schedule has recently been completed through the Children's Oncology Group (COG). Arsenic trioxide is another non-hypoxic radiosensitizer which remains in phase 1 study for pediatric gliomas.

Chemoradiation

Chemotherapeutic agents have been widely used in children with brainstem gliomas during radiation therapy in an attempt to radiosensitize the tumor cells. The major difficulties in choosing the most appropriate chemotherapeutic agent to study include:

- The independent effectiveness of any drug in children with recurrent or newly diagnosed brainstem glioma has been difficult to prove.

- Most phase 2 or pre-radiotherapy neoadjuvant studies (administration of therapeutic agents prior to the main treatment) have demonstrated minimal efficacy. Experimental data to support the synergistic benefits of chemotherapy, when added to radiation therapy in experimental models, has been limited.

- The drug(s) may have limited ability to get to the tumor site because of a relatively intact blood-brain barrier.

- The toxicity profile of the drug has to be "reasonable," given the impaired neurologic status and probable shortened life-span of the child, so as not to detract from the remaining quality time that the child and family can share.

Despite these considerations, there are multiple reasons to consider the use of chemotherapeutic agents. For example, the radiation effect on tumor cells may be enhanced by drugs that inhibit DNA repair after sublethal radiation damage. Drugs such as cisplatin, hydroxyurea, and nitrosoureas have shown this type of activity in experimental studies. Several drugs have been shown to potentially enhance the efficacy of radiotherapy by changing the cell cycling of tumor cells—putting more cells into a phase of the mitotic cycle, which makes them more sensitive to radiation therapy.

Another potential benefit of chemotherapy would be the independent effect of the chemotherapeutic agent to decrease the size of the tumor cell. This would potentially make radiotherapy more effective. Similarly, if radiotherapy made the tumor smaller, it might allow greater vascular access for the chemotherapeutic agent, resulting in a greater concentration of the drug in the tumor and increased tumor kill. Some chemotherapeutic agents are relatively effective in killing hypoxic cells. For this reason, drugs such as cisplatin may have synergistic efficacy if used with radiation therapy. Chemotherapeutic agents may also enhance apoptosis (programmed cell death) and subsequently tumor death, especially in cancer cells sublethally damaged by concurrent radiotherapy.

Delivery of Chemotherapy and Radiation

The timing of chemotherapy and radiation delivery is often based not only on the principles of when the chemotherapy may be most effective in enhancing radiation, but also the practicality of delivering such treatments to children. The toxicity of some chemotherapy agents precludes treatment throughout the entire 6 to 7 weeks of prescribed radiation therapy. In addition, the need to transport the child to the radiation therapy facility, which is often at an institution other than where the chemotherapy has been given; the time needed to sedate young children; and the concern of overburdening both the child and the family for an unproven treatment, often results in severe logistical issues and compromises in treatment schedules. In reality, these issues and compromises have resulted in chemotherapeutic agents being given with radiation therapy in a sequential fashion in order to reduce the temporal separation as much as possible.

The benefits of chemoradiation have been suggested in a variety of different tumor types, including head and neck tumors, small cell lung cancer, gastrointestinal cancers, and cancers of the genital and urinary organs. However, a clear-cut benefit in adults with primary central nervous system tumors has been difficult to prove. Pediatric tumor studies to date have been disappointing as well, with the possible exception of medulloblastoma, where a preliminary trial suggested improved survival.

Platinum derivatives

The use of platinum derivatives such as chemoradiation sensitizers is based on the ability of drugs such as cisplatin and carboplatin to inhibit DNA repair or sublethal radiation damage and to have cytotoxic effects on hypoxic cells. Cisplatin has been used as a backbone of a study comparing standard fractionated radiation to hyperfractionated radiation, without a clear survival advantage in either arm of the trial. Another study utilized carboplatin twice weekly during hyperfractionated radiation therapy without any clear-cut benefit. A subsequent carboplatin study coupled carboplatin with a bradykinin derivative to enhance delivery of the carboplatin to the brainstem. In this trial, carboplatin was given on Monday through Friday basis throughout radiation therapy with good tolerability, but overall, survival did not dramatically differ from that seen in historical controls treated with radiotherapy alone.

5-FU derivatives

The drug 5-FU has been extensively utilized in the treatment of adult cancers for both its antineoplastic effects and radiosensitization properties. 5-FU interacts with radiotherapy through disruption of cell kinetics and direct effects on repopulation of cells. Experimental work has shown that 5-FU is truly synergistic with radiotherapy. Its toxicity profile however, makes its concurrent use in pediatrics difficult. A sister drug, Capecitabine, has recently completed phase 1 and phase II testing as a radiosensitizer given concurrently with radiation therapy on a daily basis in children with brainstem gliomas. Results from the data is pending.

Topoisomerase inhibitors

Etoposide is an oral topoisomerase inhibitor that has shown efficacy in one trial of children with recurrent brainstem gliomas. The drug penetrates into the central nervous system well. However, a COG phase II trial of etoposide in combination with vincristine, concurrently with radiation therapy showed no clear-cut benefit.

Another topoisomerase inhibitor, topotecan, has been studied in a phase 1 study concurrent with radiation therapy for children with newly-diagnosed brainstem gliomas. A phase 2 study was initiated through the Children's Oncology Group but not completed.

Temozolomide

Results of adult trials with high-grade gliomas led to enthusiasm for the use of temozolomide, concurrent with radiation therapy, for patients with newly diagnosed brainstem gliomas. In children with recurrent brainstem gliomas, temozolomide has not shown significant independent activity and there is little experimental data to show that temozolomide is synergistic with radiotherapy. But based on the adult data and the relatively good toxicity profile of temozolomide when used at a low dose on a daily basis, a study was performed through the Children's Oncology Group that coupled temozolomide with radiation therapy, and followed the completion of radiotherapy. The results of this study have been disappointing.

Radiosensitization with Molecular-Targeted Drugs and Other "Biologic Agents"

Over the past decade, a host of biologic agents have become available and tested in children with brain tumors. Molecularly targeted agents have included:

1. Antiangiogenesis drugs;

2. Agents that block growth factor receptors;

3. Drugs that interfere with intracellular signaling essential for tumor growth.

The lack of biologic information about brainstem gliomas has hindered, to a great degree, a biologic rationale for deciding which drug, or drug combinations would be most effective if combined with radiation. In phase 1 trials to date, these biologic agents have demonstrated minimal ability to shrink tumors, although some have resulted in possible prolonged stable disease. Because of the relative low toxicity of many of these agents and, in some cases, theoretic evidence that they may be at least additive—if not synergistic—with concurrent radiotherapy, multiple studies have utilized biologics with, and following, radiation therapy. There is great interest in continuing such approaches, with the caveat that experimental evidence for independent efficacy or synergy is often minimal, at best.

Thalidomide and Interferon

Thalidomide is an agent that has been in clinical use for many years for a variety of indications, including sedation and leprosy, and was found to be a potent teratogen in pregnant women. Among its multiple properties, including being an anti-inflammatory agent, it is also an angiogenesis inhibitor, which probably underlies much of its teratogenicity. It has been used in combination with radiotherapy for children with brainstem gliomas without clear benefit.

Another drug that was utilized with radiotherapy is interferon. Interferon, of which various types including alpha, beta, and gamma being utilized, has shown variable benefits for adults and children with malignant gliomas. Based on radiographic objective responses in 4 out of 18 children with recurrent malignant cerebral or brainstem glioma, and clinical improvement or disease stabilization in 5 out of 9 children with recurrent brainstem gliomas treated on a beta-interferon protocol for children with recurrent disease, a study of 32 children with diffuse intrinsic brainstem gliomas were treated with concurrent recombinant beta interferon and hyperfractionated radiation therapy (7200 cGy). This study was disappointing in that not only did 30 of 32 patients develop progressive disease at a median of 5 months from diagnosis, but more than one-third of the patients required dose modifications due to a hepatic (liver related) or hematologic (blood related) toxicity. One patient developed severe neurotoxicity.

Molecularly targeted trials

A variety of biologic agents have been studied concurrently with radiotherapy. Iressa, an epidermal growth factor receptor antagonist, was studied in both phase 1 and phase 2 studies through the Pediatric Brain Tumor Consortium (PBTC). Early experience with this drug raised the issue of whether the use of such agents would increase symptomatic brainstem hemorrhage. This study highlighted how little was actually known about the rate of occurrence of spontaneous hemorrhages of brainstem gliomas prior to, or during, conventional radiotherapy. Intrabrainstem hemorrhages did occur, but it is unclear how much more frequent their occurrence was than the rate of such episodes during and after standard radiation therapy. Although there was no clear-cut benefit from the use of the drug, survival rates one year from study were more than 50%.

The farnesyl transferase inhibitors are drugs that interfere with intracellular signaling by blocking the activation of ras—a key protein involved in intracellular signaling often overactive in growing tumors. An oral farnesyl-transferase inhibitor drug was utilized in phase 1 and phase 2 studies through the Pediatric Brain Tumor Consortium with a low rate of intratumoral hemorrhage and toxicity, but no evidence of efficacy. Antiangiogenic agents are likewise in clinical use for patients with newly diagnosed brainstem gliomas. There is little data, as of yet, concerning their toxicity or efficacy.

Summary

Radiosensitization remains an appealing approach for the treatment of children with newly diagnosed brainstem gliomas. As outlined, although there are theoretic benefits to their use, there is little evidence to date to validate improved efficacy. Work continues with standard chemotherapeutic agents, hypoxic and non-hypoxic radiosensitizers, and biologic agents. Until more is known about the basic biology of brainstem gliomas, most studies will remain empiric. Delivery of agents to the brainstem remains an extremely critical and potentially limiting factor. In addition, as better agents are developed, their selective capabilities of killing tumor cells and relatively sparing the normal surrounding brain cells will remain a critical issue.

Parent Perspectives

When our daughter Ella was diagnosed with DIPG the only trial available was a radiosensitizer. So we opted to do it because we had no other options. Her first treatment was a couple weeks after diagnosis. She was to have the radiosensitizer and then radiation within a couple hours. Within 30 seconds of the radiosensitizer entering her body she began sweating, having stomach cramps and nausea. We asked the doctors to stop the treatment and were told they would give her additional anti-nausea meds and anti-anxiety meds. She finished the treatment, but due to the constant vomiting she was unable to have radiation as she would be strapped to the table and the fear was that she could choke on her own vomit. We opted out of the trial the next day.

Although our journey began a day prior to April 11th, I mark that as the day the world effectively ended for us. On that day, we were brought into a small cramped room next to the nursing station, given no more than ten minutes with the attending oncologist and told that Alexis, our then twenty-seven month old daughter, had only six to nine months to live, maybe a year at the outside. Wind taken out of our sails, devastated beyond belief, we were effectively set out to drift in the new and confusing world of pediatric cancer. We were barely familiar with the words diffuse intrinsic pontine glioma.

Within several hours, we found ourselves frantically driving from one hospital to the next to meet with another doctor to discuss treatment options and prognosis. Within a very short amount of time, we were provided with an amount of hope that, although not a guarantee of survival, at least allowed us to gain some level of comfort with moving forward.

During that initial meeting late on a Friday afternoon, we discussed several approaches and treatments. Each option was presented with its own caveat, and each was discussed in a manner which allowed us to appreciate that it was not a home run cure. Ultimately, our decision was between one of two treatment paths: a chemotherapy cocktail with overly used agents, or standard radiation with a radiosensitizer. Ordinarily, chemotherapy has proven ineffective for children with DIPG. The thought process behind this option in Alexis' case was based upon her age at diagnosis and a hunch that her tumor was low grade. This option necessitated lengthy stays in the hospital, which worried us beyond belief. Personally, we were concerned about Alexis' psychological welfare during the course of extended stays in the hospital as well as her overall quality of life. In addition, this course had no statistical efficacy. Truth is, we would have done anything in the world to save Alexis, regardless of course.

Ultimately, the decision was made to proceed with a course of thirty radiation treatments and a Phase II clinical trial utilizing a radiosensitizer. The hope was that the addition of the radiosensitizer would allow the radiation to be more effective. The theory behind radiosensitizers is that the compounds are taken up by the blood vessels in the tumor and thus direct the radiation directly to the tumor. At the time we chose this course of treatment, there was no data presented to us, either statistical or anecdotal in nature, and thus, it was simply a blind dart thrown at a wall. You hope and you pray that the dart sticks. Hindsight taught us that in rare instances a single dart would find its target with no rhyme or reason. Since Alexis was very young at the time of diagnosis, we did not believe that she could aide in any reasonable fashion with making critical decisions. Accordingly, the guiding factor in all decisions was based upon Alexis' quality of life.

At diagnosis, Alexis' main symptom was an inverted right eye that was infrequent in nature. While watching television, we noticed that Alexis had to turn her head to the side to view. We feared that radiotherapy would cause swelling and thus we would witness an increase in symptoms. Within the first three days, these fears were realized and we noticed some right-sided weakness. Obviously, this was extremely frightening and disconcerting. Thankfully, this abated within a day or so of additional treatment and Alexis sailed with flying colors through the remaining twenty six or so treatments until she "graduated" from radiation on June 19th.

Our days during radiation therapy grew to be routine, and again, we normalized life as much as possible. Each morning, we frantically rushed to the hospital by 5:45 a.m. If we were late, the entire schedule and timing of the actual radiotherapy was delayed. Upon arrival, we marched straight to one of two treatment rooms on the pediatric hematology/oncology ward. Shortly thereafter, Alexis received several pre-medications and then the radiosensitizer was brought into the room and pumped into Alexis' veins over the course of fifteen minutes. The first several times she was given this combination we sat with breath held, worried about what side effects may present. Thankfully, none ever manifested. We of course were forced to wear rubber gloves when changing Alexis due to the potential toxicities to those who came in contact with the drugs. Such an odd juxtaposition— Alexis could have these substances dripped into her veins, but there was concern over us touching them with our bare hands. After the combination was finished, we then waited three hours for the sensitizer to "find" its way throughout her diminutive little body and on to the tumor. It was always a tormenting thought: just inches inside of Alexis' head sat this uninvited beast. And nothing that we could do could ever change that. This realization continually taunted me during my waking moments and beyond.

Alexis' course was not typical in the DIPG community. Within several days of beginning radiation in combination with the radiosensitizer, all symptoms were erased and that remained true up until the end of January.

Our son was 10 years old when he was diagnosed with DIPG. Like most 10 year old boys, he was active and vibrant—full of life. He lived life to the fullest and was happiest when he was playing baseball.

There weren't many clinical trials available for children newly diagnosed with DIPG. The only trial available via the pediatric oncology clinic easily accessible for us was a Phase II COG trial involving motexafin gadolinium as a radiosensitizer. We were told that radiation therapy is the only treatment which usually makes a difference for kids with DIPG. Therefore, the most logical focus in clinical trials was to increase the effectiveness of radiation. This made sense to us, so we entered Caleb in the trial.

Each morning, Caleb received an infusion of the bright green motexafin gadolinium compound. The hour-long drive to the clinic, the hour-long infusion, and the two to five hour wait time before Caleb could have radiation all turned out to be blessings to our family. We had good times together during those days—time focused on Caleb and crafts, games or reading. Often, Caleb's brothers or his best friends would come along with us. We developed dear friendships and learned to treasure the moments.

Within a week of beginning the trial, Caleb began to develop unusual side effects. He became very sensitive to the sun; he felt a prickly sensation that quickly developed into full-fledged pain when he was outdoors. Within days of this, blisters began appearing on his face, hands, neck, arms, and ears. At first they were just little water blisters. Soon, they became huge bubbles—some of them as large as a small apple on the backs of his hands.

His fingernails turned a milky white and began to separate from his nail beds.

All the while, Caleb continued to play baseball. We saturated him in sun screen and covered his skin with cloth and bandages. The pain was intense. He could hardly stand to be in the field. After the third out was called, he raced into the dugout where we had ice chests filled with cold and warm rags in which to wrap him—one of the few efforts that brought some relief. We rubbed topical anesthetic on his skin and, when it was time for him to hit, he wore thick gloves to dull the pain of the blisters as his hands tightly gripped the bat. He wore an eye-patch on his left eye. The green chemicals gave his skin a green tint and even produced green stripes down his neck and back and across his shoulders. Add the blisters, various bandages and big gloves and he looked like quite a character. He was devoted to the game.

I greatly regret that we allowed him to suffer so—even required it of him. He never complained about the therapy; never once did he consider withdrawing from the trial. We believed it held promise and was the only hope we had of beating the evil disease.

That does bring to mind regret, however. While he never considered stopping the therapy, he did consider taking a year off from baseball. Now, I know a lot of boys love baseball, but Caleb suggesting he take a year off from baseball is akin to most of us taking a year off from food. It proves how difficult it was for him. And, because we knew that he likely wouldn't have another year, we felt we had to explain to him that he had to make the most of the current season. We were blunt—it might be his last season.

Again, in retrospect, I wish we hadn't been so forthright. He increased his resolve and will to fight. But it also caused him to be fearful at times. Caleb surely would have eventually figured out his prognosis. I wish, though, that the circumstances had been different—that we hadn't forced the knowledge on him out of desperation and baseless hope.

We do not blame ourselves or our healthcare team for these painful memories. We do, however, wish that our healthcare team had been more forthright with us and told us that radiosensitizers in general had never shown much promise in DIPG, and that this specific therapy hadn't helped a single kid. It was just the only thing they knew to try at the time.

Who knows? We might have forged on, convinced that Caleb would be "the one." That's what we all hope, isn't it? But at least we would've known.

Chapter 9

Chemotherapy and Biologics

David N. Korones, MD

The cure rate for children with cancer has improved dramatically over the past few decades, rising from less than 50% in the 1960s to close to 80% today. This is a remarkable story of laboratory research, which has given us a better understanding of how children's cancers work. It is the story of unprecedented collaboration between hundreds of pediatric cancer centers around the country and the world. It is the story of pediatric oncologists, radiation oncologists, and surgeons working together to improve the lives of children with cancer. And it is the story of strength, heartbreak, resilience, inspiration, and advocacy on the part of children with cancer and their families, who have contributed more than anyone in moving this field of medicine forward.

Yet the successes in curing children with cancer have been unequal. Remarkable strides have been made in treating some types of childhood cancers, but cure rates for others remain stagnant. Such is the case for children with brainstem glioma, for whom success has sadly eluded us. Surgical removal of this tumor is not possible. In fact, these children rarely undergo a biopsy, so tumor samples are not available to help researchers understand this disease. Radiation has proven to be quite effective, but only for a short time. This leaves chemotherapy and biologics. It would seem that for a tumor that cannot be removed surgically and that responds only temporarily to radiation treatment, chemotherapy might be the best approach to this challenging disease. But this has not been the case. Despite decades of research and clinical trials, researchers have yet to find a chemotherapeutic or biologic agent that improves the survival of children with brainstem glioma. But this does not mean we never will. In fact, it could be a new drug or some sort of targeted therapy based

Dr. Korones is Board Certified in Pediatrics, Pediatric Hematology/ Oncology, and Hospice and Palliative Medicine. He is Director of the Brain Tumor Program and the Pediatric Palliative Care Program at Gosliano Children's Hospital, Rochester, NY.

on a better understanding of the biology of brainstem gliomas that will lead to future success in treating children with this disease. That day has not yet come, but it will. This chapter reviews what chemotherapy is, why it has not worked for children with brainstem glioma, what has been tried, and what holds promise. Also discussed are biologic therapies (i.e., treatment that more specifically targets some of the mechanisms tumor cells use to grow).

Chemotherapy

What is chemotherapy?

Chemotherapy is simply any medication that kills cancer cells. Just as "antibiotic" refers to the broad class of drugs used to treat infections, chemotherapy refers to the broad class of drugs used to treat cancer. Chemotherapy can be given intravenously (IV), through an injection into the skin or muscle, orally, or even injected directly into a body cavity (e.g., injection of chemotherapy into the spinal fluid via a spinal tap [lumbar puncture]). Most chemotherapy is given by IV or orally. Chemotherapy works by targeting cells that are actively dividing thereby stopping the cancer cells from reproducing. Many different types of chemotherapy drugs exist, and each one targets one of the many different aspects of tumor cell division. For example, two commonly used chemotherapies to treat children with brain tumors, temozolomide and CCNU (lomustine), bind directly to DNA (the building block of cell division) and prevent the DNA from duplicating itself, thereby preventing the cell from dividing, leading to its death. Another example is vincristine, which targets spindle-like structures that allow one cell to become two cells.

For many pediatric cancers, it has been shown that by using combination chemotherapy—two, three, or more drugs together—the child's survival is improved. This is because several drugs together work better to kill cancer cells than any one drug alone. In addition, if a tumor is resistant to one drug, it may be killed by one of the others given.

A disadvantage of chemotherapy (particularly in treating children with brain tumors) is that it circulates everywhere in the child's body, and therefore has the potential to kill or damage normally dividing cells. This fact accounts for many of the side effects of chemotherapy, such as low blood counts, risk of infection, bleeding, fatigue, mouth sores, and nausea and vomiting.

Challenges of using chemotherapy for children with brainstem glioma

Finding effective chemotherapy for children with brain tumors is more challenging than finding effective chemotherapy for children with other malignancies. A major challenge with brain tumors is the blood-brain barrier. Blood vessels in the brain are unique; they are designed to be very selective about what can penetrate them to get into brain cells. They selectively allow nutrients to reach brain cells, but block many unrecognizable, potentially toxic substances including many types of chemotherapy. From an evolutionary standpoint, this makes perfect sense (i.e., protecting our brains from toxins), but when it comes to getting chemotherapy into brain tumors, it is a problem. Therefore chemotherapy must be designed to penetrate the blood-brain barrier. The list of drugs that can do this is small, leaving us with fewer weapons to use for children with brain tumors. It is thought (but not proven) that the blood vessels in brainstem gliomas are particularly restrictive and allow very few substances to penetrate them.

Another challenge is the tumor itself. For reasons that are unclear (and still not definitely proven), it appears that the tumor cells that make up brainstem gliomas are extremely resistant to chemotherapy. That is, even if the chemotherapy gets into the tumor, it cannot kill the tumor cells.

Clinical Trials Using Chemotherapy for Children with Brainstem Glioma

As noted above, chemotherapy has been used in every way, shape, and form possible to date to treat children with brainstem glioma. The most common approaches have been giving chemotherapy after radiation (termed **adjuvant chemotherapy**), administering chemotherapy before radiation (called **neoadjuvant chemotherapy**), and giving high-dose chemotherapy with stem cell rescue (also referred to as autologous bone marrow transplant). Chemotherapy is also used during radiation treatment as a radiosensitizer (discussed separately in chapter 8). These various approaches to using chemotherapy are discussed below.

Adjuvant chemotherapy

The first large-scale multicenter clinical trials testing the effectiveness of chemotherapy for children with brainstem glioma were published in the late 1980s. This was around the time that chemotherapy had been proven effective for children with other types of brain tumors, such as medulloblastoma, glioblastoma and low-grade astrocytoma. At that time there was considerable hope that the successes of chemotherapy for children with other brain tumors would extend to children with brainstem glioma. In one of the first studies, Jenkins et al. conducted a national clinical trial through the Children's Cancer Study Group (CCSG) from 1977 to 1980. All 74 children enrolled in the study received radiation; half received radiation alone, while the other half received radiation plus chemotherapy—lomustine (CCNU), vincristine, and prednisone (a combination used successfully for children with medulloblastoma and high-grade astrocytoma). The 5-year survival for both groups was only around 20%, suggesting that this particular combination of chemotherapy was not effective for children with brainstem glioma. It should be noted that survival in both groups was actually somewhat higher than what we see today. This is probably because the study was conducted in the pre-MRI era, and some of the tumors that were thought to be brainstem glioma may have actually been less aggressive variants of brain stem tumors that would not be classified as DIPG today.

Through the 1990s, researchers explored other types of chemotherapy for children with brainstem glioma. Walter et al. treated nine children with an MRI-documented DIPGs with carboplatin and etoposide during and after radiation. These two drugs have been shown to have activity against other types of brain tumors, so the hope was that they would also prove effective for children with a brainstem glioma. However, this treatment did not work—survival at 1 year was 44%, and at 2 years only one child (11%) was alive. In another study, Chamberlain tried an innovative approach to treatment, which comprised daily low doses of oral chemotherapy. The thought was that daily low doses of chemotherapy given orally might work better than larger IV doses of chemotherapy given every few weeks. In addition, side effects seemed to be less of a problem when this type of dosing had been used in other clinical trials. Chamberlain used this approach, treating 12 children with a recurrent brainstem glioma with oral etoposide (VP-16). Unexpectedly, the tumor shrunk in 5 of these 12 children. This result generated considerable excitement about this new approach to treatment. Based on Chamberlain's observations, the Children's Oncology Group (COG) launched a national clinical trial of oral etoposide and IV vincristine during and after radiation. Disappointingly, all 30 children on this trial died, with one and two year survival of only 27% and 3% respectively. Other types of chemotherapy have been tested, mostly in small trials, and they, too, were ineffective. Drugs including idarubicin, trophosphamide and oral etoposide, cisplatin, etoposide, ifosfamide, and oral topotecan have been tried, but none prolonged children's lives or improved cure rates. A summary of these trials is illustrated in Table 1.

One exciting new chemotherapeutic agent developed and studied extensively in

Table 1: Representative clinical trials of adjuvant chemotherapy for children with newly diagnosed diffuse brain stem glioma.

Author (see Appendix D)	Group study	N	RT dose (GY)	Chemotherapy	Median OS (mo.)	Survival (%) at 1yr	2yr	3yr	5yr
Jenkin (1)	CCG	33 37	50-60 50-60	none pCV		26* 35*			17 23
Walter (2)	St. Jude	9	70.2 (1.17 b.i.d)	carboplatin IV VP-16	10	44	11		
Korones (4)	POG	30	54 (1.8 q.d.)	oral VP-16 vincristine	9	27	3		
Wolff (6)	GPOH	20	54 (1.8 q.d.)	oral trophosphamide oral VP-16	8	40	15	5	
Wolff (7)	GPOH	37	54	cisplatin IV VP-16 Vincristine	13				
Broniscer (9)	St. Jude	33	55.8	temozolomide	12	48			
Cohen (10)	COG	63		temozolomide	10	40			

* 18 mo. survival
CCG = Children's Cancer Group POG = Pediatric Oncology Group COG = Children's Oncology Group
GPOH = German Society of Pediatric Oncology RT = radiotherapy pCV = prednisone, CCNU, vincristine OS = overall survival

the last 10 to 15 years is temozolomide (Temodar®). This drug is given orally, has fewer side effects than most chemotherapy, and has proven to be effective for adults with grades 3 and 4 astrocytomas (similar to brainstem glioma). The successes with adults led pediatric neuro-oncologists to conduct clinical trials of this drug for children with brainstem glioma. In one of the first studies of temozolomide for children with a newly diagnosed brainstem glioma, 33 children at St. Jude Children's Research Hospital received temozolomide in monthly cycles for up to 6 months. Although the 1-year survival was 48% (higher than in most studies), all 33 children eventually died. The COG conducted a similar study with children with brainstem glioma receiving temozolomide during radiation, as well as following it. The results were similarly disappointing. Of the 63 children enrolled, all but one had died after 25 months of follow-up (and that child could not be tracked down to verify whether he/she survived). In five other studies of temozolomide for children with a DIPG, (including one using cis-retinoic acid and another using thalidomide), the outcomes were also poor. In sum, as promising as temozolomide first appeared to be, and as few side effects as it has, it is not the breakthrough in chemotherapy we had so hoped it would be.

Neoadjuvant chemotherapy

As noted above, neoadjuvant chemotherapy is chemotherapy that is given before the more definitive treatment for a tumor. In the case of a brainstem glioma, neoadjuvant chemotherapy is chemotherapy given before radiation. This approach was investigated in several clinical trials in the 1990s and early 2000s. The rationale for neoadjuvant chemotherapy was based on the general enthusiasm at that time for chemotherapy for children with brain tumors. In addition, it was felt that the best way to assess the effectiveness of chemotherapy against a brainstem glioma was to give it before radiation, as it is hard to assess tumor response to chemotherapy after radiation. The hope was that effective drugs would quickly be identified and then given to children after the radiation, as well. This approach was undertaken with some trepidation, because if chemotherapy was not effective, the children might suffer from side effects of chemotherapy *and* a growing tumor, and get sicker, not better. There was concern that these children might become too sick to tolerate radiation, the one treatment known to give them a little more time.

The first clinical trial published taking this approach was a Pediatric Oncology Group study of 32 children with brainstem glioma who were treated with two to three cycles of cisplatin and cyclophosphamide before starting radiation. Although 3 of the 32 children had shrinkage of the tumor and another 23 had no increase in tumor size, the overall survival for the children was not improved compared with giving radiation alone; the median survival was only 9 months. In

Table 2: Clinical trials of neoadjuvant chemotherapy for children with newly diagnosed diffuse brain stem glioma

Author (see Appendix D)	Group study	N	Chemotherapy	Response	RT dose (Gy)	Median OS (mo.)	Survival (%) at 1yr	2yr	3yr
Kretschmar (16)	POG	32	cisplatinum cyclophosphamide	3 PR 23 SD 6 PD	66 (1.1 b.i.d.)		9	30	
Jennings (17)	CCG	32	carboplatin VP-16 vincristine	2 PR 1 MR 12 SD 12 PD	72 (1 b.i.d.)	10*	30*	18*	
		31	cisplatinum cyclophosphamide VP-16 vincristine	1 PR 4 MR 8 SD 9PD	72 (1 b.i.d.)	10*	30*	10*	
Doz (18)	SFOP	36	carboplatin	4 MR 6 SD 11 PD	54	11			
Broniscer (9)	St. Jude	16	irinotecan	10 SD 5 PD	55.8				

*estimated from Kaplan-Meier curve   PR=partial response, MR=minor response, SD=stable disease, PD=progressive disease

a second, larger study of 63 children with a newly diagnosed brainstem glioma, 32 children received carboplatin, etoposide, and vincristine, and 31 received cisplatin, cyclophosphamide, etoposide, and vincristine before going on to receive radiation therapy. Only 10 to 20% of the children had tumor shrinkage, and again, their overall survival was poor—no better than it was with radiation alone. Similarly poor results were seen when 38 children received neoadjuvant carboplatin and neoadjuvant irinotecan. These studies are summarized in Table 2.

Based on these disappointing results and the disappointing results of multiple other clinical trials of chemotherapy after radiation, the approach of trying chemotherapy before radiation has largely been abandoned.

High-dose chemotherapy and stem cell rescue

Another innovative approach undertaken in the quest to cure children with brainstem glioma was high-dose chemotherapy with stem cell rescue (also referred to as autologous bone marrow transplantation). This type of therapy is not really a bone marrow transplant at all; rather, it is simply a way to more safely give children higher doses of chemotherapy. The rationale for using such high doses of chemotherapy for children with brainstem glioma is two-fold. It was thought that 1) it might take higher doses of chemotherapy to kill the brainstem glioma cells, and 2) higher doses might somehow "push" more chemotherapy through the blood-brain barrier and allow enough chemotherapy to reach the tumor cells and kill the tumor.

Neuro-oncologists were particularly hopeful about this approach because it seemed to improve survival of children with recurrent medulloblastoma and glioblastoma. How does it work? First, the very youngest of blood cells (called hematopoietic stem cells) are removed (often referred to as "harvested") from children with brainstem glioma. This is done by taking samples of bone marrow or removing these specialized cells from the blood through a procedure called pheresis. These cells are frozen until they are needed. The children then receive 3 to 7 days of extremely high doses of chemotherapy, so high in fact that it almost destroys their ability to ever make their own blood cells again. But after they receive the chemotherapy, the stem cells that were removed and frozen are thawed and given back to the children. These resourceful stem cells are given through an IV (like a blood transfusion), circulate through the blood, find their way back to the bone marrow, and over the next several weeks, repopulate the bone marrow and the blood with new, normal blood cells, thus "rescuing" the children from what otherwise could be a lethal dose of chemotherapy.

Several clinical trials of high-dose chemotherapy with stem cell rescue were

Table 3: Clinical trials of high-dose chemotherapy with stem cell rescue for children with newly diagnosed diffuse brain stem glioma

Author (see Appendix D)	Group study	N	RT dose (Gy)	Chemotherapy	Median OS (mo.)	Survival (%) at 1 yr	2 yr	3 yr
Bouffet (21)	SFOP	35	50-55	busulfan thiotepa	10	40		
Bouffet (22)*	France	5	not stated	BCNU	10			
Jackaki (23)	Indiana U	6	54-59.4	procarbazine CCNU vincristine	13			
Kedar (24)*	U Florida	6	75.6 (1.25 b.i.d.)	cyclophosphamide thiotepa	12.5			
Dunkel (25)*	CCG	6	72-78 (b.i.d.)	BCNU thiotepa VP-16	11.4			

*Chemotherapy given prior to radiation

conducted in the 1990's, but unfortunately this approach did not seem to help. Perhaps the largest clinical trial using this approach was a study by Dr. Bouffet and colleagues. The researchers enrolled 35 children in the study, all of whom received radiation, and 24 of whom were able to then go on and receive high doses of chemotherapy (busulfan and thiotepa). All 24 of these children died, three from complications of the therapy, and the remainder from regrowth of the tumor. The average life expectancy of the group was only 10 months, not any better than the life expectancy of children who received radiation alone. Four other studies of high-dose chemotherapy with stem cell rescue included children with brainstem glioma. Although tumors shrank in a handful of children, it did not improve their overall outcome, and several children died of complications from this very aggressive approach. A summary of trials using high-dose chemotherapy with stem cell rescue is presented in Table 3.

Based on the experience with these children, high-dose chemotherapy with stem cell rescue is no longer being investigated for children with brainstem glioma. Although high doses of chemotherapy can be very effective for children with certain types of cancer, it is clearly not the case for children with brainstem glioma. We need other innovative approaches to tame this type of tumor.

Biologics

As is painfully clear from the above discussion, chemotherapy does not appear to be the answer for children with brainstem glioma. Over the past decade, investigators have come to realize the answer may lie in first gaining a better understanding of how these tumors work. Once we have that understanding, we can find drugs that target the tumor cells very specifically; this is the concept of biologic therapy. Chemotherapy is a rather blunt sword that kills any cell that divides, be it cancerous or not. Biologic therapy is more finely tuned and targeted. It is treatment that is based on the abnormal biology of a cancer cell. Biologic therapy targets the very biologic mechanisms that cause cancer cells to grow uncontrollably, and unlike chemotherapy, biologic therapy often spares the normal cells.

A big challenge in using this approach for children with brainstem glioma is that we do not know what makes these tumors tick. These children seldom undergo biopsy of their tumors, so researchers do not have many tumor samples to examine to help them understand the biology of brainstem glioma. However, this is starting to change, as some centers are doing biopsies again, others gather tumor samples at the time of autopsy, and new techniques are being used to analyze old tumor samples obtained decades ago.

A number of clinical trials of biologic therapies have been conducted. One of the first trials tested interferon, a natural substance made by the human body in response to viral infections. It was hoped that interferon would stimulate the immune system to fight the tumors and perhaps inhibit the blood supply to the tumor. In a 1991 phase I-II clinical trial that included eight children with brainstem glioma, two children had partial responses to the treatment, and in another three children, growth of the tumor was halted for several months. In a subsequent larger study of 32 children with a DIPG who received interferon along with radiation therapy, overall survival was not improved.

Another innovative approach is using agents that can "open up" the blood-brain barrier. As previously noted, chemotherapy has difficulty reaching brain tumors because it cannot penetrate brain tumor blood vessels. A substance called RMP7 was found to open up these blood vessels, making them "leaky," so that chemotherapy can go right through them and reach the tumor. There were two very small clinical trials for children with brainstem glioma using RMP7 along with chemotherapy. In one phase I study of RMP7 and carboplatin, the treatment was well tolerated but the number of children was too small to assess its effectiveness. In a second study, eight children with brainstem glioma received RMP7 along with various types of chemotherapy through an artery (instead of intravenously). These children did somewhat better, but again the number treated was small and the intra-arterial approach is not one that can be easily done at most centers. RMP7 was also studied in adults with malignant brain tumors and was not found to be effective. The drug has limited availability at this time.

One additional approach to penetrating the blood-brain barrier is the use of cyclosporine A along with chemotherapy. This drug helps "trap" certain types of chemotherapy inside brain tumor cells so the chemotherapy remains in the cells long enough to kill them. A COG trial using cyclosporine, vincristine, and oral etoposide (VP-16) was launched to study this effect, but unfortunately, the number and severity of side effects was unacceptably high.

Another promising biologic approach is anti-angiogenic therapy. This is the use of drugs that kill or inhibit blood vessel growth into growing tumors. The rationale for anti-angiogenic therapy is that if one can prevent blood vessels from growing into the tumor, the tumor will be deprived of oxygen and nutrients and stop growing. The most promising anti-angiogenic agent to date is bevacizumab, an antibody that attacks a protein called vascular endothelial growth factor (VEGF). VEGF is a natural substance that stimulates blood vessels to grow into brain tumors as the tumors themselves get bigger. This treatment has proved effective in adults with high-grade astrocytomas, and there was hope it might also prove effective for children with brainstem glioma. In a recently published study of bevacizumab and the chemotherapy drug CPT-11 (irinotecan) for children with recurrent brainstem glioma, only 5 of 13 children had a temporary halt in the growth of their tumors, and the average time until the tumor starting growing again was only 2.3 months. Although this particular anti-angiogenic therapy had little effect, there are many new anti-angiogenic drugs being developed, so there is still hope that this approach may eventually work.

Another hopeful approach to treatment is blocking growth factor receptors on tumor cells. Growth factor receptors are proteins found on the surface of tumor cells. When these growth factor receptors bind with a matching protein called a growth factor, the two proteins link together and stimulate tumor cells to grow uncontrollably. Based on studies of old tumor samples from children with brainstem glioma, investigators have learned that brainstem glioma cells seem to have increased numbers of a growth factor receptor called epidermal growth factor receptor (EGFr). Clinician-investigators are hopeful that EGFr may be a new way to attack these very resistant tumors. For example, in Germany, an antibody to the EGFr was developed; this antibody (called nimotuzumab) binds to the EGFr and seems to prevent EGF from binding to it and stimulating tumor cell growth. In a clinical trial of nimotuzumab, 22 children with a recurrent brainstem glioma were treated; 9 had stable disease and one child's tumor actually became smaller. Based on these encouraging results, a larger study of this drug was conducted, but the results are not yet available. In another recently published clinical trial, 43 children with newly diagnosed brainstem glioma were treated with erlotinib, another inhibitor of EGFr function. This drug was well tolerated, and children on this study fared slightly better than average, including three children who are alive more than 3 years from diagnosis. Blockage or inhibition of the EGFr remains a hopeful approach for treating children with brainstem glioma, but much work still needs to be done.

Other biologic therapies have been tried, but with no major successes. Some (but not all) of the agents studied include tamoxifen, cis-retinoic acid, and antineoplastons. The COG and Pediatric Brain Tumor Consortium have taken the lead in the United States in exploring new and innovative approaches to treating children with brainstem glioma. The COG is currently studying the addition of vorinostat, a drug representing a new class of biologics called histone deacetylase inhibitors (they unravel DNA), to standard radiation therapy.

Looking to the Future

As noted in the above discussion, clinician-scientists have exhaustively investigated many different combinations of chemotherapy and radiation for children with brainstem glioma. Sadly, after all this, they have discovered more about what does not work than what does. We have learned that radiation works for a short time, but chemotherapy does not seem to help at all. We have also learned that there is genuine hope on the horizon. We now have the tools to examine the most intricate details of the inner workings of brain tumor cells, including those of brainstem glioma. Furthermore, we have a rapidly growing arsenal of new biologic therapies that may be able to target the abnormal molecules/DNA/proteins that cause brainstem glioma cells to grow. It is difficult to comprehend how hard it must be for a parent, grandparent, family member, or friend to thumb the pages of this book and read through the long list of therapies that do not work. But we are on the verge of developing a list of therapies that will work, and our hope is that with the next edition of this book, family and friends will read through a long list of all the treatments that do work.

Parent Perspectives

Treatment, well really at this point there is none. You are told that steroids and radiation will most likely shrink the tumor initially and help with symptom management. Then you will get your "honeymoon period" before the tumor begins to grow again and how soon that will be is anybody's guess. Chemo you ask? Yes of course, try this, or this, or this, but we have little to no data indicating that any are effective in extending the life expectancy of the child beyond 24 months. And well there is quality of life to consider.

We also opted to do chemotherapy in the hopes that in combination there might be some added value. We agreed to known chemotherapies that were generally well tolerated by children. I'm not sure we can ever be certain how well they helped Liam's overall condition however, he had few side effects. He took all his pills orally like a champ.

When scans showed that Liam's tumor had progressed on the combination chemotherapies, we tried another course of a different combination therapy. However Liam developed an allergic reaction to one of the medications and we had to stop. His latest scan showed even further progression in parts of his brain far from the confines of the brainstem. We tried one more drug and it would prove to be his final chemotherapy. By this time Liam was not able to walk at all on his own. He had significant hearing loss, and his speech, when he spoke at all, was very hard to understand. He was growing tired. When it was discovered that this treatment too did not have the effect that was desired we decided to end treatment and begin palliative care. It was not an easy decision but one that needed to be made for Liam.

As a result of our son's chemotherapy we saw slow, steady improvement of symptoms for over six months. But we were faced with a new challenge during this time, a complication of long term steroid usage. Our son's skin began to thin, and his stretch marks opened. We were horrified to realize that the treatment regimen (Avastin) that had made such a dramatic difference against the cancer was delaying the healing of the open stretch marks. In time this issue became more of a problem than the cancer itself, and we had

to face the reality that losing our son to wounds would be no less difficult than losing him to brain cancer.

Our daughter underwent 6 weeks of radiation and chemotherapy. She did not start steroids until she was almost complete with her treatment. She had finished her treatment and 4 weeks later had to have a shunt placed due to increased pressure. The following week she had her follow-up MRI from the treatment and they saw new tumor growth in another area of her brain. That weekend we went back to the ER and she had a seizure overnight. She went into a coma and only came out once long enough to open her eyes and we were able to look into her beautiful eyes again and tell her how much we love her. She passed away exactly 3 months and 12 days from diagnosis even with a full treatment of radiation and chemotherapy.

We used Capecitabine, 1300 mg. daily for sixteen weeks. There were absolutely no benefits, just side effects. Joseph had hand and foot syndrome, gas, and diarrhea.

I knew that at that time there were no known chemo treatments that worked and had terrible guilt using my son as an experiment. My wife needed to be doing something to save our boy. I wish the doctors would have been clearer about the odds of this chemo working. I would have stopped much earlier and concentrated on quality of life over treatments.

It was exactly one year after diagnosis that we learned the tumor was growing again. With Andrew's only symptom being headaches, we chose to attempt to slow the progression of the tumor with a chemo cocktail of vincristine, irinotecan and temozolomide given every three weeks. After two cycles the scan showed continued growth, and we made the decision to try temozolomide at full dosage in 28 day cycles in a second attempt to slow tumor growth. We celebrated Christmas at home with a bald (but happy) Andrew.

A scan in January showed further progression. Andrew's doctor wondered if the combination of Avastin and irinotecan might have a positive impact against the tumor. We forged ahead with the new treatment plan, but felt that Andrew was slipping away from us. We were pleasantly surprised when Andrew's scan in March showed a significant response to therapy: shrinkage of the tumor, resolution of much of the cystic component and less enhancement. We had hoped for slowed progression or possible stability; instead we received an unexpected gift of time. Having already made peace with what we thought was Andrew's imminent death we were faced with the challenge of changing our mindset back to one of living rather than dying.

We decided not to do chemo because at the end of the day we didn't see much benefit to it. We didn't want Peyton being sick for what would be left of her short life. We didn't want her suffering more than needed. We just felt that the side effects of chemo outweighed any benefit the drugs "may" have provided.

Chapter 10

The Use of Steroids in Patients with DIPG

Eric Bouffet, MD
Ute Bartels, MD

Steroids play a major role in the management of patients with diffuse intrinsic pontine glioma (DIPG), particularly at the time of presentation. Corticosteroids have been used to control cerebral edema in various conditions, particularly in the context of aggressive brain tumors. Dexamethasone is generally considered the steroid of choice because of its superior brain penetration and longer half-life (time it takes for a drug to lose half of its pharmacologic activity). The role of steroids in the management of disease at the time of progression and during palliative care remains controversial. The aim of this chapter is to review the role of steroids during the care of patients with diffused pontine glioma.

Steroids During the Early Management of DIPG

At the time of diagnosis, steroids are usually the first treatment offered to patients with diffuse intrinsic pontine glioma. Although their role has never been properly assessed, most physicians prescribe steroids, and in particular dexamethasone, once the diagnosis of DIPG is established. The doses used may vary individually according to the clinical signs and symptoms of the child, but many physicians use large doses, up to 10 mg/m^2/per day in two or three doses. The aim of the treatment is to a) improve neurological symptoms, b) reduce the edema surrounding the tumor that may sometimes impact the flow of the cerebral spinal fluid (CSF) and cause some degree of hydrocephalus, and c) prevent or minimize the edema induced by the initiation of the radiation treatment. Traditionally, physicians would keep the dose of dexamethasone unchanged during the first week of treatment, and would then gradually decrease the dose as neurological symptoms

Dr. Bouffet is the Director of the Neuro-oncology Program and a Senior Associate Scientist in the Research Institute at the Hospital for Sick Children, as well as Professor of Pediatrics at the University of Toronto, Canada.

improve with the radiation treatment. Some physicians prefer to keep a high dose of steroids maintained throughout the 6 weeks of radiation therapy.

Steroids, however, are associated with significant side effects that may affect the quality of life of patients with diffused pontine glioma. One of the most significant side effects is hyperphagia—a feeling of extreme excessive hunger. As a result, children with DIPG often experience significant weight gain during the first weeks of treatment. The use of steroids is also associated with personality changes, such as mood swings, anxiety or sometime aggressiveness (see below). Cutaneous complications are not uncommon, particularly in teenagers who can develop severe acne and stretch marks (or striae). All of these side effects will improve within a few weeks of decreased or discontinued use of steroids. They will persist if the steroids are continued throughout treatment.

Steroids Following Radiation

Up to 50 percent of DIPG patients will present with symptoms of so called "somnolence" in the weeks following completion of radiation treatment. The onset of these symptoms is usually observed 2 to 4 weeks after the last session of radiation, but can occur earlier or later.

The somnolence syndrome consists of symptoms ranging from mild drowsiness to marked lethargy with prolonged periods of sleep, irritability, anorexia, low grade fever, nausea and vomiting, cerebellar ataxia, dysarthria, dysphagia, and headaches. For many parents who have not been informed of this complication, the somnolence syndrome is suggestive of the initial manifestations of the disease. The physiopathological mechanisms of this complication are not fully understood, but somnolence is thought to be related to radiation-induced disruption of myelination. The period of somnolence usually lasts 2 weeks, and symptoms usually subside spontaneously. However, some patients can experience symptoms for up to 4 to 6 weeks. When symptoms are significant, the use of steroids can be beneficial. The optimal dose of steroids needed in this context is unknown. However, spectacular improvement of both appetite and sleepiness can be observed with small doses of dexamethasone, in the range of 0.5 to 1 mg per day.

Steroids at the Time of Progression

Because of their beneficial effect at the time of initial diagnosis, steroids are often used at the time of recurrence of symptoms and during palliation of DIPG patients. They

Dr. Bartels is an Oncologist in the Neuro-oncology Program at the Hospital for Sick Children, and Assistant Professor at the University of Toronto, Canada.

often provide a marked improvement of recurrent neurological symptoms and are usually prescribed with the short objective to relieve the symptoms of progression. Their efficacy, however, is generally transient, and progressive symptoms recur within one or two weeks following the prescription of the corticosteroids. At this stage, the dilemma is whether to further increase the dose to alleviate these symptoms or discontinue the steroids because of their potential adverse effects. The choice is not easy for physicians and families and the decision should be made with a clear understanding of the consequences of prolonged use of steroids during palliation.

Although they can provide a transient improvement of neurological symptoms, steroids have side effects that are of particular concern in the context of progressive DIPG. Increased appetite and the resulting hyperphagia can lead to massive weight gain and body transformation, in particular the cushingoid appearance with the classic moon face. These changes can have significant cosmetic and social implications leading to stigma and isolation. They can also affect parents, siblings and relatives at the time of bereavement when they remember the cosmetic consequences of steroid usage. In addition, specific aspects of palliative care and symptom progression of DIPG patients need to be taken into account when steroids are considered. Lower cranial nerve deficits lead to swallowing disturbances and a risk of choking (see chapter 3). In this context, steroids can have an unwanted effect, as they increase the appetite and therefore the risk of choking of a permanently hungry patient. As swallowing disorders worsen, the effects of steroids on appetite can become a nuisance and an obsession for the child who is unable to eat or drink. In addition the combination of oro-pharyngeal stasis of secretions and immunosuppression often leads to the development of painful thrush that will require specific management with mouth wash and in some cases antimicrobial medications against Candida.

Other side effects of steroids can have a significant impact on the quality of palliative care. In particular the behavioural side effects can alter the quality of the interaction of the patient with his family.

Overall, the decision to use steroids at the time of progression should be made with a clear understanding of the potential consequences of this choice. This includes the risk of facing a vicious cycle as the progressive deterioration of the disease leads to increasing the dose of steroids and subsequently to increasing the side effects. Management of DIPG patients without steroids is possible, and some neuro-oncology teams prefer to avoid their use at the time of disease progression.

Side Effects of Corticosteroids

Steroids are associated with a number of potentially serious side effects. The onset and severity of these side effects usually correlate with the dose and duration of the treatment. In the context of a short duration of administration (2 to 3 weeks), most side effects will resolve after cessation of corticosteroid use. However, some children may require prolonged steroid treatment because of persistent or recurrent symptoms, or some physicians are reluctant to decrease steroids during radiation. In this context side effects may persist or even worsen over time and significantly affect the child's quality of life. Using the lowest possible dose of steroids will reduce the risk of these complications.

Cosmetic side effects include cushingoid appearance, truncal obesity, hirsutism (excessive hair), acne, and stretch marks. Other side effects include increased appetite, immunosuppression, hypertension, glucose intolerance, electrolyte disturbance, fluid retention, peripheral edema, gastrointestinal side effects, osteoporosis, avascular necrosis, growth retardation and ocular problems. Complications of corticosteroids are summarized in Table 1. Among the common side effects of steroids, weight gain, steroid myopathy, Pneumocystis carinii pneumonia (PCP) and behavioral changes are of particular concern in DIPG patients.

Hyperphagia

The introduction of high dose dexamethasone at the time of initiation of radiotherapy is associated with an immediate increase in appetite. As a consequence, children can show a dramatic weight gain within days and attempts at controlling their appetite are often difficult because of the associated mood swings and behavioural changes. The use of calorie-free drinks may help limit the weight gain. When patients can be weaned off the steroids, the weight gain is transient and most children go back to their baseline weight within weeks. However, when steroids are continued, hyperphagia may lead to massive weight gain that will limit even further the mobility of an already neurologically handicapped patient.

Mood disturbance

The neuropsychiatric effects of steroids are probably the most common and most stressful for parents and caregivers who often report that "their child is not the same." Steroids can cause anxiety, insomnia and irritability. Sometimes, discrimination of these complications from manifestations of gliomas, cerebral irradiation or changing intracranial pressure can be difficult in clinical practice, and it is not uncommon that clinicians request a CT or MRI scan to rule out complications such as intratumoral hemorrhage. However, steroids given at a very high dose have without any doubt a significant impact on behavior in some children and negatively affect their quality of life. The management of these neuropsychiatric side effects involves discontinuing or reducing the steroids as much and as soon as possible. The use of neuroleptics can be considered on an individual basis when discontinuation of steroids appears impossible.

	Common	Occasional	Rare
	Happens to 21-100 children out of every 100	Happens to 5-20 children out of every 100	Happens to less than 5 children out of every 100
Early: within days	• Hyperphagia • Insomnia	• Gastritis	
Prompt: within 2 to 4 weeks	• Immunosuppression • Personality changes • Acne	• Thinning of the skin • Stretch marks • Weakness • Infections	• Pancreatitis • Increased intraocular pressure • Hypertension • Psychosis • Vertigo • Headache • Spontaneous fractures • Growth suppression • Peptic ulcer and gastrointestinal bleeding • aseptic necrosis of the femoral heads
Delayed: usually after several months of treatment		• Cataract(s)	

Table 1: Side effects of Corticosteroids

Myopathy

Steroid myopathy is a complication that may significantly impact the quality of life of DIPG patients. The clinical manifestation of steroid myopathy is a progressive weakness affecting mostly lower limbs that can have an impact on walking abilities. Some children may require a wheelchair as a result of steroid myopathy. Other consequences include the difficulty to go up and down stairs and an inability to run. Back pain is not exceptional and seems to be the result of both myopathy and osteoporosis. Steroid myopathy usually improves when the drug is discontinued or if the dose can be reduced. However, recovery can take several months after steroid discontinuation. Not all patients will develop steroid myopathy and the exact mechanism of this complication is unknown. Some patients will present with severe symptoms of myopathy after 2 or 3 weeks of steroid use, whereas other patients treated for months may have minimal or no symptoms. It seems that regular exercise or physiotherapy programs may help reduce the severity of myopathy.

Gastrointestinal bleeding and ulcers

Patients treated with corticosteroids are also usually treated with medications that reduce the risk of gastric ulcer and hemorrhage. Although no significant association between steroid usage and gastrointestinal bleeding or ulcers has been identified in children with brain tumors receiving steroids, it is prudent to use H2 antagonists (like Pepcid) in DIPG patients treated with corticosteroids for a prolonged duration, in particular when patients are treated with unusually high doses of corticosteroids. However, in most patients treated with 1 or 2 mg. per day of dexamethasone, the systematic use of H2 antagonists appears unfounded and twice-daily corticosteroid dosing during meals reduces the risk of stomach irritation and spares the risks of side effects and the expense of H2 antagonists.

Effects of corticosteroids on the immune system

Dexamethasone and other corticosteroids can cause immunosuppression by inhibiting immune and inflammatory responses and reducing the pool of lymphocytes. The use of glucocorticoids will therefore increase the risk of opportunistic infections. Pneumocystis carinii (PCP) is a fungal infection responsible for life-threatening lung infections in immunocompromised patients. There is increasing evidence that patients with brain tumors receiving high doses of steroids have an increased risk of PCP and in several DIPG studies, cases of PCP have been reported as a result of the exclusive use of steroids (without any concomitant chemotherapy). It is therefore recommended to consider PCP prophylaxis when steroids are used for prolonged periods of time, in particular when patients cannot be weaned off steroids.

In the context of progressive disease, swallowing disturbances can cause significant oro-pharyngeal stasis of secretions. The immunosuppressive effect of the steroids will increase the risk of oral thrush (fungal infection) that can be extremely painful and difficult to treat.

Alternatives to Corticosteroids

The large number of complications associated with prolonged or repeated use of corticosteroids has led to the search for alternative therapies for the management of peritumoral edema in brain tumors, and in particular in DIPG.

Xerecept® is a synthetic analog of the naturally occurring human peptide corticotropin-releasing factor (CRF). Several animal studies have indicated the ability of CRF to reduce the brain edema caused by brain tumors. Corticotropin-releasing factor appears to reduce peritumoral edema by a direct effect on blood vessels, independent of the release of adrenal steroids. Clinical trials have shown promising activity against peritumoral edema in adult brain tumors. A randomised trial has shown that Xerecept® benefits patients with symptoms of peritumoral edema associated with primary or metastatic cerebral tumors by allowing them to reduce/stop their dexamethasone treatment, thereby reducing the incidence of the steroid-related adverse effects of myopathy, cushingoid symptoms, and skin disorders. A clinical trial is ongoing in children with recurrent brain tumors (http://clinicaltrials.gov/ct2/show/NCT01369121). Preliminary results suggest improvement in emotional, physical and fatigue scores, and the possibility to reduce or even discontinue steroids.

Cyclooxygenase-2 inhibitors (like Celebrex) have been utilized by several physicians for the management of progressive DIPG, either alone or in combination with steroids. There was indeed some suggestion that they might be effective in treating cerebral edema. However, the cardiac complications of this class of drugs have significantly reduced the use of these agents in children.

Since VEGF plays an important role in the pathogenesis of peritumoral edema, the use of inhibitors of VEGF, such as VEGF antibodies (for example bevacizumab/tradename Avastin®) appears to be a logical option in the search for alternatives to corticosteroids. In the context of DIPG a small study described the efficacy of bevacizumab in children with DIPG with suspected radiation necrosis. Four symptomatic children received bevacizumab for a period of 3 weeks to 3 months following completion of radiation at a dose of 10 mg/kg every other week for a total of 3 to 6 infusions. Treatment was well tolerated without evidence of side effects. Three of the 4 children were able to discontinue steroids and had significant clinical improvement in neurologic symptoms. Further studies are planned to better delineate the role of this agent in the management of children with DIPG.

Conclusion

Steroids and in particular dexamethasone have a major role in the management of DIPG patients. However, due to the lack of prospective studies on the use of steroids in this condition, our knowledge on the optimal dosing and schedule of administration including weaning remains limited and most physicians rely on their own experience when prescribing steroids in this context. There is currently significant diversity in clinical practice and it is hoped that future studies will provide more insight into the optimal use of steroids in DIPG, as well as potential steroid alternatives.

Parent Perspectives

Initially you see the steroids as your saving grace. You hear the side effects of extreme hunger and weight gain as possibilities but your pre DIPG self knows that you can control your child's portions and just encourage healthier choices. There is no reason for significant weight gain for your child. Sleeplessness won't be a problem because your child sleeps like a rock. Incontinence isn't even mentioned in those early days. Muscle deterioration? No problem, your child is active and strong. Anger management has never been an issue at your house, tantrums are not acceptable.

After only a few short weeks you begin to find yourself thinking that since your child is being put through all of this (until you get your miracle) he or she deserves to eat mashed potatoes at all three meals and snack times if he or she wants to. I mean carrots don't really fill you up so what made you think they would fill your child up? Slowly but surely over the course of the next six weeks you find yourself looking at a completely changed human being. The little person you took into the clinic on day one is not the same person you are taking in some six weeks later.

It was difficult to see the effects of the Decadron on Andrew's six-year-old body. His face was very full, and he did not look like himself. He saw his reflection in the mirror a few weeks after diagnosis and commented, "My cheeks are more puffy than they were." That was an understatement! The weight gain was a direct result of his steroid-induced appetite and the drastic decrease in his mobility. He liked to eat things that were good for him, but he would sometimes cry because he was so hungry.

My daughter Hope was one of the children who (with the exception of 48 hours) was never off of the steroids. She gained over sixty pounds in just six months and lost the use of her right arm. She was able to walk assisted short distances until about five weeks before she died but other than that was confined to a wheel chair. Her stretch marks were worse than any

pregnant woman I've ever met and eventually those marks became open wounds in some areas. It was her great diligence and desire to persevere that allowed her to wean off of steroids even if it was only for two days. Hope was a hero.

In some respects, I felt that I lost Mara very soon after diagnosis. Her personality was so markedly different that I felt the child I knew had already left my home due to the steroids. The steroids make these kids turn into something that they are not. That is our psychological horror as parents.

Oh, life with a child on steroids! Food becomes so important. Caleb is so hungry all of the time. He told me yesterday that even though his tummy is full, he still feels like he needs to eat. He cannot stop thinking about food.

Last night, he would not go to bed until he had two bananas on the bedside table in case he woke in the night and needed a snack. My husband assured him that we would be there and would get him something to eat if he needed it. That wouldn't do. We had to have those bananas by the bed, ready at hand.

He awoke at about 6:00 a.m. and ate a banana. I helped him with that and then fell back asleep. Every time I would drift off, Caleb would talk about what he was planning to eat today. "When I get up, I am going to eat a bowl of cereal and some scrambled eggs. Then I am going to go sit on the back porch and eat a Pop Tart. Okay, Momma?" "Okay, Caleb," I replied. "Please just let Daddy and me sleep a little bit more and then we'll get you some breakfast."

Ten minutes passed, when Caleb said, "I want to be sure you pack my lunch today when we go to the clinic. Okay, Momma? I want you to pack spaghetti and meatballs, lasagna and a Caesar salad. Will you pack that for me?" My reassuring reply was that we didn't have to leave for the clinic until noon, so he would be able to eat all of that before it was time to leave. "Then can you be sure you pack a snack?" Content for five minutes that a snack would be packed Caleb asked "Can we go to Krispy Kreme today? We can get a hot and fresh for free and then get a dozen to bring home."

...It's really quite comical from the outside, but I know he is just so tired of it already.

From the day of diagnosis until the day he passed away, Bryce took steroids to reduce the fluid surrounding the tumor. When we tried to take him off of steroids after radiation, the headaches and nausea increased, so he was always on a mild dose. We could tell the days when his cancer was on his mind. He would become irritable and he would say, "This sucks, or I hate this. Why does this have to happen to me? I don't deserve this." Our response would always be a confirmation of his feelings. And it became really difficult at times, because we knew that he was dealing with all of these emotions, and so were we, but that we still had to parent.

✝✝✝

Liam began Decadron immediately upon admission to the PICU however we did not begin to see the side effects other than an increase in his appetite until we returned home from the hospital. That's when our love/hate relationship began. Unfortunately Liam experienced many of the difficult side effects from steroids. His appetite was massive. Ask anyone whose child has had to take any significant amount of steroids and they will tell you that eventually their child can turn any conversation, TV show, game, whatever, into a conversation about food. Liam was no sooner half way through breakfast when he was asking what was planned for lunch. Fortunately for us and Liam during this time he craved only healthy things. Fruit, vegetables (You've never seen a kid devour broccoli like our boy!), seafood. He gained quite a bit of weight but thankfully not too, too much. We were worried for a bit towards the end of radiation that his big cheeks would not fir into his radiation mask and he would require a new one. Thankfully though, that never happened. Although one would think having a giant appetite would be the least of concerns when your child has cancer, it is extremely difficult to see your child's complete obsession with it. His love of all things food though was not what was most difficult for Liam during that time. Steroids brought huge mood changes, auditory hallucinations that whispered horrible things to him. His anger was heartbreaking for us to see, but also for Liam to feel. It sometimes made him lash out in ways he never would have done before. He would cry after some of these moments feeling awful that he may have hurt someone's feelings, particularly mine. Later when he would feel angry he would sit in his room and later when he would call out to me, I knew he had settled down and was ready for a big hug. Those were very difficult moments. Eventually Liam came to understand that his medication would cause these moments and we all learned ways to help him feel less out of control. As his symptoms improved, he was weaned further and further down and eventually was able to completely come off the steroids all together.

When Liam's tumor began to progress, he was put back on steroids. That was a difficult day. Liam however reassured me that it would all be ok. He didn't think he would have any of the troubles he had on the medication previously and he was right! This time however he gained a huge amount of weight. He became far less mobile in these months but the appetite continued. We did our best to give him healthy foods to help combat the lack of physical activity. Still he held a tremendous amount of weight for a little guy who started out very small. His disposition however, was always cheerful. Always. He did not have any of the problems with mood swings and anger that he had previously. What a blessing!

Steroids do just what they are supposed to do in most cases. They help alleviate swelling and really combat some of the scary symptoms that children experience but they also come with some side effects that were difficult to see. We tried our very best to help Liam manage those symptoms as best we could. We talked a great deal about all of his medication and their effects and we were careful to respect Liam's feelings about how the drugs were making him feel. After all it was his body, not ours. There were several times when we asked to make adjustments whether it was changing a dosage, changing a pill size, asking for a medication to be flavored or crushed—whatever it took. There are many, many options available and sometimes it's just a matter of asking the question of your child's provider. If your child has difficulty swallowing pills, is that medication available in a suspension? Always ask the question. Your child being diagnosed with cancer presents parents with the steepest learning curve they will ever encounter. Never, ever be afraid to ask questions!

The neuro-oncologist discussed some of their primary concerns going forward. He indicated that they were concerned about the level of hydrocephalus (an accumulation of cerebrospinal fluid on her brain) and the impact that may have on her functioning. He also recommended that Stella be taken off the steroids. While the steroids control the effect of the hydrocephalus, they also caused her to have a significantly increased appetite and to be agitated and angry. These side effects of the steroids

are problematic since one of the most common symptoms of the tumor is difficulty swallowing. There is a concern that should that occur while she is on the steroids, the anger that may result from the hunger and inability to eat may cause choking.

When Caleb was first diagnosed with DIPG he was started on steroids. At that time he took them for about three weeks during the first half of radiation. The dose was fairly small and it helped with his speech and his balance. When he first started them his initial side effect was extreme hunger and after about a week we began noticing the mood swings. I remember the first time I really saw what the steroids could do to his personality. We had taken him bowling. He was trying so hard and wanted to do well but it just wasn't going his way. He became very agitated and I can remember thinking that this was not my child. He was 8 years old at the time and although he had always had a competitive streak, he was very even tempered. Here he was having a mini tantrum after each throw of the ball. I was horrified thinking I would never see my sweet natured boy again. Of course as the steroids were weaned he became more and more like himself. I was so relieved and truly thought I never wanted to put him on that wretched drug again—he no longer looked the same and at times he certainly didn't act the same.

Once he was off the steroids he stayed off them for two months. We had learned of tumor progression the month before and had opted for a second round of radiation. He was nearly finished the second round when one morning his whole left side became paralyzed and he could barely speak. We took him to the hospital and they started him on a fairly high dose of dexamethasone again. I remember thinking it would just be temporary and I wouldn't agree to long term use. We did a slow wean but as we got closer to being off he would begin with symptoms again. We were being told the symptoms were likely due to swelling from the radiation and as the swelling came down so would the dexamethasone, so we would increase again while we waited for the swelling to go back down. This went on for months... wean the "dex," increase the "dex," wean the "dex," increase the "dex," and each time we needed to increase the dose, he would need a bigger increase to get him back to baseline.

At this point, it was thought the symptoms were likely caused by radiation necrosis. Caleb was so hungry and became agitated and food obsessed, he gained over 36 lbs. in 3 months and the weight gain continued. I remember him trying to control it. His moods were crazy at times, thankfully these bouts of insanity were usually short lived but his mood swings would upset him. He would feel so badly for acting irrational and no amount of reassurance would make him feel better about it. He knew right from wrong and sometimes the steroid would make him behave wrong. It was our double edged sword. On one hand it helped the tumor symptoms but at what cost to his quality of life? I feared if we lowered the steroids completely we would lose him faster, I wasn't ready, I knew I never would be.

So, we started Avastin, which was thought to possibly reduce the effects of radiation necrosis, in hopes that we would be able to stop the dexamethasone. I am not sure if it helped. I think it might have, as we were able to lower the dose but at this point in time no amount of the steroid would help him to walk again, He was in his wheelchair full time, had no use of his left side, could no longer swallow liquids or solids that hadn't been pureed, and his speech was greatly affected. On top of all that his skin had been stretched beyond its capabilities and he had open wounds on his body. Thankfully most of them caused no pain but he had two, one under his arm and the other between his bum cheeks that caused him a lot of pain. We were able to get topical morphine for the wounds which helped a lot. At this point we knew the steroid was causing more harm than good so we did a fairly rapid wean.

Caleb took his last dose of steroid on a Tuesday and joined the angels the following Saturday. Through it all, Caleb had tons of beautiful moments of pure joy, days when he was all smiles and would enjoy the company of those around him. He planned things and wanted to do them and it was days like this which made the steroid decision so hard for us. I know the steroids caused him a lot of anguish especially in the end but I also know it gave us a lot of beautiful, happy, loving days.

Chapter 11

Caring for Your Child at Home

Deborah Lafond, DNP, PNP-BC, CPON, CHPPN

If your child has been diagnosed with diffuse intrinsic pontine glioma (DIPG), your family will inevitably face some challenges while caring for him or her at home. For example, your child may have trouble taking or tolerating medicines or have problems with swallowing/eating, walking, sleeping, and other aspects of daily living. Many parents feel anxious about taking their child home after treatment. Figuring out what your child needs and how to care for your child at home can be very stressful.

You may have spoken with other parents of children with DIPGs and may have heard about some challenging situations. Although it is difficult, try not to compare your experience with any other child and family. Each child and family is special and each situation is unique.

To prepare you for caring for your child at home, this chapter will describe common problems you might encounter and offer advice about how you and your child can best manage these issues.

Your Child's Health Care Team is Available to Help You

Remember that your child's health care team is there to help you and your child cope with the challenges of DIPG. Your family may not encounter any of the challenges listed in this chapter, or you may experience only some of them. While the health care team tries to anticipate what you and your child might need, not all situations are easy to predict. Don't hesitate to contact your child's health care team whenever you have questions or concerns.

Know whom to call

You have likely met many members of your child's health care team since the

> Dr. Lafond is a Nurse Practitioner in Neuro-oncology and Palliative Care at Children's National Medical Center, Washington, DC.

time your child was diagnosed with a DIPG. Each person has a special role in caring for your child. Make sure you have the name, phone number, and email contact information for the person on your child's health care team that you should contact for routine questions and concerns. Also, be sure you have the contact information for those you should contact during an emergency, after hours, and on weekends. The American Childhood Cancer Organization provides a free journal entitled *Along the Way* to assist with this type of record keeping. This journal is available without charge by request to all parents of children with cancer. This journal includes designated pages to include contact information for your child's healthcare team. Keep the contact information:

- Next to every phone in your house.

- In your cell phone. (If you own an iPhone, there is a helpful "app" called iCANcer, available through iTunes, where you can store all contact information, as well as the diagnosis, treatment, and medical information of your child.)

- In your wallet or purse.

- Near your phone at work (if you have a private office or desk space).

- At your child's school—with your child's teacher and the school nurse and at your other children's school(s), if applicable.

- With people who care for your child, either at your home or theirs, while you are gone (such as grandparents, daycare, or babysitters).

Your child's social worker

Get to know your child's social worker well. The social worker is there to help you and your child navigate the many feelings and emotions you might experience as you go through the DIPG journey. If you have not been assigned a social worker, call your child's nurse and ask to have a social worker assigned to your family. Medical problems are not the only issue you, your child, and the rest of your family will face. Having a cancer diagnosis is a scary and emotional experience. There will be times when you are sad, times when you are angry, times when you are frustrated, and times when you feel joyful. Your social worker can help you and your family as you deal with these difficult emotions.

Your child's nurse or nurse practitioner

In general, social workers cannot answer medical questions about your child's diagnosis and treatment. Thus, your child's nurse is another important contact on your child's medical team. Your child will likely have a primary nurse (RN) or nurse practitioner (APN) who will take the lead in answering all your medical questions. The role of APNs is similar to the role of doctors; they can serve as a patient's primary health care provider and prescribe medications, whereas RNs do not. The nurse/nurse practitioner is usually the first person you call with routine questions and concerns. If that person does not know the answer, she or he can readily find your child's doctor. This does NOT mean your child's doctor is not routinely available to you. You may talk with your child's doctor at most any time, but your child's nurse/nurse practitioner is a great resource for practical information about the day-to-day challenges you may face. Do not hesitate to call the nurse/nurse practitioner if you have questions or concerns. The nurse/nurse practitioner usually serves as a central contact for parents and helps get them to the right person when questions or concerns arise.

Your child's case manager

Another key person to get to know is the case manager assigned to your child from your health insurance company. If a case manager is not assigned to you, call your insurance company and ask to be assigned one. Tell the insurance company that your child has "a brain tumor with complex health care needs;" this is common terminology you can use to help your insurance company understand why you are asking for a case manager. If your insurance company is not responsive, be persistent.

You will need the following information when you talk with your insurance company. This is information that you can get from your child's nurse/nurse practitioner.

- The diagnosis: diffuse intrinsic pontine glioma (ICD-9 code is 191.7);

- Date of diagnosis;

- The name of all hospitals where your child receives treatment;

- The type of treatments your child is receiving, (e.g., chemotherapy, radiation therapy, physical therapy, occupational therapy);

- The contact information for your child's doctor and nurse/nurse practitioner.

Be willing to give your insurance company permission to contact your child's doctor and/or nurse/nurse practitioner for more information about your child and the care your child will need. The insurance company may have other questions regarding your child's diagnosis. Do not hesitate to ask the insurance representative to contact your child's doctor or nurse/nurse practitioner to get answers to these questions, especially if you do not know the answers or are unsure of the details.

Having a case manager at your insurance company usually allows you to have a central contact person who can help you obtain referrals and approvals for your child's care. By having one person (your case manager) to call for help with insurance-related issues, you can often avoid the long process of trying to find the right department for needed help. Your case manager may also be able to arrange for someone to help care for your child at home.

Home care nurses

Sometimes parents can arrange nursing care in the home for a short while. This is not possible in every situation, but it may be possible for short periods of time. Talk with your child's case manager, social worker, or nurse/nurse practitioner to find out whether or not you are able to have home care nurses come in for short periods to help you, especially when your child first goes home or if your child's symptoms worsen and he/she requires more care at home.

General Physical Care

Every child is unique in the symptoms and care needs they will have at home. Your child may have none of the needs mentioned here, some of them, or all of them at any given time during the DIPG journey. At times, it may feel as if you have to be your child's at-home nurse. It is important to know what to expect and how to provide care for your child so he/she can stay at home and out of the hospital as often as possible.

This caretaking can be overwhelming at times, but the goal is for your child to live as normal a life as possible, doing the things that he/she enjoys, such as playing with friends, going to school, and being with family. Knowing how to care for your child may help prevent some of the most common problems or help resolve them sooner. This section covers such issues as prevention, medications, breathing problems, nutrition/feeding issues, constipation, skin breakdown, nausea/vomiting, pain, mobility issues, sleeping, caring for central lines, and some common symptoms children with DIPG experience.

Prevention

Discuss with your health care team any potential problems your child might have. Ask about what you may need at home to care for your child. Be sure that you understand what complications the health care team thinks your child may experience, what medications they are sending home, and the possible side effects of these medications. Also, ask your health care team what signs of medical problems to look for if your child's condition changes.

Infection

Infection can be a serious risk for your child, especially if he/she is receiving steroids, such as dexamethasone or certain chemotherapy agents. Being on certain other medications can also make your child more susceptible to infections. Having an infection can cause serious complications for your child, so ask your doctor or nurse/nurse practitioner if your child is at increased risk of developing infections. Infections can be bacterial, viral, or fungal.

You don't need to keep your child away from other people unless someone is ill. You can let your child go to school or play with other children. But if another child is obviously ill, it is best not to be around that child until he/she is well. If other family members are ill, it is often difficult to keep your child separated from them, and it is not recommended that you keep your child in another room or house. Just try to be as careful as possible about close contact.

The most important way to prevent infection is to have good hand washing practices. You may use regular soap, wash for at least 30 seconds and have several bottles of alcohol-based hand sanitizers available in your home and small ones to keep in your purse, car, and your child's backpack or diaper bag. Teach your child to wash his/her hands well (including under the fingernails) after using the bathroom, before and after eating, after playing with pets, after touching other people, or anytime his/her hands are dirty. Also ask other people including other children who are in contact with your child to wash their hands well before they interact with him/her.

Medications

Ask the nurse how to give your child his/her medications and at what times each one should be given. The nurse can make a schedule of all medications with a place for you to record the day and time you give the medications; this type of form is helpful when your child takes several medications. Having a schedule and a record of when you gave each medication will help you remember when to give them to your child. **A sample medication form is included in Appendix A. An online medication program is available at: http://www.medactionplan.com/medactionplan/mymedschedule.asp.**

Ask your doctor or nurse practitioner the following questions about **each** medication your child has been prescribed.

- Why has this medication been prescribed (why it is needed)?

- When should I give this medication to my child (what schedule)?

- How should I give this medication to my child (with or without food)?

- If pills are prescribed, can they be split or crushed for easier swallowing? Do not crush pills or dissolve pills or capsules in liquid without talking to your pharmacist or nurse/nurse practitioner first. Some medications cannot be safely crushed or dissolved.

- What are the side effects of this medication and what can I do to manage or prevent them?

- Are there any other medications, including over-the-counter medications, that I should avoid giving my child?

- Are there any foods that I should avoid giving my child that might interact with the medications?

- What should I do if I forget to give a dose of a medication or if my child vomits up the dose/pill?

If your child has any difficulty taking the medications or experiences side effects, let your doctor or nurse practitioner know as soon as possible so they can advise you about what to do. Not all medicines have unpleasant side effects or interactions with other medicines. Hopefully, your child will have no side effects with the medications he/she is taking, but it is best to be prepared for what to expect, possible side effects, and how to deal with any that may occur.

Additional tips for medications:

- Keep all medications in a safe place, out of reach of children.

- Record the time you give each medication on the daily schedule and keep track of any side effects your child experiences. Keep this list up to date and bring it with you to every doctor's appointment or emergency room visit so everyone knows exactly what medications your child is taking and the last time he had each one. This information can be documented in the iCANcer app if you own an iPhone, iPod Touch or iPad.

- Keep medications in a cool, dry, place, especially if the weather is hot and humid. Do not refrigerate medications that are not supposed to be refrigerated, but do not leave medicines in direct sunlight or in a hot car.

- If your child has trouble swallowing pills or liquid medications, ask your nurse for help in finding the best way to give them. For example, some medications can be mixed with special flavors at the pharmacy to make them taste better or can be crushed and put into pudding, ice cream, chocolate syrup, or applesauce.

- For older children and teenagers, consider getting a pillbox to organize medications to be given at certain times of the day. Most drug stores and large grocery store chains sell pillboxes in one day/time or multiple day/time versions.

- Measure all liquid medications with a syringe, if possible, rather than a teaspoon. Regular kitchen spoons can be different sizes and you want to make sure you give the right amount of medicine each time.

- Make sure you understand each medication and why it is being prescribed. In addition to your doctor or nurse/nurse practitioner, your pharmacist can provide you with information about each medication. If you use the Internet to find information, please double check that information with your pharmacist, doctor, or nurse/nurse practitioner to ensure you get accurate information.

- Do not use medications that have not been specifically prescribed for your child. And do not share your child's medicines with anyone else, even if that person takes the same prescription.

- Do not give your child any herbal or vitamin medications without checking with your doctor or nurse/nurse practitioner. Some common herbs and vitamins can interfere with chemotherapy and radiation treatments, as well as possibly interact with other medications your child is taking. More information about complementary and alternative medicines (CAM) is discussed in a section later in this chapter.

Pain

Pain can occur in children of any age and at any time. There are different types of pain depending upon the cause, the location, your child's special characteristics, the treatments your child is receiving, and your child's past experiences with pain. Not every child with DIPG will experience pain. Some children feel no pain at all. If your child does experience pain, the goal is to relieve that pain as quickly as possible, with the least amount of side effects. This section will describe some ways you can help your child manage pain.

It is important to be able to recognize when your child is in pain. Your child will experience the normal aches and pains of childhood, but sometimes it can be difficult to figure out whether a complaint of pain is a normal childhood experience, such as bumps and bruises from play, or something more serious. Depending on the age of your child, it can be difficult to figure out whether your child is even experiencing pain. For example, infants normally cry, so it can be hard to determine if a cry is from pain or something else. Older children and adolescents may not admit to feeling pain because they may associate pain with having to go to the hospital or taking more medications, which may make them sleepy or nauseated. If you think your child might be in pain, please talk with your doctor or nurse/nurse practitioner about ways to manage your child's pain. Remember that while pain is physical, it can also have an emotional component. Each child reacts differently to pain, so it is important to understand how your child expresses pain. Indications that your child may be in pain include:

- A high-pitched cry or change in an infant's normal cry;

- Changes in facial expressions;

- Rubbing particular areas on the body that may indicate pain;

- Irritability or restlessness;

- Being inconsolable;

- Being less active or mobile than usual and playing less;

- Loss of appetite or changes in eating patterns;

- Changes in sleep patterns.

If your child can talk, ask him/her if he/she has pain and ask him/her to show you where the pain is, what it feels like (e.g., sharp, stabbing, shooting, burning, cramping), what he/she thinks is causing it, and what he/she thinks will help it feel better. You may also choose to show your child pictures of faces that represent no pain to severe pain and ask him/her to point to the picture that best represents how he/she is feeling [Fig. 1]. The answers to these questions can help you decide how to help your child.

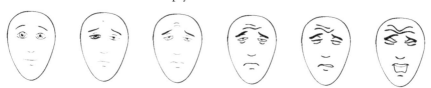

Figure 1: Faces Pain Scale, used with permission by the International Association for the Study of Pain (IASP)

Ways to treat pain **without** using medications include:

- Reassure your child that pain does not always mean the DIPG is getting worse; explain that all children experience pains during childhood.

- Create a calm and nurturing environment by turning down any bright lights, minimizing noise, and creating a comfortable room temperature. Experiment to find out what works the best to calm your child.

- Use distraction (e.g., singing, reading books, blowing bubbles, telling stories, watching a favorite movie DVD, etc.), relaxation techniques, visual imagery, or play to get your child's mind off his/her pain. Ask your child life specialist, social worker, or psychologist for other strategies to help your child.

- Apply a heat pad or ice pack, whichever your child prefers, to areas of pain.

- Run a warm bath or shower to help your child relax.

- Use massage or gentle touch, but only if your child wants to be touched, because sometimes touch is not comforting. Massaging your child's hands, feet, and shoulders can help your child relax and give you a way to connect with your child. Many hospitals offer massage classes to teach you how to perform massage techniques effectively.

- Play music—soothing music is best but use music that your child enjoys; or try a sound machine with sounds such as running water or ocean waves.

- Have your child's favorite blankets or stuffed animals or other favorite toys readily available.

- Hold your child to cuddle or rock him/her, or lie in bed next to him/her (if he/she wants you to, as older children may like to be left alone to sleep).

- Let your child cuddle up with the family pet.

Ways to manage pain **with** medications include:

- In general, start with milder medicines such as acetaminophen or ibuprofen. However, these medicines cannot be given with certain chemotherapy medications or when blood counts are low, so always check with your child's doctor or nurse practitioner before giving your child any over-the-counter pain medications.

- With prescription pain medications, read the directions carefully. These medications are prescribed based on your child's age and weight. Do not give more than the recommended dose unless you are told to do so by your child's doctor or nurse practitioner.

- If your child has more moderate to severe pain, your doctor or nurse practitioner may prescribe stronger medicines, such as opiates (morphine, codeine, methadone, etc.). Many types of opioids can be safely used for children. Your doctor or nurse practitioner will explain the directions for giving opioid medications and the expected side effects.

- In general, it is best to give pain medications throughout the day on a regular schedule, or when your child's doctor or nurse practitioner tells you to give them. Giving medicines on a regular schedule avoids the peaks and valleys that occur when they are only given when your child experiences pain. Just be sure not to give your child more medication than recommended by the doctor or nurse practitioner, or more than is recommended on the bottle for over-the-counter medications.

- If your child is experiencing increasing pain, even though he/she is on strong pain medication, other medicines can be added to help the pain medicines work better.

- Every child is unique, so the plan for managing your child's pain should be the one that works best for him/her.

Common concerns about pain medicines include:

- **Addiction and tolerance:** Children who are in pain may need strong medications to help relieve it. If your child needs pain medications for a long period of time, he/she may need increasing doses of pain medicines to help relieve the pain. This need for higher dose is known as **tolerance**, meaning your child needs a higher dose to get the same effect. Tolerance is **NOT** the same thing as **addiction**. Addiction is a physical and psychological craving for medication, usually to achieve a "high." Children in pain do not become addicted to pain medications if they are used appropriately and only as your doctor or nurse practitioner tells you to give them.

- **Medicine is too strong:** Parents may worry that if a strong pain medication, such as morphine, is prescribed it means their child is getting worse. However, morphine is a very good pain medicine and works well for children of all ages, from infants to adolescents. Morphine has been used for many years and doctors and nurse practitioners know a lot about this medication. There are other pain medications that can be used, but morphine is frequently used because it relieves pain so well. If the doctor or nurse practitioner prescribes morphine, or a similar opioid medicine, it does not necessarily mean your child's condition is getting worse. Don't be afraid to ask your doctor or nurse practitioner why a particular pain medication is being prescribed.

- **Multiple pain medications:** Sometimes medicines may not work too well by themselves, but in combination with other medicines work very well. You may even be able to use smaller doses of each medication when they are combined. Sometimes pain has several different causes, so one pain medication does not treat all the causes. Talk with your doctor or nurse practitioner about why your child is taking each medication and ask them if you can eliminate any of the medicines.

- **Side effects:** If your child is taking opioid medications, be sure to start him on a stool softener to prevent constipation. Opioid medicines slow down the intestines, which can cause constipation. Itching, nausea, and/or increased sleepiness may also be caused by certain medicines. Be sure to tell your doctor or nurse practitioner if your child has any of these symptoms so you can get advice about how to handle the side effects. Generally these types of symptoms happen in the first few days that your child is taking opioid medicines. Talk to your doctor about any other side effects that you think your child might be experiencing from other pain medications as well.

Nutrition and Feeding Issues

Good nutrition is important for your child's growth and general health. If your child is having issues with feeding/eating, it is important to find out why. For example, if your child is nauseated from chemotherapy, medicines can be given to help calm his/her stomach. If your child is too tired to eat, finding ways to deal with fatigue might help him/her have times when he/she feels better and can eat. Having a meal schedule might also help your child eat regularly, as multiple doctor appointments, other family obligations, and the chaos of daily life can be overwhelming and cause a child to lose his/her appetite or forget to eat.

If family members and friends have asked how they can help, consider letting them make meals for your family so you can concentrate on caring for your child. Your child's illness may change over time, and there may be times when he/she wants to eat more or eat less. Things that will affect nutrition and the ability to eat for a child with DIPG include the following:

- **Weight gain:** Your child may gain weight rapidly when he/she is on steroids. You may notice that he/she has a ravenous appetite often way out of proportion to what he/she normally eats. It can be very difficult to control your child's appetite, but some tips include limiting high-calorie foods and salty foods. This can be difficult, because your child may want to eat only certain foods. Let him/her eat his favorite foods but in moderation. For example, you may try saying something like, *"You can have the chocolate ice cream one time today. If you eat it now, then you cannot have any more until tomorrow. Are you sure you want to eat it now, or would you rather try _____ now and save the chocolate ice cream until later today?"* This approach does not always work because children often live in the present moment and to them "later" really does not exist; later means never! You can also try a sticker chart or some reward system so your child has to eat certain "good/healthy" foods in order to earn the privilege of eating the less-healthy foods. This can be a real challenge, so don't hesitate to talk with your child's social worker, nurse, or child life specialist about tips to help you manage your child's food cravings. Consulting with a nutritionist or dietitian may be helpful for learning ways to decrease calories in your child's diet.

- **Weight loss:** On the opposite side of the spectrum, your child may lose weight. This might happen while your child is getting certain chemotherapy medicines or radiation therapy, or when being weaned off steroid medicines. As frustrating as it may be to have your child eating all the time, many parents find it as frustrating to see their child not eating and losing weight. Things that can help counteract weight loss are using supplements, such as Pediasure©, Boost©, or Carnation Instant Breakfast©, or other supplements that your doctor or nurse practitioner recommends. Your health care team will tell you which supplements they recommend and how much to give your child each day. Consulting with a nutritionist or dietitian may be helpful for gaining tips about increasing calories in your child's diet. There are also medicines that can be used to stimulate your child's appetite, but before using any you should ask your health care team if they think an appetite stimulant would be helpful for your child. Also remember that if your child is tired and less active, his/her metabolism slows down and he/she does not need as many calories. Your child may also have cravings for a certain food and then only take one or two bites. This can be quite frustrating for parents. Try to let your child eat and drink what he/she wants. Sitting down to a big plate of food or large glass of a liquid beverage can be overwhelming for a child. Try to offer small, frequent meals. You will be surprised by how the calories add up by just taking a few bites many times a day!

- **Difficulty swallowing:** Many children with DIPG have difficulty swallowing. This is most common with thin liquids as they move more quickly through the mouth and throat which can result in aspiration, but can happen with any food or liquid. If your child coughs or chokes when he/she eats, it may be a sign that he/she is having trouble swallowing. If your child has difficulty swallowing solid foods, try cutting food up into very small bite-sized pieces, serving soft foods, and encouraging him/her to chew food thoroughly and not rush while eating. If your child has difficulty swallowing thin liquids, try using a syringe to get a stream of liquid down, using thickening agents to bulk up thin liquids, or using thicker versions of similar liquids (e.g., milk shakes or liquid yogurts instead of milk, and applesauce instead of apple juice).

- **Inability to eat by mouth:** There may come a time when your child cannot take food or liquids by mouth, so this is a challenge to think about in advance. Ask your child's doctor or nurse practitioner about the different causes of the inability to eat or drink. Knowing about possible causes will help you notice signs and make decisions about how to help your child if that time comes. If your child reaches this point, the doctor or nurse practitioner will conduct a physical exam to find out the cause of the problem. If it is a mechanical problem, such as the vocal cords not closing properly or aspiration (when food goes down to the lungs instead of the stomach), then maybe your child can receive fluids and nutrition through an alternate method, such as a nasogastric tube (NG-tube) or gastrostomy tube (G-tube). If the DIPG is quite advanced and your doctor or nurse practitioner thinks your child is nearing the end of life, then putting your child through the discomfort of having a tube placed to receive fluids and nutrition may not be the decision you want to make. If your child's DIPG is advanced, he/she may not want to eat as his/her metabolism and digestive system slow down. It is not uncommon for the appetite to significantly decrease as a child's illness becomes more advanced. More about these difficult decisions will be discussed later in this chapter.

- **Artificial fluids and nutrition:** This is the term the health care team uses for giving fluids and nutrition through a nasogastric tube (NG-tube) or gastrostomy tube (G-tube). The term "artificial" simply means that the fluids are given through a tube rather than orally. An NG-tube is a small flexible tube inserted through the nose, down the back of the throat, and into the stomach. The tube can stay in from a few weeks to a few months, and it is used as a temporary way of giving fluids and nutrition. If your child has problems with nausea or vomiting, he/she may vomit up the tube and the tube may have to be replaced more often. A G-tube is a bit larger and is placed directly into the stomach or intestines by an interventional radiologist, gastroenterologist, or surgeon, usually while your child is under anesthesia or sedation. A G-tube can stay in for about 6 months but can be easily changed by a home care nurse or—in some cases—you may be taught how to change the tube. Either an NG-tube or G-tube can be hooked up to a feeding bag to give liquid nutrition through either several bolus (large) feedings at different times during the day or by a small amount being dripped in with a feeding pump over 10 to 12 hours at night. Different types of liquid feeding formulas are used depending upon the nutritional needs of your child. Your child's nurse or nutritionist will go over the best type of schedule for your child and explain how to manage these feedings at home.

These types of feedings are not without complications, so your doctor or nurse practitioner should review the risks and benefits with you so you can make an informed decision. In general, if the benefits are great and the risks are small, a feeding tube might make a lot of sense. If your child is at great risk for complications from a feeding tube (for example, if he/she is not able to process and eliminate the feedings, causing swelling and fluid accumulation in the lungs) then a feeding tube may not be the best choice. Having open, honest discussions with your health care team will help you to make these decisions.

Nausea and vomiting

Nausea (feeling sick to your stomach) and/or vomiting can occur for many reasons. Your child may have initially had nausea and/or vomiting as one of the first symptoms of his/her DIPG. Usually this is due to increased intracranial pressure caused by swelling and pressure on sensitive areas of the brain. To combat sickness, medications such as steroids can help decrease swelling in the brain. Other things that can cause nausea and/or vomiting include constipation, fluid and electrolyte imbalances, chemotherapy, and certain medications (such as opioids). Tips for decreasing nausea/vomiting include:

- Giving anti-nausea medications, such as Ondansetron or others that your doctor or nurse practitioner might prescribe for your child, about 30 minutes before chemotherapy and/or radiation treatments and as instructed at other times of day, as needed.

- Giving your child's medications with food or after a meal, depending on the medication.

- Feeding your child small, frequent meals.

- Giving your child smaller amounts of liquids with meals and avoiding carbonated beverages.

- Avoiding greasy, fatty foods.

- Avoiding foods with strong odors.

- Putting a drop of peppermint oil or other strong-flavored oil of your child's preference (available at your local nutrition store and some pharmacies) on your child's upper lip, just below the nose.

- Using aromatherapy (described in more detail in the section below about complementary and alternative therapy).

- Taking your child outside to be in the fresh air or having your child sit near a fan.

Constipation

Constipation, or difficulty having a bowel movement, can cause discomfort for your child and lead to pain, nausea, vomiting, decreased appetite, and irritability. Constipation is generally defined as not having a bowel movement in more than 3 days, pain or crying with passing stool, or the inability to pass a stool after 10 minutes or more of trying. You may notice that your child's bowel movements are hard or small pellets, which are also signs of constipation. Constipation is a common problem in childhood and can be even more of a problem for a child with DIPG when taking certain medicines or when the tumor involves the spine. Track your child's normal bowel movement routine. For example, do they usually have a bowel movement every day, several times per day, every other day, etc.? If your child does not have a bowel movement per his/her usual routine or you notice that the stools are hard or difficult to pass, contact your child's doctor for advice.

Several things can help prevent constipation:

- Have your child drink plenty of fluids, especially water.

- Increase fiber in your child's diet and encourage him/her to eat fresh fruits and vegetables.

- Increase your child's physical activity.

- Establish a bowel regimen (i.e. having your child sit on the toilet for 5–10 minutes after meals and at bedtime).

- Consider giving your child a stool softener or stimulant (laxative), but first talk with your child's doctor or nurse practitioner for advice about which type is best for your child.

- Avoid suppositories or enemas unless recommended by your child's doctor or nurse practitioner.

Skin Issues

Skin problems are common in children with DIPG and are usually related to taking steroid medicines (e.g., dexamethasone). Common skin problems include striae (stretch marks) and dry skin. In addition, some children with decreased activity and/or decreased mobility may be prone to developing pressure sores. Common places for pressure sores to develop are on the lower back, buttocks, hips, or heels. Striae can develop anywhere on the skin surface.

Some tips to help manage skin problems in your child include:

- Changing your child's position frequently to relieve pressure on any one area (if your child's mobility is limited).

- Bathing your child daily and looking carefully at the skin for changes.

- Using moisturizing lotions/creams. (Be careful about this if your child is receiving radiation therapy. First talk with the radiation doctors.)

- Using sunscreen (SPF 30 or higher) when outside, even if your child has a dark complexion.

- Having your child drink plenty of fluids to stay well hydrated.

- Using extra padding on the bed or wheelchair.

Fatigue

Many children with DIPG feel very tired from time to time, which can be distressing for the child and family. Children want to be able to play, go to school, and do all the things they used to enjoy doing. Fatigue (feeling very tired) can be caused by muscle weakness, low blood counts, nutritional deficiencies, stress, and certain medications or treatments, especially radiation therapy. Many children experience a great deal of fatigue during and for a few weeks after radiation therapy; this is called **radiation somnolence syndrome**. Ask your doctor or radiation oncologist to explain this condition. It goes away by itself and usually does not require any treatment.

Things you can do to help your child if they have chronic fatigue include:

- Planning important activities for the time of day when your child is usually most awake.

- Giving your child pain medicines or using some of the non-medicine methods of managing pain, as pain is often a cause of fatigue.

- Making sure your child gets adequate sleep/rest; consider putting a **"DO NOT DISTURB"** sign on the door when your child is resting during the day.

- Limiting visitors to allow for rest time.

- Letting your child go to school for just one class, or half a day if he/she can; consider home schooling or a tutor (if your child is unable to go to school for a full day). Also, your social worker can help arrange for a home tutor from the school system.

- Talking with your doctor or nurse practitioner to find out if using a stimulant medication would be helpful for your child. There may be stimulant medications that can be used if the other methods do not help. Some children become more fatigued as their disease becomes more advanced, often sleeping many hours a day. This can be scary for parents and other family members. Talk with your health care team about this. Allow your child to rest, but reassure your child that you are never far away and that you will be there when needed.

Breathing Problems

Some children with DIPG have difficulty breathing. This issue can be due to increased secretions (drooling) in the mouth and back of the throat, weight gain associated with use of steroid medications, infection, coughing, wheezing, low blood counts, or the tumor affecting the nerves that control breathing. It can be scary for you and your child if he/she has trouble breathing. One of the most important things you can do when your child has trouble breathing is to remain as calm as possible and help your child remain calm, as anxiety may increase breathing difficulties.

Here are some tips to counteract common causes of breathing difficulties for children with DIPG:

- **Reduce anxiety:** Create a calm environment. Even though the moment may be frightening, take some deep breaths to calm yourself down so you can remain calm and in control. Ask your child's social worker or child life specialist to teach you techniques to help calm your child down. Sometimes playing soft, quiet music, speaking in a slow calm voice, and doing some deep breathing exercises can help your child calm down and relax so he/she is not as short of breath.

- **Combat shortness of breath:** Teach your child to take slow, deep breaths when he/she starts to feel short of breath. Other tips include using a small, hand held fan to blow air gently in your child's face; keeping the room well ventilated or opening a window; changing your child's position—such as from lying to sitting, to lying on his/her side, to elevating the head of the bed or using another pillow to raise up his/her head and shoulders.

- **Avoid smoke:** Do not smoke around your child and don't let other people smoke around your child.

- **Reduce increased secretions:** Your child may have difficulty swallowing his/her saliva, or may make noisy or gurgling sounds when he/she breathes. This is usually due to saliva pooling in the back of the throat. You may also notice that your child is drooling more from his/her mouth. There are some medicines that can be used to help dry up the saliva, and an oral Yankar suction machine can also be helpful; this device is similar to the suction straw used in your mouth at the dentist office. Ask your doctor or nurse practitioner if medicines or a suction machine might help.

- **Treat infections:** Sometimes antibiotic medicines can help if your child has a respiratory infection. If your child has a fever, a lot of coughing, or greenish sputum (coughing up phlegm), he/she may have an infection. A chest x-ray might be taken to help your doctor or nurse practitioner diagnose an infection.

- **Treat wheezing:** If your child has wheezing due to constriction of the bronchial tubes in the lungs, which can be similar to what a child with asthma experiences, your doctor or nurse practitioner may prescribe a nebulizer or inhaler medicines to open up the tubes that go to the lungs to help your child breathe better. Elevating the head of the bed or using extra pillows can help with wheezing, as well as keeping smoke away from your child.

- **Check for low blood counts:** Hemoglobin carries oxygen around our bodies. If your child has a low hemoglobin (Hgb) level, he/she may develop shortness of breath or breathing trouble. If low blood counts are found to be the cause of the breathing difficulties, a blood transfusion can be given.

Seizures

Seizures are uncommon in children with DIPGs; however, sometimes they do happen. Seizures can look different in each child. Some seizures are just mild twitching or staring spells, while others involve shaking of an arm or leg or full convulsions. Talk with your health care team and ask them if they think it is likely your child might experience seizures. If you see any behaviors that are different than normal in your child, ask your health care team if these behaviors might be related to seizures. If your child has a seizure, the most important thing is to keep him/her safe. **DO NOT** put anything in your child's mouth, such as a spoon or your fingers. **DO** keep your child safe from things in the area that might hurt him/her, for instance, move furniture away from your child and keep other people (except medical help) away. It can be very scary to watch your child have a seizure, but if you can remember, or ask someone else to remember, write down the time the seizure started and stopped and what behaviors you saw. This will help your health care team determine the best treatment for your child. Most seizures can be controlled with medications.

Sleeping Problems

Certain medications can make it difficult for your child to sleep, especially steroids. Anxiety and worry can also make it hard for your child to fall asleep or stay asleep all night. Let your health care team know if your child is having difficulty sleeping. Things you can try to help your child sleep include:

- Having a regular bedtime routine every night.

- Starting quieter activities at least an hour before bedtime to wind down an active child.

- Having your child take a warm bath or shower before bed.

- Wrapping your child in his/her favorite blanket or cuddling with him/her before bed.

- Playing quiet, soothing music.

- Avoiding use of bright nightlights.

- Reading your child a story.

- Avoiding giving medications that may cause insomnia (sleeplessness) before bedtime.

- Avoiding drinks or foods with caffeine at least 2 to 3 hours before bedtime.

- Asking your doctor or nurse practitioner if a sleep medication might help.

Other Medical Issues

Your child may have medical devices, such as a central venous access device (e.g., Broviac® catheter, Hickman® catheter, PICC line, Port-a-Cath®, Infuse-a-Port®), a tracheostomy (a surgically created hole through the front of the neck and into the windpipe), or a ventriculoperitoneal shunt (used to treat brain swelling). Not every child with a DIPG has these types of medical devices, but this section will give you some information about the use and care of some of these devices. These are only guidelines; you should follow the directions your health care team gives you about how to care for any medical devices.

This section will also discuss complementary and alternative medicine (CAM). Please discuss any CAM therapies that you might be considering with your child's doctor or nurse practitioner. Some CAM therapies interfere with chemotherapy and radiation therapy, so it is very important to let your health care team know about any supplemental medicines you are using with your child.

Central venous access devices (central lines)

Central venous access devices are longer-term intravenous (IV) lines that can be very useful for administering chemotherapy, blood product transfusions, IV fluids, total parenteral nutrition (TPN), and drawing blood. These types of lines are placed in large veins and the tip of the catheter ends in a large vein, just above the heart. It is important to know that the catheter is NOT in the heart. There are several different types of central lines, and the decision about which type of line is best will depend upon your child's age, how frequently venous access is needed, your child's activity level, and the ability of someone to care for the line at home. The vast majority of children with a DIPG do not need a central line, or if they do, it is usually for only a short period, such as needing daily IV access for approximately 6 weeks with anesthesia during radiation therapy for young children. Several different types of central lines are discussed below. Your doctor or nurse/nurse practitioner is a great resource in helping you decide if your child needs a central line, and if so, which type is best for your child. The tips provided in this section are only general recommendations. You should talk with your child's nurse to find out the specific care your hospital recommends, who is responsible for providing the care, and who will teach you how to care for the line at home.

Peripherally inserted central catheter (PICC line)

- **Use:** A PICC line is a more of a temporary line, which is often used for shorter-term IV needs, such as with radiation therapy or a few weeks of antibiotic therapy. It can be used to administer IV medications, blood transfusions, and IV fluids. A PICC line can also be used to draw blood.

- **How it is placed:** A PICC line is usually inserted under sedation or anesthesia by an interventional radiologist or a surgeon. It is a small, flexible catheter that is usually inserted in the upper arm, with a couple of sutures (stitches) to hold it in place, and then covered with an adhesive bandage over the exit site. Part of the line will be external, coming out from the exit site. The PICC line is usually loosely wrapped with an elastic bandage to hold the line up out of the way until it is needed.

- **Flushing the catheter:** A PICC line requires daily flushing of the catheter with a heparin flush solution, which keeps the blood inside the catheter from clotting. The heparin flush solution is injected inside the catheter and will not affect the ability of the blood in the rest of the body to clot.

- **Dressing changes:** The adhesive dressing over the exit site usually needs to be changed once a week, or per your hospital's policy, or if the dressing becomes soiled. Some health care teams recommend changing the dressing less frequently, or only allowing a trained nurse to change the dressing, so be sure to check your hospital's policy.

- **Restrictions:** It is recommended that children with PICC lines NOT swim or submerge themselves in water (including bathwater). In general, contact sports are discouraged. The PICC line is the easiest line to accidently pull out, so you will need to take care to protect the line and teach your child to protect it while playing or at school. If the PICC line is accidentally pulled out, hold gauze or another clean bandage over the exit site until it stops bleeding. Call your child's doctor or nurse practitioner if the line comes out and save the line so the doctor or nurse practitioner can be sure all of the line was pulled out and none remains broken off inside the body. If it is broken off, the catheter may need to be retrieved through a surgical procedure.

- **Home care:** Your child's nurse will teach you how to care for the PICC line at home, including how to flush the catheter, how to change the dressing, and how to administer medications through the PICC line (if needed). The nurse will also arrange for the supplies that are needed to care for the PICC line to be delivered to your home, and it is usually possible to have a home care nurse come to your home for a few visits to help you care for the PICC line until you are more comfortable doing it on your own.

Broviac® or Hickman® catheter

- **Use:** A Broviac® or Hickman® catheter is a longer-term central venous access device. It can usually stay in from a few months to several years, as long as it still works. A Broviac® or Hickman® catheter can be used to administer IV medications, blood transfusions, and IV fluids, as well as to draw blood specimens.

- **How it is placed:** This type of catheter is usually inserted under sedation or anesthesia by an interventional radiologist or a surgeon in an operating room. It is a small flexible catheter that is usually inserted in the upper chest with a couple of sutures (stitches) to initially hold it in place; then an adhesive bandage is placed over the exit site. Part of the catheter will be external, coming out from the exit site. This type of catheter is also called an external tunneled catheter, because the line has a cuff made out of a material called Dacron that helps your child's skin adhere to the catheter and hold it in place. The surgeon makes an incision in the upper chest and tunnels the catheter under the skin to the neck, where it is inserted into a large vein. Generally, the sutures are not removed unless they are irritating your child's skin or they fall out. Once the Dacron cuff is anchored, usually after about 1 to 2 weeks, it is difficult to accidentally pull it out. This type of catheter can have one tube or be split into two or three tubes (called lumens); each lumen requires daily care.

- **Flushing the catheter:** The catheter requires daily flushing of each lumen of the catheter with a heparin flush solution, which keeps the blood inside the catheter from clotting. The heparin flush solution is injected inside the catheter and will not affect the ability of the blood in the rest of the body to clot.

- **Dressing changes:** The adhesive dressing over the exit site needs to be changed, usually once a week, or as per your hospital's policy, or if the dressing becomes soiled. Some health care teams recommend changing the dressing less frequently, or only allowing a trained nurse to change the dressing, so be sure to check with your hospital's policy.

- **Restrictions:** Recommendations differ about swimming with a Broviac® or Hickman® catheter. Check with your doctor or nurse/nurse practitioner to see if your hospital recommends swimming with these types of central catheters. Bathing is usually allowed, but the dressing needs to be changed if it becomes wet. In general, contact sports are discouraged. If the Broviac® or Hickman® catheter is accidentally pulled out, hold gauze or another clean bandage over the exit site until it stops bleeding. Call your child's doctor or nurse practitioner if the line comes out and save the line so the doctor or nurse practitioner can be sure all of the line was pulled out and none remains broken off inside the body. If it is broken off, the catheter may need to be retrieved through a surgical procedure.

- **Home care:** Your child's nurse will teach you how to care for the Broviac® or Hickman® line at home, including how to flush the catheter, how to change the dressing, and how to administer medications through the catheter (if needed). The nurse will arrange for supplies that are needed to care for the Broviac® or Hickman® catheter to be delivered to your home, and it is usually possible to have a home care nurse come to your home for a few visits to help you care for the catheter until you are more comfortable doing it yourself.

PORT-A-CATH® or INFUSE-A-PORT®

- **Use:** A PORT-A-CATH® or INFUSE-A-PORT® (commonly referred to as a port) is a longer-term central venous access device. It can usually stay in for months to several years, as long as it still works. A port can be used to administer IV medications, blood transfusions, and IV fluids, as well as to draw blood specimens.

- **How it is placed:** A port is usually inserted under sedation or anesthesia by an interventional radiologist or a surgeon in the operating room. It is a small, flexible catheter with a port that is usually inserted in the upper chest under the skin. Initially, one or two steristrips (butterfly-type bandages) will be placed over the areas where the port is inserted in the chest and where the catheter is inserted into a large vein in the neck. This type of catheter is also called an internal tunneled catheter, because the line is totally inside the body. The surgeon makes an incision in the upper chest to put in the port and tunnels the catheter under the skin to the neck where it is inserted into a large vein. Generally, the steristrips are not removed and will fall off by themselves with normal bathing. The port does not require the same care at home as a PICC or Broviac®/Hickman® catheter.

- **Flushing the catheter:** Because the port is totally under the skin, it requires a special kind of needle (a Huber needle) to reach the port for venous access. In some cases, parents can be taught how to access the port, but in general most of the port care will be done by a nurse. A port requires a heparin flush once a month, but a flush may be needed more often if your child receives medicines through the port. The port needle should be changed once a week, if it is accessed.

- **Dressing changes:** No routine care is required for the port at home, unless the port is accessed. If the port is accessed, the dressing should be changed once a week with the changing of the port needle. Your nurse or home care nurse will generally take care of the port.

- **Restrictions:** Unless the port is accessed, there are generally no restrictions on swimming or bathing, but contact sports are discouraged.

- **Home care:** There is usually no care to provide at home, unless the port is accessed for medicines. If needed, home care nurses can come to your home to teach you how to care for the port.

Complementary and Alternative Medicines (CAM)

Complementary and alternative medicines (CAM) are non-traditional approaches to health care, but they are becoming more widely used in conjunction with traditional medical care. Some CAM therapies can help your child be more comfortable, but some can interfere with certain chemotherapies or radiation therapies, so be sure to check with your health care team before trying any CAM approaches. Make sure you go to a reputable CAM practitioner. Check out the qualifications and experience of CAM practitioners, just as you would your doctor or nurse practitioner. Ask your health care team if they recommend certain practitioners. Some of these therapies may be provided in your hospital by nurse practitioners and doctors who have specialized training in CAM. Some CAM practitioners can come to your home. Examples of CAM include:

- Acupuncture

- Aromatherapy

- Art therapy

- Biofeedback

- Herbal therapies

- Hypnosis

- Massage

- Meditation and prayer

- Music therapy

- Pet therapy

- Play therapy

- Reflexology

- Relaxation and guided imagery

- Reiki

- Tai Chi

- Therapeutic touch

Practical Care Issues

There are several other issues that may arise as you take your child home. Some children have problems with balance and walking, communicating with others, anxiety or emotional concerns, or central venous catheters or tracheostomy tubes to care for. This section will discuss how to handle these challenges and discuss other concerns for managing day-to-day life, such as traveling with your child and practical tips.

Mobility

Some children with DIPG have ataxia (poor balance) or difficulty walking due to muscle weakness. Physical rehabilitation with physical and occupational therapy may be very helpful to help strengthen your child, help your child learn new ways to walk or be mobile with his/her physical challenges, and help you to learn how to safely manage your child at home. Ask your doctor or nurse practitioner to recommend a physical medicine and rehabilitation (PM&R) doctor for an evaluation to help plan the best therapy approach for your child. Inpatient rehabilitation services may be helpful, and outpatient or in home services may be available.

Younger children can be carried, but it is helpful to have a good stroller for longer distances. Remember that your child will grow, and the stroller you had when he/she was an infant or small toddler may not be safe for him/her as he/she grows. You will want to have a sturdy stroller to hold any additional equipment or supplies your child might need. There are several companies that make heavy-duty strollers for medically fragile children. Ask your nurse or social worker to help you find the most appropriate stroller for your young child. Some insurance companies will pay for this as a medical expense.

Older children may benefit from having a wheelchair. Wheelchairs come in many different sizes, so there is one that is the right size for your child. Ask your doctor or nurse/nurse practitioner if they think a wheelchair might help your child be able to move around better. Many parents feel a wheelchair is very helpful because they can take their child outside and to places they like to visit.

Mobility concerns are not just related to walking or transportation from one place to another. Your child may also have difficulty standing or sitting, which can impact daily activities such as taking a bath or shower, watching TV or playing games, or even going to the bathroom. Discuss with your nurse/nurse practitioner what strategies you can use to help your child manage his daily life. Rehabilitation with physical and occupational therapy may improve strength and balance so your child is able to do more things independently, but in the meantime you may find some assistive equipment particularly helpful. The PM&R team may have even more suggestions, but some practical items to consider are a shower or bath chair, rails on bathtubs or showers, walkers, canes (there are many different types), hospital beds at home, and bedside toilets. You may want to consider moving your child's bed to a location in your house that is easier for him/her to manage. For example, you can place the bed in a location where your child does not need to go up or down stairs, or you can place it closer to a bathroom.

Handicap parking permits

It may be possible for you to get temporary handicap parking tags or a placard for your car to help you park closer to the hospital and other places you take your child. This is particularly helpful if your child has impaired mobility. You can obtain an application for handicap parking from your state Department of Motor Vehicle Administration. Many applications are also available online. There is a section for you to fill out with the information about your car and there is a section for your doctor or nurse practitioner to fill out to verify that handicap parking permits are appropriate for you. Usually a temporary permit is valid for 6 months but can easily be renewed. A placard is a good option if you drive multiple cars, because it can be moved between cars.

Travel tips

Traveling with children can be challenging for any parent, but it may seem overwhelming when you have an ill child. Travel is generally quite safe and your doctor or nurse/nurse practitioner can help you find ways to make things easier. The following are some helpful tips that might help traveling go a bit smoother.

- Have the name, address, and phone number of a local hospital in the area where you will be traveling, just in case your child needs medical attention.

- Ask your doctor or nurse practitioner to write a letter that summarizes your child's history, the current treatment and medications your child is taking, and how to contact him or her in case of an emergency. This can be helpful in case you have to go to a local emergency room or visit a doctor while you are traveling. If your child requires opiate medications or injectable medications and you will need to carry syringes and needles, ask your doctor or nurse practitioner to write a letter of medical necessity for you to hand carry during air travel.

- If flying, take extra medications with you and pack at least a few days' worth in your carry-on luggage in case your luggage gets lost. If medication needs to be refrigerated, remember to take cooler packs and notify flight attendants that you need to refrigerate medications if it is a long trip.

- Call the airline, train, or bus company in advance and let them know about your child's special needs. Ask for seats that have extra leg room. Also let them know if your child has a wheelchair, walker, or other medical equipment. When you arrive at the airport (or train or bus station), check in early and again remind the attendants of any special needs your child has.

- If your child has other medication equipment (e.g., suction machine, oxygen, feeding pump), ask your nurse or social worker if there is a way to have this equipment supplied in the location where you are traveling so you don't have to carry all the extra equipment with you. Sometimes this is not possible, so arrangements can be made to transport your equipment with you as needed.

- Plan activities during the part of the day when your child usually feels best. If your child needs to rest frequently, remember this and build that time into your daily vacation plans.

- Plan your meals around your child's special dietary needs, if they have any.

- If possible, take an extra person with you to help with the logistics of travel.

- Keep things simple! Many family vacations create wonderful memories, but not if everyone is stressed. Build in time to relax and take things slowly so your child does not become overly tired. Cranky children are no fun to travel with.

- Consider having friends and family travel to you. If travel is being planned to visit relatives and friends it might be less cumbersome for your child and family if visitors travel to you.

Communication Challenges

Many children with DIPG have trouble communicating at points during their treatment. These communication problems can stem from many causes such as: swelling from the tumor, weak muscles in the neck that help the tongue and mouth to form letters, or from the tumor irritating or damaging certain cranial nerves that control the vocal cords. Some children with DIPG have speech that is difficult to understand. Speech therapy may help. Children may recover their speech over time if loss of speech is due to a reversible cause, such as swelling. Sometimes speech does not improve much, even with therapy. This can be quite frustrating for you and your child. Remember to be patient and let your child have extra time to try to communicate with you. Here are some helpful hints to improve communication.

- **Speech therapy:** Ask your doctor or nurse practitioner if he or she thinks speech therapy would be helpful and, if so, to help you arrange the therapy.

- **Picture boards:** Your speech therapist can help you make a picture board to identify common things that your child may be trying to communicate. You can also do this as a family project. Find pictures in magazines, print pictures from online, or draw pictures of common things your child may want to communicate, such as being hungry/wanting food, being thirsty/ wanting a drink, wanting to go to bed, wanting to go to the bathroom, wanting to play, wanting to watch TV or a DVD movie, having pain, feeling nauseated, etc. Some speech therapists have picture boards that are already made for different ages of children. You can teach your child to point to the picture of what he/she is trying to communicate. There is an iPad application (app) called Picture Board that is available for free download from the Apple store.

- **Voice communication devices:** There are computer programs or hand-held electronic devices that allow your child to push a picture of what they want and the computer "speaks" the word or phrase. These may not be available in your hospital, but you can ask about ways to order them. There is a useful iPad application (app) that can be downloaded for free called "Talk Assist" for those children who can type text that is then converted to speech; and another free application called "Small Talk, Conversational Phrases," which provides a vocabulary of pictures that subsequently talk in a human voice.

- **Pencil and paper:** Have pencils (or markers or crayons) and paper readily available for your child to write down what he/she is trying to communicate. Save the common cards so they can be used over again. If your child cannot write but can read, consider writing common phrases out on 5 x 8 cards for your child to use to communicate what he/she needs or wants.

- **Take your time and allow your child to take their time:** Difficulty communicating is very frustrating for most children. Try not to rush your child or ask him/her over and over to repeat what he/she is trying to say. Begin to use picture boards or the written cards early, when your child is not having much difficulty communicating, so that it is natural to him/her when he/she is no longer able to speak clearly.

Chapter 12 in this book provides additional information on the communication needs of the child diagnosed with a DIPG.

Other Helpful Tips

Other challenges may arise that are not anticipated. Every child and every family is special and may have special needs. Ask your health care team about any issues that have not been mentioned here. In addition, here are a few things to consider.

- **Clothing:** Your child may gain weight or lose weight as a result of treatments. Some children develop sensitive skin, where some fabrics are irritating. Have a supply of loose-fitting clothing that is easy to get on and easy to remove. If your child has muscle weakness or is not able to stand, he/she may not be able to dress himself/herself like he/she used to. Clothing with elastic around the neck and leg openings is particularly helpful. You may also need to have several sizes of clothing available for times when your child gains or loses weight. Buying new clothing can be expensive, especially when your child may not be the same size for any length of time. Consider visiting second-hand or discount clothing stores to get basic items and save more expensive clothing purchases for special occasions. If family and friends ask how they can help, consider asking them to provide gift cards for clothing stores that your child might like.

- **Financial worries:** The costs of treatment and medical equipment can be substantial, even if you have great insurance coverage. Most insurance companies do not pay for everything your child will need. Anticipate out-of-pocket costs and try to budget for them, if possible. Ask your social worker if your child might qualify for Supplemental Social Security Income (SSI) or other possible sources of additional funding to help with some of the costs. Consider letting family and friends who are asking what they can do for you, to help with fundraising events to raise money for these unanticipated medical and personal expenses. In addition, many hospitals charge for parking and meals in the hospital's cafeteria and these can add up after a while. Extra funds can come in handy for these types of expenses, which are usually not covered by insurance.

- **Durable medical equipment:** Equipment that your child needs is called durable medical equipment (DME). It is important to know this term, because this is how benefits for payment of equipment are determined by your insurance company. Your nurse should review any equipment that your child might need at home, but most equipment is provided by an outside company that your insurance company recommends. The equipment that is used in the hospital may differ slightly from what is delivered to your home. Make sure you are given instructions about how to use the equipment, how to troubleshoot common problems, who to call 24 hours a day in an emergency, and who to call when you have routine questions. You should also ask to have a home care nurse come for a few visits to help you learn how to use any DME. If the equipment company does not provide a set of written instructions for each piece of equipment, ask for them. Keep this information in a binder or notebook in a place that is easily accessible to anyone who might be caring for your child. Be sure to put the emergency phone numbers for each company that provides DME in the beginning of the notebook or in a place that can be found quickly, if needed.

Making Difficult Decisions

Your child has a rare and challenging tumor and many difficult decisions will have to be made along the way. It is helpful to have conversations about the different types of situations that may come up before they actually do; that way your family and your child (if he/she is old enough to help make decisions about his/her health) will be able to talk about these situations openly and honestly. Some of these decisions may be difficult to talk about, so talking about them early, when there is no urgency, can make it easier if the need arises to make urgent decisions. Your social worker will be a wonderful resource to help you, your family, and your child talk together about difficult decisions. These are some helpful tips about making difficult decisions.

- **Honesty:** Have open discussions with your family and your child (if he/she is old enough to understand and participate in decisions about his/her health) about your child's diagnosis of DIPG and what the prognosis is, according to your doctor or nurse practitioner. Most children are thinking about these things, even if they are not talking about them. Sometimes your child's imagination may be worse than reality, so talking about what may or may not be happening will actually help him/her worry less. Be honest and do not lie to your child. Children are usually very good about figuring out when parents are lying to them.

- **Hope for the best and prepare for the worst:** Your health care team is working very hard to treat the DIPG and help your child. They may or may not have given you statistics about cure rates and/or relapse rates for DIPG. However, statistics really do not mean a thing, because for your one child, there will either be a 100% cure or not. Try not to let statistics keep you from enjoying life in the moment. Enjoy every day with your child. Keep your hopes up that your child will be that 100%, but talk with your health care team about what to expect if your child does not survive the DIPG.

- **Five Wishes™ or My Wishes™ or Go Wish™ Cards:** Some children and families find it hard to talk about making difficult decisions and/or facing end-of-life care decisions. Be sure to talk with your social worker about your concerns. You may also find it helpful to talk with a counselor or psychologist. Several other tools can also help you with these conversations, such as Five Wishes™ and My Wishes™, which are decision-making tools. Five Wishes™ is a set of questions for older children, adolescents, and young adults, and My Wishes™ is better suited for younger children or developmentally delayed children. These tools have several different questions about who your child might want to make decisions for him/her if he/she is not able to, and other health care decisions he/she might want people to know about. Go Wish™ Cards are like playing cards that have phrases about health care decisions written on them. Ask your health care team if you can have a copy of these tools to use at home. Your local hospital might use other tools that are equally as good as the ones mentioned here.

- **Other books and pamphlets:** Several wonderful books are available to help you with making difficult decisions. Ask your health care team to recommend some of these to you. There is also a list of books in the appendix at the back of this book that you might find helpful as well.

While the journey through DIPG treatment can be physically and emotionally challenging for both you and your child, the advice listed in this chapter can help you feel more prepared to care for your child at home. Remember that your health care team is there to support you through this difficult time, as are parent support groups led by others who have walked the same path your family is now walking. Reach out and ask for the help you need to best care for your child with DIPG.

Parent Perspectives

I didn't understand all that would be involved in Andrew's care at home until we left the hospital. There were medications to dispense. He could not be left alone for extended periods of time as he was very unstable. If he was in his hospital bed or strapped into his wheelchair, we could leave him for a short time—as long as we were close enough to hear him if he needed us. He could not walk or get down on the floor without our help. He also needed help with bathing and toileting. In the hospital we had people to help with all of these different things. At home we were on our own. This did not change how we felt about having him home; it just made being home very different from what that meant before he was diagnosed with DIPG.

Stella eats very little and requires liquids to be thickened to enable her to swallow them. Her diet at the moment consists of avocados, mashed potatoes, apple sauce, hamburgers, ice cream and milk. Since October she has been incapable of sitting up unassisted, and as of December she is unable to hold her head up without support. She drools constantly and has begun to suffer from seizures.

When our son was diagnosed with DIPG, each of our lives were impacted in some way. While he bore the physical effects of the tumor itself, each of us were changed because of it. As we lost the child we knew to steroids— not once, but twice—we grew to understand that the real boy we knew was not the body we saw with our eyes, but the soul we loved with our hearts.

I am a single parent and had to care for Warren alone. Warren's dad would take him on the weekends so that gave me a much needed break. I also had family and friends that would watch Warren when I needed to go to the store or something, but Warren didn't want me to leave him so I naturally tried not to.

I took a leave from work after Warren was diagnosed. I live in income-based housing so that worked in my favor. Even with all that, I had no way to pay other bills and pay for gas to get us back and forth to the doctor and such. Then our community stepped in and helped out with fundraisers and such. The people around where I live were so wonderful and caring and because of them I didn't have to worry about paying the bills.

From the beginning, I believed that complimentary care was an integral aspect to Alexis' overall treatment, and medical plan. In our initial discussions with Alexis' treatment team, it was important to discuss complimentary care. From those first few moments we landed headlong in the childhood cancer community, we were given the proverbial "green-light" to use supplements as long as we cleared them with the team first. Initially, we had a minor debate regarding the use of antioxidants. The conventional wisdom of the past suggested that the use of antioxidants could negatively impact the efficacy of radiation. After doing research on the topic, I was able to demonstrate that this in fact was nothing more than anecdotal information. We quickly began consulting with a nutritionist that many other pediatric and adult brain tumor patients worked with. Whether the use of supplements and the complimentary care had any impact upon Alexis' overall course we ultimately will never know of course. I certainly would like to think that it did. For around twenty months of Alexis' battle, from sun-up to sun-down, Alexis willingly took approximately twenty different natural supplements and vitamins. I tasted everything prior to administering them to her. Some were simply awful so we devised strategies for getting them into her. In the end, Alexis took everything like a trooper.

It seems to be taking more effort for our son to chew and to form words. So he is not chewing things as well as he was last week, and he is choosing not to use his words as much as he normally does. (I need to throw in here though that he uses his words quite loudly and clearly when he wants me and I'm not responding quickly enough!) He has been vomiting periodically—almost always later in the day. This has become more of a problem over the past week, so there has been some concern regarding nutrition. The vomiting is believed to be a gastrointestinal issue rather than a neurological issue, and a scope this afternoon did show delayed gastric emptying. We have made some medication changes and some food changes, and have begun using an NG tube for supplemental nutrition.

AmbuCab arrives about 7:15 a.m. on dressing change mornings. By the time we load and unload, we end up at the hospital by 8:00 a.m. The AmbuCab driver pushes my son to the fourth floor while I push another wheelchair piled high with our stuff (dressing change supplies; his Bi-PAP; a backpack filled with a change of clothes, medications, and other necessary things; my purse, and my laptop). We arrive and I begin to arrange the room in preparation for the big event. Shortly before 9:00 a.m. I set up the Bi-PAP for use while my son is under sedation. A nurse or tech prepares him by attaching electrodes to his chest to monitor vital signs. The wound team arrives to open dressing change supplies, and the intensivist arrives to administer propofol for sedation. By 9:00 a.m. the tiny room is full with at least five people, and the dressing change begins. Someone from phlebotomy arrives just after 9:00 a.m. to draw blood, and someone from the I.V. team still comes on Mondays to change the needle in the port. We have noticed that the dressing changes are getting shorter and that we are using fewer supplies. The few wounds that remain are clean and steadily improving, and my son now rarely experiences pain.

Caleb was not able to eat and I was worried he would be hungry. He hated being hungry. So, they put in an NG tube and kept food going into his tummy to make sure he would not ever feel hungry. He was restless at times and we had valium on request. If he indicated pain, we had morphine on request.

He was still able to get up (with assistance) to use the bathroom, sit in a chair, watch TV. He could not talk very well but we developed methods of communication during those days—first with hand signals, then with eye movements.

To help control her eating we implemented the use of a timer and a second hand clock that would show time running down using color. When either thing beeped Peyton knew it was snack time. We would get sneaky once in a while and add more time to the timer when she wasn't looking. We also provided little snacks and made sure we had an activity planned for after snack so she would be focused on something else. Sometimes I made stuff up like, "Oh we are out of butter to make cookies." Distractions help.

On a side note one of the best things we did during our daughter's illness was strabismus surgery. It fixed her eyes, hence eliminating the need for blacking out one lens of her glasses. Most importantly, it gave her confidence, made her feel better, and gave her a sense of accomplishment.

We are settling into a routine at home—though we are still in limbo in some ways. Our living room looks like a Pediatric Intensive Care Unit, with the focal point being our son's hospital bed. We've done our best to organize so that the medical equipment and supplies are easily accessible, but not obvious to the casual observer. We are set up to use oxygen; to administer I.V. fluids and medications; to take care of wound care and our son's port; to monitor oxygen saturation, blood pressure, heart rate and temperature; to use Bi-PAP and suction. We find ourselves using Bi-PAP and oxygen only when he sleeps; he has not required suctioning since he had a cold in early July. We do administer I.V. medications and fluids daily as there is question regarding his ability to absorb oral medications and fluids.

We met with the neurosurgeon, who explained that surgery was not possible, nor was a biopsy because of the location. She answered questions that we had written down, and ultimately told us that other children who had this tumor did not survive. When we asked how long Bryce had, we were told that with treatment, these children typically had "more or less than a year." I remember looking at my husband, and saying that one year was going to go too fast. And I remember looking at the doctor and doing what I now call the most important thing that helped us to live through this. I asked her to hook us up with anyone and everyone who could support us through this—psychologists, social workers, doctors, whomever. And she did. We thank her every day for that.

✛✛✛

We were told to talk about everything that was important, and about what was coming, so that we could be sure that we had those important conversations before speech became an issue, as it typically did with DIPG. That's not to say that we didn't continue to research, to check out a trial offered in Toronto, or search the world over for a cure. But we also decided at that point that if the treatment available would not allow Bryce to LIVE the way he chose to every day, then we would respect that. He was 13, and at that point he had already voiced that he did not want surgery, or to have chemo because he was afraid of having a port put in. So because nothing was curative, we did not have to try to change his mind.

We went back home. The thing that became obvious over the next few weeks was that Bryce just wanted to go back to school, to a regular routine, and to be a regular kid. He didn't want to be in the spotlight, babied, coddled, or have all of the attention that others wanted to give him. He even went on his Grade 8 graduation trip. And not until months later, did he know that we were also in Cleveland that day, just in case something happened and he needed to be rushed home. Thankfully, he never needed to know.

Bryce's progression surprised everyone because the doctors thought that if the onset of new symptoms were swift, that Bryce would only survive a very short time. He, however, actually survived for two months after his progression date. Over that time, he also developed pain—neuropathic pain—in his knees, and feet. We tried everything—massage, ice, heat, arnica cream, A535, Reiki, Dilaudid. Nothing gave him much relief. And we had to step up and become his advocates with everyone—medical staff and visitors to make sure that his wishes were met. That was no small feat.

At first eating wasn't much of an issue. For most of the time Warren could feed himself, but would need a little assistance. As he started to struggle I had him eat softer foods like mashed potatoes and I pureed things in the blender. His biggest problem was he couldn't get his mouth open very wide so getting food in was difficult. I had to buy smaller spoons and deeper spoons so he could get a decent bite. He also could only drink using a straw. The straw had to be placed in the right side of his lips or he couldn't get a drink.

Meal time took about an hour. Warren would eat in his "stander"—a big wooden device that I strapped him into. He was in a standing position and there was a tray in front for games and food and such. Sometimes he would sit on the floor but he couldn't hold himself up so I had to prop him up against the couch and slide our coffee table over him so he was stuck in between. I then had to put pillows on either side of him to keep him from falling over. Once Warren started taking steroids he wanted to eat more often, so rapidly began growing out of his clothes. I had to buy all new *pants (with elastic bands), shirts, underwear and jammies.*

We bathe Andrew and dress him daily. We move him—by Hoyer lift—from bed to wheelchair and from wheelchair to bed several times on any given day. We do our best to keep his hands busy because the more he uses them, the better. He enjoys shooting various Nerf guns at targets we hang from his Hoyer lift. (He also enjoys "shooting" at his brother!) Andrew has physical therapy at home three times each week. We do our best to guard that precious time with his therapists and to work with him ourselves—-as time allows—on other days.

Long shirts that look like dresses were awesome for our daughter. Paired with stretchy leggings; it was a good thing. All the name brand stores had a wonderful selection of different colored leggings. We didn't want Peyton to feel constricted in her clothes, so I usually bought the next size up as well.

I was stunned. Sick. I was left alone in a room in the PICU to take care of my very sick daughter while also trying to accept the fact that I would have to watch her die. My brain tried to reject the concept like my stomach would reject tainted food. At that point, I shut down. I let the doctors know that they should only talk to Joe, not to me. I could not handle it. I was struggling to keep myself from letting the panic and disbelief take over. I couldn't eat. I couldn't sleep. I didn't know what to do with myself. One thing I did know. No matter what I was feeling, I had to get over it and be there for Bizzie. So I did...somehow.

Our families reacted much how we suspected they would—with tears of course, but with tremendous support and strength as well. We are certain many other emotions were felt privately but in our presence and in the presence of our children there was nothing but complete strength displayed. Everyone spoke honestly about Liam's illness; however in those early days we made a decision that we would not tell our kids or Liam about the course this disease generally takes. Their little hearts were already burdened with so much. As Liam's condition improved or declined we had honest age-appropriate discussions at every step. Our kids were a tremendous help to us

and to Liam. We included them as much as we could in his care. Our oldest child, then in third grade, would read to him; his twin brother "assisted" me with dressing changes and his little brother, only three, came to every day of radiation and every clinic visit. But mostly and most importantly they continued to play and treat Liam as they always had. Liam loved this. He did not want to be different. It was a wonderful gift they gave to him.

On April 1st, my son was admitted into hospice care. With my nursing background, hospice acted in his case more as a sounding board for us as we did all of his care ourselves. In crisis moments they helped with medication calculations, gave suggestions on meds that might help ease his pain and they offered a wide range of therapies. He enjoyed Reiki and therapeutic touch. He received weekly visits from therapy dogs. This was such a blessing for a little boy who had a strong and special connection with animals. We had artists who are friends and teachers to our other children come and do art projects with our kids and at one point near the end of our son's journey a friend came with his guitar, invited all the neighborhood kids to come and they sang songs together. It was a beautiful afternoon.

Brendan welcomed the idea to have an NG tube, then G-tube then "Micky" button so we could deliver meds and nutrition easily. He felt better when he could get meds without choking and nutrition without having to chew and swallow. Keeping him hydrated and fed was key to keeping him strong and enjoying a good quality of life especially when the chemo caused GI issues and he lost his appetite.

A few weeks later, Aimee woke with a severe headache, and was partially paralyzed on the right side. When I called her new doctors, they put her back on the dexamethasone. I also began her on a drink I heard about from another mother whose child also had a brain tumor. The drink was called Vemma, which is made from the Mangosteen fruit. Once she began taking the Vemma she regained full strength on her right side.

Aimee was doing well since she began the Vemma, so she demanded to return to school in September. She was entering the 7th grade in a brand new school in a new state and knew no one in her class. I personally did *not want her to attend but she felt it was something she needed to do. A few days after school started I found a letter that she had written to her classmates.*

"Hi, I am Aimee. I am 12 years old, and I am just like you. I love reading, music, go-kart racing, cheerleading and making crafts. Yes, I may be sitting in a wheelchair, and my face may look funny and talk funny, but please don't be afraid of me because you cannot catch what I have. I have a brain tumor and the doctors say I am going to die. But I just want to be as normal as possible, just like you. So please don't be afraid of me. I am not afraid of you even when you make fun of me. I will still be your friend, so can you please be mine."

We were very busy. My son had his radiation done an hour and half from our house. So while he was doing radiation we would get up about 7:30 or 8:00 a.m., have breakfast, go to physical therapy and/or occupational therapy for 1 to 2 hours. We'd then go home and have lunch and rest and play, then leave about 3:00 p.m. for a 5:00 p.m. or 6:00 p.m. radiation appointment. We would be there for 30 minutes or so then would drive back home. We would get home about 7:00 p.m. or 8:00 p.m., eat if we hadn't already, and take a bath when needed or felt like it. Then we would go to bed because Warren would be tired.

If we had a doctor's appointment then we would skip physiotherapy and occupational therapy and drive the 3 ½ hours to the doctor, then stop on the way back home to have radiation if it was scheduled.

My son didn't go back to school after diagnosis because we were too busy with radiation and such and after that I just wanted him home. He couldn't write or walk and had a hard time speaking and would have had to have constant care with feeding and going to the bathroom.

By April he began to require the use of narcotics to manage pain as a result of steroid-induced skin breakdown. Just before he was transferred to PICU on April 9th, he was placed on a continuous drip. As we began to prepare to go home in May, the importance of oral (as opposed to I.V.) medications was discussed, and he was slowly switched from Fentanyl (by I.V.) to Methadone (by mouth). He was on such a small amount of Methadone that we began

to wean him off the medication completely last weekend. We noticed that he did not seem well, but it was not until Tuesday that we began to realize it was the lack of Methadone that was causing him to feel miserable.

We discussed the way our son was feeling with his doctor that afternoon, and she made the decision to put him back on Methadone. When he received a bit of fast-acting morphine to help him until the Methadone had opportunity to take effect, it was almost immediately as if we had flipped a switch. He went suddenly from misery to contentment. One moment he was telling us repeatedly that he could not get comfortable; the next moment he turned into a chatterbox...with a smile on his face.

Chapter 12

Communication: When a Child Can No Longer Speak

David Brownstone, MSW, RSW
Caelyn Kaise, MHSc, SLP(C), Reg.CASLPO
Ceilidh Eaton Russell, CCLS, MSc (candidate)

Supporting a child or teenager who has a brain tumor is an incredibly important and difficult job. And trying to help them understand and live with their changing abilities can be overwhelming, especially when caregivers naturally struggle with these changes themselves. The situation is also a challenge because while a child's physical abilities to communicate—including the ability to produce speech and to express thoughts and feelings—can change, cognitive abilities often stay intact. So if a child or teenager has trouble communicating because of a brain tumor, the task of supporting them becomes even more complex.

Family members and caregivers who have been in this situation often express that they did not know what to do or where to start, and they often felt helpless and frustrated. But in the end they did it. With time, patience, creativity, and support, families find ways to communicate with their children and teenagers with brain tumors, even though these young patients had, or have, trouble speaking.

This chapter includes "lessons learned" from talking with 14 families about their experiences, as well as our team's experiences working with families of children with brain tumors. (Note: Our team only interviewed families of patients younger than age 13 and our examples reflect this. While the examples may not be relevant to teens, as many issues and struggles are unique to that age group, the communication strategies are similar and can be adapted for teens.)

> David Brownstone is a Social Worker with the Brain Tumor Program and an Academic and Clinical Specialist in the Department of Social Work at the Hospital for Sick Children in Toronto, Canada.

The parents we spoke with generously shared the creative strategies and tools they developed, the most important conversations they had, and the most important lessons they learned. When we began to talk with these parents, our goal was to develop a new communication tool, yet they taught us that although tools are helpful, in the end, direct communication is more valued and helpful. Families encouraged us to share strategies and resources with families like yours so that others facing this stage of brain tumors will have ideas about where to start, what to try, and know that they—and you—are not alone.

Of course every family and every child is unique, each with their own values, philosophies, experiences, and backgrounds. Some of your family's experiences may be very different from those of the families we interviewed. However, some of the situations they faced or the strategies they tried may be similar to yours or helpful to you. We encourage you to think about the ideas outlined in this chapter and to use or modify them so they work for your family and are well suited to your child's age and developmental stage.

Most of all, the families we talked to and the members of our team sincerely hope that sharing this information will help you and your family feel, at the very least, a little more prepared and supported during this difficult time.

Quick Tips

To help you focus on how to approach and enhance communication with your child, here are a few quick tips to think about.

- Practice communication strategies **before** your child needs to use them.

- Practice more than one signal for "yes;" no response can be used to mean "no."

- Start by asking broad questions, and then ask more and more specific questions as you get an idea as to what your child is thinking about or wanting to say.

- Use simple sentences to get to the main point. For example, ask "Are you hungry?" instead of "Do you want something for dinner?" Remember the "KIS" principle: "Keep It Simple."

- Remind your child what the "yes" signal is before asking each question.

- Wait longer than usual for your child to respond.

- If your child has a hard time responding, repeat the question or simplify it. For

> Caelyn Kaise is a Speech-language Pathologist with the Brain Tumor Program at the Hospital for Sick Children in Toronto, Canada.

example, if you've asked "Are you hungry?" simplify by saying, "Hungry?"

- To make sure your child's message is understood correctly, repeat what you think he said. For example, "Okay, you are hungry," or "So you're not hungry." This gives your child a chance to confirm that his message was interpreted correctly.

- Be patient with yourself, your child, and the process.

- When exploring emotional issues, ensure that you understand your child's unique perspective rather than thinking about it only from an adult perspective. In other words, focus on how your child is thinking and feeling, not how you would think or feel in the same situation.

Communication

Preparing for the unexpected

It is hard to prepare for something when you don't know what to expect. Brain tumors affect children's abilities in different ways at different times, but some changes are more common than others and can be anticipated. For example, speech often starts sounding slurred and can be difficult to understand due to weakness or difficulty coordinating the lips, tongue, and jaw. Children's abilities to use their arms and hands may also become compromised, making it difficult for them to write, draw, or point.

Regardless of the kinds of difficulties children with diffuse intrinsic pontine gliomas (DIPGs) have, the parents we interviewed agreed that two important strategies helped maximize communication with them.

1. **Learn and practice ways your child can communicate without speech before your child needs to use them.** This is not always easy. Children can be reluctant to use communication strategies before they absolutely have to, and parents and children often do not want to think about a time when these strategies will be necessary. This reticence is natural and understandable. However, the patience and concentration that are needed to learn a new skill may not be present once your child's energy and abilities are declining.

2. **Practice more than one way of communicating without words.** This way, if some of your child's abilities change in an unexpected way, she can continue to communicate using

> Ceilidh Eaton Russell is a Child Life Specialist with the Max and Beatrice Wolfe Children's Centre at the Temmy Latner Centre for Palliative Care, and a Researcher at the Hospital for Sick Children in Toronto, Canada.

another familiar means. When practicing other ways to communicate, it is often useful to find a way to adapt a current communication tool or technique to suit your child's changing abilities rather than switching to a brand new system. By adapting a strategy that children and families are more familiar with, their experiences serve as "practice" and they may feel more comfortable and confident in their abilities to use it.

In this chapter, we present some concrete examples of communication tools and strategies to use with children who have a DIPG. This is in no way an exhaustive list, but it serves as a stepping stone to understand how to maximize communication.

Different ways to ask questions

Two techniques that are very useful when helping children express a wide range of messages are:

1. Offering two clear choices.

2. Asking questions that can be answered with a "yes" or "no."

These techniques require you to ask clear and carefully worded questions and will take thought and practice.

Offering two clear choices

No matter what a child's functional ability is, he/she is likely to be able to choose between two things, whether by pointing at or by looking at different objects. It is important to clearly tell your child what the two choices are and then ask your child to show you which one he wants.

For example: A parent can hold chocolate milk in one hand and juice in the other. After showing them to the child and saying what is in each hand, the parent then asks the child which one he/she would like, reminding him/her to point or look at the drink he/she wants. Once the child has made a choice, the parent should double-check by asking, "Do you mean that you want the juice?" then wait for him/her to show that he/she means "Yes."

When a child is choosing between two things that you cannot show him/her, try asking a series of questions to find out what he/she wants. For example:

1. "I wonder if you would rather go for a walk or take a bath?"

2. "I'll ask you about one thing at a time, and then I'll wait after each one in case you want to say "yes."

3. "So, want to go for a walk?" After asking this question, pause for at least 10 seconds.

4. If your child does not respond, say, "Okay. Want to take a bath?"

It may take your child longer than usual to make a choice, so remember to wait for a response. If your child does not respond, here are a few things to try.

1. Ask if he/she needs you to remind him/her of the signal for "yes."

2. Ask if he/she needs you to remind him/her, what the options are, then wait for him/her to respond. If he/she says "yes," repeat the series of questions above and wait for his/her response.

3. Ask if he/she does not want either of the choices that were offered, and wait for him/her to respond. If he/she says "yes," try to think of other options he/she may prefer.

Offering choices helps children feel like they have some control. Although with this method it can take a long time to find out what your child wants, it is usually worth the extra effort.

Using "Yes" or "No" questions

Even when it's very difficult for children to choose between two things, caregivers can help them express themselves by asking questions that can be answered with a simple "yes" or "no." This is a technique that can be used with a wide range of other communication tools and techniques and a method that will come up numerous times throughout this chapter.

Children can show they mean "yes" in a range of ways, including:

- Nodding their heads.

- Giving a "thumbs up."

- Wiggling a finger up and down.

- Raising their eyebrows.

- Looking up (like nodding with their eyes).

- Wrinkling their nose.

- Wiggling their toes or moving a foot.

**Remember to practice more than one signal for "yes!"

Any part of the body that the child can control can be used as a signal for "yes." **Instead of making a second signal for "no," it is easier to assume that if the child doesn't say "yes," he means "no."** This creates less confusion about which signal to use for which word. When practicing this technique, ask your child to choose a couple of signals, then ask him/her five "yes" or "no" questions that you know the answers to and make sure your answers match his/her signals. If they match, you're ready to start!

Some questions may have more than one meaning, so it is very important to ask in a way that is clear and direct. For example, asking your child, "How are you feeling?" can be confusing, because it could refer to physical or emotional "feelings." Instead be specific; ask "Are you sad?" or "Does your body feel okay?" This allows your child to respond with a clear "yes" or "no."

When there are fewer clues about what your child wants or needs, start by asking broad questions, then ask more and more specific questions based on your child's responses. For example, if your child seemed upset you could start by asking, "Is something bothering you?" If the answer is "yes," you can ask more specific questions one at a time until she says "yes" again. The following is an example of a progressive series of questions.

1. "Is it something in your body that's bothering you?"

   - If she says "yes," ask, "Is it your head?" or "Is it your stomach?" continuing to ask about different body parts until she says "yes." Remember to pause after each question to wait for a response.

     o Once your child says "yes" about a particular body part, ask, "Is it sore?" "Is it itchy?" or "Is it hot?" etc.

If he/she does not say "yes" to any part of the body, say "Okay, maybe it's not something in your body that's bothering you. Are you feeling upset about something?" If he/she says, "yes," ask questions about specific feelings, such as, "Are you sad? Are you feeling frustrated?" until he/she says "yes" to something. If your child does not say "yes," try asking, "Is it something you're thinking about?" or "Are you worried about something?"

This example illustrates that it is often easier to know what to ask when the topic is concrete, such as physical sensations or finding out what a child wants to do. Talking about more abstract concepts, such as emotions and ideas can be much more complicated because there are many more possible questions. Because of this, you will need to ask a lot more questions when discussing these topics.

If you continue to ask questions without being able to figure out what your child wants and he/she becomes frustrated, it is good to talk with your child and explain in the following way.

1. "I know that you know what you want to say. This is really hard for both of us, but I want to try to help."

   - Then ask, "Should I keep trying to figure out what you're thinking or should we take a break? I'm going to ask you that again and wait for you to show me "yes" after the one that you want me to do."

     o Then repeat these two options, pausing in between for your child's response.

It is especially important to be patient with the process, and with yourself and your child, during these discussions.

Figuring out what to ask

Although interactions may feel different when a child has trouble speaking, he/she is still the same person as before. Try to consider past experiences with your child, including his/her typical behaviors, preferences and needs, to give you clues about what he/she would want now.

Facial expressions and body language

When you recognize a familiar facial expression, it probably means the same thing it used to mean. In addition to telling you about their feelings and moods, a child's face or body can also show you whether he/she is comfortable (through a relaxed body) or uncomfortable (through a tense body or face).

Tumors may affect facial muscles for some children, making facial expressions look different than they used to. However, parents often say that even with these changes they can recognize what their child is expressing, especially because the children's eyes continue to show a lot of emotions.

Routines and preferences

Time of day, familiar routines and the context of a situation can offer clues about whether your child is tired, hungry, wants to bathe, go outside, or play. Although children may have to do these things in a different way than they used to, if they are losing some of their abilities it is still helpful and comforting for them to participate in familiar activities as frequently as possible. Thinking about the situation—where you are, who's around, and what you are doing—will also help narrow down the questions or the needs the child may currently have.

We have found that while it may feel like there are a million things a child could want or need; it is often the simplest things that the child wants. Try to always start with basic questions, such as whether the child wants to sit up or change position. If the child has a communication tool, check to see if that's what the child is asking for.

Coping with the challenges of communication

If you feel daunted, frustrated or overwhelmed, try to remember that although this can be an incredibly difficult task, **YOU CAN DO IT**. In fact, you have probably done it already, before your child learned how to speak as a baby. Although he/she has developed intellectually since that time and now has more complex ideas to express, remember that with your help, your child was able to learn a new way of communicating once before and will again. Try to be patient with yourself, keeping in mind that the difficulties you may face with this new way of communicating are caused by this enormously challenging situation; always remember that you're doing the best job you can. If you need to, take breaks to manage your own stress. Young people can sense your anxiety, stress, or frustration, so allow yourself the time to refocus and know that this is a challenging process for any parent.

Communication Strategies

Families have shared with us a range of creative communication strategies they have used, which fall into two categories:

1. **Tools:** meaning there is an actual "thing" to help the child express himself.

2. **Techniques:** referring to a special way of communicating without using a physical tool.

Please note: this may be an overwhelming list of possibilities. We've included these to assist you in finding what will work best in your situation; you are not expected to use them all.

Tools

- A bell or buzzer: These can be used to get someone's attention if the child is in a different room, or be used as a way to say "yes."

- Paper and pencil/markers: For kids who have learned to print or write, this is a familiar way to express their thoughts.

- **Magna Doodle:** Children can write messages, draw pictures, or draw an arrow to point the Magna Doodle at what they want. Kids typically enjoy these because they are familiar and feel like using a toy rather than a "special device," and because they are easy to use.

- **Laptop/tablet:** Children who know how to type like using laptops because they can send emails or type messages for someone to read while they type. They also tend to like that they can watch movies on the same device, although for some the laptops are too heavy.

- **Keyboard:** A few children have used regular keyboards that are not connected to computers. They press a series of letters to spell a message while someone else watches and reads what they typed. Special keyboards that have the letters in alphabetical order can also be used. These tools help children express a wide range of messages, but some people who have used the keyboards say it can take a long time to type messages and a child can forget what letters they have already typed. Many families create their own keyboards by clearly writing the alphabet in large letters on a piece of paper or cardboard for the child to point to.

- **Picture books or boards:** These can be like scrapbooks or a piece of cardboard with photos or drawings and words, made by family and friends. Children can point to a picture or word, or parents scroll through, pointing to one message at a time and waiting for the child to say "yes" when they point at the right message. Some people find it frustrating to search for the right message, especially when the child wants to say something that is not included in the book or board.

- **Feelings faces:** A chart showing a variety of faces, including happy, sad, angry, frustrated, lonely, bored, excited, hopeful, etc., can help children to express themselves by pointing (or having their parents point) to the feeling they are having. The number of faces to include depends on a child's age and abilities; faces can be added or taken away as a child's needs change.

- **High-tech communication devices:** These devices usually have buttons for children to press, with each button causing a different message to be spoken, allowing kids to express a range of messages. While some children like using these, others do not, because certain devices are complicated, seem unfamiliar, and are sometimes hard to use or learn or feel impersonal.

Tips about tools

- For kids who are able to read, include words as well as pictures or symbols in communication tools. Children will associate the words with the symbols so if it later becomes difficult to read the words, they are still familiar with the meaning of the symbols.

- Include your child in creating their communication tools (such as books, boards, high-tech devices) as much as possible. By choosing which images will represent different words, feelings, activities, etc., your child maintains some control and will feel more connected and involved in the process. Involving children also promotes familiarity and makes them feel more invested in using the tools.

- As much as possible, consider your child's individual voice. For some families this means recording the child's voice on a high-tech device or a voice recorder, saying common messages so he/she can hear his/her own voice. Families who have done this typically treasure the recording and encourage other families to do this as early as possible. When such a recording is not possible, families can record another child's voice that sounds similar in age and gender. Many parents have said that it wasn't just about the sound of the child's voice but the kinds of things that he/she would have wanted to say. By including jokes, sayings or common phrases, a child's unique personality is able to continue shining through in a meaningful way.

- If you are using a tool that has preset messages or pictures in it, such as a picture book or a high tech device, your child may want to express something that is not included in the tool. In this case, be sure to ask your child about messages that are not in the tool. Ask, "Is it something that isn't in here?" to find out if that's the case. Then you can use "yes" or "no" questions to find out what your child is thinking, and to decide whether or not to add that new message to the tool.

Techniques

Most families we interviewed said they use special ways of asking questions, such as offering two choices, asking "yes" or "no" questions, and reading their children's body language and facial expressions. Some families also used the following techniques:

- **Signs and signals:** They use their hands or their faces, or adapt sign language, especially by using the first letter of a person's name to refer to that person. An example of a signal would be a child holding an imaginary cup up to their mouth to show she is thirsty.

- **Pointing:** Children can point to things to show what they want, such as pointing to a window to say they want to go outside. If a child is uncomfortable, he/she can point to the part of his/her body, or a picture of a body, to show others where he/she feels discomfort.

- **Lip reading:** Some children have trouble producing sounds or words but are still able to make the shape of words with their mouths. For children who have trouble hearing, a few parents say that by mouthing words slowly, and exaggerating their mouth's movements, their children can figure out what they are saying.

- **Physical presence, touch and hugs:** When it is too hard to use words, being close to one another and sharing affection are great ways of expressing emotions and love.

- **Lists:** Many parents said it was very important to keep three kinds of lists, and to keep adding to them, including:

  1. Signals, such as what the signals look like and what they mean, (i.e., "pointing to mouth means hungry or thirsty").

  2. Common questions that caregivers ask, things that the child frequently asks or says, or issues or needs that the child has.

  3. Clues to a child's needs, such as body language, time of day, or anything else that can help caregivers figure out what the child wants or needs.

These lists may help you remember or think of what to ask, and improve communication when someone else, who is less familiar with his communication strategies, is caring for your child.

Tips about communication in general

- When possible, try to adapt familiar communication tools to meet a child's changing needs rather than introducing new tools.

- Keep talking **to your child**. Avoid asking questions that they can't answer; stick with "yes" or "no" questions, but keep including your child and asking her opinions.

- Teach siblings how to communicate using the new tools or techniques. This helps to encourage interaction and maintain sibling connection.

- Use communication strategies to play games with your child to improve comfort using the strategies. Children who are able to say "yes" can play twenty questions; children who are using a communication book can choose a message while others try to guess what it is. Play charades by having your child point out one message for another person to act out.

- Try to be patient with yourself, your child, and the process. There is no easy way to do this. Try to stay calm, take deep breaths, and take care of yourself. Parents and their children can often feel frustrated and helpless. In the midst of this difficult process, one of the most important things for children to hear is: "I know that you know what you want to say."

Challenges

Some children are reluctant to use tools before they are needed and may feel the tools undermine their current abilities. If a child refuses to use a certain tool, try telling him/her that he/she does not have to use it right now but that you want to show him/her how it works anyway. That way if you need to reintroduce it later, it will be familiar.

While we do not want to force children to use a communication tool they don't want to use, if their abilities change unexpectedly and they have not already had the chance to learn and practice communication strategies, it can be even more challenging for them to use new techniques to express themselves. For these reasons, we recommend that families talk about and practice a range of communication strategies rather than focusing only on one.

Try adopting old strategies as much as possible so your child can keep using the same approach in a slightly different way, rather than learning something completely new. For example, start with a picture board with many small pictures, and if your child's vision starts to change, narrow down the number of pictures, spread them out, and enlarge them so they're easier to see. Practicing a variety of techniques and adapting them (rather than starting something totally different) are ways of helping children feel familiar with different communication strategies.

Sometimes you may need to communicate in the midst of a crisis situation or while your child is distressed; these moments may be brought on by physical and/ or emotional pain that the child is feeling. It is important to know how to calm yourself and your child so you will be able to work together and communicate effectively to manage these situations. Practice calming techniques together on a regular basis. Some examples are deep breathing, blowing bubbles, soothing touch, or focusing on each other. These techniques are helpful because when you and your child are calm, you will be able to communicate more effectively, which is especially important in an urgent situation.

Deciding what to try

Choosing a strategy for communicating with your child depends upon the child's abilities and personal preferences. Consult with your child's team to find out what strategies might be the best suited to your child's needs, abilities, and preferences. Then, considering your child's personality, decide which ones to try. Together you can decide which ones work best. Some children are open to using familiar tools that feel like play, such as drawing, writing, or using a Magna Doodle. Remember that the emphasis of communication should be on the connection between you and your child rather than the content of the messages.

While it is often easier for a child to keep doing what is familiar rather than trying something new, sometimes there is no choice. If a communication strategy is no longer working, or if your child is getting too frustrated, it is time for a change!

Communication Topics

Parents we spoke with felt it was important to be able to talk about "everything:" physical comfort, feelings, worries and "regular conversations" about friends, jokes, hobbies, and daily activities. Some messages were more concrete—hunger, discomfort—which are easier for children to express by pointing to a picture or an object, or answering "yes" or "no" questions. Abstract topics such as emotions, spirituality, and the future are more difficult to discuss, requiring caregivers to ask more questions in order to help a child express what he/she is thinking and feeling.

Parents described some of the most important topics they addressed with their children, and strategies they used to do so. It may seem overwhelming to think about all of the topics or messages your child may want to express, and the charts, lists, or strategies you could create. Remember that becoming familiar with communication strategies will happen over time and with support from family, friends, and your child's team at the hospital.

The way you communicate throughout this time will be shaped by your family's values, belief systems, personalities, and previous experiences communicating, especially about difficult topics. While we know sharing information and discussing feelings helps children and families cope and support one another, there is no "right" way to go through this experience.

Physical and health needs

Parents described important conversations they'd had with their children about how their abilities had changed and that the changes would continue. Although these can be difficult discussions, children cope better when their questions are answered than when they are left to wonder and make up their own answers. To assist with talking with, or responding to your child's physical needs, below is a chart [Table: 1] outlining some issues and approaches.

Child's Messages	Parents' Questions
Ouch/I'm in pain/Something's hurting.	"Is something hurting?"/"Are you in pain?" If "yes," ask: "Can you show me where it hurts?" Point to different parts of your child's body, or to a picture of a body, or even name different body parts—"Is it your head?"/"Is it your stomach?"—and ask your child to let you know when you've said, or when you have pointed at the part of the body where he/she feels pain. Remind your child how to signal "yes."
I'm uncomfortable.	"Are you uncomfortable?" If "yes," ask (one at a time, slowly, until your child indicates "yes"). "Do you feel stiff/numbness/itchy/dizzy/hot/cold/weak?"
I need to move/I need to change positions.	"Do you want to move/change positions?" If "yes," ask (one at a time, slowly, until your child indicates "yes"). "Do you want to sit up/lean back/lie down/roll over/move over/sit somewhere else/lie down somewhere else/go outside?"
I need to go to the bathroom.	"Do you need to go to the bathroom?" If "yes," ask (one at a time, slowly, until your child indicates "yes"). "Do you need to use the toilet or a new diaper/take a shower or bath/brush your teeth/brush your hair/wash your face?"
I'm hungry.	"Are you hungry?" If "yes," offer food choices, one at a time, slowly, until your child indicates "yes."

Child's Messages	Parents' Questions
I'm thirsty.	"Are you thirsty?" If "yes," offer various drink choices, one at a time, slowly, until your child indicates "yes."
I need my walker/wheelchair.	"Do you want your walker/wheelchair?"

Table 1: Questions and responses

Medical needs

Children we spoke with wanted to know about medical equipment, tests, and procedures, including the use of different medical equipment, how it works, and what procedures will feel like. When a procedure will be uncomfortable, people may be afraid of upsetting children by telling them the truth. Unfortunately, when children are caught off guard by a needle or other unpleasant things, they do not have the chance to react and then calm down and then try to cope with the experience before it is time for the procedure. Children may also begin to doubt caregivers and to think that things are being kept from him even when they're not.

Children benefit from knowing what to expect—where a procedure will take place, who will be there, what steps are involved, and what it will feel like. This information gives kids a chance to prepare for what will happen and practice coping strategies, such as deep breathing, blowing bubbles, holding your hand, listening to music or a story, using guided imagery, or squeezing a stress-ball. Children may also benefit by watching a simulated procedure on a play-therapy doll or stuffed animal like American Childhood Cancer Organization's Cozy, the "Port-a-Cat."

When explaining medical procedures to children, it is important to be honest, to use language that is clear and simple, and to check in with them by asking "Does that make sense or would you like me to try to explain it in a different way?"

Children may also want to know why treatments are needed, how to know if they're working, and what happens if they don't work. When a child finishes or stops a certain treatment, he/she may wonder what that means, whether it is because the disease is gone or because it can't be cured. These are difficult concepts to explain, but if a child has a question, it is better to explore the answers honestly and openly together than for a child to rely on his own imagination. These issues can be overwhelming for children to think about on their own; talking about them together offers reassurance and support for the child even when there aren't clear-cut answers.

It is helpful to talk to children about what kinds of information they want to be told about their illness, treatment, and side effects, before communication gets more difficult. That way you have an idea of what your child wants to know about and you can continue to provide the information your child wants and needs throughout his/her journey.

Emotions

To talk about feelings you can use charts with pictures of different facial expressions or use a list of feelings. Your child can point to the face that shows how he/she feels, or you can point and look for your child to indicate when the right answer is selected.

It is helpful to offer a wide range of feelings so your child can express his/her true emotions, rather than settling for one that is "close but not quite right." On the other hand, if your child is getting overwhelmed, use a shorter list or chart with four to eight simpler feelings such as happy, sad, scared, mad, bored, etc. Try to use words that are familiar to your child and make sense given her age. If possible, try to include your child in creating this list of feelings to ensure she is familiar with all the words and that she has some control.

Strategies for talking about emotions

Ask your child if he/she feels a certain way. For example, "Are you feeling happy?" or "You look frustrated, are you feeling that way?" This offers your child the chance to express an emotion and to offer some control by answering "yes" or "no."

Share how you are feeling and then ask your child whether he/she is feeling the same way. This helps a child express his feelings and reassures him/her that others feel that way, too. However, it is important to recognize that children may feel differently than the people around them; this is perfectly normal. Try to say something like, "I've been feeling pretty sad and I wonder if you have, too. You know, it's okay to feel sad and it's okay not to, too."

Children need to be reassured that all of the feelings they have, no matter how intense, unfamiliar or conflicted, are natural. Let your child know that even though these are not "easy" feelings to have, they are natural, understandable, and "okay." A lot of emotional messages can be conveyed through hugs and touch. Being close and making eye contact also helps children feel more connected and comforted.

Activities

When a child's abilities change what he/she is able to do or play with, it is helpful to have a list of things that your child **can** do to choose from. Lists also help parents so they don't always have to remember all of the options. Some of the most common activities that parents we interviewed said their children enjoyed were: listening to music, watching a movie, hearing a story, going outside, playing a game, writing to someone, making food, or visiting friends.

People and pets

Maintaining relationships with family and friends is very important for young people. Parents and caregivers can help by giving children a way to ask to see a special person, or to send them a message. Create a chart with names and photos of family members, friends, and even pets, for children to point to.

Many children ask about people they know who have died, wondering where they are now, whether they are "okay" and commenting that they miss these people. It is natural for a child who has a serious illness to start thinking about life and death and loved ones who have died. It can be a safe way to wonder about these things, an indirect way for children to show you that they're thinking about death, and a way to start a difficult conversation. Also, when children realize their loved ones are still remembered and loved after they've died, it offers them the reassurance that they, too, will be remembered and loved after their death.

The Future and Spirituality

It is natural for children to wonder about these topics, especially as they feel their bodies changing and sense the emotions in the people around them. It can be very hard for children to initiate conversations, especially when they fear that talking about these things will be upsetting for others. They may ask questions in indirect ways, such as asking about the death of a pet, or the death of someone else, or general questions about what happens after you die. Because of how difficult it can be for children to bring up these topics, it is very important to support them when they want to have these conversations, rather than avoiding or changing the subject.

If your child has questions about death and spirituality, try to answer his/her questions as honestly, clearly and calmly as you can. He/she may ask you questions you don't have answers to. That's okay. You can say you're not sure, that many people wonder about questions like that, and that it's okay to wonder about these things together, even without finding any answers.

In interviewing parents, some of the biggest struggles they said they faced were about whether or not to tell a child that he/she could or would die and how to do that. Research and our own clinical experiences suggest that children and families benefit from having open and honest conversations. Families who do this said they did not later regret having had these conversations. Many parents said that even though it was so hard for them to talk about these things, after they had spoken with their child about death or spirituality, they realized the child seemed comforted and relieved, and that they—as parents—did as well. Whether you decide to talk with your child about death and spirituality and how you do this is up to you and will be a very personal decision based on your experiences and your beliefs.

About the future

For some children, thinking about the future can include writing a will, exploring organ donation, or planning a memorial celebration. Parents often worry that talking about these things with their children will cause them to lose hope. On the contrary, if a child is already thinking about these things, the opportunity to share his/her thoughts and feelings about them with loved ones can offer tremendous comfort and relief, a sense of control, and the opportunity to plan his/her own legacy.

You can also talk about how you will remember and honor your child at holidays, family events, birthdays, and other special times. Some families have a special meal or celebration, wear a special piece of clothing or jewelry, listen to a certain song or musician, or make up their own unique rituals for these special times. Others may plant a memorial tree or garden, hold a fundraiser, or create a scholarship in the child's name. Some children have their own ideas about how they want their family to remember them, and many children want to be involved in family discussions about this. Not only does it reassure the child that he/she will not be forgotten but it gives him/her a clear idea of exactly how her family will remember and feel connected to him/her.

About spirituality

Some children ask their parents questions about what happens after someone dies, what they will do when they are in heaven, or how their families will feel their presence. Whatever your beliefs are, you can share them with your child. Many people don't know what they believe, or may believe that there is nothing after death. If this is the case for you, you can explain to your child that many people have different beliefs and that you're not sure what will happen, or that you're not sure whether any of them will happen; either way, ask your child what he/she thinks, or would like to think.

Regardless of what you believe about what happens after death, you can talk with your child about how he/she will always be part of your family even though he/she will not be physically present. Things he/she taught others, personality traits, his/

her values, and hobbies that he/she shared with others, are all deeply meaningful ways that his/her life will continue to impact his/her loved ones.

Caring for Your Children and Yourselves

This is a very difficult and challenging experience for parents and children. Developing strategies to manage the impact of the ongoing loss of abilities can be as important as developing communication strategies. This section is meant to assist parents and caregivers in thinking about and addressing some of these challenges.

Supporting the child with a brain tumor

Here are examples of some of the challenges and concerns that parents described and the things that can help kids deal with them. Strategies from the previous sections will assist in dealing with these issues.

Feeling frustrated

When a child finds that he/she can no longer do something that used to be easy to do, or realizes that so much about his/her body or his/her life is beyond his/her control, frustration is a natural reaction. The loss of independence or needing help with things such as eating or going to the bathroom can be very upsetting, especially as children realize they will not regain the ability to do those things on their own. This kind of frustration might be expressed in different ways, such as being impatient or getting angry. One way to help children cope with these feelings is to help them find ways to express themselves with words added to a communication board or book, or physically using a stress ball made out of Play-Doh.

People often want to cheer kids up when they are feeling upset; sometimes they try to distract them by talking about something fun or focusing on an activity. But when children have these strong feelings, they need ways for their feelings to be expressed and heard—and to know that someone else understands—before they are ready to move beyond these emotions. It's important to be patient and let your child know that you will work together to figure out what he/she wants or needs, whatever it may be.

Feeling self-conscious

As their bodies and their abilities change, it is common for children to feel less comfortable around others. Children, particularly teenagers, are often fearful about being seen as "different" or being treated "differently" than others.

Educating a child's peers about his/her illness, explaining that a tumor is not contagious and that it is the reason for his/her changing abilities, and helping them learn useful communication techniques can be a very good way to help them understand and relate to one another. There may be someone at your child's hospital—such as a nurse, a child life specialist, or a social worker—who can visit your child's classroom to talk about these things. Teachers and other school staff are often very helpful in organizing this kind of classroom experience. On the other hand, some children feel strongly that they do not want other people to know about their illness and would not be comfortable having someone speak with their classmates. Sometimes it helps to talk with your child about what he/she is afraid would happen if others found out, and you may be able to dispel these fears and facilitate the connection.

However, if your child does not change his/her mind, it is important to respect his/her wishes in order to avoid your child feeling embarrassed, helpless, or even vulnerable. There are so few things that a child in this situation can control that deciding what information to share with others may be one of the few things that he/she can control.

A few parents described their children feeling self-conscious about communication. MSN and other online chat systems, email, social networking sites, text messages, or even written letters can be great ways to help children keep in touch with their friends without having to feel so self-conscious. Also, if your child is comfortable with you teaching others how to use the specific communication strategies your family has developed, with time and practice, his/her feelings of self-consciousness may decrease.

Missing familiar people and activities

Familiarity provides so much comfort to children. When it's possible to help children continue to participate in these kinds of activities, even if it means participating in a different way than they used to, it can be very helpful for them. On the other hand, some children may find that there are some things they don't want to continue being involved in. If this is the case for your child, try to help him explain why he feels this way. It may be that he/she is self-conscious and afraid of how others might treat him/her, in which case you can talk to him/her about anything that can be done to help make the situation more comfortable or inviting. In some cases a child may feel uncomfortable or even unsafe in different environments. Whatever the situation, respecting your child's wishes as much as possible will help him/her feel more comfortable and safe and give him/her a sense of control.

Coping with medical experiences

Play is a great way to help children cope with difficult experiences. In times of stress, play may be the furthest thing from our minds, but it may also be the most valuable tool. Blowing bubbles, bringing paper and crayons to draw or play tic-tac-toe, a deck of cards, or even a list of games such as "I Spy" or "Twenty Questions" are all simple and useful distractions. For older children and teenagers, think back to what has helped them before; listening to music, playing a video game, or reading a book may be useful distraction techniques.

Guided imagery, deep breathing, and other relaxation techniques can also help children of all ages cope with anxiety related to medical issues. Talking with your child about what is happening, what medical procedures might feel like, and any other questions or concerns they might have will help them better manage these experiences.

Knowing they will be cared for

Parents highlighted that it was extremely important for their children to know that they would be well cared for. This concept included three things.

1. Knowing that the health care team would continue to care for them. When they know that a disease or a tumor is not curable, children may think that means there will be no more medical care.

2. Knowing that they will still be looked after and that their pain and other symptoms will still be managed is very important.

3. Knowing that they are not alone and that their parents and their family will always be with them and love them "no matter what." When children are struggling with how they're feeling and the ways their bodies are changing, this may be the most valuable comfort you can offer them.

Children's concern for others

Another common and important concern parents told us about is children's worries about whether their parents and their families will be okay after the child dies. Parents said it is very important to address these concerns by letting your child know two things: that the family will be sad and will miss the child after he/she dies, but at the same time, the family will be alright. Families did their best to try to ease the child's burden of worrying about how his/her loved ones will cope. It's important to express one's love for the child while acknowledging the impact of his/her loss.

The importance of communicating

Parents told us that they often feel helpless and frustrated that they are not able to change the situation and protect their child from what is happening. Of course this feeling is natural. Sometimes in an attempt to protect a child, parents avoid talking with their child about his/her illness or letting him/her know that he/she is going to die. Although this is done with the best intentions, it does not have the impact parents hope for. Some of the unintended, possible consequences are:

- When children are not invited to talk about their illness, they learn from others' example not to raise the issue themselves. Without having someone to talk to about their thoughts and worries, they are left to wonder on their own, using their imaginations to answer their own questions.

- Children are very sensitive to the emotions of the people around them and know when others are upset. They can recognize when something is being kept from them and can only wonder what that might be, often imagining the worst.

- Children are more aware than anyone of the changes occurring in their own bodies. Although they may not know what will happen in the future, they have learned that unpredictable changes can continue to occur. If they do not feel able to talk about their illness or the future, they are left to face these questions and fears on their own.

With these things in mind, it is clear that protecting a child from talking about his/her illness does not protect him/her from the difficult experience he/she is already living. Instead of letting this fact make you feel helpless, try to see that it actually offers you an important opportunity. You are not helpless. Even though no one can change what is happening, there is a great deal that you can do to help your child through this experience. As we've discussed in this section, there are some very important messages that will offer your child comfort, reassurance, and security. Make sure your child knows the following.

- Your child is not alone. You will be there to support him/her throughout this experience.

- Your child can trust you. You can truthfully prepare him/her for things such as medical procedures and other events so he/she feels less anxious and surprised by these things. Your child's health care team at the hospital can help you figure out how to do this.

- Your child will be well cared for. You can reassure your child that you, your family, and your child's health care team will all be working to make sure that he/she has what he/she needs to feel comfortable and taken care of.

- Your child will always be part of your family. You can talk about all of the things you will remember and all of the ways that your child will continue to have an important place in your family.

- Your family and people who know and love your child will be incredibly sad when he/she dies, but your family members and friends will support one another through their grief.

Although these things cannot change what is happening to your child, they can make him/her feel supported in the knowledge that he/she will not be alone. Nothing can take away the pain that your child and your family will struggle with, but these important messages can offer your child support and strength as you face what is happening, together.

Supporting siblings

As a parent, you may not only be supporting a child who has a DIPG but also his or her siblings. There are some issues that are common for children who have a sibling living with a serious illness, and these can vary depending on the age of the children. For example, many children in this situation have questions about why this happened, worries about their own and/or their sibling's health, and concerns about their parents' emotional struggles. It is also very common for children to wonder if they are somehow to blame for a sibling's illness and to worry that they may also "catch" the illness. Even if a child has not expressed these worries, it is helpful to say something like, "I just want to make sure you know that there is nothing you could have done to make this happen and that this is not the kind of illness you can catch from someone else."

Siblings may also have questions about the future. The suggestions in this chapter about how to talk with a child about his or her own illness and the future, as discussed in the previous sections, also apply to talking with the child's siblings.

Many of the parents we spoke with shared their suggestions about how to help brothers and sisters.

- Make sure the siblings are able to continue spending time together at home or in the hospital.

- Help all of your children learn how to use the new communication strategies, as it can help children continue to interact with each other and maintain their relationships.

- Encourage siblings to say "hello" and "goodbye" to their sibling when they come home and when they go out.

- Encourage interactions that help a sick child continue to feel recognized and included in the family's day-to-day activities despite their changing abilities.

Brothers and sisters may be reluctant or nervous about learning new communication strategies, and may be afraid of doing it "wrong" or looking silly if they do. Just like teaching communication strategies to a child who is sick, it can also help to use games to teach these strategies to their siblings, and to practice with them until they feel more comfortable using them. They may also need your help to understand why their brother or sister isn't able to talk the way they used to. Because they may not be able to see any physical evidence of something stopping their sibling from being able to speak, some children wonder why their brother or sister just doesn't try harder. It helps to explain that our brains are like computers that send signals or instructions to all of the other parts of our body to make it work, including our arms, legs, stomach, heart, lungs, eyes, ears, mouth, etc. When a person has a brain tumor, it interferes with, or "mixes up," some signals so that things don't always work the way they're supposed to. This is why some children who have brain tumors aren't able to speak the way they used to.

Similarly, children may not know how to interact or play with their brother or sister since their abilities have changed. They may also believe that their sibling doesn't want to play with them anymore. Again, it is important to explain that these changes are caused by the tumor rather than being the child's choice. Then you can help your children find new ways of playing or being together. Healthy siblings can read stories to their brother or sister, watch movies or listen to music together. They can also play "for" their sibling; some examples of this are making a beaded bracelet or building a LEGO tower by asking their sibling what color bead or LEGO block to use next. They can also draw a picture or write a story based on their sibling's ideas about what to draw or write. When thinking about how to help children play together, consider what they used to do together and try to find ways to adapt those activities. Children may have a hard time trying new things; it can be easier and more comfortable to do what feels familiar.

Some other considerations we've learned about siblings are:

- Healthy siblings need opportunities to play for themselves.

- They will need your assistance to find a balance between feeling helpful without taking on too much responsibility for their sibling with a brain tumor.

- Even when they understand why their brother or sister needs the extra attention, siblings need support to make sense of, and express, their emotions and possible feelings of jealousy about the extra attention their ill sibling is getting.

- Sometimes siblings are asked to be patient, helpful, and understanding for a long time, which isn't easy. This is a challenging experience for children of all ages, and their frustrations can be expressed differently at different developmental stages.

- All children need to know that their needs will be met.

- Children of all ages need love and support from their parents, though how they express this need changes at different ages.

- It is important to recognize and tell each child how much you appreciate all that he or she has done throughout their sibling's illness, including specific examples when possible.

- Let them know that you recognize how challenging it has been and will continue to be and encourage them to let you know when they're struggling and need help.

Talking with your other children about how they are feeling, helping them to understand that all of their emotions are natural, and encouraging them to express any questions or fears that they have is very important and beneficial. There may be people at the hospital or at school, such as child life specialists, social workers, counselors, or volunteers who can help support children when their sibling is ill. There may also be local organizations that can provide support.

Parents' Advice for Other Parents

The parents we spoke with shared some very personal insights into their experiences that may be helpful advice for others parents. Some of these are reflections or quotes about a parent's outlook or important things that they tried to keep in mind while going through this same process with their child.

About relating to children

- Know your child, their personality, interests, coping styles, and preferences for support.

- Have important conversations sooner rather than later. Have important conversations about topics such as illness, life, death, your love for them, and spirituality as early as possible. Although these can be emotionally difficult conversations to have, they get even more difficult once children have a harder time communicating.

- Keep communicating. When a child can no longer express themselves to others, it can be hard to know whether or not to continue to talk to them. Communicating through story-telling and touch (including a hug, gently squeezing or rubbing a child's arm) can convey love, warmth, affection, and provide great comfort to a child.

About relating to one another as parents and as a family

Try to work together—as a couple, as parents, and as a family.

Asking questions and asking for help

- Whatever you want to know, ask. If there is anything you have wondered or worried about, do not hesitate to ask a member of your child's health care team.

- Whatever you need, ask. Different services will be available depending on the hospital or the community where you live. Ask a member of your child's health care team to help you find resources near you.

Acknowledgements

We want to express our sincerest thank you to the families who participated in this research and who shared their experiences and insights. Thank you to our colleagues, Dr. Eric Bouffet, Dr. Ute Bartels, Cindy Van Halderen and Dr. Tom Chau. Funding for this research and the creation of a handbook for families and caregivers has been generously provided by B.r.a.i.n.child at www.sickkids.ca/brainchild.

Parent Perspectives

Caleb was diagnosed with DIPG January 28th, 2010. At the time of diagnosis his speech was slightly slurred. Within a week of starting steroids and radiation this cleared completely until progression. In December 2010 we noticed his speech became very nasal; progression was confirmed January 13, 2011. Steroids and a second round of radiation helped but not completely.

In June 2011 he began having a lot of trouble with speech, to the point that no one, other than his father, his sister and me could understand 75% of what he was saying. Caleb was nine and a half years old at the time. This frustrated and upset him far more than any other symptoms, including the loss of strength in his left side and the ability to walk. He told us he could hear himself perfectly clear and could not understand why no one could understand him. He said that if he could hear what we heard then he would know how to try to fix his words, but since he heard himself "clear as a bell," he had no idea how to help us understand. This was extremely frustrating for him.

Initially he would speak one word at a time and we would repeat what we thought he had said until we guessed what that word was before moving on to the next word. Caleb was very witty—a funny little man who had the best "one-liners," so it saddened him so much when he would try to speak and no one understood. He told me that things are not funny when they have to be repeated over and over. That was when he began to withdraw.

We bought a small white board that we carried everywhere we went so he could write down whatever he wanted to say. It helped, but he missed talking and being part of conversations. When he spent time with friends he would become so sad because whenever he wanted to say something he would begin to write but by the time he was done writing, his friends had moved on to a new topic. That is when we insisted on more one-on-one visits instead of group visits with friends and family. This helped a lot because he didn't feel he had to compete to get his thoughts across and he didn't lose the chance to have his point heard.

As time went on and he began losing the ability to write (some days he could, and some days he couldn't) he would lose his interest in communicating and he didn't want those around him talking or communicating either. We found it very important to match his mood. If he was in a good mood it was okay to laugh and talk a little, but when he wasn't we tried to keep the house quiet and low key. Up until this point his relationship with his sister, Avery (seven and a half years old at the time) had held strong, but once Caleb's ability to communicate had diminished he did not want her around much and she avoided him as well. She learned very quickly to only ask "yes or no" questions and she would always ask if she could tell him something instead of bombarding him with her conversation. Giving him that choice helped him feel some sense of control. This helped with his patience and his willingness to listen to her.

We also made up small cards with words on them so he could pick out one or two that would help us guess what he was thinking. In the end when he was not able to move at all we wrote the letters of the alphabet on a white board, we would point to the letters and he would either nod or blink when we had the right letter, then we would move on to the next letter, spelling each word out. It was extremely slow but we only used this method when he needed something new or out of the ordinary.

Throughout the process of Caleb losing his ability to communicate, I become acutely aware of his needs. I learned his expressions and could usually guess fairly accurately what he wanted or needed through them. All of this was extremely hard for all of us to adjust to, but with these tools we were able to keep as much fun in his days as we could.

When Ella started to lose her ability to speak, we created a picture book with photos of all sorts of things she liked to do, needed to do, and feelings. When we couldn't understand her speech we would pull it out and flip the pages. She had just enough strength to point to the pictures. My favorite was the "I Love You" picture because I missed hearing her sweet voice say those words to me.

Warren's speech wasn't very good. People had a very hard time understanding him. I had a hard time too. He would have to repeat things a lot and he would get frustrated. Other than listening hard I didn't know what to do. Looking back both of us learning some simple sign language

such as drink, eat, bathroom might have helped.

Whereas in August and prior, Stella was speaking in full sentences with a huge vocabulary, now it takes her up to 30 seconds to squeak out one word, which is generally difficult if not impossible to comprehend.

We find it necessary to be close to him and looking directly at him to understand his speech. He is not at all frustrated by this and patiently repeats himself as often as necessary so that we know exactly what he wants to tell us.

It was Monday, Nov. 29th, when our 4-year-old Julian woke me at 5 a.m. I noticed he wasn't finishing his sentences as he kept repeating, "Mommy, I just wanna... I just... Mommy, I just wanna..." Crediting the early hour and perhaps a still sleepy state, we pulled him into our bed to sleep a little longer. When he woke again, this time vomiting, lethargic and still speaking as if confused, we knew something was terribly wrong.

Three months after that dreaded day and diagnosis, while searching for signs of hope on the internet, I came across a site filled with text by a father who had lost his daughter. He detailed DIPG treatment options and what to expect during "end of life" care. I read a passage about how most children lose the ability to speak in the last month or so due to tumor progression or, in the author's daughter's case, a "stroke-like" episode. I recall wanting to throw my computer across the room. Julian was famous for his sweet, raspy voice and endless chattiness. Our conversations were treasures and I could not bear the thought of not hearing his voice let alone him not being able to tell us what he needed or wanted.

A few weeks later, Julian did suffer a series of seizures that left his speech slowed but intact. In his final two weeks, he spoke less and less, but was still able to point and nod in answer to our questions. We were fortunate in that he still shared a few beautiful words right up until his last day.

Like many children with DIPG, Caleb was unable to speak during the final days of his life. At first, we developed a system of communication involving

both side to side and up and down eye movement. Then, he lost the ability to even move his eyeballs from side to side. After that, up was "yes" and down was "no."

We were at home, with Caleb set up in a hospital bed in the living room. His school principal (who had been his 5th grade teacher) contacted classmates she knew would want to see him and established a visitation schedule. The children were precious. They sat beside his bed and talked to him, read to him, remembered. The memory of his best friend sitting beside him on the bed is seared into my mind. His buddy was scared, unsure what to say, so I was trying to help. I explained something I'd been doing and concluded with, "but that gets on Caleb's nerves." Immediately, Caleb's eyes began moving up and down, up and down forcefully. He was clearly saying "YES IT DOES!" What a gift that even in those final hours and with such limited abilities, he continued to bless us with his quick wit and sense of humor. He helped his best buddy realize that even though his body was no longer cooperating, our Caleb was with us at that moment.

Chapter 13

Overcoming Research Hurdles in DIPG

Patricia Baxter, MD
Susan Blaney, MD

The treatment of childhood brain tumors remains a tremendous challenge for pediatric oncologists, particularly the treatment of aggressive brain tumors such as high-grade gliomas (e.g., anaplastic astrocytoma or glioblastoma multiforme [GBM]). This challenge is even greater when the tumor is located in an area of the brain that is not amenable to surgical resection, such as the hypothalamus or brainstem (pons). The subsets of pediatric glial tumors that are located in the brainstem are also known as brainstem gliomas (BSG), or diffuse intrinsic pontine gliomas (DIPGs). As discussed in previous chapters, the diagnosis of DIPG is most commonly made by a radiologist after reading the magnetic resonance imaging (MRI) scan, rather than by a pathologist after a neurosurgical procedure such as biopsy or tumor resection.

So how do we know that DIPGs are high-grade glial tumors if there is no biopsy or other surgical procedure to determine the tumor pathology? And because treatment progress for many other types of cancer has been the result of laboratory studies of human tumor tissue, how can scientists advance research on this type of tumor and develop effective treatments for children who have a DIPG without tissue from a biopsy or surgery? These important questions will be addressed in this chapter.

DIPG Research Hurdles

Physicians and scientists are optimistic that with modern scientific tools, progress will be realized in the treatment of children with DIPGs. Patients, parents, physicians, and scientists must all work together to overcome the research hurdles associated with DIPGs,

> Dr. Baxter is an Assistant Professor of Pediatrics at Texas Children's Cancer Center, and Baylor College of Medicine, Houston, TX.

one of the most, if not **the** most challenging childhood tumor.

Biopsy tissue challenges

The diagnosis of a DIPG is particularly difficult for many parents to accept because tumor biopsies with resulting pathology are not routinely performed for DIPGs in the majority of pediatric oncology centers. Surgical resection of DIPGs is not performed because the brainstem serves as the main roadway for all information that travels to and from the brain. The brainstem is critical for vital functions such as breathing, maintaining blood pressure and heart rate, along with other physiological functions essential to life (see chapter 3). DIPGs are physically located within the brainstem, and the tumor itself is intertwined with the non-cancerous cells that conduct these vital life functions. There is not a definitive border that distinguishes the tumor from the normal brain tissue, so DIPGs cannot be surgically removed.

Several decades ago, neurosurgeons routinely performed diagnostic biopsies on children with symptoms of a DIPG and found that these tumors were, with rare exception, high-grade glial tumors. With the advent of improved imaging technology and the widespread availability of MRI, it was found that a diagnosis of DIPG could reliably be made through a history, physical examination, and MRI. As a result, the practice of diagnostic biopsy was abandoned because of the small, but very real, risk of severe or life-threatening complications associated with a biopsy and the fact that past biopsy results have not changed treatment recommendations. This lack of available tissue from biopsy specimens however, creates an enormous research hurdle for investigators who need tumor tissue to perform essential molecular analyses of this unique tumor.

In the future, physicians may routinely recommend biopsy for children with a clinical and radiographic diagnosis of DIPG. Currently, this recommendation only occurs when a child's physician believes the potential benefit of a biopsy outweighs the potential risks, for example, if the MRI findings are not classical for a DIPG. In the future, the most likely situation in which biopsies would be recommended would be if scientists were able to analyze the tumor tissue and identify a set of tumor genes or other characteristics specific to the tumor that could suggest one treatment may be of greater benefit to a child with a DIPG than another. In this case, a physician and parent would want the child to receive the treatment that has a higher likelihood of benefit. Scientists make constant advances through research that have made such scenarios a reality for a variety of other tumors. Our hope is that such advances will

Dr. Blaney is a Professor and Vice Chair for Research in the Department of Pediatrics at Texas Children's Cancer Center, and Deputy Director, Baylor College of Medicine, Houston, TX.

occur sooner rather than later for DIPGs. However, this requires ongoing intensive research by the best scientific minds and access to tumor tissue, which will be discussed below.

Challenges associated with the tumor location

Progress has been made in the treatment of some high-grade glial tumors, particularly those that can be surgically removed. However, progress has been slower for tumors that cannot be surgically removed, such as DIPGs. As noted above, the location of DIPGs deep in the brain impedes ready access by the surgeon to tumor tissue. Tumor tissue is essential to the work of research scientists who are trying to acquire a better understanding of the tumor's basic biology and unlock the key for figuring out how a DIPG first develops. This understanding is needed for the development of better treatments for this disease. Once scientists understand the tumor's biology, they can develop strategies to destroy the tumor cells or to convert them to cells that no longer behave in a malignant fashion.

Tumor cells can be destroyed in a variety of ways. However, the location of a DIPG within the central nervous system (CNS) makes all potential treatment approaches even more challenging, because the CNS has natural mechanisms (the Blood-Brain-Barrier) that isolate it from other parts of the body. This isolation protects the brain from damage or side effects associated with chemicals in the blood, including chemotherapy. Yet this isolation also means that most anti-cancer drugs in the blood do not get into the central nervous system to any appreciable extent. In everyday life this isolation is good, because it protects the brain. But this isolation is a major obstacle in the treatment of brain tumors because the target of the therapy is in the CNS. Thus, researchers are developing strategies to ensure drug delivery to the tumor. This can be accomplished by delivering a drug directly into the CNS, by making drugs that can more readily enter the CNS, or by developing special carriers (e.g., nanoparticles) that can deliver the anti-cancer drug to the tumor.

Clinical trial challenges

Despite the many challenges in treating DIPGs, doctors and scientists, assisted by patients and their families, continue to work diligently toward finding new and more effective therapies for children with DIPGs and other brain tumors. While progress has been slower than desired, we continue to make incremental advances in understanding the biology of these challenging cancers. While we are working to unlock the keys to determine what makes a DIPG develop, we are simultaneously evaluating new drugs in clinical trials to determine whether or not they should be used in the treatment of DIPGs.

Because the survival rate for children with DIPGs is unacceptable, doctors and scientists are constantly evaluating new drugs, biological agents, and immunotherapeutic strategies to improve survival. The best way to evaluate new treatments is through clinical trials. Clinical trials are a scientifically rigorous way to determine the best dose and schedules of new agents and treatment strategies, and to ultimately determine whether a new treatment is of benefit for a particular disease. As such, many patients with aggressive cancers such as DIPGs are offered the option of a clinical trial either at diagnosis or relapse, if a trial is available.

Local radiation to the brainstem is the standard treatment for children diagnosed with a DIPG. Because the benefits of radiation in DIPGs are temporary (typically less than 1 year), and because there are no chemotherapy agents that have a known beneficial effect for DIPGs, many of the current clinical trials for children with a DIPG are early phase clinical trials (Phase 1 or Phase 2) where the goals of therapy are to: a/ find the appropriate dose of medication to give with radiation therapy; b/learn more about the side effects of the medications when given with radiation therapy; and c/ find early information about the effectiveness of a new treatment.

There are many contributing factors associated with clinical trial participation that create additional hurdles for DIPG research. Not all patients will qualify for participation in clinical trials. All clinical trials are conducted using strict guidelines to minimize the risk to patient safety. Patients must also have a physical and neurological examination, laboratory tests, and imaging studies (scans) to determine if they are eligible to participate in the trial. These additional tests and the clinical trial itself might be regarded by the family as interfering with the quality of life of their child. Trial requirements may also result in disappointment or frustration if a child is not eligible to participate or if no open slots are available for trial enrollment.

The decision to participate in a clinical trial, if eligible, is also a personal one. The decision may be influenced by the potential for benefit from the treatment; the potential side effects of the treatment; a need to travel to a new treatment facility that is far from home; a desire to help children in the future; and other factors. When balancing the pros and cons of participation, the family must decide what is best for their child. This might mean that participation in a clinical trial is not the decision that they choose to make.

Clinical trial phases and institution challenges

Clinical trials are normally divided into three phases—Phase 1, Phase 2, and Phase 3. Phase 1 trials are most frequently performed in a limited number of pediatric oncology centers that have specially trained clinical research personnel. In North America, the institutions that perform these studies are comprised of a small group of institutions that have been designated by the National Cancer Institute to work together to perform these trials. These groups include the Children's Oncology Group Phase 1 and Pilot Consortium (comprising 20 pediatric treatment centers) and the Pediatric Brain Tumor Consortium (comprising 11 pediatric treatment centers). The formation of these consortia facilitates patient access throughout the country to a treatment center closer to home and allows trials to be conducted more efficiently. After the optimal dose and schedule of the new therapy have been determined in Phase 1, Phase 2 trials are conducted to evaluate whether or not the new treatment is effective for children with DIPGs. Phase 2 trials are typically conducted by the Children's Oncology Group, which is comprised of more than 200 children's oncology treatment centers in North America. At this stage, access is more widely available to children throughout the United States. Because the Phase I trials are conducted at fewer sites, this might make participation difficult for many families. Traveling distances to participate in a trial can seem overwhelming when there is no clear benefit from a Phase I trial for the participating child. Additional mobility challenges, as well as communication issues impacting consent and assent that are common with DIPG children make participation in clinical trials even more difficult. Delays to clinical trial enrollment prolong the time to completion of the study and analysis of the trial to determine the efficacy of the new therapy being tested.

Benefits, risks, and accrual challenges of clinical trials

There are benefits and risks of participating in a clinical trial. This too can impact a parent's decision to not enroll their child into a study, leading to delays in study accrual and research progress. Participation gives patients access to new therapies that are promising, but the best dose is often not yet known and side effects may be present without ultimate direct benefit for the patient. However, all clinical trials lead to information that helps future patients. The dramatic success in the treatment and cure of other childhood cancers such as leukemia, lymphoma, Wilms tumor, and many other types would not have occurred without the participation of patients and physicians in clinical trials. All clinical trials in children with cancer have scientific rationale and the potential for benefit, but no guarantee of benefit. This is a challenge to families as they are faced with the decision of participating or not.

Another challenge to progress in the treatment of DIPGs is the length of time it takes to complete a trial. DIPG is a rare tumor and it may take several years to accrue an adequate number of patients for a trial. A drug or therapy may sound very promising based on information about its use in other tumor types or in an individual patient, but to determine whether or not there is an actual benefit for patients with a DIPG, there needs to be a scientific evaluation through a clinical trial. If children are treated with new therapies at random—meaning outside of clinical trials—there is risk of exposing them to serious side effects, without the benefit of learning whether the treatment is effective and safe. To be scientifically valid research, there needs to be a sufficient number of patients entered into the study to determine the benefit of any therapy. Given such a small patient population, it takes time to accrue the required number of patients in order to give definitive scientific validity to the study. This too can be a difficult research hurdle to overcome.

In the future, we hope to have enough understanding of DIPG biology to tailor the treatment for each individual child based on an analysis of a tissue sample (biopsy) from his or her tumor. We do not have that knowledge today, and such knowledge will only come from rigorous scientific studies, which includes clinical trials.

How Can the Barriers be Removed?

As already noted, many barriers exist to progress in the research and treatment of DIPGs. Because of the tumor's location, surgery and biopsy are generally not performed. The resultant lack of tumor tissue from patients at diagnosis limits researchers' ability to understand the biology of these tumors. Scientists must therefore make inferences from what we know about similar tumors in adults and children in our treatment approaches, which may or may not be appropriate. So, how can progress be realized?

Parents of pediatric cancer patients are the advocacy voice of their children. It has been through the initiatives of parent advocates that progress has been realized in many types of childhood cancer treatment. In the early 1970s, a group of parents of children with cancer formed Candlelighters Childhood Cancer Foundation (now the American Childhood Cancer Organization) and lobbied Congress for childhood cancer research funding. Their efforts led to 1) an increase in awareness of the devastation of childhood cancer, 2) designated pediatric oncology program funding within the National Cancer Institute (NCI), 3) the inclusion of pediatric oncology language in President Nixon's National Cancer Act of 1971, and 4) the development of information and support programs within Candlelighters.

Similarly, parents of children diagnosed with DIPG have a tremendous opportunity to make a difference in the future outcome of this disease. A number of families have responded by forming non-profit organizations in memory of their children. Some of these organizations provide funding for promising research, some offer financial help to families, some have websites populated with invaluable DIPG specific information, and others raise awareness of this disease in the community and amongst national funding agencies such as the federal government and the NCI. Individual parents have dedicated their time to the creation and administration of online groups in an effort to provide support and allow families to connect with one another. All of these efforts contribute to progress toward making life better for children with DIPG.

For some parents, donation of their child's post-mortem tumor tissue is a way to make a difference. This selfless act provides tissue that would not otherwise be available for research. As a result, scientists have recently been able to establish DIPG cell lines and animal models, and to advance their understanding of the biology of these challenging tumors. It is hoped that this progress will make it possible to quickly develop, test and prioritize DIPG treatments for evaluation in clinical trials. Tissue donation is perceived by many families as a way for their child to finally be free from the ravages of DIPG, while giving hope to those children who will follow in their path. Sandy Smith and Kimberlee Spady are two DIPG parents who, along with others, have devoted themselves to providing families with information regarding, and/or assistance with, the planning of autopsy tissue donation. It is their goal to ensure that once a family has made the decision to donate tumor tissue, they will not be burdened with the details of arranging the donation. They also offer support to families from the time of diagnosis, helping with treatment information, and hoping for the best possible outcome for each child.

Individuals and foundations are working with determination to raise much needed funds for on-going research efforts. One way a family can make a big difference is to team up with an established organization or group of organizations, because as organizations grow, they are able to make more of an impact by funding larger research projects. Individual families and groups of families around the world have been able to fund national and international summits for researchers. These forums have provided opportunities for scientists to come together to share data and ideas. An important factor to consider when teaming up with another organization or foundation, is whether or not the organization has a scientific advisory board that advises the organization. This helps to ensure that the research projects that are funded are addressing the most important issues in the field and are of the highest quality.

In summary, there are many ways that families can honor their children with DIPG by helping to promote progress toward improving current treatments. It remains clear that ongoing research is required to develop a cure for children with DIPGs. This research requires tissue to understand the biology of DIPGs, participants in clinical trials to evaluate new treatment approaches, increased awareness of the devastation of this disease, and financial support for basic science and clinical research. Although there are hurdles and barriers related to DIPG research and treatment, they will continue to be overcome as scientists, physicians and families work together to overcome them.

Chapter 14

The Future of Genomics and Proteomics in DIPG

Mark W. Kieran, MD, PhD

The sequencing of the human genome has resulted in a revolution in biology and medicine that offers enormous possibilities leading to an improved understanding, diagnosis, and treatment of human diseases. These advances have largely been achieved in two major domains. First, the development of new technologies that can rapidly and cheaply analyze DNA, RNA, and proteins has lead to an explosion in our understanding of the building blocks of the cells, and how they interact with each other through the process of growth and development. The second major advance has occurred in the area of bioinformatics. Developments in computational sciences have permitted the storage and analysis of the billions of fragments of tumor data that result from these technologic advances, and provide the opportunity to place them in the context that better approximates complex biologic systems. Thus, we now have the opportunity to examine the genome of cancer as well as begin to understand it. The goal of this chapter will be to review the technical advances, specifically genomics and proteomics, and place these in the context of future therapeutic developments for diffuse intrinsic pontine gliomas (DIPG). These important advances are just now being applied to DIPG and like most other advances, will take some time before their impact is felt in the clinical treatment of DIPG.

Genomics

In its simplest form, genomics refers to the reading of the genetic code of cells. DNA is the genetic material that acts as the blueprint for making new cells as well as all of the

Dr. Mark Kieran is the Director of Pediatric Medical Neuro-oncology at the Dana-Farber Cancer Institute and Children's Hospital, Boston, MA.

information needed to maintain the current ones. Tumors often alter their DNA (the blueprint), and divide into multiple "daughter" cells which then inherit the same altered DNA, leading to the propagation of the cancer. When a cell divides, the two new cells formed are called daughter cells and when they divide, four daughter cells will be created etc. Alterations in the DNA occur via changes in the genetic code which is made up of four nitrogen bases identified by the letters: **A** (adenine), **G** (guanine), **T** (thymine), and **C** (cytosine). These 4 letters spell out all of the proteins that need to be made (called the coding regions) as well as the intervening sequences of DNA that contain the control regions (called the non-coding regions) that determine when proteins are made. When an error occurs in the code of a cell, not only does it have the potential to affect that cell, but that error is also transmitted to every new daughter cell. Thus, errors can accumulate, increasing the malignant phenotype of the tumor, as well as its resistance to therapy.

How do Mutations in the DNA Sequence Cause Cancer?

There are generally two types of genes that can sustain mutations leading to cancer: tumor suppressor genes and oncogenes. In normal cells, tumor suppressors make proteins that keep cells "in check" (e.g. suppress tumors). However, if errors in the DNA of tumor suppressor gene(s) are acquired, and these errors destroy the function of the tumor suppressor, then tumors are no longer suppressed, and the cell is not kept "in check" any longer. While tumor suppressors cause cancer by their absence, oncogenes cause cancer by their presence. Mutations occur to oncogenes that impart new abilities of the protein to cause cancer. The alteration in the DNA of oncogenes results in a protein that instructs cells to continuously divide, with uncontrolled proliferation.

The cell that possesses these types of mutations determines the kind of cancer observed. When these mutations happen in blood cells for example, leukemia results. If they happen in a brain cell of the pons, the patient is diagnosed with a diffuse pontine glioma. Thus, we consider cancer (tumor) a result of the accumulation of abnormalities in the DNA of cells. The major types of alterations of the DNA that can occur in pediatric brain stem gliomas (and all other cancers) are described below.

Mutation: Genes contain the sequence code necessary to make proteins, and the proteins make up all cells and tissues. Mutations in the DNA occur such that the sequence (blueprint) for a protein has an error in it resulting in defective functioning. In other words, mutations in the genetic code result in no protein being produced, or a defective protein being made. Mutations may involve alternations in only one letter of the code (point mutation), many letters

(nucleotides), or the entire gene (deletions, amplifications, see below). If the altered protein has a critical role in cell proliferation, then the first step toward development of a tumor has occurred.

Translocation: Translocations of the DNA occur when certain parts of the DNA coding for a protein, break into two and rejoin at a site belonging to a different protein. This can sometimes result in a new molecule that tells the cell to do the wrong thing. For example, if the protein responsible for rapid proliferation of immune cells during infection accidently gets linked to the gene that makes astrocytes (the cells of the brain that hold everything in place), you may create a new "molecule" that accidentally tells astrocytes to rapidly divide.

Deletions and amplifications: Deleting or amplifying regions of the DNA is a common way in which errors can be introduced into the genetic material of the cell. If a piece of DNA coding for the molecules that stop cellular proliferation is lost (deleted), then uncontrolled cell division can result. In a similar way, if a segment of DNA that codes for the protein that makes cells start to divide is amplified, then the cell is stimulated to proliferate and tumor growth ensues.

Truncation (partial deletion of a gene): Many genes are organized such that one part possesses the functional part of the molecule (stop or start cell division) while the other end possesses the control sequences. Thus, knocking out bits of a gene, rather than the whole thing, can sometimes have a significant impact on the function of that molecule. For example, if the control region of a molecule is lost, it may continue to activate the cell even at times when it should be in the "off" position.

Epigenetic control of methylation and acetylation: Some cells are out of control not as a result of some assault on the integrity of the DNA but because a perfectly normal protein is expressed in the wrong place or at the wrong time. For example, during early embryogenesis, the fertilized egg must rapidly divide billions of times as the fetus grows. This is an example of normal proliferation. If an astrocyte that has finished dividing accidently turns on the embryonic signal for a cell that is supposed to be dividing, then it will begin to divide even in the absence of any mutations, translocations, deletions, or amplifications. The process of abnormal expression or timing of a normal gene may be of particular importance for pediatric cancers where the proliferation of many cell types associated with growth and development are still active.

The field of genomics is typically divided into two major components: structural and functional. Advancements in the evaluation of the structural organization of the DNA required technology that could rapidly, inexpensively and reproducibly

analyze the genetic code of both normal and abnormal tissue. This would then allow for the identification of the mutations, translocations, amplifications, or deletions of the DNA discussed above. Improvements in this technology are happening rapidly, and genomic analysis can now be done at both large and small academic institutions around the world. Many of these techniques are performed on small inert platforms (often called "chips") where millions of reactions can be performed simultaneously. The complexity of each chip determines how much information can be gathered from the sample being tested. Chips are available for the study of DNA (the genetic material), RNA (the intermediate code derived from the DNA) and proteins (the translated end product of the RNA code into amino acids). Simply finding an alteration in the DNA, RNA, or protein however does not prove that it is responsible for disease. Thus, clinicians and scientists must map the genetic abnormalities identified, onto the tumors ability to divide, infiltrate, and escape treatment. For example, a mutation in a protein not expressed in the tumor is unlikely to be responsible for the tumor. Thus, each abnormality in the DNA, RNA, and protein must be assessed for its active role in the tumor. Once identified, the relevant abnormalities can then be considered for targeting with drugs or other therapies.

Proteomics

Changes in DNA, RNA, or epigenetic events may be responsible for the abnormal function associated with many tumors, but the analysis of the proteins themselves is the most direct method to assess for critical changes in a cell's function. Recall that the purpose of DNA is to provide the code (via RNA) for all proteins. The field of proteomics uses a variety of techniques that allow for the separation of the thousands of proteins in a cell, as well as the structure and function of many of these molecules. Proteomics is usually divided into two critical phases. First is the separation of the different proteins in a sample—typically achieved by their size and overall charge (basic or acidic); and second is the identification of the different proteins—usually achieved through a technique called mass spectroscopy. As with genomic analysis, tissue is necessary for proteomics; however because many tumors shed their proteins in the blood or cerebral spinal fluid (CSF), these samples can sometimes act as surrogates to tumor tissue. Our increasing ability to identify the location, quantity, and activity of different proteins in a tumor sample has provided the pharmaceutical industry with the targets on which tumor specific inhibitors can be developed. In fact, a number of these drugs are already being used for a variety of different adult cancers and have started testing in pediatric patients as well.

Genomics of DIPG

A primary requirement for genomic analysis of cancer, is actual tumor material. While the biopsy of pontine gliomas was frequently performed in the 1970s (before any of the current genomic techniques were available), a change in national policy occurred in the 1980s for sound scientific and clinical reasons (see chapter 19). The diagnosis of DIPG was becoming easier to define radiographically through CT scans in the 1970s and in particular with MRI scans in the 1980s. Furthermore, with the very poor prognosis of these tumors with or without biopsy, the lack of justification for a biopsy, in which patients could experience significant neurosurgical damage, resulted in a moratorium on this procedure. Over the intervening 30 years, innumerable clinical trials of radiation alone or in combination with chemotherapy, biologic therapy, anti-angiogenic (anti blood vessel) therapy, gene therapy, immunotherapy, etc. have been performed. None of these approaches have significantly altered the outcome of this disease when compared to treatment with radiation therapy alone. Because none of these children had a biopsy, the reason these combination therapies failed remains unknown. When biopsy was performed, this was generally done because the tumor was atypical and histologic assessment was needed. The majority of these atypical lesions were discovered not to be DIPG. These studies were important at they demonstrated the relative safety of biopsy in this region.

Adult DIPG and animal models of pontine gliomas (not all of them are diffuse and intrinsic) are helping guide our understanding of the important genomic changes that help maintain a tumor's growth and resistance to therapy. Unlike most diseases, adults rarely get DIPG and in the few reports of this disease in these patients, the clinical course appears different than in children—a finding that suggests that DIPG prefer the environment of the pediatric pons. While it is quite easy to start tumor growth in animals for lung, breast, prostate, or colon cancer, mice do not develop DIPG spontaneously. Fortunately, a number of groups have been working on the development of animal models and the first reports of possible contenders are now available (see chapter 15). While these models are likely to be useful in extending our understanding of this disease, they are unlikely to provide all of the answers. As we discovered many years ago, we have cured just about every tumor type in mice many times over and yet those same results have often not been realized in humans. They may, however, become good animal models for "proof of principle discoveries" once pediatric DIPGs are analyzed for their genomic changes.

To overcome the lack of fresh tumor material derived from the time of diagnosis of patients with DIPG, many centers have initiated genomic analysis of autopsy material. While these studies will provide some important insight into the biology of these tumors, they all suffer from the fact that the molecular analyses performed post-mortem are altered by the initial treatment of the tumor with the variety of procedures mentioned above (radiation, chemotherapy etc.), and by the relatively limited sample size of these studies. For example, in a study of 11 cases (9 autopsy and two newly diagnosed DIPG), abnormal expression of PDGFRα in 4 cases and PARP1 in 3 cases were identified. Equally important in these studies was the identification that the genetic abnormalities in DIPG were different from malignant gliomas in other parts of the brain. Thus, molecular profiles of supratentorial malignant gliomas cannot always be used to identify appropriate pathways for the treatment of DIPG, which perhaps helps to explain the three decades of failed clinical trials. These studies also support a commonly held belief in the field that DIPGs are a heterogeneous population of tumors, and that one treatment is not likely to be useful in all cases.

Another approach to the molecular classification of DIPG has used imaging. Both MRI/MRS and PET/SPECT can identify individual markers in a tumor without the need for biopsy. For example, an 11year old female with a large pontine tumor demonstrated strong uptake of In-111-pentreotide, which identifies the presence of somatostatin receptors in the tumor. Similarly, PET imaging allows for the detection of glucose metabolism in tumors and can provide some important metabolic information in DIPG. As new pathways in DIPG tumors are identified, the ability to follow tumor growth or response with these types of imaging markers will likely make these modalities of greater importance in the near future.

With significant advances in neurosurgical technique and previously performed biopsies (in selected cases), the ability to safely biopsy brainstem tumors is becoming better recognized. In a landmark study demonstrating the safety of biopsy of DIPG, 24 consecutive children successfully underwent this procedure in Paris. Not only did the patients not suffer long-term consequences of the biopsy, in two patients, a diagnosis other than a DIPG was identified. The rapidity of improved neurosurgical techniques is now opening the door to direct administration of therapy into the brainstem, not just biopsy. As our improved molecular understanding of these tumors continues, the ability to administer drugs directly into the pons will likely play a greater role in treatment. A major regulator of cellular proliferation known as p53, has been extensively evaluated in both newly diagnosed and autopsy cases of DIPG, as well as other brainstem tumors. This critical regulatory gene was abnormal in over half of the cases in two different studies. Unfortunately, there are currently no drugs targeting p53. While only limited information on the molecular phenotype of pontine gliomas is currently available, the opportunity to change this is rapidly approaching.

We now find ourselves at an important crossroads to the molecular classification of DIPGs. For the last 30 years, it has been felt that the diagnosis of DIPG is easily made by imaging and clinical evaluation. The risks of biopsy within the pons were felt not to justify routine biopsy, and the moratorium on biopsy was considered appropriate. Today, with improved neurosurgical techniques and the availability of sophisticated genomic technologies that can derive extensive data from very small biopsy samples, the tide has turned. DIPG is not a single disease caused by a single mutation. Rather, there are a large number of abnormal pathways that likely account for these tumors and only by identifying them can we expect to develop the kinds of interventions that will be successful.

In this regard, two exciting developments have recently been discussed at national meetings but not yet published. The first is the experience of the French group that has expanded their biopsy program from 24 to 70 patients, and has completed a prospective trial with an EGFR inhibitor in these patients. A difference in the outcome of children expressing abnormalities of the EGFR pathway was significantly better than in those who received the same therapy but without the abnormality (suggesting their tumors were being driven by something else). Thus, we may have the first indications of an approach that can begin to make small improvements in the time to progression of DIPGs. While this may seem like a small step, if validated, it may represent the first time a therapy has really impacted the time to progression of this aggressive disease.

The second important development is the initiation of a 20 institution clinical trial within the United States run through the Dana-Farber Cancer Institute, in which all patients with DIPG will undergo biopsy and extensive molecular profiling, and the treatment of these patients will be based upon the expression of certain pathways in their tumors. Thus, rather than a single treatment for everyone, each patient will receive a treatment designed for the expression pattern of their specific tumor. From this trial, we will have the opportunity to fully evaluate the molecular profile of newly diagnosed DIPG, while at the same time, begin to adapt personalized therapy based on these unique patient profiles.

The outcome for patients with DIPG remains poor. Thirty years of guessing at treatment has not helped improve the outlook and has subjected countless thousands of these children to toxic therapies that had no benefit. With recent advances in molecular technology and neurosurgical techniques, we are now poised to investigate the underlying biology of DIPG—the first step toward rational and effective therapy.

Chapter 15

Animal Models for DIPGs

Oren J. Becher, MD

Diffuse intrinsic pontine glioma (DIPG) is a rare tumor that arises in the pons of children and is currently incurable. The only active therapeutic agent is radiation, which unfortunately provides only temporary relief. Clinical trials for the past 30 years evaluating novel agents have failed to identify additional active and effective agents against this tumor. In recent years, molecular genetic technologies have been quite successful in identifying new molecular targets in numerous cancers which has led to targeted drug development, and an increasing number of promising targeted agents. The challenge is how to determine which novel agents or combination of agents should move into clinical trials for DIPG. As this is a rare tumor, it is impossible to test every new agent and combination of these agents in these patients. There are not enough patients to accomplish this feat. An additional complexity to new drug development is that DIPG tumors are heterogeneous and may be comprised of multiple different subtypes, where each subtype may respond differently to specific drugs.

Why Do We Need Animal Models?

One idea that scientists thought might be helpful is to develop animal models that would allow for screening of novel agents and combinations. The results from these animal models could be predictive of anti-tumor activity in children with DIPGs, leading to the discovery of the most promising drugs for human DIPG trials. At this point in time, this ideal has yet to be fully realized. There is currently one main obstacle that must be overcome so that predictive animal models can be developed. Scientists need a better understanding of the genomic alterations that drive the growth of human DIPGs so as to guide the development of accurate animal models to potentially treat

Dr. Becher is an Assistant Professor in the Departments of Pediatrics and Pathology at Duke University School of Medicine, Durham, NC.

it. Unfortunately, scientists do not have a good understanding of the drivers of these tumors, although there are several research groups who are currently working on this, and it is believed that answers to these questions are within reach.

In spite of the limited understanding of the biology of human DIPGs, there are several animal models that have been described, although it is not clearly known if they are predictive. In the next few paragraphs, I will review the various DIPG models that currently exist, and the advantages and disadvantages of each.

DIPG Animal Models Available

Most of the current animal models for DIPGs are rat allograft models and only recently a genetically engineered DIPG mouse model was developed as well.

The three main types of animal models for glioma are:

1. **Allograft:** Chemically induced tumors in rats that mimic DIPG.

2. **Xenograft:** Human tumor from patients, transplanted into mice or rats.

3. **Genetically Engineered Mouse Model/GEMM:** Mice given new genes (transgenics) that cause tumors appearing similar to DIPG, and sharing some molecular signatures of the human tumor.

Allograft: There are several rat glioma cell lines available, which were generated by injecting rats with repeated dosing of chemotherapy until the rats developed gliomas, which were then cultured and propogated. There are currently several rat glioma cell lines available. Three of these cells lines (C6, 9L, and T9 gliomas) were induced by repeated injections of methylnitrosurea (MNU) to adult rats. Two other cell lines (RG2 and F98 gliomas) were chemically induced by administering ethylnitrosurea (ENU) to pregnant rats. In this case, the progeny developed brain tumors that subsequently were propagated in vitro and cloned.

Both MNU and ENU are alkylating agents, which mean that they damage DNA by adding alkyl groups to it. Most of the above mentioned rat glioma cell lines are being used to generate brainstem gliomas by direct injection into the brainstem of either rats of the same strain or immunodeficient rats. Depending on the number of cells injected, the cell line used, and the age of the rats at the time of injection, the rats go on to develop brainstem tumors one to several weeks later. A head-to-head comparison between 3 week-old and 10 week-old rats injected with the same cell line and the same number of cells into the brainstem demonstrated that the microenvironment of young rats allows for the formation of diffuse pontine tumors, while the microenvironment of older rats allows for the development of focal brainstem tumors. Interestingly, there have not been many trials testing systemic chemotherapy using such models. This is most likely due to the belief that systemic chemotherapy for the most part does not get into the brain tumor due to the blood-brain barrier (BBB). Therefore, most of these models have been mainly used to test for CED (convection enhanced delivery) of chemotherapy such as carboplatin. A detailed description of CED is given in chapter 17 of this book.

Xenograft: Recently, a rat xenograft model was developed whereby adult human glioma cell lines were implanted into 6-week old immunodeficient rats. Prior to implantation, some of the cell lines were maintained in media with serum (these are usually grown as cells adherent to plastic); some of the cell lines were maintained as subcutaneous xenografts (grown under the skin of immunodeficient rats); and one cell line—the GS2 cell line was maintained as neurospheres (these are spherical colonies in suspension in media).

It is well documented that gliomas which are cultured in epidermal growth factor (EGF) and basic fibroblast growth factor (bFGF), and are grown as neurospheres, have genomic signatures that most resemble the signatures of naturally developing (*in vivo*) gliomas. While an advantage of such a model is that the tumor cells are human, the disadvantage is that adult glioma cell lines have different genetic alterations than DIPGs. In addition, the *in vitro* culturing step likely alters the biology of the cells even in neurosphere conditions. Lastly, such models remove the role of the immune system in DIPG tumorigenesis.

GEMM: Genetically engineered mouse models for brain tumors have been developed since 2000 and are a more recent addition to the animal modeling toolbox. The advantage of such models is that the genetic alterations which initiate and drive tumor formation are known and recapitulate the genetic alterations present in the respective human tumors. Therefore, the genetic alterations of the respective human tumors should be determined so as to guide the development of the genetically engineered mouse model. Such models are helpful in determining if a particular genetic alteration can drive tumor formation. Not all genetic alterations are equally meaningful and scientists divide genetic alterations into "drivers" and "passengers" to imply that only certain genetic alterations can drive tumor growth (so-called driver mutations) while the role of other genetic alterations is less clear (so-called passenger mutations).

There are numerous technologies that can be used to generate these mice. One brain tumor model uses conditional knockout mice where mice that have lost one copy of p53, PTEN, and NF-1 develop brain tumors through loss of heterozygosity. A second system is the RCAS-tv-a system, which allows for oncogene delivery by injection of virus producing cells into areas of interest such as the brainstem. Normal mice do not express the receptor (called tv-a) and so are not susceptible to infection by RCAS vectors. However, two transgenic mice were developed that express the tv-a receptor in progenitor/stem cell of the brain compartment: nestin tv-a mouse and GFAP tv-a mouse. (A transgenic mouse is a mouse which integrates an additional piece of DNA in its germline called a transgene, and so every cell in the mouse acquires this extra piece of DNA.)

Recently a genetically engineered mouse model for brainstem gliomas was developed which recapitulates the genetic alterations of a subset of the human disease. It was recently observed that PDGFRα is amplified in 20% to 30% of DIPGs which means that the receptor for PDGF ligand is expressed in high levels in a subset of DIPGs. The derived mouse model uses the retroviral delivery system described above, whereby a virus is used to deliver oncogenes to specific areas in the mouse brain. Tumors are generated by the over-expression of PDGF-β in nestin positive cells which line the floor of the 4th ventricle at postnatal day 1 to 3. Nestin positive cells are cells that express nestin, an intermediate filament that is expressed in progenitor cells in the brain. Overexpression of PDGF-β results in the formation of low-grade brainstem gliomas. The addition of Ink4a-ARF null genetic alteration (which has been described as a common alteration in human DIPGs and normally restrains cell division), together with PDGF-β overexpression, results in the formation of high-grade brainstem gliomas, or DIPGs, with high incidence by six weeks of age.

Advantages of genetically engineered mouse models are that a) the genetic alterations are clearly defined; b) the tumor forms in the right microenvironment (the brainstem); and c) the tumor forms at the right time period (pediatric). It is generated completely *in vivo* and develops *de novo* in the mouse. As tumors are a complex cellular setting, it is important that this environment is as close to reality as possible. Another advantage of the genetically engineered mouse model is that it can be used to determine the cells-of-origin for a particular tumor. The cells-of-origin for the recently developed DIPG mouse model were derived from cells lining the floor of the 4th ventricle and aqueduct. However it does not tell us with any certainty that the cells-of-origin for human DIPGs are similar cells. One disadvantage of this animal model is that it is probable that this genetically engineered DIPG model may be oversimplified, as human DIPGs likely contain more genetic alterations than simply PDGF-β overexpression and Ink4a-ARF loss. It remains to be determined whether therapeutic agents with antitumor activity in this animal model will also be active in children with DIPGs.

There is no perfect animal model. Ultimately there is a need for a predictive model of activity in the clinic. An added complexity is that the human tumors are heterogeneous and so it is likely that we will need to classify them into several groups based on their genetic alterations. Each subtype will then require specific therapy and an associated specific DIPG animal model. Of note, adult gliomas have recently been subdivided into three groups based on the genetic alterations of the tumors.

One advantage of rat brainstem glioma models is that the rat brainstem is larger than the mouse brainstem. As a result, it may be easier to conduct CED preclinical studies. The disadvantage of rat allograft models are that in most cases the genetic alterations of the tumors are not clearly defined and may change over time. Most of the cell lines are maintained on plastic dishes that are quite artificial. In addition, as mentioned, human tumors are complex with several cell types interacting including tumor cells and various stromal cells such as blood vessel cells, support cells, and immune cells. Therefore it is ideal for the animal to develop the tumor within a normal immune system and with all of the support cells being present from tumor onset.

Preclinical Testing

The question that often arises, is how much preclinical evidence is needed before a decision is made to move a new agent into the clinic for DIPGs? There are several levels of preclinical evidence and I personally believe that novel agents should move to the clinic after full preclinical testing has been done. This means that a novel agent has been tested in cell lines; in DIPG xenograft rat models where the xenograft originated from a DIPG tumor that has been propagated *in vivo* or, second best, neurospheres; and has also been tested in genetically engineered DIPG subsets. Depending on the therapeutic agent, some agents cannot be tested in cell lines at all and can only be tested in vivo or in neurospheres. An example is the sonic hedgehog pathway inhibitors, which cannot be tested in cell lines grown on plastic dishes, as the pathway is not functional in such conditions.

Once an agent shows strong promise in preclinical testing, a decision is then made to test it in patients with DIPGs. The first clinical study is a phase I study which is used to determine the correct dose to use in the clinic, as well as assess for toxicities of the drug. Even if a drug has already been tested in adults, it will still need to be tested in a phase I trial for children as children at times metabolize drugs differently than adults. Usually phase I studies are open for children with diverse cancers but it does not mean that a particular drug will not be active in DIPGs. Once the safety and dosing are established in a phase I study, then a phase II trial is designed to determine if the drug or drug combination is active against DIPGs. Phase II studies are usually done on a selected tumor subtype. Phase III studies are large studies that are used to confirm promising results from phase II studies (see chapter 5).

Conclusion

At this point in time, most clinicians do not believe that animal models can help guide which therapeutic agents or combination of agents will be active in the clinic. The burden of proof lies with the animal-modeling field to continue to improve the animal models so that eventually they will be predictive of activity in the clinic. Similar to what has been done in adult gliomas, in the near future DIPGs will also be grouped into genomic subgroups, and genetically engineered animal models will be developed for each subtype. It is my hope that these genetically engineered DIPG mouse models will be predictive of activity in the clinic, but it remains to be seen if this will indeed be the case.

Chapter 16

Neural Stem Cells and DIPG

Michelle Monje, MD, PhD

Diffuse intrinsic pontine gliomas (DIPG) occur strictly in the ventral pons and typically during a relatively specific period during mid-childhood, peaking between ages 6 and 8. The age and location-specific nature of DIPG suggests that the underlying pathophysiology may involve dysregulation of a developmental process. In this context, it makes sense to approach DIPG from the vantage of neural stem and precursor cell biology.

Normal Neural Stem Cells

Neural stem cells—cells that can renew themselves and also can make all types of neural cells (neurons, oligodendrocytes and astrocytes), are well-recognized in the brain and spinal cord of both children and adults. Two populations of neural stem cells are very well studied. These two populations reside in the hippocampus, a brain structure important in memory function, and in what is called the subventricular zone (i.e. just below the ventricular walls) of the lateral ventricles. It is known that, at least in mice and rats, stem cells exist throughout the ventricular system of the brain and spinal cord, but little attention has been paid to those in the subventricular zone of the third and fourth ventricles. The fourth ventricle sits immediately behind the pons. The term "neural precursor cell" includes both true stem cells and cells that are somewhat further along the path of differentiation but still give rise to daughter cells. Both types of cell—stem and "precursor" are important to developmental processes in the brain both before and after birth.

Cancer Stem Cells

Cancer stem cells (CSCs) represent a subpopulation of cells that can generate all

> Dr. Monje is an Assistant Professor of Neurology and Neurological Sciences at Stanford School of Medicine, and Practicing Pediatric Neuro-oncologist at Stanford Hospital, and Lucile Packard Children's Hospital, Stanford, CA.

cell types found within a tumor and are thought to be responsible for tumor growth and spread. Like normal stem cells, cancer stem cells possess the capacity for self-renewal and multi-potency. (Multi-potent cells can make all the cell types in a tissue. In this case the tissue is the tumor.) The first cancer stem cells were described in acute myeloid leukemia, and have now been shown in many solid tumors, including many brain tumors such as glioblastoma and ependymoma. CSCs isolated from primary brain tumors possess many of the characteristics of normal neural stem cells, and can recapitulate the tumor *in vitro* and *in vivo*, whereas other cell types from the tumor cannot. CSCs are thus a small proportion of a tumor, but are solely responsible for tumor propagation.

The relationship of normal neural stem cells to cancer stem cells is somewhat controversial, but there is an emerging consensus that **many brain tumors arise from stem or precursor cell populations** in both children and adults. Excellent examples of this point include "radial glia" cells (a type of stem cell) giving rise to ependymoma and subventricular zone neural stem cells giving rise to central neurocytomas. With respect to more lineage-restricted precursors, Shh-responsive granule cell precursor cells of the cerebellum give rise to medulloblastoma in many cases, and recent animal model data indicate that oligodendrocyte precursors give rise to periventricular low grade gliomas in a mouse model of platelet-derived growth factor (PDGF) overexpression. Brain tumor stem cells exhibit many of the same marker proteins and utilize many of the same signaling pathways as normal neural stem cells. Understanding normal neural stem or precursor cells in the brainstem may thus shed light on brainstem tumor pathogenesis.

What Stem Cells Need to Thrive—the "Stem Cell Niche"

Normal stem cell niche

Neural stem cells in the childhood and adult nervous system reside in a niche of signaling factors, extracellular matrix composition and specialized cell types that support neural stem cell function for that brain region. Perhaps best studied is the stem cell niche that supports forebrain neurogenesis in the hippocampus. This specific microenvironment necessary for stem cell production of new neurons is referred to as the neurogenic niche. Transplantation experiments demonstrate that neurogenesis is restricted in the postnatal brain to regions in which it occurs naturally, namely the subventricular zone (SVZ) and the subgranular zone (SGZ) of the hippocampus. In general, microenvironmental determinants of neurogenesis include the presence of the trophic signals required for progenitor cell proliferation, differentiation and survival, and the absence of inhibitory factors. Neural stem/precursor cells form a close anatomical relationship with the small vessels in the neurogenic region, and this neurovascular relationship—the so-called "vascular niche"—is believed to be crucial not only for nutritional but also for growth factor support. Vessel cells (endothelial cells, pericytes) and glial cells (astrocytes) all contribute to the stem cell niche. Hippocampal astrocytes play key roles in creating and maintaining the neurogenic niche. As noted above, many of the signaling pathways central to prenatal neural development are conserved in postnatal neurogenesis, including pathways called Wnt, Shh, and Notch. Additional molecules with potent pro-neurogenic effects include fibroblast growth factor (FGF), vascular endothelial growth factor (VEGF) and certain neurotransmitters. An important negative regulator of the neurogenic microenvironment is microglial cell inflammation, particularly in disease states. Pro-inflammatory cytokines elaborated by microglial cells in certain states of activation, including IL-6 and TNF-alpha, inhibit neurogenesis via a specific blockade in neuronal differentiation mediated by Notch signaling, as well as a non-specific increase in precursor cell death. The effects of inflammatory cells on neurogenesis are complex and depend on the microglial phenotype involved; microglia stimulated by cranial irradiation or systemically-administered lipopolysaccharide (LPS, also known as endotoxin) inhibit neurogenesis, while microglia stimulated by IL-4 or interferon gamma promote neurogenesis.

Cancer stem cell (CSC) niche

Just as cancer stem cells share many properties with normal stem cells, so the cancer stem cell niche is similar to the normal stem cell niche. The vascular niche appears to be recapitulated in human brain tumors. Cancer stem cells, defined molecularly by expression of the proteins CD133 and Nestin, are localized in close proximity with tumor microvessels in human medulloblastoma, glioblastoma, oligodendroglioma and ependymoma. The relationship between cancer stem cells and tumor microvessels is bidirectional: glioblastoma cells induce angiogenesis (new vessel cell growth) via VEGF elaboration, and vascular endothelial cells supports glioblastoma cell tumoriogenicity. Treatment of a mouse orthotopic glioblastoma model with the VEGF blocking agent bevacizumab (Avastin) depletes CD133+ cells, decreases tumor vascularity and reduces tumor growth rate. Accordingly, bevacizumab has shown modest clinical efficacy in glioblastoma, at least in adult glioblastoma of the forebrain. Highlighting the differences between DIPG and adult glioblastoma, bevacizumab is not efficacious for DIPG. Important determinants of the DIPG cancer stem cell niche are yet to be defined.

Stem Cells in DIPG

Cell of origin

Presently, intense research is underway to identify the cell type in the normal childhood pons from which DIPGs originate. The cell type that transforms and gives rise to DIPG could be a neural stem cell, a neural precursor cell type (that is destined to give rise to glial cells or neuronal cells) or a differentiated cell type (glia or neurons). Lessons learned from other pediatric brain tumors teach us that the most likely candidate would be a neural stem or precursor cell. Neural stem and precursor cells are not well described in the brainstem, but current research will soon shed light on candidate cells of origin for DIPG. Understanding the cell of origin for DIPG is of fundamental importance to elucidate mechanisms by which DIPG may form, and thus potential targets for treatment.

DIPG cancer stem cell

Researchers are working to identify and characterize a cancer stem cell in DIPG. This research requires fresh tumor samples for cell culture, and scarcity of tissue for research has limited progress in this area until very recently. Donation of tumor in the early post-mortem period after the loss of a child allows for successful cell culture of both normal brain and brain tumor tissue. This strategy can allow crucial research to be done without putting a child through an additional procedure such as a biopsy. Identifying and studying the cancer stem cell of DIPG may elucidate new targets for therapy that are at the core of DIPG growth and propagation.

A few words on hematopoietic stem cell and bone marrow transplant

Hematopoietic stem cell transplant (HSCT) and bone marrow transplant are designed to rescue the bone marrow after intensive chemotherapy or to provide cell replacement therapy for certain genetic diseases. At present, there is no role for either HSCT or bone marrow transplant for DIPG.

Chapter 17

Convection-Enhanced Delivery in DIPG

Zhiping Zhou, MD, PhD
Mark M. Souweidane, MD

Diffuse intrinsic pontine glioma (DIPG) is locally highly infiltrative. In this type of tumor, cancer tissue cannot be distinguished from normal brain tissue macroscopically. This infiltrative nature makes effective therapy extremely difficult, if not impossible. To be clinically useful, a therapy must have the ability to selectively target and kill tumor cells without significant damage to the normal brain tissue. Given the need for cell specificity, surgical resection and stereotactic radiosurgery have limited utility, pose a great risk of injury and are therefore rarely an option to consider. Conventional radiation therapy is currently employed routinely as a palliative approach. The improvement of newer chemotherapeutic agents' tumor selectivity and the development of targeted therapeutic agents in recent decades raise hopes that improved chemotherapy will lead to improved outcome. Paralleling this development has been the promising advance in drug delivery to the central nervous system via local delivery systems to overcome the blood-brain barrier (BBB), one of the major hurdles in delivering drugs to the brain.

In this chapter, we will be discussing the application of convection-enhanced delivery (CED), also known as interstitial infusion, in the treatment of DIPG. CED is a technique designed to deliver drugs directly into the tumor at high concentrations. This avoids or at least greatly reduces systemic exposure to the drug. Drugs being studied for delivery through CED include conventional chemotherapy drugs, novel small molecule agents and macromolecules such as therapeutic antibodies, immunotoxins, and viral vectors, some of which would otherwise never gain access to the brain.

Dr. Zhou is an Instructor in the Department of Neurological Surgery at Weill Cornell Medical College, New York, NY.

Blood-Brain Barrier

Chemotherapy may be administered systemically or locally. In systemic chemotherapy, the drug is administered orally or intravenously. An important limitation of systemic chemotherapy in the treatment of brain tumors is the existence of the blood-brain barrier (BBB). The BBB isolates the circulating blood from cerebrospinal fluid (CSF) in the central nervous system (CNS). It occurs along cerebral capillaries and consists of tight junctions (zona occludens) that do not exist in systemic circulation. Endothelial cells joined by tight junctions restrict the entry of microscopic objects (e.g., bacteria) and large or hydrophilic molecules into the CSF, while allowing the diffusion of small hydrophobic molecules (O_2, certain hormones, CO_2, etc.). Typically, molecules with molecular weight greater than approximately 40kD are unlikely to penetrate the intact barrier. For the brain's supply of nutrients and removal of metabolites, cells of the barrier actively transport substances such as glucose across the barrier with specific proteins (transporters). The BBB acts effectively to protect the brain from many common bacterial infections and some toxic substances. Yet it presents a major challenge in delivering therapeutic agents to specific regions of the brain for the treatment of brain tumors and other disorders. Most cancer drugs are not able to permeate the BBB because they are polar in structure or too large in molecular weight. Even for drugs that are able to cross the cerebral capillary bed, it is difficult to achieve optimal concentrations due to systemic toxicity.

Another difficulty in the delivery of drugs for the treatment of brain tumors is how to direct those agents to the specific anatomic region or tumor mass to reduce the disturbance of normal neurological functions. Several strategies have been developed in an attempt to overcome this barrier, including: 1) the temporary disruption of the BBB, 2) modification of drugs to enhance their ability to permeate the BBB and 3) local delivery methods such as intratumoral/intra-cavitary embedding of drug-containing polymers or microchips, intra-arterial injection, direct injection of drugs into the tissue or CSF in the ventricles or subarachnoid space, and CED to deliver drugs directly into the extracellular space.

Local Delivery

Direct injection into the tumor or CSF is one of the earliest local delivery methods attempted. When injected into the tumor, it relies on diffusion for the drug to reach the cancer cells not directly adjacent to the injection site. Therefore the drug has an uneven distribution and can only reach the

> Dr. Souweidane is the Director of Pediatric Neurological Surgery at Weill Cornell Medical College and Memorial Sloan-Kettering Cancer Center. He is also Vice Chairman and Professor of Neurological Surgery and Professor of Neurological Surgery in Pediatrics at Weill Cornell Medical College, New York, NY.

tumor tissue that is a short distance from the injection site. With small molecules, depth of distribution is often limited to several millimeters, with an exponential decay in concentration from the point source. Thus, the distribution of therapeutic concentrations of a drug is limited to a small volume of tissue around the injection site, often with very high and sometimes toxic concentration at the center. Drugs can also be injected directly into the CSF, and the drug is usually only able to reach a shallow layer of the brain using this technique.

Drug-containing polymers and microchips are a more recent development and they can be embedded at the time of surgical resection of brain tumors. As in the case of direct injection, this method relies on diffusion for the drug to spread past the embedding site and has similar limited and uneven distribution.

Convection-Enhanced Delivery

Convection-enhanced delivery (CED) is a novel drug delivery method first developed by a research group directed by Edward Oldfield at the National Institute of Neurological Disorders (NINDS) in the early 1990s. This method was named convection-enhanced delivery because the therapeutic molecules are distributed into the extracellular space driven by a small, persistent hydrostatic pressure generated by an infusion pump, essentially, forced convection of a fluid containing a therapeutic agent. In contrast to diffusion which depends on a concentration gradient to distribute the molecules, the use of hydrostatic pressure in CED allows for the distribution of a homogeneous concentration of small and large molecules over large distances by displacing extracellular fluid with the infusate (fluid infused). In practice, the agent is delivered into the parenchyma or tumor through a microcatheter, or multiple microcatheters, inserted into the tissue. Infusion rates typically range from 0.1-10μl/min. The distribution from a single point source results in an elliptical to spherical distribution and spatial distribution is in some degree dependent on the tissue type (i.e., grey matter versus white matter). In a given tissue type, distribution volume is approximately linear to infusion volume.

CED into brain parenchyma, both white and gray matter, has shown reproducible large volumes of distribution with homogeneous drug concentration. Oldfield group's initial work showed that the concentration fall-off at the border is steep, resulting in a potentially large benefit in the delivery of cancer drugs in reducing toxicity to surrounding normal brain tissue.

Several factors influence the distribution volume. One key factor to achieve a large volume of distribution is the stability of the agent in the extracellular space.

Lipophilic agents may be exported transvascularly through blood vessels leading to a high efflux of the drug and limited distribution. Some other drugs may be prone to enzymatic degradation in the extracellular space. Another important determinant for distribution of macromolecules is the surface characteristics of the molecule and the extracellular matrix, i.e., the substances in the extracellular space within tissues that serve various purposes, including but not limited to serving as scaffolding to hold tissues together and helping to determine the behaviors of the cells. Binding of the molecule to the extracellular matrix or surface receptors may limit distribution. Binding to cell surface receptors may be overcome by saturating receptors with excess ligands. Binding of macromolecules to extracellular matrix has been overcome with some success by co-infusion of heparin.

Size of the molecules also affects volume of distribution. Early CED studies by Oldfield group and others suggested that 180kD, the size of immunoglobulin G (IgG), appeared to be the largest size that could pass through the extracellular space without the need of surface modification to the extracellular matrix. Recently, with the help of surface modification, adeno-associated virus (AAV, 40nm) and liposomes (50-200nm) have been distributed to large volumes of brain tissue. Surface modifications used were pegylation with liposomes and heparin co-infusion to saturate heparin sulfate proteoglycan (HSP) binding with AAV.

The volume of distribution is also affected by the retrograde movement of fluid along the outside of the catheter (backflow or reflux). Reflux is determined by catheter diameter, infusion rate, and tissue density among other factors. The larger the diameter of the catheter, the greater is the backflow along its outer wall. If reflux reaches a low pressure zone (necrosis or CSF space), the fluid will inadvertently be lost into these spaces. This leads to the accumulation of the drug in these regions which may cause toxicity. Finally, increasing the infusion rate can increase the overall volume of distribution; however, this may also increase backflow, potentially shunting fluid away from the target region.

Ideally, agents delivered via CED should be contained within the target region of brain parenchyma or tumor mass. However, there are low pressure regions in some tumors along which infusate will flow, sometimes into ventricles or subarachnoid space. This phenomenon is usually referred to as leakage and has often been observed in both humans and experimental animals. One study indicates that this can happen in 20% of CED procedures. This obvious waste of therapeutic agents will consequently reduce the volume of distribution and drug concentration in the planned target region. It may also cause untoward effects on normal brain tissue. It is therefore critical to follow the flow of the infused agents. When this happens, it might be helpful to adjust the placement of the catheter to move the opening away from the low pressure region. It is also not known yet whether this leakage is reversible. If reversible, pausing infusion for a period of time and subsequently restarting the infusion could eliminate leakage.

Although the physical parameters influencing drug distribution by CED have not been thoroughly clarified, the ability of CED to achieve high concentrations of a therapeutic agent over large volumes of brain tissue has led to several clinical trials in patients with neurodegenerative disorders and malignant gliomas. Therapeutic studies for malignant gliomas have focused on delivering targeted macromolecules (monoclonal antibodies, recombinant toxins, etc.) or currently available small molecule drugs.

Catheter Design for CED

Metal needles have been used as the infusion tool since the early studies of CED in laboratory animals. Most of the recent clinical trials of CED in the treatment of malignant gliomas have used ventricular catheters made of Silastic® rubber. Ideally, a catheter for CED should be reflux-free; does not adsorb therapeutic agents to its wall, especially when expensive novel targeted agents are used; and should have tip configurations that direct the drug to desired regions. In certain instances, it may be required to confirm catheter placement before drug infusion with magnetic resonance imaging (MRI) where MRI-compatible catheters are needed.

As briefly discussed above, reflux negates the bulk flow of infusate in the extracellular space that is produced by CED. In the presence of reflux, an increase in infusion volume does not produce an increase in distribution volume accordingly. Reflux causes the drug to flow into ventricular or subarachnoid space where it may cause toxicity. While reduction in infusion rate may reduce the chance of reflux, it would be ideal to have the option of infusing at various flow rates, i.e., up to 10μl/minute or more if possible, to achieve desired volume of distribution in a reasonable period of time.

Simple infusion tools such as metal needles have high rates of reflux. Several groups, including Souweidane group at Weill Cornell Medical College, observed that a step-design cannula significantly reduces, or even effectively prevents, backflow. The group used a 22 gauge guide cannula with a 28 gauge internal cannula, both of fused silica. The internal cannula extended beyond the end of the guide cannula by 5 mm. The cannula set was left in place for 5 minutes before infusion started. At flow rates as high as 8μl/minute of an [124]I-labeled monoclonal antibody, no reflux was observed on positron emission tomography (PET) imaging. Presumably the tissue surrounding the extended internal cannula sealed off the entry tract. There might be a threshold that this design can withstand the pressure, but infusion rates higher than 8μl/min have not been attempted with this tip configuration. Nevertheless this design offers an attractive improvement over the cannula design previously used. This fused silica cannula set is not and probably will never be approved for clinical use due to its insufficient mechanical strength. Ventricular catheters currently used in CED clinical trials have larger diameters and would produce a higher chance of reflux based on laboratory observation of the relationship between reflux and cannula diameters. Advances in biocompatible materials such as polymers and ceramic may eventually make small diameter MRI-compatible step-design cannulas and catheters strong enough for clinical use.

Tip Configuration

A standard cannula only has an opening at its tip. In certain instances, such as after radiation therapy where scars may form inside the tumor, this may not allow for sufficient flow of infusate. Considering infusates will follow the path of least resistance, a multi-tipped cannula may provide better pressure output, and therefore, achieve a better volume of distribution. The effectiveness of the multi-opening configuration has been questioned by studies showing that a multi-port catheter delivered most of the infusate through the proximal port and thus behaved like catheters with only one port.

One research group constructed a 3-mm long porous hollow fiber catheter to increase the surface area of the brain in immediate contact with the drug releasing area. The hollow fiber has innumerous pores of 0.45μm along its walls. This theoretically avoids clogging, which happens in certain instances. The hollow fiber catheter offers up to a threefold increase in the distribution volume of the drug into the normal mouse brain when compared to a needle which has a single macroscopic pore. The tiny microscopic pores do not have the same pressure-shunting properties as the macroscopic pores do; therefore a long length of the porous wall is effective in delivering drugs. In large animal and human applications, it is more reasonable to have this porous hollow fiber configuration at the tip for a few millimeters to a few centimeters rather than the entire catheter being porous. The porous wall and step design could even be combined to reduce reflux during drug administration.

In certain other instances, it may be desirable to direct the infusate preferentially in a specific direction. Due to the pressure-shunting properties of the proximal port on the regular multi-port cannulas, it may not be effective to direct infusate distribution via such a tip configuration. One potential design is to construct a catheter with independent cannulas inside. Each cannula has an opening at a predetermined location and direction with its pressure being independently controlled. This design will require additional engineering and testing to determine its feasibility.

Monitoring Drug Distribution

Monitoring the distribution and concentration of an infused drug is critical for numerous reasons. In order for the delivered therapeutic agent to be effective, in addition to its biological effectiveness, it must be distributed within the tumor in therapeutic concentrations. Exposure of normal tissue to the drug should be controlled to reduce the probability of toxicity. It is also highly desirable to monitor for possible backflow and leakage so that cannula placement can be adjusted to correct for any problems that may arise. The importance of monitoring *in vivo* distribution and concentration is highlighted by the difficulty in achieving optimal therapeutic efficacy in recent clinical trials. In the recent TGFα-PE38 study and the phase III PRECISE trial for glioblastoma (see below), poor drug distribution was cited as one of the reasons for the unsatisfactory efficacy results. Monitoring the distribution and concentration of CED infusate in humans is difficult due to the fact that the majority of therapeutic agents cannot be seen on any of the clinical imaging methods. Nevertheless, distribution can be visualized under certain circumstances. T2-weighted magnetic resonance (MR) images are helpful in identifying infusate distribution in regions of relatively normal intensity, but distribution cannot be identified with certainty when infused into already hyperintense regions, such as in the case of DIPG.

Another choice is to use visible surrogate tracers. Gd-DTPA and ^{123}I-albumin have been co-infused as surrogate tracers, viewable on T1-weighted MR and single photon emission computed tomography (SPECT) images, respectively, in clinical studies. The shortcomings of surrogate markers are that they are only able to track the initial distribution accurately. Differences in biological activities and clearance can confound their ability to follow the volumetric distribution of the therapeutic agent over time. Moreover, neither T2 MRI signals nor surrogate tracers are able to provide information on the concentration of the infused therapeutic agent. The ideal scenario is to directly image the therapeutic compound. With calibration, the concentration of the drug can be determined as well as the distribution. Utilizing serial imaging, clearance can be followed over time. In an ongoing clinical trial at Memorial Sloan-Kettering

Cancer Center and Weill Cornell Medical College, a therapeutic monoclonal antibody is labeled with [124]I to treat DIPG. [124]I is a positron emitter that can be visualized using PET imaging at a high resolution. The spatial resolution of [124]I PET is significantly higher than that of ^{123}I SPECT. [124]I has an intrinsic spatial resolution loss of only 2.3 mm. It is expected that much more detailed information regarding the distribution and concentration of CED infusate will be acquired. This approach of labeling a therapeutic agent with imageable radionuclide can be applied to some other agents and applications. For some other therapeutic agents, novel tags such as paramagnetic particles may prove useful in labeling the drug for quantitative *in vivo* imaging.

Predicting and Planning CED Distribution

It is critical to define the relationship between the volume of infusion (Vi) and the volume of distribution (Vd) to understand the expected distribution of an agent delivered into the brain via CED. This relationship is approximately linear and has variable slopes depending on the anatomical site of administration as well as the therapeutic compound. For instance, the Vd/Vi ratio is 8.2 in the non-human primate (NHP) striatum compared to a ratio of 4.1 in cerebral white matter for small molecules. A ratio of 8.7 was observed in the NHP brainstem for Gd-albumin (72kD). This ratio can serve as an estimate to match tumor volume in clinical trials.

BrainLAB AG (Feldkirchen, Germany) has developed a software package called iPlan Flow specifically for use in planning CED. The software takes data obtained via MRI regarding brain tissue characteristics of individual patients as input. Then the software helps in determining cannula placement, calculating the infusion parameters and predicting distribution. The plan for treatment can be visualized in three dimensions, including the number and position of catheters. One study retrospectively tested the ability of this software using MR diffusion tensor imaging to predict patient-specific drug distributions by CED. ^{123}I-labeled albumin was co-infused as a surrogate tracer with the targeted recombinant cytotoxin IL13-PE38QQR in patients with recurrent malignant gliomas. The spatial distribution of ^{123}I-albumin was then compared with a drug distribution simulation provided by iPlan Flow. The algorithm had a high sensitivity and specificity in identifying catheter trajectories that resulted in reflux or leakage. The mean concordance of the volume of distribution between the actual ^{123}I-albumin distribution and the simulation was 66% and the mean maximal inplane deviation was less than 8.5 mm. The use of this simulation algorithm was considered clinically useful in 85% of the catheters.

Even though albumin does not have a specific affinity towards malignant tissue compared to targeted agents, this simulation showed that software with the ability to take into account characteristics of an individual patient's anatomy and pathophysiology is helpful in the planning of CED. iPlan Flow has yet to be tested in CED in the brainstem.

Safety of CED in the Brainstem

The concept of using CED for DIPG is appealing given that this particular tumor is relatively compact, has growth patterns simulating white matter tracts, seldom metastasizes before local relapse and has no definitive therapy. The Souweidane group first established the feasibility of this delivery route in the brainstem in small animals for potential clinical application in 2002. Subsequently, the safeties of inert agents, characteristics of distribution and toxicity of potential therapeutic agents in the brainstem of small animals and non-human primates have been studied. This approach has also been used safely in a small number of patients with brainstem diseases. These studies showed that CED does not cause clinically relevant mechanical injury to the brainstem and this approach has a promising therapeutic application in humans. In clinical practice, image-guided frameless stereotaxy can be utilized to target the brainstem in children for biopsy or cannula insertion with high accuracy and low risks of temporary or permanent morbidity. These will help establish CED as an accepted drug delivery method in the treatment of DIPG.

Therapeutic Efficacy of CED

CED of chemotherapeutic molecules has shown considerable promise in phase I and phase II clinical trials in patients with recurrent malignant gliomas. However, phase III results are less encouraging. CED in the treatment of DIPG has produced encouraging results in preclinical studies. A few phase I trials of CED in DIPG are recruiting patients or in the planning stage.

Several factors that are critical in achieving good therapeutic efficacy require further elucidation. The convective force used in CED facilitates drug distribution to larger volumes of brain tissue. However, malignant gliomas may contain areas of fibrosis and necrosis, especially after receiving external beam radiation therapy, which is currently part of the standard of care. CED, as an investigational therapy, usually is not started until the completion of radiation therapy. The fibrosis and necrosis may cause chaotic pressure gradients within the tumor and therefore an unpredictable distribution of the drug. Even within the peritumoral margins, targeting infiltrating tumor cells may be limited by the normal anisotropy of the brain tissue resulting in preferential flow of fluid away from the intended target. Furthermore, the presence of areas of disrupted BBB either by the pathological changes or by previous treatment such as radiation therapy may increase efflux of drugs out of the CNS. A better understanding of drug distribution will become a critical part of evaluating future studies employing CED. Another concern is that the drugs infused in a single session may maintain their therapeutic concentration for a period too short to be effective before being cleared out of the target region. Once we have a better understanding of drug distribution and clearance, other unsolved questions including optimal catheter design and placement, infusion rate and duration, and the benefit of repeat infusions can be better addressed.

The use of targeted macromolecules allows for either intratumoral or peritumoral treatment in malignant gliomas. Some of these agents may not be specific enough, potentially leading to injury to normal tissue. This was seen with IL4-PE, which initially started at a concentration of 2μg/ml. The potential benefit of targeting multiple molecules by combining different recombinant toxins, or combining these agents with other chemotherapies, remains unknown. Despite these limitations and uncertainties, significant responses have been observed in all of the CED clinical trials described below.

CED Clinical Trials for the Treatment of Brain Tumors

Theoretically, any antineoplastic agent can be delivered through CED for the treatment of brain tumors, including standard chemotherapeutic agents and novel macromolecules such as monoclonal antibodies and viral vectors. One unresolved issue is that CED, in its current form, is a surgery and typically performed as a single session. It is unknown how long the infused drugs remain at therapeutic concentrations after a single session of CED. Imaginatively, it is more like a bolus dose, and predictably only a portion of the cancer cells are killed by such a bolus dose and the remaining cancer cells will continue to grow, ultimately resulting in failure of treatment.

For various reasons, most standard chemotherapeutic agents do not cross the BBB in sufficient amounts to have a significant effect on the cancer. CED of such small molecules showed that these agents have observable antitumor responses. However, more neurological complications have been observed when these agents were delivered via CED compared to systemic chemotherapy. There are efforts to improve formulations of these agents for local delivery to reduce neurotoxicity and enhance therapeutic response. These efforts, if successful, will make CED of small chemotherapeutic molecules applicable on a larger scale.

More effort is focused on delivering recombinant toxins via CED in the treatment of brain tumors. These toxins are recombinant proteins and have two components, a targeting moiety, typically a monoclonal antibody or a ligand to an over-expressed cell membrane receptor, and a toxin, which can be bacterial toxins. Bacterial toxins frequently utilized in recombinant toxins are *Pseudomonas* exotoxin (PE) and *Diphtheria* toxin (DT). These polypeptide toxins have strong cytotoxicity against mammalian cells by inhibiting protein synthesis. They do not show selectivity in killing cancer cells over normal cells. But by attaching them to a targeting moiety directed to cancer cells, the recombinant toxins can become highly selective in killing cancer cells while sparing normal cells. For this purpose, these bacterial toxins have been genetically modified to make them easier to attach to targeting moieties. Genetic modification also reduces the activity of these toxins to give a wider therapeutic window. One targeting moiety widely studied for adult malignant brain tumors is interleukin-13 (IL-13), because the IL-13 receptor is known to be over-expressed in a high percentage of these tumors. Binding of a recombinant toxin on the cell surface triggers internalization of the toxin, which enzymatically arrests protein synthesis and ultimately causes cell death. Several recombinant toxins have been utilized in clinical trials for adult malignant brain tumors delivered via CED. These toxins are attractive in that they have strong cell-killing capabilities and resistance rarely develops.

Transferrin-CRM107

Several recombinant toxins have reached the stage of clinical study. The first cytotoxin that was used in brain cancer therapy via CED was Transferrin-CRM107, a thioether conjugate of human transferrin and CRM107, a mutant form of *Diphtheria* toxin. The compound was developed by a group led by Richard Youle at the NINDS and is commercially available as TransMID™ from Celtic Pharma (HM, Bermuda). Transferrin-CRM107 targets tumor cells by binding to the transferrin receptor, which is over-expressed on rapidly dividing cells.

In a multicenter, open label phase II clinical trial, 44 adult patients received intratumoral CED at 0.67 µg/ml of Transferrin-CRM107 delivered directly into the tumor bed. Numerous significant clinical responses were observed. Of the 34 evaluable patients, five had a complete response and seven a partial response. The median survival for all 44 patients was 37 weeks. However, the tumor-selectivity of this recombinant toxin is not high, shown by its toxicity to normal tissues. In eight of the patients, increased cerebral edema was noticed. Those with clinical neurotoxicity also had MRI changes suggestive of microvascular injury, perhaps related to the higher levels of transferrin receptors on normal blood vessel walls. A phase III multicenter, randomized study in recurrent, nonresectable glioblastoma multiforme (GBM) was opened but withdrawn prior to patient enrollment due to the toxicity data from the phase II trial.

IL4-PE

Another recombinant toxin clinically examined is IL4-PE, which is commercially labeled as NBI-3001 (Neurocrine, San Diego, California) and PRX321 (Protox Therapeutics, Vancouver, British Columbia, Canada). More accurately called IL-4(38–37)-PE38KDEL, the agent uses a mutant interleukin-4 (IL-4) as the targeting moiety and a modified *Pseudomonas* exotoxin as the cytotoxic effector.

A phase I study of intratumoral CED of IL4-PE started at a concentration of 2μg/ml and was dose escalated to determine the maximum tolerated dose (MTD). Drug-related grade 3 or 4 CNS toxicity was seen in a total of 39% of patients in all groups, and no systemic toxicity was seen. A phase II, multicenter randomized study of intratumoral IL4-PE followed by tumor resection between 2 and 7 days after the completion of toxin infusion enrolled a total of 30 adult patients. The accrual was completed in 2003 and the objective clinical responses were not as good as Transferin-CRM107. A phase II trial of CED of IL4-PE with real-time imaging for therapy of recurrent glioblastoma (the study is referred to as CLARITY-1) has been approved but not recruiting patients as of November 2008, the last time the status of the trial was reported. There are no plans for a phase III study.

TGF-α-PE38

TGF-α-PE38 is another recombinant toxin that entered clinical phase. It is labeled as TP-38 commercially (TEVA Pharmaceuticals, North Wales, Pennsylvania). TGF-α-PE38 is composed of transforming growth factor-α (TGF-α), a native epidermal growth factor receptor (EGFR) ligand, and a 38kD fragment of the *Pseudomonas* exotoxin. TGF-α-PE38 binds to the EGFR, which is over-expressed in the majority of GBM and is naturally present in many normal organs.

Moderate or better responses were recorded in several patients in clinical trials. A phase I study of intratumoral and peritumoral infusion of TGF-α-PE38 was performed in 20 patients with recurrent malignant glioma with a concentration escalation of 0.025 to 0.1μg/ml. Two catheters were initially placed during tumor resection and then a total volume of 40 ml was infused. TGF-α-PE38 was well tolerated and a MTD was not established. At the completion of the study, four patients had no recurrence of tumor over 55 weeks after treatment.

The overall median survival for all patients being treated was 28 weeks. For those without radiographic evidence of residual disease at the time of therapy, the median survival was 33 weeks. One GBM patient remains alive and without progression more than 211 weeks after CED therapy, and another GBM patient went 198 weeks without progressive disease after a nearly complete response to TGF-α-PE38 and remains alive more than 260 weeks from CED therapy. In the majority of patients imaged using SPECT, infusate distributions were significantly influenced by leakage and failed to produce any significant intraparenchymal distribution. This highlights the importance of accurate catheter placement and drug distribution monitoring.

A phase II multicenter randomized study was conducted in adults with recurrent GBM. Patients were randomized into two groups treated with peritumoral CED of 0.05 or 0.1µg/ml of TGF-α-PE38. The total volume infused was approximately 40 ml. Post-infusion MRI changes were seen 1 to 4 months after treatment, geographically associated with the site of catheter placement. These changes usually resolved by 20 weeks post-treatment. There were no grade 3 or 4 toxicities related to TGF-α-PE38. Only 20% of patients retained the cytotoxin within the tumors by imaging. A phase I/II clinical trial evaluating TGF-α-PE38 in treating young patients with recurrent or progressive supratentorial high-grade glioma was terminated prematurely. Further clinical trials are pending resolution of issues encountered in the phase I and II trials, with catheter placement and infusate leakage as the most important concerns.

IL13-PE38

IL13-PE38 was developed by a research group led by Waldemar Debinski in the mid-1990s. It is a recombinant toxin consisting of human IL-13 with PE38QQR, a 38kD fragment of the *Pseudomonas* exotoxin. It is labeled commercially as Cintredekin Besudotox by NeoPharm (Lake Bluff, Illinois). High levels of the IL-13 receptor have been found in more than 90% of glioblastoma, whereas expression of the receptor in the normal brain is not present or at low levels. This toxin demonstrated efficacy in several preclinical GBM models before moving into clinical study.

Intratumoral and peritumoral CED of IL13-PE38 has been investigated in four separate phase I studies. In the largest peritumoral phase I study, a maximum tolerated concentration of 0.5µg/ml was observed. In this four-stage study, histological efficacy, maximum tolerated concentration and maximum infusion time were assessed. The final stage explored the stereotactic placement of catheters after tumor resection to improve targeting the peritumoral brain tissue.

A total of 51 patients with malignant gliomas were treated including 46 patients with GBM. IL13-PE38 and procedure-related adverse events were primarily limited to the CNS, including those associated with increased edema. With the administration of steroids, all patients tolerated infusions of 40ml through 2 to 3 catheters lasting up to 6 days. The maximum tolerated concentration was 0.5µg/ml and tumor necrosis was observed at this concentration. There were no grade 3 or 4 adverse events associated with drug infusion at concentrations lower than 0.5µg/ml, and no systemic toxicities were observed. Delayed radiographic changes were observed in some patients 2 to 4 months after therapy, which responded to steroids and may represent an inflammatory response or nonspecific activity.

The overall median survival for GBM patients was 42.7 weeks. Catheter placement was variable in the early portion of the study, with some catheter tips placed in CSF spaces. Catheter placement was correlated with survival. The 27 GBM patients with two or more catheters placed optimally without loss of drug into the CSF compartment had a median survival of 55.6 weeks with follow-up extending beyond 5 years, and 5 of these patients (18.5%) survived beyond two years after a single treatment. These trials showed that most of the effective drug deliveries were achieved by infusing into the parenchyma surrounding the gross total resection cavities rather than into the remaining tumors themselves. They also demonstrated that the chance of successful delivery without reflux or leakage was enhanced if the catheter tip was at least 2cm deep from the last traverse pial surface and 5mm from the nearest non-traverse pial or ependymal surface.

These encouraging results led to a phase III multicenter, randomized study (known as the PRECISE study) in patients with first recurrent GBM. The patients were randomized 2:1 to surgery followed by peritumoral infusion of IL13-PE38 versus surgery and Gliadel wafer (MGI Pharma, Inc., Bloomington, Minnesota) implant. Gliadel wafer contains carmustine (bis-chloroethyl-nitrosourea [BCNU]) and is approved by the Food and Drug Administration (FDA) as a standard therapy for GBM following surgical resection. Fifty-two medical centers participated in this trial worldwide. Total enrollment was targeted at 300 patients to demonstrate a 50% improvement in overall survival in the experimental arm. Enrollment was completed in December 2005.

Analysis of follow-up data showed that this goal was not achieved. The median survival of the 184 patients in the CED arm was 36.4 weeks compared to 35.3 weeks for the 92 patients in the control arm. When the dataset was restricted to sites having enrolled more than six patients progressing to drug delivery, the results are more encouraging. In this case, the CED arm had an overall survival of 46.8 weeks versus 41.6 in the control arm, even though statistical analysis showed that this cannot be said with sufficient certainty. However, it is significant that progression-free survival was 17.7 versus 11.4 weeks in favor of CED. The investigators believe poor drug distribution in some patients is a major factor that adversely affected the therapeutic response. The trial implies that a uniform method must be applied in participating centers to ensure exact and reproducible drug delivery. Future trials will probably benefit from improved catheter placement, drug distribution and screening of expression level of IL-13 receptor chain α2 (IL-13Rα2). IL-13Rα2 is expressed specifically by glioma cells. The next generation toxin has been developed to bind the tumor-specific IL-13Rα2 rather than the IL-13 physiological receptor, and should be studied clinically.

[131]I-chTNT-1/B mAb

[131]I-chTNT-1/B mAb is an ^{131}I-labeled humanized murine monoclonal antibody (mAb). It binds to a universal intracellular antigen, histone H1. Histone H1 is in the assembled DNA double strand and is exposed and accessible for antibody binding in the necrotic core of solid tumors. This antigen provides an abundant insoluble anchor for the mAb. [131]I emits γ rays with sufficiently high energy to penetrate and kill adjacent tumor cells. From the principle of how the drug was designed, ^{131}I-chTNT-1/B mAb is not as specific as those targeting specific receptors (e.g., the EGFR or IL-13 receptors) expressed by tumor cells, but rather delivers cytotoxic radiation to the tumor mass as well as to tumor cells invading the surrounding tissue. "TNT" in the name of the agent stands for "tumor necrosis therapy." ^{131}I-chTNT-1/B mAb is commercially labeled as Cotara (Peregrine Pharmaceuticals, Tustin, California). The effect of ^{131}I-chTNT-1/B mAb in patients with malignant gliomas was investigated in several clinical studies. The results of two non-randomized, open-label studies have been published: a phase I study in 12 patients with recurrent anaplastic astrocytoma (AA) and GBM, and a phase II study in 39 patients with newly diagnosed or recurrent malignant gliomas.

The 51 patients enrolled in the two studies included 37 recurrent GBM, eight newly diagnosed GBM and six recurrent AA. All patients had previously undergone radiation therapy, 42 had previously undergone at least one surgery and 31 had a chemotherapy regimen. More than half of the patients (53%) had a tumor volume of ≥ 30 cm³. One or two catheters with slit openings near the closed distal end were placed with tips at or near the center of the enhancing tumor. ^{131}I-chTNT-1/B mAb was infused using CED over 1 to 2 days at a rate of 0.18ml/h. In the first six patients, 1.5mCi/cm^3 clinical target volume (CTV) was prescribed, which was calculated to deliver a dose of 137 Gy. For subsequent patients, the dose was based on tumor size and the prescribed activity was 0.5 – 3.0mCi/cm^3 administered in 1 or 2 infusions.

The phase I study showed that more than 130 Gy could be delivered to the tumor with 34 ± 9% dose retention at 24 hours and a biological half-life of 46 ± 16 hours. Imaging and dosimetry studies on a subset of six malignant glioma patients in the phase II study showed that infusion of 13.2 – 71.1mCi of activity produced a calculated absorbed dose of 55 – 135Gy.

Treatment-emergent, drug-related central nervous system adverse events included brain edema (16%), hemiparesis (14%) and headache (14%). Most of these were reversed by corticosteroids. Systemic adverse events were mild.

Treatment with ^{131}I-chTNT-1/B mAb in the phase I study resulted in three of nine GBM patients having stable disease at 60 days, and all nine patients with progressive disease at 90 days. The median time to progression (MTTP) and median survival time (MST) were 8.7 and 27.3 weeks, respectively. Of the three patients with AA, one achieved a partial response and the other two had stable disease 90 days after treatment. The 28 recurrent GBM patients in the phase II study had an MTTP of 8.4 weeks (historical control 8.0 weeks) and an MST of 23 weeks (historical control 24 weeks).

The phase II study contained patients with more diverse conditions. In an effort to "normalize" findings in this study, efficacy data from a subset of 12 recurrent GBM patients who received a total activity between 1.25 and 2.5mCi/cm^3, which was considered a therapeutic window based on efficacy versus toxicity, were examined. The median survival for these patients was 37.9 weeks. In addition, seven of the 28 recurrent GBM patients and one of the three recurrent AA patients survived for more than one year. Further research is required to determine the value of ^{131}I-chTNT-1/B CED in these patients.

Two other phase I trials of ^{131}I-chTNT-1/B CED in patients with recurrent or relapsed GBM have been completed recently and the results have not been published. A dose confirmation and dosimetry phase II study for GBM patients at first relapse is ongoing. The dose is a single 25-hour infusion of 2.5mCi/cm^3 CTV. Brief interim results for a subset of 14 patients were reported in October 2010 and the median overall survival was 86 weeks.

Current and Upcoming CED Clinical Trials in DIPG

There are no completed CED clinical trials for DIPG and only a small number of CED trials for DIPG are under way or in the planning stage. This is in contrast to the application of CED in the treatment of adult malignant gliomas, where a number of clinical trials have been completed as summarized above. Institutions sponsoring CED trials for DIPG have spent significant efforts in studying the safety of CED into the brainstem in small and large animals, including non-human primates.

CED of IL13-PE38 for DIPG

The NINDS is sponsoring a phase I clinical trial led by Dr. Russell Lonser, using CED to deliver IL13-PE38QQR into DIPG [Fig. 1a, 1b]. This study started recruiting patients in 2009 and is expected to finish in early 2013. It is an open label dose escalation safety study. IL-13 is an immune molecule normally occurring in the body. About 90% of malignant gliomas have high levels of IL-13 receptors while the normal brain tissue has only a low level of these receptors. The experimental drug, IL13-PE38QQR, which combines the modified PE with human IL-13, has been discussed above.

This study recruits patients 3 to 17 years of age with DIPG or supratentorial high-grade glioma that have not responded well to standard radiation therapy. 20 patients are expected to enroll in this study. The planned doses are 0.125, 0.25 and 0.5µg/ml. Safety and tolerability are the primary endpoints with secondary endpoints including imaging changes and treatment responses.

CED of [124]I-8H9 for DIPG

Memorial Sloan Kettering Cancer Center and Weill Cornell Medical College are conducting a phase I clinical trial led by Dr. Mark Souweidane, using CED to deliver [124]I-8H9 for the treatment of DIPG. This study is ongoing and expected to be completed in 2014. This is an open label dose escalation safety study. [124]I is a radionuclide with a half-life of 4.18 days. It emits γ rays and positrons, both of which having energies high enough for therapeutic purposes. Positrons will eventually be annihilated in the tissue resulting in the release of photons that are detected in PET imaging. 8H9 is a monoclonal antibody that binds to membrane protein B7-H3, which is expressed in high levels in most DIPG but not by normal brain tissue. In principle, this antibody conjugated to [124]I potentiates the antineoplastic effects of the radionuclide by directing therapeutic irradiation preferentially to cancer cells.

This study recruits patients with DIPG ages 3 to 21 years old. The enrolled

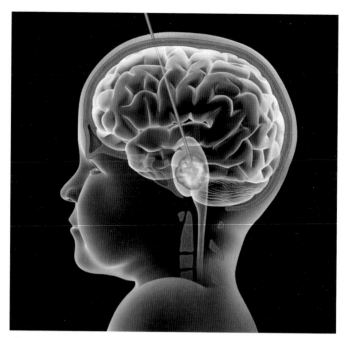

Figure 1a: Illustration demonstrating convection-enhanced delivery (CED) in the treatment of diffuse intrinsic pontine glioma (DIPG). An infusion cannula is inserted through the transfrontal approach into the pons. The tip of the cannula will be at, or near the center of the tumor. This is achieved by image-guided high-precision stereotaxy.

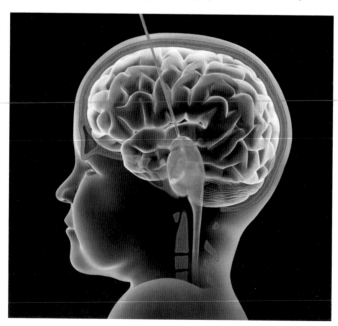

Figure 1b: With the cannula in place, drugs are infused into the pons driven by a precision pump. Ideally, the drug infused area encompasses the tumor and the surrounding infiltrated area.

patients will have undergone standard external beam radiation therapy but have not shown signs of progression. A maximum of 24 patients will be enrolled in this phase I study. The planned doses are 0.25, 0.5, 0.75 and 1.0mCi of the radio-antibody ^{124}I-8H9. Safety and tolerability are the primary endpoints. Uniquely, this study uses PET to image drug distribution and calculate radiation dose, which will provide invaluable information to correlate with tolerability and therapeutic response. The usefulness of other imaging modalities in CED planning in the brainstem will also be assessed as a secondary objective.

Future Directions

CED of therapeutic agents in the treatment of malignant brain tumors has shown considerable promise in preclinical and some clinical studies. Future advances will occur on two fronts: 1) the development of more effective therapeutic agents for delivery via CED and 2) the improvement of the technique of CED.

A promising advance in the development of therapeutic agents for the treatment of DIPG is the recent molecular characterization of this tumor. Three groups independently discovered that the platelet-derived growth factor receptors (PDGFR) are over-expressed in the majority of DIPG. Therapeutic agents targeting the PDGFR signal transduction pathways will be studied for therapeutic efficacy. These include anti-PDGFR antibodies and inhibitors of the receptor tyrosine kinase (RTK) and downstream pathways. Another over-expressed growth factor receptor is the EGFR. Like in the PDGFR pathway, agents targeting the EGFR pathway include anti-EGFR antibodies and inhibitors of the RTK and downstream pathways. The Sonic hedgehog (*Shh*) pathway is over-activated in many cancers, including malignant gliomas. Its study in DIPG is less in depth than in adult malignant gliomas. Inhibitors of this pathway could also be potential therapeutic agents. Like in adult malignant gliomas, IL-13Rα2 is highly expressed in DIPG therefore recombinant toxins using IL-13 as a targeting moiety are also potentially effective therapeutic agents for DIPG. The safety of CED of IL13-PE38QQR in the brainstem has been investigated by the Souweidane group in preclinical studies and a clinical trial sponsored by the NINDS is studying this agent in DIPG patients. Even though biopsy of DIPG is far from being routine, when these targeted therapies based on molecular profiling of tumors come to clinical use, it would be ideal for the tumor to be pre-screened for the targets that the drugs are designed for.

Increasing evidence shows that each individual tumor harbors multiple mutations. For instance, there are on average 60 mutations per glioblastoma. There is no reason to believe DIPG contains a much smaller number of mutations than other malignant gliomas. Targeting one therapeutic target rarely causes death to 100% of the cancer cells. RTK, downstream and parallel signal transduction pathways may be regulated in complex compensatory fashions that reduce the chance of cell death when the tumor is treated by aiming at only one therapeutic target. Therefore it is not surprising that drug resistance has been inevitable in almost all single-drug targeted therapies. We believe it is worthwhile to characterize defects in parallel and downstream signal transduction pathways and devise multi-targeting therapeutic regimens based on such characterization.

On the technical front of the delivery method, there is a need for better designed cannulas and more accurate stereotactic placement of cannulas into the tumor to achieve optimal drug distribution. The use of computer algorithms may help in planning the cannula placement and infusion parameters by taking into account anatomical structures and structural changes induced by the disease and prior treatment. Perhaps more important, imaging should accompany CED to ensure effective drug distribution and concentration as well as to determine how long the therapeutic agents are retained in the tumor and tumor-infiltrated brain tissue in individual patients. This requires the improvement of current imaging techniques or the development of new imaging methods.

As discussed above, the current single session CED is more like delivering a bolus dose. Clinically feasible methods to deliver multiple cycles of CED or continuous CED lasting up to several weeks are desired. This will require the development and engineering of catheters suitable for these purposes and desirably also pumps that can be embedded and allow patients to remain ambulatory.

CED-based therapies will continue to evolve, with a need for additional preclinical and clinical research.

Chapter 18

Vaccine Treatment Strategies

Christopher Moertel, MD

Over the last 40 years, incredible advancements have taken place in the treatment of childhood cancer. The overall cure rate for childhood acute lymphoblastic leukemia is approaching 90 percent and some pediatric cancers have exceeded that mark. New treatment strategies for medulloblastoma, a malignant brain tumor of childhood, have increased the cure rate while managing to decrease the dose of radiation necessary for cure. The history of cancer therapy has seen first advancements in surgical techniques, then radiotherapy, then chemotherapy.

Despite improvements in surgery and radiation delivery for some types of brain tumors, the survival rates for one type of brain tumor known as glioblastoma multiforme (GBM) has changed little over the years. The incorporation of temozolomide in the treatment of adult GBM was heralded as a great treatment advance, but it did little more than extend survival by about two and one half months. Temozolomide has been used to treat children with the same tumor, but little to no benefit has been seen. Specifically, children with DIPG (which looks like GBM under the microscope) have seen no benefit from the addition of temozolomide, let alone any chemotherapy added to classical radiation therapy. Hence, the need to keep looking for new answers to old questions. Is there any way we can find a new tool to treat brain tumors like GBM and its pediatric equivalent, DIPG?

Tumor Immunology to Treat Cancer

We are in a new era in which we are witnessing a great leap in the knowledge of chemical pathways at work in cancer cells and are now able to create designer drugs known as targeted therapies to attack these pathways and, hopefully disable the cancer cell. Another novel area for cancer therapy has been the focus on tumor immunology. The hope of

Dr. Moertel is a Professor of Pediatrics and Clinical Director of the Pediatric Brain Tumor Program at the University of MN, and Children's Hospital in St. Paul, MN.

tumor immunology is built on the premise of taking advantage of the body's own weapons to attack foreign invaders and tumor cells. Some of the immunologic tools in this arsenal are antibodies, immune stimulators and vaccines.

Vaccines have been used in medicine for decades to boost the body's own immune response to protect against invading foreign diseases, particularly infectious diseases. In this case, the vaccine is given prior to the individual becoming severely ill with the disease—hopefully with the result that the individual only exhibits a very mild form of the disease or no symptoms at all. There are currently two vaccines available which prevent virus infections leading to the development of cancer. The first is against hepatitis B, a virus that can cause liver cancer. The second is against human papilloma virus that is designed to stop specific strains of the virus leading to cervical cancer.

Tumor immunotherapy to treat childhood cancer is no longer just theory and research taking place in the lab. A recent breakthrough in the treatment of neuroblastoma—another difficult childhood cancer to cure, employs an antibody against the tumor cells. One monoclonal antibody, called chimeric (Ch) 14.18 attacks a molecule on the neuroblastoma cell surface called GD2. The body can then recognize this antibody-tumor cell complex and attack it using its own immune system to destroy the cancer. To enhance this immunological response from the child's own body, the children are also given 'immune stimulators' to excite their own immune system eliminating even more antibody-tumor cells complexes. The immune stimulators include interleukin 2 and granulocyte-macrophage colony stimulating factor (GM-CSF). Some children can have significant side effects, but the benefit of cure far outweighs the risks in the setting of this otherwise lethal disease. This approach has helped saved many more children's lives. Indeed, antibody therapy has become part of the standard of care for treating advanced-stage neuroblastoma.

Tumor immunology to treat brain tumors

Researchers hypothesizing about the possible use of vaccines to treat brain cancer were concerned about the established belief that the brain was "immunologically privileged." That is, the immune system could do little across the blood brain barrier. However, our laboratories here at the University of Minnesota, in addition to other labs across the country, have shown that immune system cells and antibodies can go into the brain fairly easily. In fact, it has been shown that malignant brain tumors can train cells called myeloid (bone marrow) derived suppressor cells to "dumb down" the immune system. A lot has been learned about the immune system's relationship with the brain and the body's ability to mount an immune attack within brain tissue. This body of science has encouraged many to pursue immunotherapy strategies against brain tumors. Recently, there has been significant energy put into vaccine therapies for brain tumors, with GBM being the main target.

One group at Duke University has studied an antibody against a protein found in excess on the cell surface of brain tumors called Epidermal Growth Factor Receptor (EGFR). Indeed, about 20% of GBMs have a mutant variant of EGFR called EGFRvIII. So if EGFR is found in abundance on tumor cells and EGFRvIII is a unique mutation on tumor cells, why not use this as a target for a programmed immune attack? That is what the Duke group did. First, they conducted a clinical trial combining their EGFRvIII protein with cells from the patients' immune system called dendritic cells (DC) and re-injected them into the patients with newly diagnosed GBM. This led to an overall survival rate that was better than expected. They then went on to do a study in partnership with MD Anderson that used their EGFRvIII vaccine combined with KLH, a protein that excites the immune system. None of the patients' dendritic cells were removed and re-injected in this study and everyone received "standard" temozolomide in addition. The results of this trial were somewhat encouraging. Immunotherapy for brain tumors burst onto the scene and a great deal of enthusiasm and interest was created in the brain tumor community. Currently there is one trial open at Stanford for newly diagnosed children with DIPG that uses an EGFRvIII vaccine. This vaccine trial was initiated after Dr. Li and colleagues reported 50% of DIPG tumors had EGFRvIII on their cell surface.

While the Duke group was working on their specific protein-based approach, another group in California was using a patient's own tumor cells to make a vaccine. Dr. Linda Liau and colleagues resected the patient's own tumor, cultured it in the lab and separated proteins from the surface of the tumor cells. They then removed cells called mononuclear cells from the patient's circulating blood through a process known as apheresis and separated cells called dendritic cells (DC). The patient's own tumor surface proteins were then combined with his or her DCs, incubated for up to an hour, and re-injected into his or her body. This treatment is best called an acid-eluted glioblastoma multiforme peptide-pulsed dendritic cell vaccine. Dr. Liau's group showed that the vaccine was safe and, resulted in longer survival for a number of patients. This work has now been commercialized (Northwest Biotherapeutics, Inc.) and is available to adult patients with GBM through a phase II trial at participating centers. This therapy is not yet available for DIPG patients.

Another group led by Dr. Hideo Okada at the University of Pittsburgh has had significant experience with glioma-associated antigen-derived synthetic peptides that excite cytotoxic T cells. Okada's work also employs dendritic cells incubated with the peptide and given along with a substance that excites the immune system called Poly-ICLC (polyinosinic-polycytidylic acid). This peptide strategy is available only to individuals with a specific HLA subtype, A2. Unfortunately, HLA-A2 is present in only 45% of the population. One of Dr. Okada's vaccine studies conducted with Dr. Regina Jakacki, who has participated in and run a number of DIPG clinical trials, target DIPG specifically. Dr. Okada has reported (unpublished data) that at least one vaccine patient exhibited significant tumor regression after initial worsening of the MRI abnormality in the brainstem.

At the University of Minnesota, we have developed a dendritic cell vaccine based on a brain tumor initiating cell (BTIC) line called GBM6. This cell line has surface characteristics on the cells that match the surface characteristics of initiating cells in many types of brain tumors, including glioblastoma. The cell line also more closely mimics the growing conditions of human brain tumors by being grown in 5% oxygen rather than the usual room air or 20% oxygen seen in most lab environments. While our research is still early, we are in the midst of a phase I trial that is showing that patients with brain tumors have immune responses to our vaccine and may have tumor regression or stabilization without any unusual toxicity. Indeed, the stronger immune responses have been noted in our younger patients. Based on this early data, we are going on to start a phase I trial targeting patients with newly diagnosed DIPG using a lysate of our GBM6 cell line and topical Imiquimod, another immune system-enhancing agent. Initially, we will be treating adult patients with GBM so that any unusual toxicity will be dealt with before kids are exposed to this new treatment modality. We feel this treatment approach has three specific advantages for the DIPG population. First, there is no need to obtain tumor tissue to create the vaccine (a nearly impossible task in patients with DIPG). Second, the vaccine is not HLA restricted, as is the case in most peptide-based vaccines, being available to the entire population. Third, this new vaccine trial will not use dendritic cells. Hence, there will be no need for apheresis and all of the difficulty that entails.

The common experience among those conducting brain tumor immunotherapy trials is that minimal residual disease is optimal at the beginning of treatment. Because DIPG cannot be surgically removed, we will need to depend on radiation therapy to create minimal disease. Unfortunately, this means that immunotherapy strategies will generally not be optimal for those whose disease has relapsed, unless caught at a very early stage.

All of this is very early and may certainly end up not providing what we and all parents of children with DIPG ultimately desire, but the early experience with GBM immunotherapy tells us that there is a glimmer of hope for patients with DIPG that has not been realized with classical radiation and chemotherapy–based approaches. At the very least, we hope that new pathways to a cure will be revealed.

Chapter 19

DIPG and Tissue Donation

Cynthia Hawkins, MD, PhD
Eric Bouffet, MD
Ute Bartels, MD

Before magnetic resonance imaging (MRI) became available, surgery was usually recommended to confirm the diagnosis of brainstem tumors including diffuse intrinsic pontine glioma (DIPG) to provide both histological and prognostic information. However, surgery was associated with significant morbidity and the benefit of this approach was questioned when it became evident that the MRI scan was able to provide images that were basically diagnostic of DIPG. Therefore, since the early 1990s, the frequency of biopsy has significantly decreased and most DIPG children are currently treated without histological confirmation.

Although this approach is the result of a consensus, over the years there has also been increasing awareness that progress in the management of this deadly disease will only occur with more biological information on DIPG. In this context, several teams have explored ways of collecting tissue material, in particular at the time of death, from limited brain or brainstem autopsies.

Early Experiences

Autopsy

Autopsy was a standard practice for in-hospital deaths in many institutions until the late 20th century. Autopsies were a standard procedure in former times. They were performed to identify the cause of death, and the contribution of autopsies to the understanding of many conditions has been significant. However, there has been a steep decline in

Dr. Hawkins is a Principal Investigator at the Arthur and Sonia Labatt Brain Tumour Research Center, an Assistant Professor at the University of Toronto, and Neuropathologist at the Hospital for Sick Children, Toronto, Canada.

autopsy rates over the last decades as, in many cases, the cause of the patient's disease was felt to have already been identified. A drawback to this practice, however, is that it limits researchers' ability to study diseases at the tissue level particularly for diseases such as DIPG, where no surgical procedures are ever undertaken. Thus, until recently there has been no experience with systematic collection of brain or brainstem tissue to advance research in DIPG. Now groups from Canada and the U.S. have reported this experience and demonstrated the possibility to use postmortem material for genome-wide studies and even for generating cell lines.

In the Toronto experience, the concept of autopsy was discussed by the treating neuro-oncologist after radiation therapy, at the time of progression or later during palliative care. Sometimes this discussion was initiated during a home visit. Explanation included the different types of autopsies, in particular the possibility to restrict the autopsy to the whole brain or to the brainstem tumor according to the family's preference. In cases where only the tumor was removed, a small biopsy of the frontal normal brain was also performed. To obtain appropriate tissue, in particular RNA (ribonucleic acid), the autopsy needs to be done relatively early following death. In the St. Jude experience, there was minimal RNA degradation when the autopsy was performed within 5 hours of death; however, the quality of RNA dropped significantly beyond that delay. Similarly the possibility to grow cell lines from tumor tissue is strongly related to minimizing the delay between the time of death and autopsy.

Interestingly, in both the Canadian and U.S. experiences, most patients died at home (88% and 84%, respectively). If a family or patient consented to an autopsy, the process was carefully organized ahead of time in order to avoid any delay in the funeral. At the time of death, a transportation service was arranged to pick up the body and transfer it to the academic center or to a local hospital where the autopsy was performed within hours. The autopsy itself was carefully performed in order to avoid any visible scars, in particular in the context of viewing visitations and open casket services, which are an important part of bereavement in the North American culture. The body of the child was brought back to the funeral home. This organization allowed privacy for the family and a timely funeral without delay.

The issue of the consent for post mortem tissue collection has been described in detail in one publication from the Toronto group. In this experience, 10 out of 21 parents who were approached gave their approval. For the 10 families who consented, their main motivation was to support research and to contribute to breakthroughs in scientific research on DIPG to benefit future children.

> Dr. Bouffet is the Director of the Neuro-oncology Program and a Senior Associate Scientist in the Research Institute at the Hospital for Sick Children, as well as Professor of Pediatrics at the University of Toronto, Canada.

In this experience, 2 children (11 and 10 years old) expressed their own wish to donate their brain for research purposes. The main reasons for declining autopsies were ethical and/or religious reasons or related to the level of emotional distress. Only one family felt upset by the request for brain donation. In all cases, when an autopsy was performed, a face-to-face meeting took place between the treating physician and the parents once the results of the autopsy were available. No parents expressed any regret from having given consent. All expressed their hope that their child's death may help research and contribute to the development of new treatments.

The scientific results of the research conducted on postmortem material have been reported since 2009 in several important publications. Researchers have been able to identify a number of potential targets for new treatments. This work has also shown that DIPG is not a single entity and that different types of treatments may be needed according to the underlying biology of the tumor.

Stereotactic biopsies

In parallel, other teams have decided to reintroduce the concept of biopsying DIPG at the time of presentation. The neurosurgical team from Necker Hospital in Paris has reported on the feasibility and safety of stereotactic biopsies of patients with newly diagnosed DIPG. In their initial report, 2 out of 24 patients presented with a transient deficit associated with the procedure. They have subsequently reported and updated their experience and have confirmed the safety and feasibility of DIPG biopsy in more than 80 patients. This work has also provided new information regarding the biology of DIPG. Interestingly, the results of studies conducted with tissue obtained at the time of diagnosis or at autopsy (therefore after radiotherapy in most cases) do not differ considerably.

What Have We Learned So Far About DIPG From Autopsy Studies?

Three genomic studies have now been published on autopsy series of DIPG. While still somewhat limited when compared to genomics studies conducted in adult cancer, several important conclusions can be drawn from the data available from these DIPG studies which can help in the development of future clinical trials. First, the studies support differences at both the copy number and expression level that distinguish pediatric DIPG from both adult and pediatric glioblastoma multiforme (GBM) elsewhere in the brain. This confirms that DIPG must be considered as a separate biologic entity

Dr. Bartels is an Oncologist in the Neuro-oncology Program at the Hospital for Sick Children, and Assistant Professor at the University of Toronto, Canada.

for the purpose of clinical trial design.

Second, receptor tyrosine kinases (RTKs) appear to be upregulated at the genomic or expression level (or both) in the majority of pediatric DIPGs. The most commonly amplified RTK in pediatric DIPG is *PDGFRA*, occurring at the genomic level in at least 30% of DIPGs with an even larger number showing over-expression at the RNA and protein levels. Gain of *EGFR* does not appear to be a frequent event in pediatric DIPG. However, two other RTKs are reported to be frequently gained in DIPGs: *MET* and *IGF1R*. Interestingly, in many cases more than one RTK is amplified in the same tumor, a finding that may have implications when using single RTK-inhibitors.

Based on their work on stereotactic biospies, the team for Necker (Paris) has described two distinct subgroups of DIPG. The first subgroup shows mesenchymal and pro-angiogenic characteristics. The second subgroup displays oligodendroglial features, and appears to be driven by *PDGFRA*. This later group had a significantly worse outcome and shorter survival expectancy. This suggests that different treatment strategies may be needed as DIPGs do not appear as a uniform disease.

Current Situation

These experiences have generated significant hope and enthusiasm in the DIPG community and also amongst parents and support groups. In April 2009, the FDA held an open public hearing specifically to discuss the science and ethics regarding pediatric DIPG biopsy in the United States. The purpose of the FDA hearing was to address a research initiative proposed by a U.S. based children's hospital that wanted to biopsy newly diagnosed DIPG children to compare similarities between their tumors and pediatric cerebral glioblastomas. Several issues were addressed during the 2009 FDA hearing including the concern of a number of the panel members that the risk of biopsy of DIPG was not balanced by certain benefit for the individual child. As a way to bridge this issue, several experts suggested that an initial effort be made to evaluate port-mortem tissue. This would alleviate concerns regarding safety of biopsy and also make more tissue available for research purposes. Several groups (Dana Farber of Boston, UCSF of San Francisco, the National Cancer Institute of Bethesda, the Institut Gustave Roussy of Paris) are currently working on biopsy driven protocols. In these protocols, the results of the biopsy will be taken into account to stratify patients and allocate their treatment accordingly.

Concurrently, an increasing number of institutions, including Sick Children's

Hospital in Toronto, St. Jude Children's Research Hospital, and the National Institutes of Health (NIH), already have research procedures in place for autopsy tissue donations from families whose children were treated under their care or in outside institutions.

Where Do We Go From Here?

Autopsy studies have triggered a tremendous enthusiasm in the pediatric neuro-oncology community. Several protocols have been developed or are about to open following the publication of the first genomic studies that have identified potential targets. However, most protocols target one mechanism only and it is likely that the successful management of DIPG will require combination therapies. In this context, recent development of genetically and histologically accurate preclinical (animal) models is critical, as this will allow the testing of targeted therapies that may eventually be brought to the clinic. A number of models are currently being tested that may contribute to selecting the most appropriate agents or combinations for future clinical trials. There is no doubt that the coming years will see an explosion of new DIPG protocols based on the data generated by the collection of autopsy material. Everyone hopes that, as a result, we will observe for the first time a difference in the dismal outcome of children with DIPG.

Parent Perspectives

I know this is such a difficult thing to consider while a child is fighting, but planning for tissue donation is not giving up in the fight. It is just one of the many ways we can prepare for our children's memories to endure and for their lives to make a difference, even as we hope and plan to never reach the day.

None of Caleb's doctors ever approached my wife or me about a donation of Caleb's tumor. Through reading the web blog of another family whose son had passed away, I learned that they had donated his tumor and I became aware of the medical value of the tumor. I would not have known the tumor had any value, or that a doctor would want it, if I'd not stumbled across that web page.

While we were on a routine monthly trip to the NIH, I raised the subject with Caleb's doctor. Caleb was still doing well, but I knew the prognosis of his disease and I wanted to begin the discussion with his doctor. She seemed hesitant to discuss it, but simply said that when the time was right, there were some studies that could use the tumor and we could certainly discuss it later. I also asked Caleb's doctor in Houston about donating the tumor, wanting to make sure they knew of my interest. Since my wife had not yet accepted the possibility that Caleb could die, I did not discuss my questions with her.

When Caleb began to worsen, and it finally became clear that he would not survive, I raised the topic with my wife. She was open to making the donation, but wanted Caleb's doctor to be at the hospital to receive him, and so I more seriously pursued the topic with Caleb's doctors at the NIH and in Houston. They informed me that there were studies that could use his tumor, and they would be glad to receive it. I know recent cases where parents selected the studies and beneficiary institutions for the tumor tissue, but at the time, I didn't know this was possible. So we simply donated it to the hospital in Houston where Caleb was treated, making sure our doctor at the NIH knew of the donation and could obtain the tissue she needed for her studies as well.

I also talked with our funeral director early on. I was concerned about Caleb having an open casket funeral, and I didn't want to do something that would disfigure him noticeably. Both the doctors as well as the funeral home assured me this should not be a problem.

We signed the paperwork for the study, and there were no expenses at all which were charged to us for either the surgery or the transportation of Caleb's body to the hospital for the removal of the tumor.

Caleb passed away at home, and we kept him there for a few hours afterwards. Then, the funeral home brought him to the hospital for the removal of the tumor. Caleb's doctor agreed to my wife's request and was present during the tumor removal, to ensure he was lovingly taken care of. We did not see Caleb again until he was embalmed and ready for viewing.He looked amazing, and angelic. The doctors and the funeral director were right—there was no evidence whatsoever of the tumor removal; they must have done a very discreet incision on the back of his head (which was resting on the pillow). He looked beautiful.

In hindsight, we would do this all over again. Knowing that Caleb might help other children fighting the disease, even in his death, brought us some peace. And, having the tumor removed from him was also important to us. We wanted it gone, even if that were only possible in his death.

Five years have passed now, and there are many more options available. Some parents have selflessly made themselves available to help others through this experience, and I wish we would have had that help with our decision. There are many studies, well known, which will accept tumor tissue donations. Parents can have a say which studies benefit from the donation, and the tumor can be divided among several studies. Every parent must make their own decision, but for us, this was the best decision.

Probably mid-way through Mara's diagnosis with DIPG we heard about the need for tissue samples. For us, the decision to donate seemed easy and quite frankly it seemed like the only way we could make a difference for the future of this disease. To us, donating meant that if Mara were to pass away, it would not be in vain, for perhaps someone else could live even though she could not. Initially though, we prayed to be THE MIRACLE and didn't want to think about crossing that bridge.

It wasn't until Mara's pediatric oncologist set up a palliative care meeting for Mara at the end of August (approximately 1 month before her passing) that the issue was discussed directly with them. As I recall, we were the ones in this meeting to bring up tissue donation. As I look back, I was a little surprised that our medical team never mentioned it to us directly. However, I see their wisdom in it now. What kind, compassionate doctor can tactfully ask a parent for a tumor donation when their child is still living and the family is still fighting? So, my husband and I brought up the issue of having Mara's tumor donated upon her passing as well as any other organs that could be donated.

Mara's doctor was honored that we would suggest donation. He explained to us that we'd have to sign a consent form and we did that at Mara's next CT scan, which was a few weeks later. The consent form we signed was a rather generic form. It was a form that anyone would sign to release tissue, whether it is due to the child's passing or just a simple donation derived from a biopsy. We made it clear at this time that we'd like samples to be sent to St. Jude and to the NIH, as well as the researchers at Seattle Children's Hospital. He did communicate with us the need to have Mara transported post mortem and taken from our home up to Seattle (about an hour away). He told us that any cost associated with the transportation would be paid for by the hospital.

As the week continued, we realized that we should probably at least touch base with a funeral home to let them know about our situation and that transportation would be an issue. Bryan made this excruciating call, an act I can never imagine doing myself. It seemed against every parental inclination to arrange for our child's death when she had not yet passed. This phone call occurred only 2 days before Mara left her earthly home. The funeral home assured us that this would not be a problem. We gave hospice the funeral home information, which worked out well because when Mara did pass away they took care of everything. We didn't have to think about it anymore after this phone call. It made the decision much easier in the long run.

The day Mara passed, we received a phone call from her doctor and from our nurse practitioner telling us that the autopsy was being performed and that the transport went smoothly. They cried with us, and thanked us. Later, we also received a note in the mail from Mara's doctor thanking us once again and letting us know that in his opinion, we did everything possible to help Mara. Reassurances like that mean the world to grief-stricken parents.

In the end, nothing about this disease is easy, nothing. I understand that the decision to donate is most personal in nature. However, the pride in my heart for my daughter's offering is beyond description. For us, this was the best decision and will allow Mara's legacy to live on.

We had already made arrangements to donate Caleb's tumor for research. So, after my husband and our other boys and our friends had had some time with Caleb's body, my husband called our oncologist to let her know of his death and to make plans to meet her at the hospital. Our funeral home director is our neighbor and was prepared to hear from us. He came to the house when my husband was ready. They rode to the hospital with Caleb's body and delivered it to our oncologist (with our friends following behind). After my husband was sure that our oncologist had Caleb's body and was prepared to supervise the harvesting and preservation of the tumor tissue, he left the hospital with our friends. After the autopsy was complete, the funeral director took Caleb's body back to the funeral home.

Our son Andrew died on December 4, 2009. We donated his tumor to his neuro-oncologist at the NIH, and tissue was shared with Hopkins and Children's National Medical Center.

I have been helping with DIPG and other brain tumor tissue donations since November, 2008. As a result of tumor tissue donation over the past few years, researchers are beginning to have an understanding of DIPG biology which means that treatments can now actually be developed and chosen in a scientific way. Though we do not yet have a cure for DIPG, we are headed in the right direction. We could not say this in October 2007 when my son was diagnosed.

It was almost seven months after Ethan passed when I happened to email his oncologist. His oncologist shared information with us that he had received from a researcher at Texas Children's. I wanted more information, so I emailed the researcher directly. I wasn't sure I would hear back, but he was very willing to share with me the progress of his research with Ethan's tumor and the mouse model he had created with it.

I believe in miracles but I am also a realist. As we sat in the exam room listening to the doctor tell us our daughter had a brain tumor for which there was no real treatment much less a cure, I remember thinking I want this thing out of her head. If we don't get our miracle someone has to

study this beast so no one else has to do this. I had no illusions that our donation in and of itself would be the magic bullet for DIPG patients but Hope was special and her life mattered. Her grey matter would be studied and knowledge could be gained.

While I am positive that our doctor would have brought tumor donation to our attention at the time he thought appropriate, I beat him to it. I always put reality in the driver's seat with hope firmly strapped into the passenger seat. I wanted to know up front what all my options were. When he said, "Don't go online I will answer your every question," I raced to the computer. I trusted him completely but I needed to know ahead of time what potentially could or would happen. We had conversations throughout Hope's battle regarding tumor donation. These conversations were always welcomed by our team but were initiated by me. I felt compelled to be sure they understood how important it was to me. They felt bound by compassion to be gentle with me.

As Hope appeared to be nearing the end of her life we had our most serious conversation regarding our donation. Hope's doctor assured us that he would stay with Hope during the entire autopsy and made sure her "blankie" was nearby. He asked us for permission to share her tumor with other researchers, which we happily agreed to. We did not ask where he would send the tumor or how it would be used as we had complete confidence in his professional judgment. We have no regrets. Hope's tumor is being studied at some of the finest institutions in the country.

If I had any suggestions to give, I would suggest that doctors be upfront with families about tumor donations and for families to understand why they need to do so. These relationships are built out of respect and honesty. It is unfortunate that the time line for our kids is so short that doctors really can't afford to wait for the "right time." Just like a clinical trial is fully explained as an option, so should tumor donation be explained as an end of life option. I wish I had known more about the need for live cell lines and what they have to offer research. While I know that Hope's tumor, having been frozen, is offering much to the research community, it would have made my heart happy to know that somewhere the evil thing that took my child's life was alive and potentially being used for the good of our kids.

Throughout my daughter's battle with DIPG, I constantly struggled to balance my ultimate hope that she would somehow survive, with my acknowledgement of the reality of the disease and the likelihood that

she would not. By nature, I am a planner. Subconsciously, I think that I somehow believe that if I can think through all of the possible outcomes and scenarios and plan for all contingencies, then it will be easier to deal with whatever actually happens when the time comes. Of course, I knew that I could never prepare for my daughter's death.

So, it wasn't long after my daughter's diagnosis that I learned about tumor tissue donation and began to think about whether it was something I would want to do. Our daughter's medical team did not mention it for a long time; in fact, they didn't mention it until very close to the end. But long before they brought it up, we had considered it. We learned of other families who had donated, and how comforted they were in knowing that perhaps their child's death was not in vain—that the donation might help another child someday. Throughout my daughter's battle, my husband and I occasionally discussed the issue. He was hesitant to do it, while I thought it would be comforting. In the end, we discussed it with our clergy, other parents who had donated, and with a few very close friends and family. We were reassured that it would not affect our funeral plans or how long we would be able to stay with our daughter once she had died. We also were told that the logistics would be handled and that it would not require any additional burden on our part at such a difficult time.

Despite all of that, ultimately we decided that donating our daughter's tumor tissue was not the right decision for us or for our daughter. It was not an easy decision by any means; but it is one with which we are comfortable and do not regret. Throughout the course of her battle, she had participated in four clinical trials. She had sacrificed so much already in her short life. She went through extra weekly pokes, prods, and tests, and never complained. She had scars from various surgeries. She took drugs that caused her side effects but gave her no benefit. She had suffered enough. My husband and I also struggled with the thought of picturing our daughter after the donation. We wanted to remember her as the beautiful little girl that she was, and not be clouded with images of her "less than whole." While I, no doubt, would have found great comfort in possibly helping to find a cure through donation, that comfort may not have outweighed the emotional distress that such a donation may have caused me and my husband. Whatever parents decide; it will be the right answer for them and their family. But parents should know that it is okay if they choose not to donate.

✚ ✚ ✚

Our decision to donate our daughter's tumor tissue was easy in comparison to the other decisions we had to make at that time. We had just been dealt the news that her tumor had progressed and we were dealing with being removed from a clinical trial, setting up hospice care, and looking for other treatment options. Other parents of DIPG children mentioned they would be willing to help set up the tumor donation. I asked my husband what he thought and he said we should go ahead with it. I agreed. I contacted the parent/advocate who had offered to help and we began the process. Of all the decisions we had to make at that time, we gave that one the least amount of thought. We did not realize the positive impact it would have.

Because our daughter's condition deteriorated so quickly, our involvement in setting up the donation was minimal. We made important choices, such as where the tumor would ultimately be donated, but the DIPG mom who was helping us let us know that she could take care of the logistics if we did not have the time. We were able to choose our level of involvement so that we could focus on our daughter during her last days on earth.

After she passed away, we signed some paperwork and the donation was made. The donation did not disrupt our plans for her Catholic mass and burial. We laid our daughter to rest tumor free. We opted to have her tumor go to Dr. Monje at Stanford. Once the donation was done, I thought that would be it. But Dr. Monje has graciously shared her progress in research using Bizzie's donation. She took the time to provide us with details about our daughter's tumor and how she was using the tissue. Within weeks of our donation, Dr. Monje shared with us that Bizzie's tumor was used to confirm an important finding in DIPG research. To know that our decision to donate has, along with other donations, facilitated a finding that could help develop an effective treatment for future DIPG kids is something that honors our little girl's memory in a way that nothing else could. No amount of fundraising could provide the same value. While we could not help our daughter beat cancer, we can help other kids have a chance at growing up.

Brendan knew there was no cure and that he would die from the tumor. He also knew that donating the tumor could lead to a cure in the future. His tumor tissue was donated to Children's Hospital and a pathology report was shared with us. His post mortem tissue is going to be useful for future research.

Chapter 20

Organ and Tissue Donation by Pediatric Brain Tumor Patients

Angela Punnett MD, FRCPC

Some patients with brain tumors and their families may wish to explore the potential for organ and tissue donation following an expected or unexpected death. This is a complicated decision and it is helpful when planning to understand the background of organ donation in the context of a cancer diagnosis; issues specific to patients with brain tumors; the process for donation; and implications of organ donation at the time of death.

History of Organ Donation and Cancer

There are a significant number of patients awaiting solid organ transplantation at any given time and 5% to 7% of these patients will die while awaiting transplant. Lack of consent to organ donation by the population at large is the main limiting factor to transplantation.

It is generally accepted that individuals with a diagnosis of cancer are not eligible to donate their organs because of the risk of transmitting cancer to the organ recipient. This risk of transmission has been documented since the early days of solid organ transplantation, with reports of close to half of recipients developing the donor's cancer, resulting in death.

However, not all cancers are equally likely to spread, and recognizing the need to balance pre-transplantation life-threatening conditions with post-transplantation malignancy risk, an International Consensus document was written in 1997 (Council of Europe, 1997).

Dr. Punnett is an Assistant Professor in the Department of Pediatrics at the University of Toronto, and Program Director of the Pediatric Hematology Oncology subspecialty training program at The Hospital for Sick Children, Toronto, Canada.

The group of experts who crafted this document recommended consideration of donors with primary brain tumors that very rarely spread outside of the central nervous system (CNS).

Risk of Spread of Primary Brain Tumors

Spread of a primary brain tumor outside of the CNS, or extracranial metastasis, has been considered unlikely because of anatomical and biological features of the CNS itself. The CNS is a relative sanctuary with the so-call "blood brain barrier" and has few lymphatic channels. As a brain tumor grows it invades surrounding tissue, collapses existing blood vessels, and really has nowhere else to go. However, studies have shown that brain tumor cells can grow in other types of tissue and invasion of blood vessels and lymphatic drainage has been documented.

The most important and consistent risk factor for extracranial spread is the cell type and grade of malignancy. The tumors most likely to demonstrate extracranial spread include ependymoma at about 6% of patients, medulloblastoma at about 5% of patients, and glioblastoma at about 0.5% of patients. These numbers are based on relatively limited and older data however, and are difficult to interpret. In addition, a number of other risk factors for extracranial spread have been proposed, including duration of disease, receipt of chemotherapy and/or radiation therapy, and history of craniotomy and/or ventriculosystemic shunt.

Donor transmission of primary brain tumors

There are a number of case reports in the literature documenting transmission of tumors from donors with primary brain tumors to their organ recipients, in some cases causing death. Recipients of heart, lung, or liver transplants, were more likely to die from transmitted malignancy, as kidney transplant recipients could be saved with chemotherapy or removal of the transplanted kidney.

A number of transplant centers have reviewed their local experience in an attempt to understand the risk of transmission. The resulting analysis showed that donors with a history of a primary brain tumor accounted for 1% to 4% of all donors. Among those donors with a history of a primary brain tumor, the risk of transmitting a tumor to an organ recipient was 0% to 3%.

Larger experience is available through mandatory reporting to national organ transplant registries. In the United States, the United Network for Organ

Sharing (UNOS) has published its experience, which shows donors with primary brain tumors consistently represent approximately 1% of all donors. Out of 642 transplant recipients, 3 developed a fatal tumor from one donor with glioblastoma multiforme (0.5% transmission rate). When comparing survival curves for recipients of kidney and liver transplants from donors with and without primary brain tumors, there is no difference. Donors with primary brain tumors represent 2.6%, 2%, and 1.5% of all donors in the Australia/New Zealand, Czech Republic, and United Kingdom registries respectively, with no cases of donor-derived malignancy reported.

Somewhat different data is available through the Israel Penn Tumor Registry, an international, voluntary reporting registry based in the United States that started in the very early days of transplantation. It is not possible to estimate the incidence of transmission with this registry data, but it is possible to look at risk factors for transmission. Among 62 organ recipients from 36 donors with primary brain tumors, 14 (23%) developed a tumor; almost half of the donors had glioma/glioblastoma. Risk factors for transmission from this data include the presence of ventriculosystemic shunt, extensive craniotomy, high-grade histology, and the presence of a cerebellar lesion.

When organ donation is being considered, the local Organ Procurement Organization (OPO) and the transplant team must consider all of this information in the context of the patients awaiting transplantation. The risk of transmission of a tumor from a donor with a primary brain tumor is difficult to quantify but appears to be low, with identifiable risk factors that increase the risk. It has been recommended that potential organ recipients be counseled around the small but definite risk of transmission of malignancy, as well as the chance of survival if they choose to remain on the waiting list for their needed organ. With donors considered to be higher risk, transplant teams may exclusively request certain types of tissue donation (for example, heart valves, cornea, bone, other), where the risk of transmission is practically nil.

The Process of Organ and Tissue Donation

As parents of a child with a brain tumor, you may be considering organ and tissue donation at different times during the course of your child's illness. It is helpful to speak with the health care team sooner rather than later in order to explore options and the implications for your child's care around the time of death. The health care team will then refer your family to the local OPO and a representative will meet with you to discuss the donation process.

Organ donation occurs following confirmation of a donor's death with the goal of maintaining the organs in a healthy state until the time of transplantation. The process of removal of the organs from the donor is called organ retrieval. With brain death, there is confirmation of irreversible brain damage but continued heart activity, such that the organs are still perfused, or receiving their blood supply from their donor. Donors are maintained on artificial life support until organ retrieval occurs. Some hospitals will offer donation after cardiac death, after careful ethical consideration. In those situations, a donor is removed from all life support and death is confirmed by lack of heartbeat and breathing effort. Organ retrieval occurs immediately thereafter. In either case, death must occur in the hospital for donation to occur.

Current guidelines recommend careful review of a donor's medical history for the risk factors discussed above, as well as careful exploration at the time of organ retrieval to assess for metastatic disease. The areas to assess may include sites of previous surgery, related lymph nodes, and the shunt tract, including the chest, abdomen, and pelvis. In the unlikely event that spread of malignancy outside of the brain is confirmed by pathology, the transplant team will be notified immediately and the organs retrieved will likely not be used for transplantation.

The process around tissue donation depends on the tissues to be donated and will require discussion with the OPO representative. For cornea donation for example, the tissue is less sensitive to lack of oxygen and retrieval can take place hours after death. In this situation, there is more flexibility for families around the time of death.

At the time of death

Every family will have their own needs and wishes for their child at the time of death, and organ donation may not be appropriate or possible for many families.

For those families who do want to pursue the opportunity to donate, it is important to understand the small possibility that your gift of organs may be denied. (This is much less likely for gifts of tissue.) It does appear that transplant teams now have better data to appreciate how small the risk of tumor transmission actually is, and to counsel potential organ recipients appropriately. There is an urgent need for organ donors worldwide and patients with primary brain tumors and their families have developed an extraordinary legacy with their gifts of life.

Parent Perspectives

Parents do need the option of organ donation; therefore, they need to know the right questions to ask and when to ask them. It's so difficult because in asking the questions we are admitting that we are going to lose our children—something we try to condition ourselves not to think about.

When we thought we were going to lose Emma I asked about organ donation but was told we couldn't donate. Tissue donation was possible—hence the corneal donation. The morning she earned her wings, our palliative care medical team was connecting with the agency and we received the news that they would accept Emma's corneas. It was so bittersweet to hear that decision. Emma had an amazing way of seeing the world, people and events. And now, there are two people that will be able to see their world, through Emma's eyes. We take comfort in knowing this, and knowing that part of Emma lives on in this world.

Soon after Mara's passing we received a phone call from the donation center verifying our intent to have the corneas donated. We could have missed this phone call had it not been for others answering phones for us at the time. Just a few weeks later, we received a letter from the donation center indicating to us that Mara's corneas were indeed used. We cried tears of joy knowing that a small piece of our daughter was still alive. It made us want to find the person and gaze into their eyes. It was made clear to us through the letter that anonymity was paramount in this situation, however. I understand why this has to be and appreciate that we can write an anonymous letter to the recipient telling them about Mara.

I want to start by telling everyone a story about my family. My Mom lost her husband, son, and mother all in a car accident on Mother's Day in 1963. It was before I was born. My mom and my two sisters lived but the others died. My brother's name was Max. Ironically, Max was 8 years old when he passed away, the same age as my son Ethan. Max was killed instantly and the one thing that my mother always said when I was growing up was that she wishes she would have been able to donate Max's organs. That

even though it wouldn't have taken the pain away of losing him, it would make her feel like his death had some purpose. And so when Ethan was diagnosed with DIPG and his tumor later progressed, I felt a very strong need to donate whatever organs, or cornea, or tumor that I could.

Like most of you, I always thought if you were a cancer patient you could not donate your organs. In reading other children's websites I noticed that many were donating their tumors and their corneas. So as Ethan's health declined, I emailed his oncologist and asked him what we needed to do to make pre-arrangements for this. At that point in time, he emailed me back and said, "Lets cross that bridge when we get to it."

A few weeks before Ethan passed away; we sat down with Ethan's oncologist and asked him again about tumor and cornea donation. He told me that as Ethan's tumor is a glioma, they are known to not spread to other parts of the body, i.e., the organs. He thought that Ethan may be able to donate all of his major organs. He made some phone calls and put us in touch with the Gift of Life Organization.

They told us that if Ethan was to be a candidate for donation, he would have to pass away at the hospital. We had been on hospice with Ethan since October so it would mean that the plans we had made for Ethan to pass away peacefully at home would have to change if we wanted to donate. So in talking with Ethan's father, he at first was not sure if he wanted to donate but would think about it. I believed in leaving this to God, so decided that if we were meant to donate Ethan's organs we would make it to a hospital and he would die there. If we weren't, then he would pass away at home.

During Ethan's final days, he was in so much pain due to headaches. He had never complained hardly ever of headaches previously, only very minor ones. These were "over the top," leaving him hollering in pain. Hospice gave him morphine but it was not easing his pain. The hospice providers kept in close touch with Ethan's doctor and on Tuesday, he suggested we should bring Ethan to the hospital to get his pain under control. So we packed him up for the 1 hour 15 min ride to the hospital. The car ride up there I rode in the back seat with him stroking his hair and forehead and holding his hand.

When we got to the hospital, and laid him on the bed, I noticed his fingers and toes were a bluish color. They hooked up the pulse oximeter and he only had 10% oxygen saturation. So he was admitted to PICU and was eventually put on a ventilator. A CT scan of his head showed that the tumor had grown and was compressing areas of the brain that controlled breathing, but that the brain had not herniated or hemorrhaged. The doctors told us that the brain had been pushed upwards and that it was blocking the flow of spinal fluid throughout the brain. This was something he could not recover from and if taken off the ventilator he would not be able to breathe on his own. But also that he probably would not have brain death for quite some time, (days or weeks).

We were forced to make a decision: 1) continue to support him, knowing he will not recover and that he is in discomfort; 2) make a decision to remove support in his hospital room, and let him pass away as it would occur, knowing he would not be able to donate any organs, or 3) plan to remove life support in the operating room, with my husband and I present. They would allow him to take his last breath and his heart to stop beating, and then life support would be placed back on. At that point in time we would have to leave the operating room so that the transplantable organs could be removed (this is called a post-cardiac death transplant). If Ethan did not pass away within a certain time frame of removing life support, then he would be brought back to his room in the PICU, and we would be with him until the very end, but not able to donate his organs.

There had only been four previous post-cardiac death organ donations done at this hospital in 10 years. Ethan's case had to be brought to the Ethics Committee to make sure it was ethical in his case. It was decided it was, so we planned for him to be taken off the ventilator at 6:00 p.m. the following evening in the operating room and donate his organs.

The Gift of Life Organization was able to locate one match for Ethan's kidneys from someone who was willing to take them from a cancer patient, and two recipients for his corneas. It was decided later that his tumor would go to research.

So at 6:45 p.m. we were changed into scrubs and taken into the operating room where Ethan was already prepped for surgery. They had all of the surgical instruments covered up, and had Ethan draped with the exception of his face and hands. His dad and stepmom stayed at one side and his stepfather and I at the other. At 7:30 p.m. they removed the breathing tube and we waited holding his hands for him to pass. He took several last gasping breaths but then did not breathe again for several minutes even though his heart was still beating. His heart would flatline but then register and then flatline and then register. Finally it stayed flatlined and the doctor confirmed he had passed. We said our goodbyes and left the OR, while the surgical team recovered the organs. Afterwards, they cleaned him up and we were able to come and see him before leaving the hospital. He looked very much at peace.

We had to give up the chance to have him at home for his death but I know we made the right decision. I know in the end that Ethan would have wanted his organs to save other lives, and I know he would have been proud of us for making this difficult decision. It was evident when they removed the tube that he could not breathe on his own enough to sustain his life. I think his time to go was Tuesday evening, we just were fortunate to get two more days with him while making preparations for his Gifts of Life. While it may have changed where he died, we were able to see that he was at peace, and know that someone else was able to live and see because of our sacrifice.

Chapter 21

Integrating Palliative Care and Making Difficult Decisions

Justin N. Baker, MD, FAAP, FAAHPM
Adam J. Tyson, MD
Javier R. Kane, MD

As you have read in prior chapters of this book, diffuse intrinsic pontine glioma (DIPG) is a serious disease. The majority of patients with DIPG and/or their families are told that the tumor cannot be removed with surgery because of its location. They are also told that the tumor is rarely sensitive to chemotherapy, and that while the tumor may decrease in size with radiation therapy, the disease often continues to grow despite best efforts. What this means is that DIPG is usually an incurable and progressive disease. When presented with such difficult news, most families want their child to receive the best possible treatment for this terrible disease, hoping that their child will beat the odds. Most families also realize that serious illness often comes with pain and suffering, and they want to avoid this for their child as much as possible.

Parents in these circumstances often report that making decisions regarding their child's care is extremely difficult because it requires balancing the dual goals of care that include cancer-directed goals and care that provides comfort-directed goals. Parents often wonder how they can possibly prepare for such an overwhelming and difficult situation and how to plan for their child's care in such a way that hopes for the best but allows for consideration of all possible outcomes, thus allowing a balanced approach to decision making. In these difficult situations, parents must often think about what is most important

> Dr. Baker is the Director of the Quality of Life and Palliative Care Division, Director of the Hematology/Oncology Fellowship Program, and an Attending Physician for the Quality of Life Service at St. Jude Children's Research Hospital, Memphis, TN.

for the child and family. Based on what is happening with the tumor, available medical treatment, and the child's experience, the parents must decide the most important goals in the care of their child. Families may also have important life goals they would like to accomplish with their child. These goals are critical and should be taken as seriously as evaluating blood levels or assessing the side effects of medications. Every attempt should be made to integrate these goals into the overall plan of care for children with DIPG so as to balance the use of treatments to fight the tumor, and the efforts of the family and the care team to preserve comfort and the best quality of life (QOL) possible for these children.

Establishing Goals of Care and Making Difficult Decisions

Most families start treatment with the hope of attaining a cure for their child with DIPG. Having hope is very important, as it sustains patients, families, and their caregivers during extremely difficult times. Unfortunately, this disease makes cure highly unlikely and in reality most therapies for DIPG are either experimental or are only intended to prolong life. This does not mean the team will not remain hopeful with you that a cure can be attained, but it does mean that you and your team must hope for the best possible results while planning for all possibilities, including the possibility that the tumor will continue to grow in size despite everyone's best efforts.

If and when the tumor begins to grow despite the treatment, parents may know with greater certainty that the child's tumor is incurable. During this time it is appropriate to continue to hope for the best possible outcome. If you come to realize that your child has a disease that cannot be cured, it is also critical to work on deciding the goals you would like to try to achieve while your child is alive.

You may want to think about what is most important to you and your family, and how you would like to spend the remaining time you have with your child. You will once again face many difficult decisions. It may be easier for you to make decisions at this time if you think about whether or not the possible treatment choices presented to you will help you achieve the goals you have for your child and family. Parents report that the most difficult decisions they have to make for their child happen at this stage and include whether or not to stop fighting the tumor and stop cancer treatment or to enroll their child in a phase I research trial [Table: 1].

> Dr. Kane is the Director, Pediatric Hematology/Oncology and Professor in the Department of Pediatrics at The Children's Hospital at Scott and White, and Texas A&M Health Science Center, Temple, TX.

Chapter 21: Integrating Palliative Care

Goal to prolong a life of good quality—minimal morbidity
Values discussion regarding location of care and cancer-directed treatment options: • Phase I trial possibilities   • IV or oral cytotoxic chemotherapy with hopes of tumor response   • "Palliative" chemotherapy   **Values discussion regarding priorities and life plan goals:**   • Discussion with your child about DIPG progression   • Hospice enrollment   • Placement of a DNAR order
Goal to optimize comfort
Values discussion regarding priorities and life plan goals: • Discussion with your child about progression   • Hospice enrollment   • Placement of a DNAR order

Table 1: Goals and values discussion

Parents may also choose to avoid further pain and suffering caused by invasive treatments such as breathing machines or other aggressive and potentially uncomfortable life-sustaining treatments and have a "Do Not Attempt Resuscitation" (DNAR) order (see questions 6 to 8 in addendum below for more information about DNAR orders) placed in the medical record, or to decide against certain treatments that may not help achieve the primary goals of care. Other important decisions to consider include whether or not to enroll their child in hospice, to speak to their child about the fact that the disease is worsening or the possibility of death, choosing a desired location of death, deciding whether an autopsy should be performed, and other important life choices such as whether or not to continue going to school, traveling, or pursuing other goals the child and family would like to achieve. While these are some of the most difficult decisions you will ever have to make, the specific goals of care you have set for your child and family will help minimize distress for your child and help

Dr. Tyson is a Family Medicine Resident Physician at the Bryn Mawr Hospital, Bryn Mawr, PA.

to ensure his or her comfort.

Your Team and Individualized Care

You and your child are part of a team. In fact, you are the most important members of this team. Your health care team is taking this journey with you, and everyone's desire is that you and your child should never feel alone. Your care team may not be able to fully put themselves in your shoes, but they have likely walked through this very difficult time with many other families and will draw on those experiences to help you. You should encourage your medical team to be very open with their thinking as they make recommendations to help accomplish the various goals of care that you have for your child and family. This process may look different for your family than it does for others [Fig. 1]. Discussing the individualized aspects of care is difficult, but the better the team knows you and your child, the better the care plan can be matched to your and your child's needs.

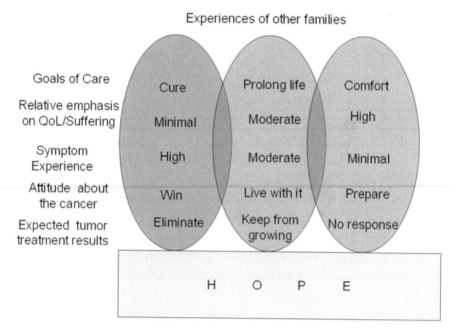

Figure 1: Decision-making schematic

Most children with DIPG enroll in a research treatment plan or receive treatment following a specific cancer treatment plan. You may be wondering how this individualized approach to palliative care can work within the context of a research protocol or a predesigned cancer treatment plan. Remember that these treatments are only one aspect of the overall care plan. A care plan includes a medical plan and a life plan, both of which should be individualized to your and your child's unique needs. A specific research protocol or cancer treatment plan may be a part of the medical plan, but other aspects of the care plan can be highly individualized, such as medications to relieve pain and other distressing symptoms. Any specific needs that are unique to your situation, such as rehabilitation needs or spiritual needs must also be addressed.

Communicating your needs and perspectives

Communication with your child's physician and other members of the care team about all of the before-mentioned issues is extremely important. As your team (remember this means your child, family, and medical care team) starts out on this journey together, you can facilitate better communication and understanding by talking to the medical team as much about your child and family as possible.

Do not hesitate to bring your child's and family's needs to the attention of your care team, because they cannot address your needs if they do not know what your concerns are or what is most important to you. The better the team knows you and your child, the better the team can make an individualized plan of care along with you.

You may not automatically know what information is important to share. It will be helpful for the team to be able to judge your level of understanding of the prognosis, goals, and treatment options as treatment begins, and at other key points in time if the illness progresses. It will also be very helpful, for example, to hear about whom your child is, how your family is doing, and what the illness experience has been like for each of you.

Questions to consider when talking to the team about these things are listed in Table 2.

Category	Questions to Consider
Understanding your perspective	What does good quality of life mean for you and your child?
	What are you hoping for? What is your child hoping for?
	What is most important for you and your family?
	What are you most concerned about?
	What is your definition of being a good parent to your child?

Category	Questions to Consider
Information and decision making	What information do you or your child need right now?
	How do you like information to be delivered/handled?
	How much does your child want to participate in decision making and difficult conversations?
Specific needs: symptoms	What are your child's most concerning or distressing symptoms that interfere with good quality of life?
Specific needs: spiritual	Are you or your child experiencing spiritual distress? Do you feel abandoned by God? Do you feel angry toward God?
Specific needs: emotional	Is anyone in the family experiencing emotional distress that is interfering with good quality of life?
Specific needs: social	Are there any family needs that if not addressed will lead to increased distress?
	Are there any sibling needs that are currently not being addressed?
Chance for treatment success	What is your family's understanding of your child's chance for cure and overall life expectancy?
Goals	What are your goals for treatment?
	What other goals do you have for your family and your child?
Treatment alternatives	What is your understanding of the availability of cancer-directed treatment options?

Table 2: Helpful perspectives for your child's health care providers

Reconsider these questions from Table 2 periodically and tell the rest of the care team of any changes. The diagnosis of a DIPG is overwhelming for all families, and the way you look at the tumor and its impact on your child and family is likely to change as time goes by and as symptoms resolve and/or progress.

Some key moments when most families should consider these questions include:

- at diagnosis and the beginning of treatment;

- at the end of radiation therapy;

- upon returning for the first magnetic resonance imaging (MRI) scan following radiation;

- when symptoms seem to be returning;

- upon confirmation that the tumor has progressed on imaging;

- as your child's condition declines or the symptoms continue to progress, or worsen.

Your family's level of understanding is likely to shift during any and all of these events and your goals of care for your child and family are also likely to change. The medical team will not be aware of these changes unless you help them understand your evolving thoughts and goals.

The key to establishing goals of care is open communication between you, your child, and the primary medical team.

Some examples of goals of care are noted here:

- Cure of disease;

- Prolonging life, while having the best quality of life possible;

- Providing comfort;

- Maintaining or improving the ability to perform activities of daily living;

- Attaining specific life goals (e.g., going to graduation, camp, wish trip);

- Support for family and loved ones;

- Advancing medical knowledge (i.e., helping contribute to a cure);

- "Knowing we did all we could" (i.e., that we did not give up);

- "Being the best parent that I can be" (i.e., making the best decisions for my child).

These goals are not necessarily mutually exclusive. Many families will choose different goals of care at different points in time, and the list above is only a sample of the large number of possibilities. Table 3 contains decisions you may need to make for your child, along with possible positive and negative aspects of these decisions.

Decision	Potential Positive Aspects	Potential Negative Aspects
Further cancer-directed therapy.	• Slow progression of the tumor. • Fullfills a need to continue to fight against the tumor.	• Introduces or increases suffering due to side effects. • Continued need for medical care primarily provided through outpatient clinic or hospital setting, so less time to pursue other life goals.
Enrollment in a phase I study	• Further understanding of how the medicine works. • Involvement in research →altruism; a chance to give back. • Closer monitoring of clinical status. • Fulfills a need to continue to fight against the tumor.	• No studies may be available. • Introduces or increases suffering due to side effects. • Continued need for medical care primarily provided through outpatient clinic or hospital setting, so less time to pursue other life goals.

Decision	Potential Positive Aspects	Potential Negative Aspects
Hospice enrollment	• Home-based provision of care. • Expertise in pain and symptom management. • Interdisciplinary team approach to care—availability of chaplain, physician, nurse, social worker, and volunteers. • 24/7 call coverage for symptom-related or other emergencies.	• May be viewed by others as "giving up," because hospice is sometimes viewed by the general public as being for people dying soon. • Another team working with you and your child; meeting new people may seem difficult. • May not allow for blood product transfusions or continuing cancer-directed therapies.
Placement of a DNAR order	• Tells all team members that benefits of aggressive resuscitation efforts are outweighed by the suffering such efforts may inflict. • Focuses the final moments on comfort and mourning. • Can be changed/reversed at any point in time.	• May be viewed as "giving up," or not doing everything possible. • Because it is a piece of paper, it may not be followed unless presented to medical personnel when the patient is actively dying. • Can be a statement of acceptance that the end result will likely be death.

Decision	Potential Positive Aspects	Potential Negative Aspects
Aggressive symptom control	• Decreasing symptoms allows one to focus on other important aspects of life and the things that can be enjoyed. • Helps decrease suffering.	• May cause drowsiness or sleep. • Certain pain medications may cause unintended consequences (e.g., significant constipation) if not treated properly.
Location of death: home	• Allows the child to be in a familiar environment. • Limited interruptions (e.g., no nurse taking vitals constantly, noisy alarms going off, doctors being paged overhead). • Ease of access for friends and family (no visitor hours). • May decrease costs.	• May feel less supported (i.e., we tend to look to hospitals or clinics for medical support instead of having it delivered in the home). • Limited gatekeepers (e.g., hospital staff and nurses who can help control who has access to family/patient).
Location of death: hospital	• May allow staff to help control visitors (keeping visits to a minimum). • Continual access to nursing staff and physicians at the bedside.	• Noisy with many interruptions. • An unfamiliar environment. • Limited and confined space. • May increase costs.

Decision	Potential Positive Aspects	Potential Negative Aspects
Speaking to my child about death and dying	• Allows you to address/relieve the fears and concerns your child may not express without being invited to share. • May provide a sense of closeness and understanding between you and your child during this process. • May relieve your child to know that you will be okay and will be able to cope.	• Difficult emotionally. • Takes time. • Requires facing the fears of saying "the wrong thing."

Table 3: Specific decisions, along with positive and negative aspects of each decision

Pediatric Palliative Care

Children with DIPG often benefit from palliative care. Palliative care is specialized health care designed to relieve suffering and provide the best possible quality of life for people facing the pain, symptoms, and stresses of serious illness. If your child has DIPG you may decide that having access to palliative care resources is the right option. Palliative care aims to promote healing and increase the quality of life throughout a child and family's journey through serious illness. The aims of pediatric palliative care are not limited to a disease process (e.g., DIPG), but rather become helpful for improving quality of life, maintaining dignity, and attending to the suffering of seriously ill or dying children in ways that are appropriate to their upbringing, culture, and community.

Pediatric palliative care promotes a team approach to care focused on addressing the patient's and family's needs and on providing the highest quality of care. This care should help with difficult decision making and care planning; attend to suffering from physical or psychological symptoms; address social, emotional, and spiritual needs; improve communication and coordination of services; be a point of continuity no matter where the child is receiving care; provide the highest quality hospice and end-of-life care; and address grief and bereavement issues.

Hence, palliative care is about giving the child the best quality of life possible, regardless of whether or not the child is receiving cancer treatment. In this regard, a child with DIPG may have access to palliative care services provided by members of the primary oncology care team while he or she receives cancer-directed therapy. Adding pediatric palliative care resources and principles into the overall plan of care helps the primary care team and your child and family work together, with the ultimate goal of providing the best possible treatment for the disease while creating the most comfort and best quality of life. In your hospital, your primary care team may also be able to consult with a specialized pediatric palliative care team to help you and your child achieve the best quality of life possible.

Addendum

The following section provides some specific examples of some frequently asked questions and possible decisions.

1. What are some of the things you want to consider in making difficult decisions?

Every decision and situation is unique. However, some things that parents think about include:

*   What your child wants;

*   Care team recommendations;

*   Your personal feelings, such as how to be a good parent;

*   Faith/beliefs;

*   How the decision affects the family.

Some reasons children give for making the difficult choices they make include:

*   Avoiding treatment that will make them feel worse;

*   Specific life goals (e.g., going to graduation, prom, camp, wish trip);

*   Pursuing comfort when cure is no longer an option;

*   Pursuing specific care-directed goals, including not wanting to continue therapy;

*   Seeing how other patients around them have suffered.

2. Who can help me make these decisions?

Your child's primary medical team is generally looked to for the most support. Many families also ask for help from other health care staff, family, friends, and spiritual leaders. Also, other families you have come to know through the DIPG journey with your child may have helpful insights. It will be important to recognize that these decisions are understandably very difficult, and because they are so difficult, it is important to realize when you need help making them. You may need help in getting information or talking with others who have more experience with this process. Any time you realize that you need help making these decisions, ask your clinical team for assistance. Ongoing communication is crucial in every aspect of this process. Recalling your specific goals of care will be helpful in directing these decisions. Once you have identified those goals, share them with your team regularly so they can maintain your goals as they suggest a course of treatment for your child.

Depending on your child's age and situation, it may be appropriate to discuss these decisions with your child. He or she may bring insight and revelation that the team can draw on when making decisions. If you have doubts about whether or not to discuss these decisions with your child, ask for help in determining whether or not it would be right or helpful.

3. What kinds of decisions will I be making?

Some decisions, in general terms, are centered on whether or not to:

- Enroll in phase I or II experimental clinical therapies, which do not have a curative goal but may offer more quality time for the patient;

- Try treatment to prolong life (e.g., radiation, chemotherapy, surgery);

- Pursue aggressive symptom control for improved quality of life;

- Create a DNAR order for your child;

- Choose the location of your child's death;

- Speak with your child about death and dying.

4. How can I help the medical team help my child?

Many times the treatment decision and plan are based on specific goals of care as established by you and your child. These goals may be as simple as "aggressively treat pain," or as complex as "I want my child to be able to perform normal activities for a child his/her age." Presenting these goals clearly to the medical staff needs to be a top priority. These goals should be agreed upon by you, your child, and your child's primary care team. From these goals, a particular care plan can be established.

The medical staff will never know your child as well as you do. You must continue to be his or her strongest advocate. This cannot be over-emphasized. You are very likely to be more in tune with your child's needs than anyone else, so you must be his or her advocate. Any time you think there is something different the team should be doing, share it with them. Any time you think your child is suffering or could be doing better, tell the team. Ongoing communication is the key.

5.   Where should my child receive the remainder of his or her care?

Your child will continue to receive medical care to fight against pain and other symptoms, no matter where you decide to receive care. Choosing to continue receiving cancer-directed therapies on a study may limit your location options (e.g., your ability to return home or be close to home). This must be considered in the context of overall goals of care. If being at home is important to your child and family, plan ahead and organize a team of providers who are your best allies—work toward this transition before an emergency or crisis arises that might hinder or completely prevent you from going home (e.g., your child being in the intensive care unit on a ventilator). Every effort will be made to help coordinate your child's and family's goals of care throughout the treatment course.

6.   What is a "Do Not Attempt Resuscitation Order" (DNAR) and should I have my doctor place a DNAR order on my child's chart?

A DNAR order is a request to allow a natural death for your child rather than performing cardiopulmonary resuscitation (CPR) if your child's heart stops or if he or she stops breathing. You and your child's primary medical team will consider such an order in light of the goals of care for your child. It is best to make this decision when the goals of care are changing, rather than during a time of crisis. If you decide a DNAR is best for your child, the order is put in your child's medical record by your primary medical team. A DNAR order is most appropriate when using medicines, procedures, or machines to restart your child's heart or breathing are unlikely to benefit your child or when such measures may actually be harmful. This decision is usually the case when the DIPG has started to grow again and your child's physical decline is due to the growth of the tumor.

As patients go home to receive care, many of them have an out-of-hospital DNAR in place. It is best to plan for these events in advance, because unless given other instructions, medical staff (i.e., hospital staff or emergency medical staff) will attempt to resuscitate all patients whose hearts have stopped or who have stopped breathing.

7.   Can I change my mind about the DNAR order for my child?

Yes, you can change your mind about the DNAR order. Feel free to discuss changing or canceling the DNAR order with hospital or medical staff at any time. These decisions should again be considered in view of the goals of care for your child and can be reversed at any point in time. Children are treated on a case-by-case basis, and all types of treatment can be given, whether or not a DNAR order is in place. The condition of your child and the agreed upon goals of care will determine the clinical decision making for your child.

8. This is a very difficult decision; how do most parents decide?

Most children who have died from DIPG had a DNAR order in place at the time of their death. Some parents know early on in treatment what they will decide about a DNAR; others prefer to speak with their family, friends, their child's pediatrician, other parents of children with cancer, or their ill child, when possible. This is a very difficult decision and it should be made with the goals of care for your child in mind and with the help of your primary medical team. Your primary team can help you look at all the options from different perspectives to help you make the best decision with/for your child and your family.

9. How much do I tell my child?

Every situation is different and the level of understanding for children varies greatly. There is no right or wrong answer to this question. You know your child best, and over the course of your child's illness you have learned how much your child wants to know and how your child handles information. Children as young as 9 or 10 years old, or even younger in some cases, understand complex situations and can help in making difficult end-of-life decisions. Some families regret not speaking to their child about these issues, especially if they feel their child knows or wants to discuss such topics further. Studies have shown that parents who have discussed death and dying with their child do not report any regrets about doing so. On the other hand, some parents who did not discuss these issues with their children report wishing they had done so.

10. What if I change my mind about the decision I have already made?

As time goes by it may be very appropriate to change your mind, or it may be important to stay the course. If you want to change your decision or shift the focus of care, the medical staff will do their best to support that decision. The first thing that will likely occur is to suggest a revisiting of the goals of care. From these goals, you can decide as a team the best way to proceed. It is always important to consider all aspects of these decisions and ask if these decisions will lead to more harm than good.

11. What if I want to pursue "complementary and alternative medicine" (CAM) or other non-standard therapies such as herbs, nutritional and vitamin supplements, acupuncture etc.?

Talk openly with your child's doctor and care team about this option. Often these therapies have not been studied for their potential benefit or harm to your child. If the therapy is not seen as harmful, and you feel strongly about pursuing a particular option(s), the team can try to watch for possible side effects and cross reactions with other medications your child may be receiving.

Parent Perspectives

The following, are stories written by parents of children with DIPG. Some of the stories may be emotionally difficult to read. As editor, I felt they were important to include in the book in order to help you gain what I hope will be a balance of perspectives, through the experiences of other parents who have endured this stage of the journey. My intent is to provide you with information that you can discuss ahead of time with your health care team, and assist you with making decisions that are appropiate for your child. Ruth I. Hoffman, MPH

No one's path with DIPG is the same, and the only thing you can strive for is that you don't regret any of the decisions you've made.

We have been extremely lucky to be connected to an excellent palliative care doctor who visits us weekly at home and gives us an incredible amount of information and support. Although Stella is not receiving treatment, she receives morphine on a daily basis to eliminate the pain in her head, PEG flakes to counteract constipation, Zofran for nausea, and Ativan for seizures. So far we have been able to give her all her medications orally... mostly hidden in ice cream!

When we decided against treatment, doctors told us to expect Stella to live 3 to 4 months maximum. We are 8 months into the diagnosis, and Stella is still with us. She has seen her brother being born, lived through Halloween, Christmas, New Year's, Valentine's Day, etc. She still smiles on a daily basis, and although she is declining, the decline is slow and often stalled.

We have been open and honest with Andrew about his situation. Conversations regarding dying and Heaven have become fairly common over the past couple of months. When you are dealing with cancer, especially one with such a dismal prognosis, there is already a sense of isolation. We have not lost hope, but we do understand the reality of what we are facing. And we do not want to isolate Andrew further by making him feel that he

cannot talk to his own family about the things that are on his heart. When a child—or anyone—expresses his feelings, we do not help by making light of those feelings or attempting to explain away those feelings. When Andrew says he doesn't want to die, we can honestly respond, "We don't want you to die."

Bryce was told that first week that other children who had had this kind of tumor had not survived. My husband and I decided at this point that if we were going to ask him to go through all of this treatment, then we were going to have to be hopeful, even knowing what we knew, and after researching on my own, I knew that the doctors were right. We decided that we were going to follow Bryce's lead, and so we asked his care team to not talk about dying until Bryce wanted to know about it. That meant informing every doctor who saw him that we were choosing this path before they spoke to Bryce. How could we ask him to do all of these treatments and still know that he would probably not survive?

It wasn't until the end of June that he finally asked us about his future. Children do things in such an uncanny way. He and I were at the gas station when he finally asked. (We had some of our best talks in the car.) He said, "Mom, what is going to happen now?" I asked what he meant, even though I already knew where he was going with it. "Now that I'm done treatment. What if it comes back?" So, at that point I reminded him about what we had been told—that radiation could not be done in the same spot for a few years; that they did not have any chemotherapy that was working for this kind of tumor; and that surgery was not an option either. With tears in his eyes, he responded with, "You mean they are just going to let me die?" My response was, "I hope not Bryce. We will have to see if something new comes along, but for whatever comes our way, we are going to just try to enjoy every single day." Next, he said, "Mom, go pump the gas."

As Bryce began to feel worse, it was then that we started to talk about dying. It would often be that Bryce chose to speak to me about it. He began asking questions about things like: Would he be here for his birthday in December? Would he be here for Christmas? Would he be here for his cousin's birthday next summer? My response would always be, "I hope so Bryce." I tried to be as honest as possible, and also let him know how much I loved him at the same time.

He continued to go to school right up until December 19th. And on

December 20th he fell at home. We contacted the hospital because over the weekend we were seeing a decline in his speech, abilities, and mental capacity. An MRI was scheduled for Dec. 23rd. His oncologist called with the results on December 24th to confirm what we already knew. The tumor had progressed. At that time, she indicated that once the tumor progressed, that it would more than likely be swift. So she referred Bryce to hospice care and we signed papers for Care at Home. Life at that point felt like it was spiraling out of control for all of us. Over the Christmas holidays, Bryce progressed from walking on his own, to a walker, to a wheelchair, to spending most of his time in bed as his ability to walk and move declined.

We decided at that point that our daughter would only go to school for half a day. She needed the normalcy of going to school, but we felt that she also needed some time at home with Bryce, without visitors. It was one of the best things that we did, and it allowed her to feel like she was part of his daily care. She would often crawl into bed with him and we would hear them talking away. This was a stressful time for her too, and she was full of questions about what was happening to him. We tried not to give her too much information at once, or to let her know more than she needed to hear at the time, because we felt that it would frighten her. But we always felt that we needed to answer her questions clearly and honestly. We watched her grow up in the process of watching her brother's decline and throughout his palliative care. It was almost as if she felt that she became the older sibling throughout the process. She knew as much as we did by the end because she even felt comfortable asking the nurses who came into our house what was happening. I look back, and now feel that this is honestly how she learned to cope with losing him too.

Talking about dying would pop up at the oddest moments, and catch me off guard. I would make a point of stopping whatever I was doing because I was afraid that he would not ask again, and I wanted him to have the answers. One day he asked if his head was going to just explode. It became very important then that we discuss what was going to happen medically. As Bryce became unable to walk, the questions changed to what happens after one dies and whether or not he would still be sick. He asked, "Will I be able to walk in heaven?" I took this as some kind of acceptance of his fate, and tried to follow his lead.

In reflection, we did make one mistake. One day, when Bryce referred to the day when his head would explode because the tumor would not have anywhere else to grow, it became very important to explain medically about what would happen to him. None of us had really asked the BIG question—we were afraid of the answer. I mentioned to him that eventually he would just become tired and that his body would begin to shut down and that that would be when he would be dying. He began having trouble sleeping. We finally figured out, with help from our palliative care team, that he was afraid to sleep because he thought that he was going to die in his sleep. Obviously not a good choice of words to explain what was going to happen to him.

One of the most difficult things about watching Bryce go through this was that as his tumor progressed, he became more anxious, and had more pain. As this happened, Bryce began talking of dying more freely. Every morning, because his mental capacity and memory became affected, he would wake up and yell out "I'm scared!" We would ask him what he was scared about. He would say "I don't remember what you told me about heaven!" So we would spend time every morning reminding him of what our family believes happens when someone dies. And we began having to give him Ativan for his anxiety. He then began asking us to put his hands together every night, so that he could say his prayers.

About two weeks before Bryce's passing, he was in pain and very anxious and he actually looked at me, and asked me if I would kill him. I thought I was going to die myself with heartbreak. But I looked at him, held his hands very tightly, and said "Bryce, I know that you are frustrated, and angry with what is happening to you, and that you can't find the right words to tell us how scary and awful this is. When you are ready to go because you are tired of fighting, I want you to know that it's okay. I love you with every breath that I take and every beat of my heart, but I can't kill you—it's illegal." And he laughed, but I knew that he was serious. I feel that that was the day that he honestly tried to show us that he accepted what was coming.

Talk about dying changed into making us promise that he would be buried near his grandparents or by the pond at the cemetery, and into making us promise to go there to visit him every day. He was afraid of being forgotten, which is apparently normal for most teenagers.

I had been diagnosed with colon cancer in late June and was scheduled to have the cancer resected on July 13th. So, the plan was that I would have

surgery in the morning and as soon as I came out of recovery, my husband and Caleb would drive to Memphis so Caleb could start treatment the next day. Caleb snuggled up in bed with me for a while before they hit the road and then they were off.

Caleb began declining rapidly during the drive. By the time they got to Memphis at about midnight, my husband was worried that Caleb wouldn't be able to qualify for the study. He was declining quickly. By the next morning, the only concern became whether they'd be able make the hour trip home before he died. He was declining quickly and obviously could not be treated. My husband and I discussed it and decided we would take the risk. We wanted him to be home.

As we left the hospital, Caleb was in a wheelchair. His breathing was more labored and he'd just been placed on oxygen that day. We arrived home and the hospice nurse and equipment was there and ready to be put in place. The guy who brought the hospital bed had quite a time getting it put together. He made the comment that it was an old bed and so heavy. He had no idea why he'd been required to bring it for Caleb. Our nurse told us that she has a 10 year old son and she knew that if her son was dying at home, the whole entire family would want to be piled in bed with him. She wanted to make sure to get us the strongest and biggest bed she could so that we could all pile in whenever we wanted. I carry that memory with me as an example of the blessings so many people gave us along the way.

So, Caleb was set up in the living room. We had an open door policy. Friends and family were welcome to come and stay as long as they liked. Some of our closest friends were with us the entire time. Some of Caleb's closest friends came and just sat by his bed for hours. By this time, Caleb could only communicate by moving his eyes up and down. Even the side-to-side movement was gone. I will never forget that I was sitting on his bed, talking with his best friend Samuel, and Caleb managed to make a joke by moving his eyes up and down during our conversation! Caleb's 5th grade teacher came by to check on him often, and we asked her to contact any of his classmates who would like to spend some time with him and let them know they were welcome to come and visit. So, we had many children come through our home to spend time with Caleb over the next two days.

By the following morning, Caleb was not very responsive and did not really interact with anyone. The home health aide came mid-morning to check on him and she and my husband gave Caleb a bath. My husband noticed that Caleb's breathing changed and knew the end was near. He called our other boys in to be with Caleb and the friends who were here went into another room. Caleb peacefully took his last breath with his brothers and daddy holding him in their arms.

Our hospice care was subpar, at best. We felt that our highly recommended hospice staff was not adequately trained to deal with children, especially children with this type of brain tumor. We also felt the staff was lacking in compassion, the ability to read parents, and deliver the proper care to our son. Sadly, we did not get the privilege of time to adequately research hospice care, so we trusted our medical staff and their recommendation.

I wish I could say our Connor passed away peacefully, but after my many urges that he was still suffering, I was simply dismissed. The end was even more horrific and it really hurts to talk about it. We had a hospice nurse trying to get an oxygen tank for his much labored breathing (which we had been requesting for days). After suffering for a long time, he died. Our hospice nurse, who was on the phone at the time trying to secure an oxygen tank, simply said, in a calm manner, "No, never mind, we no longer need it...the patient has expired." Really? My sweet, precious little boy has "expired" to you? I will never forget those final moments and have to say the hospice staff was unbelievably unprofessional and lacked compassion in our situation.

It has been 22 days since my son's passing and we still haven't had a response from a hospice bereavement counselor.

When I had time, I would send an email or call a friend telling them about the conversations I was having with my kids. I didn't know if I was saying the right thing and I wanted a counselor to help me navigate these land mines. I have a couple of friends in the counseling profession so I knew I could trust their perspective. St. Jude offered professional counseling through the child life specialist or the social worker if I needed more support for myself or my kids.

I learned that giving my kids the opportunity to talk about what was in their heart gave them the freedom to heal and move in and out of the stages of grief just like I moved through these stages. Children have immature ways of handling emotions and if I can help my kids by listening without criticizing or interrupting and asking questions, then it makes them feel loved and safe, and they are able to handle their grief until a professional counseling environment can be offered.

Scan results confirmed our growing fears. Julian's doctors braced us with the news that the "relentless" disease had taken over and that we had less than a month left with our sweet boy. Turns out, we only had five days. Barely five years old, we spared Julian unnecessary fear and anxiety, and never really explained that we would soon have to say good-bye. Wonderful hospice nurses and doctors coached us on comfort care and what to expect as the end drew near. We, intent on keeping Julian happy and at ease, surrounded him with his favorite toys, books, movies, music and most importantly, his favorite people.

In his final moments, we assured him over and over that it was ok to go, that he was safe and loved and that we would be ok too. I held him in my arms, and my husband held us both in his, and together we ushered our child out of this world, just as we had ushered him in. Julian, ever the generous of heart, left us with one final gift just moments after he passed. He wore on his beautiful face the most serene, almost blissful expression, in which he seemed to be telling us, "We did it. I'm in a wonderful place now. And you guys aren't even going to believe how good this gets!"

Liam passed away at home in my arms with his daddy and siblings whispering their "I love You's" in his ear, and with his extended family in the rooms nearby. Nearly 14 months after his diagnosis he finally won his peace. He is a magical boy and dearly, dearly missed.

Mara passed away after a 12-hour intense struggle, at 8:12 a.m. on September 22nd. Both sets of grandparents, 2 aunts, her siblings and Bryan and I were all nearby when Mara slipped away. Our hospice nurse arrived very soon after Mara's passing (Hospice nurses had been in and out throughout the course of the night) and started making preparations. I began the process of getting my little girl ready for nearly the last time.

When the moment was right (probably an hour after she passed) I began to bathe her, dress her, and do her hair. Grandma helped Natalie (Mara's younger sister) pick out the right nail polish for her fingernails. We put on just the right dress and picked out her favorite jewelry. We took some precious pictures of the kids' hands together. This time with her was so very painful, yet it was peaceful. It was excruciating but sacred. I would not have traded this precious time for anything. The funeral home came at approximately 10:00 a.m. to pick up Mara. We held a family prayer and then Bryan carried his baby girl for the last time to the van (rather than use a stretcher) in a final act of love and compassion.

Looking back, there are moments when I wished I had perhaps one more hour with Mara's body before they took her away. However, things were beginning to happen to her body (blood was starting to pool—something we were told is very normal) and I'm not sure that I'd like to witness every detail of nature taking its course. We did everything we could have done.

We did have the privilege of dressing her at the funeral home 4 days later before her viewing. It was nice knowing that we'd have one more chance to see her alone. Sure, it was not the same but in some ways Mara looked more beautiful at the funeral home than she did at our home. I don't think as a mom that I realized how sick Mara truly was. That probably sounds silly, how could I not know, right? But I just think that we kept picking up and moving forward so many times that I didn't absorb completely what was happening. It wasn't until I looked back at pictures of her last days that I could see how sick she was. At the time, I just saw my perfect angel without any imperfections. Even to this day when I think of memories with Mara, I think of her running and playing...not lying on the couch with a feeding tube in her nose.

Our oncologist was brutally honest, which we appreciated to no end. But even when things were stable, they kept reminding us, "It will come back; it's just a matter of time." We wanted to celebrate the small things, even if it was just for a couple of hours, but were usually crushed before leaving the hospital room. This is after getting "good" news, i.e. stable tumor. We all know it is "coming back," but do the doctors really need to constantly drill it in? Trust me no parent EVER forgets that this tumor usually comes back.

✛✛✛

Imagine that you had a cherubic, mischievous, energetic and moody two year old with flashing blue eyes, a brilliant smile and curly red hair. Imagine that each morning she got you up at 5:15 am by standing up in her crib and shouting, "Maaamaaa, I'm awaaaake! Maaamaaa, where are you??" Imagine if when you went into her room she threw both her arms up towards you in a great big hug and chattered her way into the living room, telling you she wanted Cheerios for breakfast...with banana...and milk... and when is Auntie Heather coming...and can we paint now...and watch Caillou. Imagine if when you tried to get her dressed in the morning, she ran away from you laughing, no matter how exasperated you got. Imagine if she insisted on picking out her own clothes and you let her, rather than fight about it. Imagine if she could sing the entire theme song to "Golden Girls," could go down the slide on her own, could pee on the potty, catch a ball, dance and chase her friends. Imagine when you step off the subway after work and walk into her daycare room, all the kids turn to look at who has entered the room, and when she sees you she flashes the most brilliant smile and comes running with her arms up, saying "Mama! Mama! Mama!" Imagine if no matter how many times she had a tantrum and demanded things from you and exhausted you, she ended each night with a snuggle and a kiss and you breathed in the smell of her curls and felt warm happiness all over. Imagine if you could never love anything as much as you loved your first born child, your dream come true, your daughter.

Now imagine it's 9 months later. Imagine she is lying next to you in your bed. She can't walk. She can't use her arms or hands. She can't hold her head up. She can't see the television. She can't tell you she loves you. She can't hug you. She is lying in the bed sound asleep, but coughing on her own saliva, which she is starting to choke on because she can barely swallow. Imagine she was dying and there was nothing you could do to change it. Imagine if you knew that one day soon you would never get to see her again. Never see her smile, feel her hand slip into yours, kiss her warm cheek, feel her sigh into your chest.

That is the simple reality of what we are living with. And it's hard. No matter how many good things happen to us, no matter how much we believe in a bright future for ourselves and a time of healing, we are being tortured. No matter how well or easily we manage to get through the days, to talk with our friends, to laugh and joke and even fight sometimes, we are broken inside. It's a very strange way to live. We need to not focus only on what we are losing, but on all we have gained, but despair creeps in nonetheless.

It is never the same in progress...always the same in result. It is the cessation of the brain signal to breathe that causes the death of each child. That time can come swiftly as with my daughter Savannah...4 1/2 months from diagnosis with absolutely no slowing of symptom progression...or it can move more slowly like in so many kids. I hate it...I hate it!

✛✛✛

I think I've said before that despite the large groups of people who surround us, sometimes grief feels incredibly lonely. One of the realizations I've made this past week, is that there never seems to be a good time to cry. All these people come in and out of our house and they bring hugs and kind words and delicious foods and generosity and beautiful friendships, but no one ever comes in and just cries. I guess it's human nature to want to avoid being sad in front of one another, but I feel like crying all of the time and it's difficult to find the "right time" to do it. You can't do it when you're out walking on the street...you shouldn't really do it when you have company... it upsets our daughter if you cry in front of her. The only safe spaces left are at night when the darkness blankets my room and I fall asleep with hot tears pooling at my neck, or behind my dad's house on a small swing that lies hidden from sight.

This is the saddest thing in the world, but no one wants to cry with me. I understand it on some level, but sometimes it makes me feel as though no one else is sad, or they are able to push it out of their minds. I am jealous. I wish I could also ignore the grief, but to me it's palatable in the air we breathe day in and day out within the white walls of our house.

I wonder if the issue is that we live in such a superficial culture that often seems uncomfortable with true depths of feelings, in particular grief. I feel there is a certain amount of intolerance of acute sorrow and intense mental anguish that makes up the bulk of my life right now. Sorrow is something to be medicated, as I'm doing right now, or something to be divided into five recognizable stages that I can read about, label and rate my growth with. Grief is too complex an emotion to be ignored, pushed away, or forgotten about. I have been grieving my daughter since June 24th and have learned that for me to grieve is to let sorrow and tears invade my soul so that it permeates my pores like a heavy perfume. I am always stunned that no one else can see and smell the sadness that is so obvious to me.

Chapter 22

Journey of Sadness and Hopes: A Letter to Parents

Tammy I. Kang, MD, MSCE
Chris Feudtner, MD, PhD, MPH

Dear Reader,

As this book draws to a close, following many pages filled with information about the diagnosis, prognosis, scientific advances, and emerging treatment options for diffuse intrinsic pontine glioma (DIPG), what can we add that would be worthwhile to parents? Is there anything we can say that would help in this journey of sadness and hopes?

After wondering and worrying about these questions, we thought that the best place to start would be to tell you, from the bottom of our hearts, that we wish your child did not have this cancer. We wish that you did not have to embark upon this journey. We wish that we knew with certainty what your questions and concerns were, that we understood what you might find potentially helpful. And we wish that we knew you, so that we could say all of this face-to-face.

We decided that the best way to proceed was to write the final entry for this book as though we were writing a letter to distant friends who had asked for our thoughts and suggestions. Thus we write with the hope that some of what follows may be of help to your child, to your family, to you. At the same time, we know that no single conversation, no single approach, can work for everyone; so if our ideas aren't working for you, please put this aside and accept our apologies.

Dr. Kang is the Medical Director of the Pediatric Advanced Care Team at Children's Hospital of Philadelphia, and Assistant Professor of Pediatrics at the Perelman School of Medicine at the University of Pennsylvania, Philadelphia, PA.

The Breadth of Hopes

If we were able to sit down and talk, we might ask a question that we often pose to parents as a way to start a conversation. Given your child's situation, what are you hoping for? There are many answers to this question, and none of them are wrong. We encourage parents to relay as many hopes as they have. This takes time. Some hopes may feel much more important than others. When working with this question, at this point, the goal is to get all the hopes to surface and to set them out in front of us, as though spread upon a table, so that they can be discussed.

Indeed, some of our patients want to do this. Once, a cheerful, bright-eyed 11-year-old girl, meeting her oncologist for the first time said, "Before you start asking me a lot of questions, you should know a few things. I know I have a brain tumor called an intra-pontine glioma. I know most people can't be cured of this and that I have had a lot of problems because of it, more than most. I was in the hospital for a long time and didn't like it much. I already had radiation and am excited to move here because it will be easier here for my mom." As if this wasn't already remarkable enough, she finished by saying, "I hope for lots of things, some of them maybe I can have, and some I can't. Even though I know my cancer probably won't go away, there are still things I want, like I would really like to be able to get rid of this trach and g-tube before I die. I want to go to school and, no offense, I'm sure you're really nice and everything, but I would rather not see you too much." Remarkable. In one conversation this patient illustrated, and illuminated what we have learned over decades—that inherent within us, no matter how difficult the circumstances, we harbor hope. Not a singular hope, but many hopes.

Hope for the best

One of these hopes can always be—and, in our conversations with parents, often is—to hope for the very best. These hopes take many forms, and are often the first thing that parents mention when asked about their hopes. Some of these hopes are as large as life, or even larger. I hope that the cancer goes away. I hope that the treatment cures this awful disease. I hope that this is all a bad dream. I hope for a miracle. Parents also have other hopes which, in some situations, may seem quite small in comparison; but to those who hope such hopes, they brim with life. I hope to go home. I hope my child gets this

> Dr. Feudtner is an Attending Physician and Director of Research of the Pediatric Advanced Care Team at the Children's Hospital of Philadelphia, and Associate Professor of Pediatrics at the Perelman School of Medicine at the University of Pennsylvania, Philadelphia, PA.

tracheostomy and gastrostomy tube out. I hope to celebrate my child's birthday. I hope to see my child with those whom I love and who love my child. Hoping for something that may not happen does not mean you "don't get it" or have unrealistic expectations. For many parents, these hopes are one clear way they show their love and devotion for their children. And while we cannot say for sure for you, for many parents, there are other hopes as well.

Hope against the worst

Hopes can also be shields of sorts against the potential worst. We cannot begin to imagine the emotions that have entered your life. Parents have shared with us their intense, painful feelings of fear, anger, desperation, and sadness. Hopes swirl aloft in these wild winds. They do not tame the feelings, but they can help to ride them out. Some hopes will be that certain events do not happen. Other hopes will be that, if those events do happen, plans will be in place to assure that the child is well cared for, as protected as possible, comfortable and not afraid. Modifying the old adage, hope for the best and plan for the worst so that you can hope that the true worst does not happen. Although difficult to discuss these fears, mentioning them to health care providers and asking, "What would we do if this happened?" can start the process of making these plans tangible, forging a clearer pathway toward the hope that the worst will be prevented. Although the hope that arises to counter these fears may seem grim, this type of hope is full of deep commitment and resolve.

Everyday hopes

When the diagnosis of DIPG enters the lives of many families, for a time life may seem to stop, to be put on hold, consumed by the chaos and emotions surrounding the diagnosis and coordinating and coping with the early stages of complex medical care. How can life resume? There is no single right answer, and every potential answer is difficult; yet one recurring answer we hear from parents is this: one small everyday hope at a time. Start by hoping to simply take a deep breath and let it out. Then hope to get outside and see the sun straight overhead or the first stars at dusk. Parents have told us that even seemingly insignificant things like running a short errand without worrying about not being at their child's side, or being able to attend to another child without feelings of guilt, is something to hope for in a day. Name these hopes to yourself and to others, and then work toward them. One small hope at a time can make a large difference. Ask for help if needed and accept the help that is offered.

Hopes to be a good parent

Many parents we have spoken to wonder—and worry—about what they need to do in order to be, in their own view, a good parent for their child with serious illness. This is usually not a topic of conversation that comes up spontaneously, arising only when we ask whether parents think about this, and then they often say words to the effect of "yes…all the time." Cast upon a journey that no parent ever anticipates, and none are prepared for, parents often have told no one about these furtive thoughts, which arise from confronting the uncharted enormity of this disease and the inevitable doubts and confusions. Our hope when broaching this topic is simply to be a companion and help to dispel some of the loneliness that accompanies these private worries. What do I need to do? Am I doing the right thing? Am I doing enough? Again, there are no right or wrong answers. We find that parents usually can name a few things that they feel that they must do for their child, and hope fervently that they can do these things. Our job, as we see it, is to gain an appreciation of what these things are, help the parents to achieve what they are hoping to do, and offer feedback and reassurance that they are indeed doing them.

Hopes for health care providers

"Given your child's situation, what are you hoping for?" Sometime during the days or week after receiving the news that their child has a DIPG, when the initial shock of the news has started to lift, this question should be routinely posed to parents. Yet typically, medical providers don't ask. Is it because they are sure they already know the answer? Because they cannot bring themselves to imagine with this family what hope might look like in even the most difficult of circumstances? Or is it because they are afraid of not being able to aid in making those hopes a reality?

Quite often physicians assume—or, more blatantly, assert—that parents have only the capacity for one hope: hope for cure, the hope for a miracle. In this regard, physicians and other health care providers are not alone. Studies of the social construct of hope as portrayed by print media suggest that the public dialogue in the newspapers and magazines around hope for patients with advanced cancer conveys the message that only one legitimate hope exists for persons with cancer—hope for a cure.

What are the origins of this notion that, when given a diagnosis of advanced cancer, hope becomes a singular entity? Perhaps this concept is just a self-reassuring shared myth, consoling all of us, who do not have to confront cancer personally, that one need only hope for cure. Perhaps this notion is a way to push aside the health care provider's own feelings of failing their patients and families. Or perhaps this is an optimistic—and thus effective—way to market and advertise medical innovations.

Whatever the origins, this notion is a conceptual straightjacket, causing us to underestimate a parent's ability to harbor, frame, and hold hope while still being grounded in reality. Certainly parents have voiced that what is important to them is honest communication with their child's medical providers about their child's medical issues, regardless of prognosis. Health care providers may need to be encouraged that one of the most valuable things they can give to patients and parents is permission to hope—and that they themselves can hope to participate in the care of a patient and family, offering to help in ways that extend beyond the physical or biological treatment of disease, all in the pursuit of hopes.

Completing a Circle of Hopes

Not all of the aspects of hope outlined in this chapter may come readily to you or your child or your family. And some aspects may not be what you need. What is right, hope-wise, is what is right for you and your child. In the profusion of what you hope for, your hopes are intertwined with your values, your loved ones and your goals. Take a look, from time to time, at what your hopes have become, building your hopes until you can envision your child, your family, and yourself surrounded by a protective circle of hopes, 360 degrees of commitment and compassion, capable of moving forward with purpose.

We started by asking whether there was anything that we could do that would be helpful, and here at the end we still worry that our words may not have sufficed to bring clarity of thought or comfort of feeling to you. Yet we, too, live in hope, as we all must, and hope that you have found something of value in this letter, something within you or around you that can help carry you, your family, and your child forward with hope.

Parent Perspectives

Julian was diagnosed with an atypical brainstem glioma because of the way his tumor was growing up and out of his brainstem. We clung to the hope that this tumor would prove "atypical" in its behavior and that he could be an exception to the grim statistics.

Another brain tumor parent asked me, "How do you walk the line between accepting the reality of this and staying hopeful?" It was the internal struggle we faced every day. Walking the tight rope between fear and optimism, we found balance by taking it practically one hour at a time, savoring the small, beautiful moments and committing to the task of keeping him feeling safe and loved.

Early on, a friend and pastor made me tell him the prognosis. He said, "You need to be honest with me before I can help you." It was the first time I said it aloud, "Typically patients have less than a year."

His advice that followed stuck with me throughout our 7-month battle. He said, "You need to prepare your heart, but make no plans to lose." Encouraging us to stay hopeful, he continued, "You will not start planning the funeral. You find him the best care you can, and you will not stop searching for a breakthrough."

Keep your head where your feet are was my motto. You can spend your time searching the world over for a wonder cure or treatment, but if you use your time wisely you will quickly see what is important. Assign that role to someone else. Keep in mind your priorities and don't lose sight of quality over quantity. Don't ever lose hope but please put reality in the driver's seat so that you don't miss out on one single happy moment with your child. Ask for your miracle but some part of you must come to terms with the "what if you don't get it" part. Don't think you are giving up if you decide to end treatment or follow a different path. You are never going to give up. You are always going to do what you think is best for your child.

It was at the end of radiation that we did another good thing. We were

asked, and agreed, to meet with the pediatric palliative care nurse, before going home. I can say that I was in complete dread of meeting Bryce's palliative care nurse, because she was going to tell us all the terrible things that we couldn't and didn't want to even imagine yet, including how and when Bryce would die. I wasn't ready for it, didn't want to hear it. The day that my husband and I met with her I was physically sick. We walked in, and the first thing that she asked us was to tell her about Bryce, which threw me off kilter. She didn't want to know about his symptoms like every other person we had encountered. She wanted to know about him as a person, and as a child. She wanted to know what his interests were, and about our family. After being submerged in the cancer world and on "a mission" to treat him, this was somewhat shocking, and even refreshing.

She then looked at us and asked if we knew what palliative care was all about. We said yes, it was about dying. She said, yes, that was part of it, but it was also about so much more. She looked at us and told us that palliative care was about choosing to LIVE, for as long as possible, and in the best manner possible with the time that is left. It was about making each day a choice to live, not about waiting to die. And at that moment we made a choice. We decided that we would do just that. We would go home and LIVE Bryce's days with him, and make those days everything that they could be—and it became our new mission. Our hope changed.

We knew there was no cure, but we also knew that our hope became about making whatever days we had left with our son be good ones. Those days would have to be so good that for him, and for us, and for his sister there would be no regrets.

Once we were home, we contacted hospice right away. We were trying to find a connection at home for Bryce and for our family that was local. We all started to see the social work team there. It was one of the good things that we did. Bryce met with the social worker every couple of weeks. She suggested that they work on a scrapbook together, one page every session, about Bryce's life. So we would get fancy papers and pictures ready for the theme of the week, and during their sessions, they would talk—alone. It was nice for Bryce to have someone to talk to who was not a family member, and to have someone to tell how he really felt about what was happening, without being afraid of hurting anyone at home. They worked on the scrapbook for almost 6 months.

Over that summer and into the fall many wonderful things happened.

Bryce got his "Wish" for a camper from Make-a-Wish Foundation. We camped and traveled. He spent time with his friends, and he did his best to be a regular kid. He continued to have double vision, so some activities were no longer possible, but he was determined and found ways to compensate. His balance generally improved, so he still rode his bike. As dirt-biking was too fast, much to the dismay of his doctors, we got him a four wheeler, which he was allowed to ride on flat fields with his friends. This was probably his most prized possession that summer. For the most part it was a good summer, when he felt good.

He never really wanted to discuss his illness except on the days when he wasn't feeling well. He even started high school. He attended two classes in the morning. He went to the gym with special permission in the afternoon with his dad, and we got him a personal trainer. This really helped to keep his strength and balance up, too. He continued to hang around the arena, skated when he felt up to it, and even coached his own team with his father. He always amazed us with how hard he fought to be a regular kid every single day. He wouldn't accept any less from the rest of us either.

Not only were we on a mission to help Bryce no matter where this journey took our family, but we were also dealing with the reality of losing a child. And you do what you have to do to help your child, no matter what—because that's what he expected of us. There were many days when I would just want to crawl into bed and never get up again. We were already grieving and he was still here. But he would say, "Mom, go take a shower, you look like crap." And I remember crying one day all the way home from the hospital, and cuddling with him when we got home that night. He was accepting of me being sad, but then, he suddenly looked at me, and said "Mom, you can cry today, but you can't cry tomorrow." I asked why not. He said, "Because I just need you to be mom every day." And that was when I decided that no matter what happened, if my son was going to have to do this, that I would be present every step of the way. What choice was there? He needed us to be.

It was at this point that we decided that we needed to fill in a booklet that was given to us about what Bryce wanted for end-of-life care. As Bryce's progression developed, his speech became quite affected, so we were glad to have this booklet full of answers to help us to make sure that his wishes were being met. It also helped for planning his celebration of life thereafter.

As Bryce lost his gross motor ability to hold up his head and to sit, we found the right wheelchair for him so that we could still do things with him. He wanted to go for a walk around the block one day. We had to wait until all visitors left, because they thought it was a terrible idea taking him out. It was unsafe, he would get sick, they argued. But that was what he wanted. These adventures took 2 to 3 hours from start to finish. He wanted his snowsuit on because it had snowed. So we did that. We went for a walk, and he wanted us to lay him in the snow. So we did. He wanted to lie in bed with his hockey skates on, so he did. He wanted to hold his skateboard in bed, so he did. He wanted a remote control car, so we searched the earth and found it in Australia. He got it with a lot of help. He wanted to go to Walmart for an F150 dinky car. So we did. One of the biggest adventures was that Bryce wanted to go and watch his sister play hockey. It was her first hockey tournament. The arena where she was playing did not "support" a viewing area for individuals in wheelchairs, so, with the help of Earth Angels, 6 police officers came out to lift Bryce and his wheelchair up a flight of 25 stairs to the viewing area. He watched his sister play, and at the end of the game he said, "You forgot to tuck in one side of your jersey, Bailey." Those officers came back an hour later to lift him back down. Another day former NHL player Bobby Orr showed up at our house to visit.

I have to say that as a parent, and not a health care professional, it was the scariest thing that we will ever experience, but we could only have survived it because of the communication and support that we received from the healthcare team. You see, for the entire 361 days that Bryce fought this cancer, we were supported. We were able to talk to people who could help us and explain things to us, so that we could in turn explain it to Bryce and his sister, and ultimately live through what was happening. Everyone was only a phone call away, or a visit away. Once in Care at Home, Bryce's care team continued to support us by calling us regularly in the evenings. This meant so much to us, because this would be when we felt that much more separated from medical staff and when truthfully after dealing all day, we were most vulnerable and scared of what was to come. What if it happened at night?

I can tell you that now, 20 months later, I still feel that we did what was right for our Bryce and for our family. All of the decisions and conversations that we had were right for us. We have no regrets that we didn't get to talk about things, or that we didn't get to spend time doing the things that Bryce chose to do, or that he didn't LIVE every single day that he was given. That is not to say that we do not miss our boy every second of every day, or that our life will ever be the same without him. We said what we needed to say, and did what he needed us to do. In the meantime, we LIVE as he showed us how to—with hope for a cure, much courage to get through our days, strength in making good decisions, and with the peace of knowing that we will one day be together again.

As I look back on this journey, my advice to parents that may have a newly diagnosed child with DIPG is to not give up. There are survivors of this—not many. It is crucial, in my opinion, to send out your child's scans to doctors that know this tumor. Join the DIPG yahoo group online for a list of exceptional doctors with expertise in DIPG, for other families that have gone through this and are in the battle, for the most up-to-date treatment options from around the world, for clinical trial information, for alternatives that others have tried, and for understanding. Please know there are people that will help you and will listen and will understand. Finally know that as the parent you will make the right decisions for your child in this very difficult journey.

Things were as normal as they could be with all the appointments and the anxiety of knowing that this reprieve was probably going to be a short-lived gift. Although we held out hope that Miguel would be the one to beat this, we were realistic. We were able to enjoy him fully for 18 months from diagnosis. It wasn't easy, especially when progression occurred almost one year from diagnosis, just like the doctors said it would. While he was able to compensate for many of the symptoms prior to diagnosis, after progression, things changed one by one: loss of mobility, difficulty swallowing, loss of speech, and the loss of fine motor skills to name a few. Although the deterioration was difficult to watch and endure, Miguel's short life has made a profound impact in many lives. Miguel is a precious yet rare gift and it is an honor to be his grandma—always.

"Honey, I am scared Johnny is going to die too. Right now, I don't know if he will or not, but I do know he isn't going to die today. So each day I have with him, I am going to love him and make it as special as possible.

Does that sound like a good plan?" At this point, we were both crying. Through our tears, a small smile came to her face and we headed back up to the room to check on the one boy we couldn't stop thinking about.

We had been at St. Jude for about three weeks. We had a routine of radiation, chemotherapy and clinics. We were beginning to accept that Johnny had cancer, and although there was no cure, we were given more time with him, and we all wanted more time. One afternoon, we were in the truck driving back to the Ronald McDonald House. Johnny's stomach was upset and he was lying down in the back. Johnny speaks up from the back, "Mom, am I going to die?" I felt the stabbing dagger of pain once again. My son knew he was going to die and no one needed to tell him, but he needed to talk.

Since I had already talked with my daughter, I knew how I would respond. I went on to ask more questions from him and then closed the conversation by telling him his feelings were normal and good, his dad and I felt the same way, there were some things we can't control and don't have the answers to, how much we love him and how special we will make the time we do have with him. We were taking life one day at a time. We had no guarantees about tomorrow, but today we were living it for all it was worth.

The questions from my other children continued, "It's not fair. Why did he get sick? What did we do wrong? We are good people. I mean we do some bad things but not really bad. Why is God punishing us?" I didn't know what to say. Having questions about faith and spiritual matters is normal. The intensity of this pain is going to bring to the surface questions that most people can go a lifetime without addressing. One option is to ignore or avoid my child's questions. A second option is to seek out the answers and wrestle with the questions. Option one gives immediate relief but the questions will resurface throughout their life because they go unresolved and unanswered. Option two is a more difficult path, but when the wrestling is over and the tension is resolved my other children will be able to move through their grief in a healthy pattern.

So, this was my reply. "I don't know why God is allowing this to happen to us. This is what I do know. I know all the stories of people helping us. I know dad's friends from his childhood live in Memphis and have a house so you kids can stay here with us. Most families have to live apart from each other all this time. I know that grandpa and grandma have the time to live here with you, so that dad and I can take care of Johnny. I know dad's work is letting him stay here the whole time Johnny is at St. Jude and still paying him so we don't lose our house. I know our neighbors are mowing our grass and taking care of the dog. I know people are sending you kids gifts and cards. I know that every time we turn around someone is doing something special for us, and a lot of those people don't even know us because we just moved to Arkansas three months ago. I know these things mean something."

I could not offer many answers to my son that day. I still cannot offer many answers. But my answer offered hope to him. Hope that there are good things in the face of tragedy. Living one day at a time, hope was enough to calm my child's heart.

In the days that followed his diagnosis we would tell Liam he had cancer. We felt it was incredibly important to tell him the truth, to use that word. As hard as it was, we wanted him to know he could always trust us to be honest with him going forward.

We called family and close friends. We had family bring our other three children to the hospital. We told our kids that Liam had brain cancer and that they could not take it out but that we were going to do everything we could to make it smaller. Liam's neuro-oncologist allowed the kids to visit Liam very briefly. Liam's identical twin brother asked his doctor what would happen if the medicine didn't work. The doctor reassured him that they had lots of things they could try to help Liam feel his best. We felt grateful for this small offering of hope.

I would have liked to have a group of individuals to talk to about our daughter's specific tumor type during her treatment. We were following another DIPG child's story and were very inspired at how long he was able to live after treatment. We never gave up hope and we always believed that something would come up to save our daughter. We never really thought she would really die from this even though that's what they told us.

Things are changing for our kids, for your child. There are viable alternatives to current steroids and new therapies on the horizon. I know that there is always hope.

We have found it incredibly helpful to hear from other parents that have lost a child. Their advice is always so heartfelt and honest. The only advice we can come up with at the moment is to listen to your own heart and make decisions based on your knowledge of your child, individual circumstances and personal convictions. Grieving is such a personal journey, and the patience you need to have with yourself is infinite. No one's path with DIPG is the same, and the only thing you can strive for is that you don't regret any of the decisions you've made. We think the best way to do this is to trust your instincts and be at peace with the journey as much as possible.

Stella is many things. As was evident early, she is a force to be reckoned with. She is inquisitive. She is intelligent. She is hilarious. More than anything else, Stella is her aptly given middle name: Stella is "Joy." Stella proves that cancer can't take away everything...her smile is our lifeline!

✦✦✦

Aimee asked me last night if I thought we would ever be happy again. It's an interesting question. It's not that we haven't felt happiness these last 8 1/2 months; it's just that all happiness is tinged with a pervasive sadness as well. I had to think for a while before answering, because the truth is I have no idea if I will ever feel true happiness again. I think we will definitely have many moments in the future of being happy. But feeling happy? I think they are two different things. My best guess is that each joyful moment will come with a small shadow of wishing that our daughter was there to experience it as well. Every family vacation and holiday, every accomplishment in our lives, every celebration (big or small) that she should have been there for. I imagine that eventually the shadow around your heart just becomes who you are and happiness and sadness cease to exist as separate entities and your new norm is to just accept that happiness and sadness are not mutually exclusive, but intertwined in one another—bitter and sweet.

What is keeping us moving forward right now, even when our hearts are completely broken, is watching how our daughter has chosen to live her short life. How she treats each day as a new adventure, pushes herself both physically and mentally to ensure that she accomplishes what she wants on that particular day. Sometimes it's something big—painting *with her mouth and visiting the pigs at the farm. And sometimes it's just being able to mouth the words "ice cream," and then napping most of the day. But she is always true to herself, and even though things are hard for her, she ignores the barriers of DIPG and chooses to forge her own path. Most importantly, she believes that when life gives you a hundred reasons to cry, you need to find a thousand reasons to smile...**And in my own smiles, I have become familiar with the bittersweet taste of getting to parent my precious daughter—the best experience in the world, but like a spring day that is much, much, too short.***

Appendix A

Medications Form

Appendix A: Medications

Name of Medication and Strength	Instructions/Dose (Include all details, dose, and times)	Purpose	Prescribing Doctor
Ex: Tylenol liquid (acetaminophen) 160 mg/5 ml	Takes 3 ml every 4 hours by mouth as needed	For fever or pain	Dr. Smith

It is strongly recommended that you take any medication that your child is receiving at home to each doctor or hospital visit. The medications will be reviewed and any changes can be made at that time.

Appendix B

Glossary of Terms

The following terms were referenced by the authors throughout the book. They are listed here to provide additional information to assist with understanding.

Accessible: Tumors that can be approached using a surgical procedure.

Active Immunization: This is the kind of vaccine we are most used to. The MMR, influenza, DPT, and Polio vaccines all depend on active immunization by presenting an antigen to the immune system and inducing an immune response and long-lasting central memory.

Adaptive Immunization: This comes into play when the innate immune system is evaded and an invader (a pathogen or cancer cell) gains a foothold. The adaptive response recognizes these invaders and enables the immune system to mount a stronger response each time they are encountered. This response involves all branches of the immune system, both B cells and T cells, working together in balance. The adaptive response can be trained through dendritic cell vaccine strategies.

Adjuvant Chemotherapy: Administering chemotherapy after the primary tumor has been treated by some other method, for example after radiation.

Adoptive Immunization: The transfer of mature circulating lymphocytes to treat certain diseases.

Anaplastic Astrocytoma: A synonym used interchangeably for WHO grade 3 astrocytoma (glioma).

Angiogenesis Inhibitor: An agent that inhibits the growth of new blood vessels.

Apraxia: Inability to perform activities such as making gestures, speaking in spite of the person's willingness to do so; inability of the brain to correctly communicate instructions to the body.

Astrocyte: One of two types of glial cells in the central nervous system that help support the neural cells. The other type of glial cell is called an oligodendrocyte.

Astrocytoma: A tumor developed from the glial type of cell called an astrocyte. These tumors are oftentimes further described by location or appearance under the microscope. The microscopy appearance can be into one of 4 grades using the World Health Organization classification.

Ataxia: Uncoordinated and clumsy appearing walk that is associated with balance issues.

B Lymphocytes: Cells in the immune system responsible for the humoral immune response. That is the production of antibodies that attack foreign antigens (like bacteria) or tumor associated antigens.

Blood-Brain Barrier (BBB): Protective barrier separating circulating blood from the brain's extracellular fluid thereby preventing substances in the blood from entering into the brain. The BBB is created through tight junctions around the capillaries of the linings of the blood vessels of the brain.

Brainstem Glioma: The broadest term to describe all histologic grades of glial tumors that are located in any part of the brainstem (pons, medulla, tectum and cervicomedullary junction). Brainstem gliomas can always be classified more specifically by particular location (e.g. pontine glioma, tectal glioma, cervicomedullary glioma) and by certain descriptive terms (e.g. diffuse, focal, intrinsic, exophytic and extrinsic).

Biopsy: Surgical procedure to remove a sample of tumor tissue to establish diagnosis. Tissue can be further utilized to determine specific molecular analysis for research purposes as well as potentially used to develop personalized treatment plans.

Cerebellar Ataxia: Loss of muscle coordination brought on by a lesion in the cerebellum.

Cerebral Spinal Fluid (CSF): Clear, colorless fluid that circulates around and inside the brain and spinal cord.

Contrast Enhancement: Use of an agent administered to a patient prior to an MRI scan to increase the visibility between the tumor and surrounding tissue.

Computerized Tomography (CT) Scan: A medical imaging procedure using x-ray technology from a series of different x-ray angles, which are then processed through computer technology to create cross-sectional images of bones and soft tissue including the brain; also referred to as CAT scan.

Cranial Nerves: Twelve pairs of nerves originating in the brain, and often included in the designation of central nervous system (brain, spinal cord, and cranial nerves.)

Cytoarchitecture: The typical arrangement of cells within a particular tissue or organ.

Cytotoxic: Toxic to cells. Any agent or process that kills cells.

Cytotoxic T Cells: T lymphocyte cells that directly induce the death of tumor cells or virus-infected cells; also known as killer T cells.

Daughter Cell: Cell(s) that result from cell division. Daughter cells are genetically identical to the originating parent cell.

Dendritic Cell: These cells are unique to mammals and function to capture foreign invaders (antigens) and present them to the immune system. Activated dendritic cells from the nose, lungs, or skin migrate to the lymph nodes to tell B and T cells what to do.

De Novo: New—for example a de novo mutation is a new genetic mutation.

Diffuse: An adjective that can be used to describe an infiltrative nature of a tumor as opposed to focal tumors which are more confined or circumscribed. Diffuse tumors are usually a higher histological grade (3 or 4) but can be low grade. Except in the cases of leptomeningeal spread or gliomatosis cerebri, diffuse is also intrinsic. These tumors cannot be removed as they are like "sand in grass" or "pepper in Jello" i.e. being too difficult to remove the tumor without severely disturbing the normal tissue of the pons.

Diffuse Brainstem Glioma: This is an infiltrative tumor of glial origin located anywhere in the brainstem. Approximately 80% of these tumors will be in the pons. Thus most, but not all, diffuse brainstem gliomas can be more specifically called diffuse pontine gliomas or diffuse intrinsic pontine gliomas.

Diffuse Pontine Glioma: A glioma (usually an astrocytoma) located in the pons which intermingles and infiltrates normal pontine tissue. Synonyms include diffuse intrinsic pontine glioma or diffuse infiltrative pontine glioma.

Diffuse Intrinsic Pontine Glioma (DIPG): A glioma (usually an astrocytoma) located in the pons which intermingles and infiltrates normal pontine tissue. Synonyms include: diffuse pontine glioma or diffuse infiltrative pontine glioma.

Diplopia: Double vision

Dorsal Exophytic Pontine Glioma: Tumor that grows from subependymal glial tissue out into the 4th ventricle; typically presents with hydrocephalus.

Dysarthria: Speech disorder resulting from defects in the central or peripheral motor nerves leading to an impairment of neural transmission to the muscles involved in speech. Can include impairment to all processes involved in the production of speech including respiration, phonation, and articulation.

Dysphasia: Loss or impairment of the ability to speak, read, or write; understand or interpret speech or written language.

Edema: Excess bodily fluid leading to swelling.

Embryo's Yolk Sac Endoderm: The germ layer that lines the yolk sac.

Endoscopic Third Ventriculostomy (ETV): Surgical procedure in which an opening is created in the floor of the third ventricle using an endoscope through a burr hole. This allows for the cerebrospinal fluid to flow directly into the basal cistern, thereby used as a means to treat obstructive hydrocephalus.

Extrinsic: An adjective to describe a tumor that is located on the outside.

Exophytic: An adjective to describe a tumor that is growing out of the brainstem— like the top part of an iceberg sticking out of the water.

Focal: An adjective used to describe a tumor that is well defined and does not seem to intertwine with normal tissue. Focal brainstem gliomas are usually histologically grade 1 (also called pilocytic astrocytoma).

Glial Cell: One of the supportive cells in the central nervous system. These can be either astrocytes or oligodendrocytes.

Glioma: A tumor arising from glial cells, either astrocytes or oligodendrocytes. If one can differentiate the cell line from which the tumor derived from, then it may be called by a more specific name, i.e. an astrocytoma, oligodendroglioma or a mixed tumor. Different adjectives can be applied to the term glioma to convey a more descriptive, specific understanding of the tumor.

Glioblastoma Multiforme (GBM): A synonym used interchangeably for WHO grade 4 astrocytoma (glioma).

Helper T Cells: T lymphocyte cells that help the immune system recognize what to attack.

Hemiparesis: Muscle weakness on one side of the body.

Hirsutism: Abnormal hair growth on face and body.

Histologic: A term referring to the classification of tissue based on microscopic examination. With gliomas, there are 4 grades based on the WHO classification.

Hydrocephalus: Excess fluid in the brain resulting from a blockage of the CSF pathways.

Hyperphagia: Abnormal increased appetite for food.

Hypoxic Cells: Cells that are deprived of oxygen.

Hypoxic Cell Sensitizers: Compounds that selectively sensitize hypoxic tumor cells to the effects of radiation.

Immunohistochemical: Pertains to an assay used in research analysis that shows specific antigens in tissues through the use of fluorescent markers.

Infiltrative: An adjective used to describe a tumor that is intermixed with normal tissue. A synonym for diffuse.

Intrathecal: An area sometimes used to administer drugs, which is located in the space under the arachnoid membrane that covers the brain and spinal cord.

Intratumoral: An area within a tumor.

Intraventricular: An area located within a ventricle of the brain.

Intrinsic: An adjective used to describe that a tumor is located on the inside.

In Vitro: A preclinical study or experiment done within a test tube or laboratory dish.

In Vivo: A study, medical test, or procedure that is done on a living organism, such as a laboratory animal or human.

Lumbar Puncture (LP): Insertion of a needle into the subarachnoid space of the spine to either administer drugs or to withdraw a sample of CSF for biopsy; also referred to as spinal tap.

mAB: Monoclonal antibody.

Magnetic Resonance Imaging (MRI) Scan: Medical imaging technique that uses magnetic field and radio waves to generate computer imaging data; produces high contrast images of the soft tissue of the body with useful application to the brain.

Malignant: Another term meaning cancerous.

Memory B Cells: The cells that most childhood immunizations depend on. Memory cells are created from activated B cells the first time an antigen is encountered (like a tetanus vaccine). When one encounters the same antigen again (like stepping on a rusty nail), even years later, the memory B lymphocyte cells will respond quickly to create an immune response before things get out of hand.

Memory T Cells: Experienced lymphocyte T cells that have previously encountered virally infected cells or tumor cells. They are more effective than naïve T cells are when encountering an immune target for the second time, i.e. they hit harder and faster. Memory T cells are divided into central memory and effector memory subtypes.

Mitotic Cycle: The transferring of the parent cell genome through cell division into two identical daughter cells.

Necrosis: The death of living cells or tissue(s) due to disease, injury, loss of blood supply, radiation or chemical agents.

Neoadjuvant: Induction therapy that is given to a patient prior to the main treatment; can include chemotherapy, radiotherapy, hormone therapy. The goal is to reduce the size of the tumor prior to the radical therapy.

Neoadjuvant Chemotherapy: Administration of chemotherapy in order to decrease the tumor burden prior to treatment by other modalities such as radiation.

Neurospheres: A free-floating (non-adherent) in vitro spherical cluster of neural stem cells.

Neurotoxicity: A damaging effect on the nerves or nervous tissue.

Passive Immunization: Fetuses acquire antibody from the mother via the placenta of breast milk and are more able to cope with specific infections during the first weeks of life. Artificial passive immunity can be used to treat transplant rejection, rabies or tetanus.

Peritumoral: Area around the margins of a tumor.

Peritumoral Edema: Swelling around a tumor.

Pilocytic Astrocytoma: The lowest histologic grade of tumor. When in the brainstem these tumors tend to be more confined and less infiltrative. They possibly could be operable. These are WHO grade 1 astrocytomas.

Plasma B Cells: Large B lymphocyte cells that have been exposed to a specific immune target and make lots of antibodies against it.

Pons: A specific area of the brainstem located below the midbrain and above the medulla which is connected to the cerebellum through the cerebellar peduncles.

Pontine: An adjective used to describe the specific location as being in the pons.

Pontine Glioma: A tumor of glial origin which is located in the pons.

Progenitor Cell: Cell that is an early offshoot of a stem cell but one that is more differentiated than a stem cell.

Radiation Necrosis: The death of living cells or tissue(s) caused by radiation.

Radioresistant: Tumors that do not respond well to conventional radiation therapy.

Radiosensitive: Tumors that do respond to conventional radiation therapy.

Ras Protein: A protein involved in signal transmission within cells which typically promotes normal cell division. Abnormal ras, caused by gene mutation(s) results in increased cell division leading to cell proliferation.

Resect: Surgically remove.

Spiral CT Scan: CT scan technology using a helical/360 degree capture of the x-ray image which results in increased resolution, also referred to as a helical CT.

Stem Cell: Master cell that is undifferentiated within the human body, capable of growing into any one of more than 200 cell types, allowing them to replace defective or lost cells/tissues in patients with disease or defects.

Stereotactic: Surgery or radiation therapy that is directed by 3D scanning device to enhance procedure accuracy.

Sublethal Radiation Damage: Radiation that damages but does not kill the tumor cell.

Suppressor T Cells: T lymphocyte cells that maintain immune tolerance so we don't attack ourselves or overly respond to everything we come in contact with; also known as Regulatory T Cells (Treg).

Teratogen: Drug that can disturb the development of an embryo or fetus.

T Lymphocytes: Cells within the immune system which are responsible for the cell-mediated immune response.

Tumor Necrosis: Death of tumor tissue.

Tumor Vasculature: Arrangement of blood vessels within tumors; vascular-targeted therapies are being studied to destroy the blood supply to cancer cells within tumors.

Ventricle: A small cavity located within the brain.

WHO Grading of Glial Tumors: The World Health Organization has criteria in categorizing glial tumors by the way they appear under the microscope. Those that appear closer to normal cells are lower grade (1 or 2) and are generally considered less aggressive. Those that look more abnormal are higher grades (3 or 4) and are typically considered more aggressive.

Grade 1-pilocytic astrocytoma

Grade 2- fibrillary astrocytoma

Grade 3- Anaplastic Astrocytoma

Grade 4- Glioblastoma Multiforme

The number grade and the corresponding terms are considered synonymous and used interchangeably.

Resources

Many resources exist for families of children with diffuse intrinsic pontine glioma. This appendix contains a sampling of some especially helpful books, organizations, videotapes, and websites.

Books

General

Keene, Nancy. *Chemo, Craziness, and Comfort: My Book About Childhood Cancer*. American Childhood Cancer Organization, 2002. Provides clear explanations and practical advice for children ages 6 to 12 with cancer. Warm and funny illustrations, by Trevor Romain, help the child (and parents) make sense of cancer and its treatment. Free to children with cancer.

Dodd, Michael. *Oliver's Story, For 'Sibs' of Kids with Cancer*. American Childhood Cancer Organization, 2004. A practical book written to celebrate the ways in which siblings of children with cancer can help during this time of family crisis. Free to families of children with cancer. Available in English and Spanish.

Hoffman, Ruth I. *Along the Way*. American Childhood Cancer Organization, 2010. This coil-bound journal provides a place for contact information for doctors, school and other caregivers essential to caring for the child with cancer. It also includes information about clinical trials, informed consent, medical terminology, blood counts as well as forms to log the child's temperature and out-of-pocket expenditures. An extensive journal section is also included. Free to families of children with cancer.

Hoffman, Ruth I. *Cozy Cares Journal*. American Childhood Cancer Organization, 2010. This 122 page journal includes illustrations by Trevor Romain. The drawings of Cozy the 'Port-a-Cat' include hand gestures such as 'high five,' 'ok,' and 'thumbs up' to encourage the child to draw strength from within themselves as well as those around them. Writing prompts throughout the book help the child cope during their diagnosis and express their thoughts and feelings during this difficult time. Examples of writing prompts include: I am special because ...; When I'm bored in the hospital my family and I ...; When I'm feeling sad it helps to ... etc. Free to children with cancer.

Romain, Trevor. *Lift Me Up*. American Childhood Cancer Organization, 2008. This 24 page book with inspirational text is filled with wonderful illustrations to color. Free to children with cancer.

Grief in school

Gliko-Braden, Majel. *Grief Comes to Class: A Teacher's Guide*. Centering Corporation, 1531 N. Saddle Creek Rd., Omaha, NE 68104. (402) 553-1200. Comprehensive guide to grief in the classroom. Includes chapters on grief responses, the bereaved student, teen grief, developmental changes, sample letter to parents, and sample teacher/parent conferences. Also available on Amazon.com

The Compassionate Friends. *Suggestions for Teachers and School Counselors.* P.O. Box 3696, Oak Brook, IL 60522. (630) 990-0010.

Romain, Trevor. *What on Earth Do You Do When Someone Dies?* Minneapolis, MN: Free Spirit Publishing, 1999. Warm, honest words and beautiful illlustrations help children understand and cope with grief.

Harvey, Diane. *Why the Snowman Melts.* Sandstone Publishing Saint George, UT, 2010. Through the story of the melting snowman, young children gain understanding of change and loss.

Brown, Laurie Krasny and Brown, Marc. *When Dinosaurs Die: A Guide to Understanding Death.* Little Brown and Company, New York, NY, 1996. For children ages 5 to 8 years. Direct answers to children's questions about death such as "Why does someone die?" Available through Amazon.com.

Wilhelm, Hans. *I'll Always Love You.* Crown Publishers, 1985. The loving story of a little boy and his love and loss of his dog Elfie. Available on Amazon.com.

Heckert, Connie. *Dribbles.* Clarion Books, New York, NY, 1994. For ages 5 to 8. This picture book addresses death as told by three household cats living with an aging owner and aging feline. Available on Amazon.com.

Grootman, Marilyn. *When a Friend Dies: A Book for Teens about Grieving and Healing.* Free Spirit Publishing, Minneapolis, MN, 1994. Practical guide for teens that addresses and validates emotions associated with death such as guilt, fear, anger and confusion.

Wolfelt, Alan. *Healing a Child's Grieving Heart: 100 Practical Ideas for Families, Friends and Caregivers.* Companion Press, Ft. Collins, CO, 2001. Practical guide that provides suggestions on how to help those who are grieving by offering sensitive responses to "what to say and do" and "what not to say and do." Available on Amazon.com.

Hearing loss

Poitras Tucker, Bonnie. *IDEA Advocacy for Children Who Are Deaf or Hard of Hearing: A Question and Answer Book for Parents and Professionals.* Singular Publishing Group, 1997.

IEP school advocacy

Siegel, Lawrence. *The Complete IEP Guide: How to Advocate for Your Special Ed Child.* Harbor House Law Press, 2001. Spells out the IEP process for families and includes helpful sample letters and forms.

Anderson, Winifred, Stephen Chitwood, and Deidre Hayden. *Negotiating the Special Education Maze: A Guide for Parents and Teachers.* 3rd ed. Bethesda, Maryland: Woodbine House, 1997. Excellent, well-organized text clearly explains the step-by-step process necessary to obtain help for your child.

Susan Gorn, Editor. *Special Education Dictionary.* LRP Publications, 1997. (215) 784-0860.

Wright, Peter, and Wright, Pamela. Wrightslaw: *Special Education Law.* Hartfield, VA: Harbor House Law Press, 1999. Text of key laws and regulations.

Wright, Peter, and Wright, Pamela. *Wrightslaw: From Emotions to Advocacy: The Special Education Survival Guide.* Hartfield, VA: Harbor House Law Press, 2001. Full of information on special education law, advocacy tactics, and IEP tips.

Speech and language

McAleer Hamaguchi, Patricia. *Childhood Speech, Language and Listening Problems: What Every Parent Should Know.* John Wiley & Sons Inc., 1995.

Schoenbrodt, Lisa, ed. *Children with Traumatic Brain Injury: A Parent's Guide.* Woodbine House, 2003.

Schwartz, Sue, and Joan E. Heller Miller. *The New Language of Toys: Teaching Communication Skills to Special-Needs Children.* Rockville, MD: Woodbine House, 1996.

Videotapes

Paul and the Dragon. Powerful 25 minute video created to help children, siblings and friends understand the world of childhood cancer in a safe way, with humor but also with truth. Through watching Paul's battle with his dragon, the child with cancer will understand that scary things will happen to them as they fight their "cancer-dragon." They will learn that the doctors, nurses and even the blue "medication-men" and purple "chemo-blobs" are there to help them beat their cancer. Available through the American Childhood Cancer Organization. http://www.acco.org

Why, Charlie Brown, Why? Tender story of a classmate who develops leukemia. Available as a book or videotape. For video availability, call the Leukemia and Lymphoma Society, (800) 955-4572 (4LSA).

Cancervive Back to School Kit. A comprehensive package of materials developed to assist children and adolescents re-entering the school setting. The kit contains a "Teachers Guide for Kids with Cancer" and two award-winning documentary videos: "Emily's Story: Back to School After Cancer" and "Making the Grade: Back to School After Cancer for Teens." http://www.cancersourcekids.com/parents/schoolintro.cfm?usertypeid=3

Drying Their Tears. Produced by CARTI. For information, call (800) 482-8561. Video and manual to help counselors, teachers, and other professionals help children deal with the grief, fear, confusion and anger that occur after the death of a loved one. Has three segments: one about training facilitators, one for children ages 5 to 8, and one for ages 9 to teens. Each section includes interviews with children and video from children's workshops. http://www.hopkinschildrens.org/tpl_rlinks_nobanner.aspx?id=828

Back to School: Teens Prepare for School Re-entry. Produced by Starbright Videos with Attitude, call (800) 315-2580. Teens who have been there share their stories and advice on how to get back into the groove of school. Also discusses how teens can get the extra help they may need to make returning to school a successful experience. http://www.starbright.org

Organizations

ACCO would like to acknowledge the many non-profit organizations that have been founded in memory of children diagnosed with DIPG. It is because of the work of so many of these organizations that DIPG has received increased awareness as well as heightened research interest. The following is a list of organizations that support DIPG research and/or provide resources to families on a national basis, whether financial, emotional, or informational. It is provided as a starting point to assist families, and is not to be regarded as a comprehensive list.

Air Care Alliance
Email: mail@aircareall.org
(888) 260-9707
http://www.aircareall.org

The Air Care Alliance promotes, and provides public benefit flying through facilitation of flights for health, compassion and community service. These groups do not fly patients or supplies when insurance or other funds can provide commercial transport via air ambulance, charter or airline. The public benefit flying volunteers fly when financial need or other special circumstances mean a compelling human need would go unfulfilled.

American Childhood Cancer Organization®
10920 Connecticut Ave. Suite A
Kensington, MD 20895
(855) 858-2226
http://www.acco.org

Founded in 1970, ACCO has more than 70,000 members. Some of the free services provided by ACCO include a toll-free information phoneline, an e-bulletin, childhood cancer books to help children with cancer and their families, diagnosis kits, local support group affiliates, and national advocacy.

American Speech-Language-Hearing Association
2200 Research Blvd.
Rockville, MD 20850
(800) 638-8255; TTY: (301) 296-5650
http://www.asha.org

ASHA's mission is to ensure that all people with speech, language and hearing disorders have access to quality services to help them communicate effectively. Canadian organization can be found at http://www.caslpa.ca

Believe in Tomorrow Children's Foundation
6601 Frederick Road
Baltimore, MD 21228
(800) 933-5470
http://www.believeintomorrow.org

The Believe in Tomorrow Children's Foundation provides hospital and respite housing services to critically ill children and their families.

Brain Tumor Foundation of Canada
620 Colborne Street, Suite 301
London, ON N6B 3R9
(800) 265-5106; 519-642-7755
http://www.braintumour.ca

The Brain Tumor Foundation of Canada provides up-to-date brain tumor information materials, educational events and support groups. Important brain tumor research is supported through annual grants, a fellowship and the brain tumor tissue bank.

Childhood Brain Tumor Foundation
20312 Watkins Meadow Drive
Germantown, MD 20876
(877) 217-4166
http://www.childhoodbraintumor.org

Founded in 1994, the Childhood Brain Tumor Foundation funds scientific and clinical research for pediatric brain tumors, and sponsors educational conferences.

Children's Brain Tumor Foundation (CBTF)
274 Madison Ave. Suite 1004
New York, NY 10016
(866) 228-HOPE
http://www.cbtf.org

Founded in 1988, the CBTF provides information, support and advocacy to children with brain tumors and their families. They fund scientific research leading to better treatments and cures of pediatric brain tumors, as well as research leading to improved quality of life.

Compassionate Friends
900 Jorie Blvd. Suite 78
Oak Brook, IL 60523
(877) 969-0010
http://www.compassionatefriends.org

Compassionate Friends provides personal comfort, hope and support through local chapters for bereaved family members experiencing the death of a child.

Just One More Day
1853 Surrey Court
Viera, FL 32955
(321) 698-8538
http://www.justonemoreday.org

Just One More Day is committed to providing information and support for families affected by diffuse intrinsic pontine glioma, promoting awareness, and funding research leading to a cure.

Kids v Cancer
4646 Hawthorne Lane
Washington, DC 20016
(646) 361-3590
http://www.kidsvcancer.org

Kids v Cancer is committed to the creation of legislative initiatives leading to pediatric cancer drug development, as well as the parent-led effort to making autopsy tissue donations more widely available for research.

Make-A-Wish Foundation®of America
4742 N. 24th Street, Suite 400
Phoenix, AZ 85016
(800) 722-9474
http://www.wish.org

Founded in 1980, the Make-A-Wish Foundation has enriched the lives of children with life-threatening medical conditions, and their families, through their wish-granting program.

National Association of Hospital Hospitality Houses (NAHHH)
P.O. Box 1439
Gresham, OR 97030
(800) 542-9730
http://www.nahhh.org

NAHHH is a nation-wide association of 200 non-profit organizations that provide lodging and support services to patients and their families who are receiving medical treatment far from their home communities.

Pediatric Brain Tumor Foundation
302 Ridgefield Court
Asheville, NC 28806
(800) 253-6530
http://www.pbtfus.org

The PBTF, founded in 1991, provides education and emotional support for children with brain tumors and their families. They seek to find the cause and cure for childhood brain tumors by supporting medical research and increasing public awareness of childhood brain tumors.

Reflections of Grace Foundation
P.O. Box 298
Irwin, PA 15642
Email: contact@reflectionsofgrace.org
http://www.reflectionsofgrace.org

Reflections of Grace Foundation is dedicated to providing financial, emotional and educational support for children and families fighting pediatric brain tumors; and funding the search for a cure for DIPG and other forms of pediatric brain tumors.

Smiles for Sophie Forever Foundation
31722 Leeward Court
Avon Lake, OH 44012
Email: info@smilesforsophieforever.org
http://www.smilesforsophieforever.org

Smiles for Sophie Forever is dedicated to providing financial support to families burdened by pediatric brain tumors, as well as increasing global awareness of the devastation of pediatric brain tumors.

SuperSibs!
660 N. First Bank Drive
Palatine, IL 60067
(888) 417-4704
http://www.supersibs.org

SuperSibs' mission is to support, honor and recognize brothers and sisters of children with cancer. They provide numerous "Advocacy and Support" services, including journals for siblings, guides, scholarships and a monitored teen chat internet room. SuperSibs also sponsors "Surprise and Delight" services such as special sibling activities and giveaways for siblings ages 4 to 18. Services are provided free of charge.

The Cure Starts Now Foundation
10280 Chester Road
Cincinnati, OH 45215
(513) 772-4888
http://www.thecurestartsnow.org

The Cure Starts Now Foundation fights for the cure for children with brainstem glioma through public awareness and media campaigns, as well as the funding of research leading to new treatments for DIPG.

Online Support Groups

ACOR, The Association of Cancer Online Resources, Inc.
http://www.acor.org

ACOR offers access to mailing lists that provide support, information, and community to everyone affected by cancer and related disorders. It hosts numerous pediatric cancer discussion groups.

American Childhood Cancer Organization's Inpire Online Community
http://www.inspire.com/groups/american-childhood-cancer-organization

ACCO's Inspire online commmunity connects patients, families, friends and caregivers. It provides a platform for support and inspiration from diagnosis, through treatment and beyond. Discussion topics include: newly diagnosed; treatment; emotional support for children with cancer, siblings, parents and caregivers; financial and insurance issues, and more.

Apraxia-Kids Mailing List
Listserv@Listserv.syr.edu
http://www.apraxia-kids.org

This website and mailing list covers oral motor apraxia and related disabilities. To subscribe, send an email with the message "subscribe apraxia-kids FirstName LastName."

Cerebellar Mutism Brain Tumor Listserv Yahoogroup
http://health.groups.yahoo.com/group/cerebellarmutism

Listserv providing online support for parents and caregivers of children who suffer from cerebellar mutism and posterior fossa syndrome after brain tumor surgery/resection.

DIPG Listserv Yahoogroup
http://health.groups.yahoo.com/group/dipg

This group is primarily for parents of children diagnosed with diffuse intrinsic pontine glioma (DIPG). The membership includes parents who are in all stages of the DIPG journey.

Educating Brain Tumor Kids
http://groups.yahoo.com/group/EducatingBTKids

A group with links and files dealing with neuropsychological testing, school re-entry, school options, late effects etc. There is an associated listserv with archives.

Home Schooling Special Needs Children
http://groups.yahoo.com/group/special-needs-homeschool

This group supports parents who choose to home school their children with special needs. Most members have medically fragile children dealing with challenges in speech, motor development and learning disabilities and home school full time or part of the time.

Hydrocephalus (HYCEPH_L)
http://neurosurgery.mgh.harvard.edu/pedi/hyceph-l.htm

This list is open to all people interested in hydrocephalus.

IEP Guide and Listserv Yahoogroup
http://groups.yahoo.com/group/IEP_guide

This is a very large listserv that offers special education support and has a free IEP guidebook.

Pediatric Brain Tumor Angels Listserv Yahoogroup
http://health.groups.yahoo.com/group/PBTAngels

Listserv providing online support for parents and caregivers who are facing end of life issues with a child who has a brain tumor and extended support for parents of children who have died after battling a brain tumor.

Pediatric Brain Tumor Facial Paralysis Listserv Yahoogroup
http://health.groups.yahoo.com/group/PBTFacialParalysis

Listserv providing online support for parents and caregivers to gain information and support regarding facial nerve paralysis after surgery for pediatric brain tumor surgery/resection.

Pediatric Brain Tumor Listserv Yahoogroup
www.yahoogroups.com/group/pediatricbraintumors

Listserv providing information and online support for parents and caregivers of children diagnosed with pediatric brain tumors including: astrocytoma, atypical teratoid/rhabdoid, glioblastoma multiforme, pleomorphic xanthoastrocytoma, craniopharyngioma, diffuse intrinsic pontine glioma, gangliocytoma, ganglioglioma, germinoma, glioma, medulloblastoma, metastatic brain tumor, neurocytoma, oligodendroglioma, juvenile pilocytic astrocytoma, pineocytoma, pineoblastoma, PNET, primitive neuroectodermal tumor, teratoma, and ependymoma.

Websites

Bandaids and Blackboards-When Chronic Illness Goes to School
http://www.lehman.cuny.edu/faculty/jfleitas/bandaides/contkids.html

Wonderful, fun and informative website about ill children and school.

CaringBridge
http://www.caringbridge.org

Free, personal and private websites to help families experiencing a health crisis connect with family and friends.

Children's Hospice and Palliative Care Coalition
http://www.childrenshospice.org/coalition

Children's Hospice & Palliative Care Coalition is a social movement led by children's hospitals, hospices, home health and grassroots agencies and individuals to improve care for children with life-threatening conditions and their families.

Children's Oncology Camping Association International
http://www.cocai.org

Website listing the more than 65 children's oncology camps located across the U.S. as well as camps for children with cancer in Canada, New Zealand and Europe.

Children's Oncology Group
http://www.childrensoncologygroup.org

The Children's Oncology Group (COG) unites more than 7,500 experts in over 200 children's hospitals, universities and cancer centers into a global team dedicated to working towards a cure for all children with cancer. Includes a list of all COG treatment centers.

Clinical Trials.gov
http://www.clinicaltrials.gov

Clinical Trials.gov is a registry and results database of federally and privately supported clinical trials conducted in the U.S. and around the world.

DIPG Collaborative
http://dipg.org

DIPG Collaborative provides information on numerous foundations whose mission is to support DIPG research and support children and families diagnosed with DIPG.

DIPG Registry
http://dipgregistry.org

Comprehensive website dedicated solely to DIPG. Divided into two portals, one for patients and their families, and one for medical professionals. Information includes upcoming conferences, DIPG research studies, available clinical trials, registry enrollment form, up-to-date information on the diagnosis and treatment of DIPG as well as contact information for DIPG specialists in Canada, U.S., Australia and Europe, providing second opinions.

iCANcer Electronic Medical Record
http://itunes.apple.com/us/app/icancer/id389815342?mt=8

Personal electronic medical record created for iPhone, iPod, and/or iPad app that stores diagnosis, treatment and health care provider information. This app manages medical information including current and past medications, side effects, lab results (graphed over time), and it organizes and syncs doctor's appointments, and conveniently exports medical information to an email format for easy communication to a health care provider prior to an appointment.

Monkey In My Chair
http://www.monkeyinmychair.org

Monkey In My Chair is a program for preschool and elementary aged children who are away from school because of a cancer diagnosis. Each child is provided with a "monkey kit" which includes a teacher's guide and classroom book, a backpack and a big stuffed monkey that takes the child's place when he/she is unable to be in school.

Pediatric Brain Tumor Consortium (PBTC)
http://www.pbtc.org

The PBTC is a multidisciplinary cooperative research organization devoted to the study of correlative tumor biology and new therapies for primary CNS tumors of childhood.

Pediatric Preclinical Testing Initiative
http://pptiohsu.blogspot.com/2011/12/open-science-forum-dipg-preclinical.html

Research blogspot including postings on the Rapid Preclinical Development of Targeted Therapy Combinations for DIPG.

Autopsy tissue and organ donation

Oregon Health and Science University CCURE-FAST

http://www.ohsu.edu/xd/health/services/doernbecher/research-education/research/pape-family-pediatric-research-institute/ccure-fast.cfm

A helpful site to assist families with information about tumor tissue donation. Includes dowloadable information on tumor banking, Q&A about legacy gifting, religion and tumor banking, as well as guidelines for medical professionals.

U.S. Government Information on Organ and Tissue Donation and Transplantation
http://www.organdonor.gov

Comprehensive website dedicated to providing information on organ and tissue donation and transplantation, including statistics, information on how to become an organ donor, legislation, associated research and grant opportunities.

Trillium Gift of Life Network
http://www.giftoflife.on.ca/en/organandtissuedonation

Website to assist Canadian families with information about organ and tissue donation.

Behavior

Behavior Problems of Children who have undergone Treatment for Brain Tumors
http://www.childhoodbraintumor.org/index.php?option=com_content&view=article&id=59:behavior-problems-in-children-who-have-undergone-treatment-for-brain-tumors&catid=38:late-effects-a

Cerebellar mutism

Cerebellar Mutism and Posterior Fossa Syndrome
http://groups.yahoo.com/group/cerebellarmutism

There is an annotated bibliography from a medline search on cerebellar mutism, a bibliography on radiation and cognitive effects and several articles from a speech pathologist.

Disabilities

Council of Educators for Students with Disabilities, Inc. (CESDI)
http://www.504idea.org/Council_Of_Educators/Welcome.html

CESDI provides Section 504 and special education training and resources to educators.

Protection and Advocacy
http://www.disabilityrightsca.org

Group that works to advance the human and legal rights of people with disabilities. Website includes a page on assistive technologies.

Pacer Center Parent Advocacy Coalition for Educational Rights
http://www.pacer.org

A national coalition of parents working for educational rights.

Family Village: A Global Community of Disability Resources
http://www.familyvillage.wisc.edu

A huge site that provides informational resources on specific diagnoses, communication connections, adaptive products and technology, adaptive recreational activities, education, health issues, disability-related media and literature.

Distance learning

Talia Seidman Foundation
http://www.taliaseidman.com

An organization dedicated to using technology to bring hospitalized and homebound chronically ill children back into the classroom.

Hearing impairment

Hard of Hearing & Deaf Students: Resource Guide to Support Classroom Teachers
http://www.bced.gov.bc.ca/specialed/hearimpair/intro.htm

Homeschooling

A to Z's Cool Homeschooling
http://www.gomilpitas.com/homeschooling

Huge site with information on introduction to home schooling, curricula, home schooling laws, support groups, methods, and philosophies.

National Home Education Network
http://www.homeschool-curriculum-and-support.com/national-home-education-network.html

A source for home schooling information, support group listings, home school news, and related resources.

Nonverbal learning disabilities

Nonverbal Learning Disabilities
http://www.nldontheweb.org

A comprehensive site on nonverbal learning disabilities.

Siblings

SuperSibs
http://www.supersibs.org

A national program dedicated to the interests of brothers and sisters of children with cancer. Includes online activities for children at http://supersibs.org/the-sib-spot/index.html.

Siblings of People with Disabilities
http://www.iidc.indiana.edu/index.php?pageId=2458

A list of books and videos that help siblings of people with disabilites.

Special education law

Consortium for Appropriate Dispute Resolution in Special Education (CADRE)
http://www.directionservice.org/cadre

CADRE provides support and materials that can help parents and educators implement the mediation requirements under IDEA 97.

Department of Education Information about IDEA
http://idea.ed.gov

Comprehensive information about the Individuals with Disabilities Education Act.

Wrights Special Education Law
http://www.wrightslaw.com

This extensive and well organized site is probably the best place to start to gather information on special education law. Includes sections on advocacy, law, books and other resources.

Educational Rights/Educational Law
http://edlaw.org/wordpress

This site provides publications and services for attorneys, advocates and parents who need to know about educational law, including a section that deals with transportation.

Americans with Disabilities Act Homepage
http://www.usdoj.gov/crt/ada/adahom1.htm

National Information Center for Children and Youth with Disabilities
http://www.nichcy.org

Includes helpful resource sheets for every state.

Speech and language

IntelliTools
http://www.intellitools.com

This firm has a great catalog of assistive technology and communication devices.

Sports

Disabled Sports USA
http://www.dsusafw.org

An organization that gives people with physical, neuromuscular and developmental impairments the opportunity to participate in a variety of activities including water/snow skiing, camping, and whitewater rafting. Adaptive equipment information available.

American Hippotherapy Association
http://www.americanequestrian.com/hippotherapy.htm

Hippotherapy is therapeutic riding for those with motor disturbances.

North American Riding for the Handicapped
http://www.narha.org

An organization that promotes the benefits of horseback riding for those with physical, emotional or learning disabilities.

Appendix D

Research Articles

The following journal articles were referenced by the authors in specific chapters throughout the book. They are listed here to provide direction for additional reading for those individuals who wish to delve deeper into a specific topic.

Further Reading

References from Chapter 4, Imaging DIPG

1) Jallo GI, Biser-Rohrbaugh A, Freed D, (2004). *Brainstem Gliomas.* Childs Nervous System, 20: 143-153.

2) Barkovich AJ, Krischer J, Kun LE, et al., (1990). *Brain Stem Gliomas: A Classification System Based on Magnetic Resonance Imaging.* Pediatric Neurosurgery, 16: 73-83.

3) Moghrabi A, Kerby T, Tien RD, et al., (1995). *Prognostic Value of Contrast-Enhanced Magnetic Resonance Imaging in Brainstem Gliomas.* Pediatric Neurosurgery, 23: 293-298.

4) Fischbein NJ, Prados MD, Wara W, et al., (1996). *Radiographic Classification of Brainstem Tumors: Correlation of Magnetic Resonance Imaging Appearance with Clinical Outcome.* Pediatric Neurosurgery 24: 9-23.

5) Freeman CR, Farmer JP, (1998). *Pediatric Brain Stem Gliomas: A Review.* Int. J. Radiation Oncology Biol Phys 40(2): 265-271.

6) Fisher PG, Breiter SN, Carson BS, et al., (2000). *A Clinicopathologic Reappraisal of Brain Stem Tumor Classification: Identification of Pilocytic Astrocytoma and Fibrillary Astrocytoma as Distinct Entities.* Cancer 89(7): 1569-1576.

7) Hargrave D, Chuang N, Bouffet E, (20 08). *Conventional MRI Cannot Predict Survival in Childhood Diffuse Intrinsic Pontine Glioma.* J. Neurooncol 86: 313-319.

8) Liu AK, Brandon J, Foreman NK, et al., (2009). *Conventional MRI at Presentation Does Not Predict Clinical Response to Radiation Therapy in Children with Diffuse Pontine Glioma.* Pediatr Radiol 39: 1317-1320.

9) Kornreich L, Schwarz M, Karmazyn B, et al., (2005). *Role of MRI in the Management of Children with Diffuse Pontine Tumors: A Study of 15 Patients with Review of the Literature.* Pediatric Radiology 35: 872-879.

10) Nelson MD, Soni D, Baram TZ, (1994). *Necrosis in Pontine Gliomas: Radiation Induced or Natural History?* Radiology 191: 279:282.

11) Fenton LZ, Madden JR, Foreman NK, (2003). *Misleading Leads: Brain Stem Glioma in a Child: False Diagnosis of Radiation Necrosis With FDG PET.* Med Pediatr Onc 40: 260–262.

12) Krieger MD, Bluml S, McComb JG, (2003). *Magnetic Resonance Spectroscopy of Atypical Diffuse Pontine Masses.* Neurosurg Focus 15(1): 1-4.

13) Panigrahy A, Nelson MD, Finlay JL, et al., (2008). *Metabolism of diffuse intrinsic brainstem gliomas in children.* Neuro-Oncology 10 (1): 32-44.

14) Mullins ME, (2006). MR Spectroscopy: *Truly Molecular Imaging; Past, Present and Future.* Neuroimag Clin N Am 16: 605–618.

15) Curless RG, Bowen BC, Pattany PM, et al., (2002). *Magnetic Resonance Spectroscopy in Childhood Brainstem Tumors.* Pediatric Neurology 26(5): 374-378.

16) Smith JK, Londono A, Castillo M, et al., (2002). *Proton Magnetic Resonance Spectroscopy of Brainstem Lesions.* Neuroradiology 44: 825-829.

17) Panigrahy A, Bluml S, (2009). *Neuroimaging of Pediatric Brain Tumors: From Basic to Advanced Magnetic Resonance Imaging.* Journal of Child Neurology 24(11): 1343-1365.

18) Laprie A, Pirzkall A, Hass-Kogan DA, et al., (2005). *Longitudinal Multivoxel MR Spectroscopy Study of Pediatric Diffuse Brainstem Gliomas Treated with Radiotherapy.* Int. J. Radiation Oncology Biol. Phys. 62(1): 20-31.

19) Law M, Oh S, Johnson G, et al., (2006). *Perfusion Magnetic Resonance Imaging Predicts Patient Outcome as an Adjunct to Histopathology: A Second Reference Standard in the Surgical and Nonsurgical Treatment of Low-Grade Gliomas.* Neurosurgery 58(6): 1099-1107.

20) Bisdas S, Kirkpatrick M, Giglio P, et al., (2009). *Cerebral Blood Volume Measurements by Perfusion-Weighted MR Imaging in Gliomas: Ready for Prime Time in Predicting Short-Term Outcome and Recurrent Disease?* Am J. Neuroradiol 30: 681-688.

21) Law M, Young RJ, Babb JS, et al., (2008). *Gliomas: Predicting Time to Progression or Survival with Cerebral Blood Volume Measurements at Dynamic Susceptibility-weighted Contrast-enhanced Perfusion MR Imaging.* Radiology 247(2): 490-498.

22) Cha S, (2003). *Perfusion MR imaging: Basic principles and clinical applications.* Magn Reson Imaging Clin N Am 11: 403–413.

23) Macapinlac HA, (2006). *Positron Emission Tomography of the Brain.* Neuroimag Clin N Am 16: 591–603.

24) Pirotte BJM, Lubansu A, Massagner N, et al., (2007). *Results of positron emission tomography guidance and reassessment of the utility of and indications for stereotactic biopsy in children with infiltrative brainstem tumors.* J. Neurosurg 107(5 Suppl Pediatrics): 392–399.

25) Kwon JW, Kim IO, Cheon JE, et al., (2006). *Paediatric brain-stem gliomas: MRI, FDG-PET and histological grading correlation.* Pediatr Radiol 36: 959–964.

References from Chapter 8, Radiosensitizers for DIPG

1) Shrieve DC, Loeffler JS, (1995). *Advances in radiation therapy for brain tumors.* Neurol Clin 13(4): 773-793.

2) Stieber VW, Mehta MP, (2007). *Advances in radiation therapy for brain tumors.* Neurol Clin 25: 1005-1033.

3) Sanghavi SN, Needle MN, Krailo MD, Geyer JR, Ater J, Mehta MP, (2003). *A phase 1 study of topotecan as a radiosensitizer for brainstem glioma of childhood: First report of the Children's Cancer Group-0952.* Neuro Oncol 5(1): 8-13.

4) Packer RJ, Krailo M, Mehta M, Warren K, Allen J, Jakacki R, Villablanca JG, Chiba A, Reaman G, (2005). *Phase 1 study of concurrent RMP-7 and carboplatin with radiotherapy for children with newly diagnosed DIPGs.* Cancer 104(6): 1281-1287.

5) Turner CD, Chi S, Marcuc KJ, MacDonald T, Packer RJ, Poussaint TY, Vajapeyarn S,

Ullrich N, Briody C, Chordas C, Zimmerman MA, Kieran M, (2007). *Phase II study of thalidomide and radiation in children with newly diagnosed brain stem gliomas and glioblastoma multiforme.* Journal of Neuro-Oncology 82: 95-101.

6) Packer RJ, Prados M, Phillips P, Nicholson HS, Boyett JM, Goldwein J, Rorke LB, Needle MN, Sutton L, Zimmerman RA, Fitz CR, Vezina LG, Etcubanas E, Wallenberg JC, Reman G, Wara W, (1996). *Treatment of children with newly diagnosed brain stem gliomas with intravenous recombinant B-interferon and hyperfractionated radiation therapy. A Children's Cancer Group Phase I/II study.* Cancer 77(10): 2150-2156.

References from Chapter 9, Chemotherapy and Biologics

1) Jenkin RDT, Boesel C, Ertel I, et al., (1987). *Brain-stem tumors in childhood: a prospective randomized trial of irradiation with and without adjuvant CCNU, VCR, and prednisone.* J. Neurosurg 66: 227-233.

2) Walter AW, Gajjar A, Ochs SJ, et al., (1998). *Carboplatin and etoposide with hyperfractionated radiotherapy in children with newly diagnosed diffuse pontine gliomas: a phase I/II study.* Med Ped Oncol 30: 28-33.

3) Chamberlain MC., (2993). *Recurrent brainstem glioma treated with oral VP-16.* J. Neurooncol15: 133-139.

4) Korones DN, Fisher PG, Kretschmar C, et al., (2008). *Treatment of children with diffuse intrinsic brain stem glioma with radiotherapy, vincristine and oral VP-16: a Children's Oncology Group Phase II study.* Pediatr Blood Cancer 50: 227-230.

5) Dreyer ZE, Kadota RP, Stewart CF, et al., (2003). *Phase 2 study of idarubicine in pediatric brain tumors: Pediatric Oncology Group study POG 9237.* Neuro-oncology 5: 261-267.

6) Wolff JEA, Westphal S, MolenkampG, et al., (2002).T*reatment of paediatric pontine glioma with oral trophosphamide and etoposide.* British Journal of Cancer 87: 945-949.

7) Wolff JEA, Driever PH, Erdlenbruch B, et al., (2010). *Intensive chemotherapy improves survival in pediatric high-grade glioma after gross total resection: results of the HIT-gBM-c protocol.* Cancer 116: 705-712.

8) Minturn JE, Janss AJ, Fisher PG, et al., (2011). *A phase II study of metronomic oral topotecan for recurrent childhood brain tumors.* Pediatr Blood Cancer 56: 39-44.

9) Broniscer A, Iacono L, Chintagumpala M, et al., (2005). *Role of temozolomide after radiotherapy for newly diagnosed diffuse brainstem glioma in children.* Cancer 103: 133-139.

10) Cohen KJ, Heideman RL, Zhou T, et al., (2011). *Temozolomide in the treatment of children with newly diagnosed diffuse intrinsic pontine gliomas: a report from the Children's Oncology Group.* Neuro-Oncol 13:410-416.

11) Chiang KL, Chang KP, Lee YY, et al., (2010). *Role of temozolomide in the treatment of newly diagnosed diffuse brainstem glioma in children: experience at a single institution.* Childs Nerv Syst 26: 1035-1041.

12) Jalali R, Raut N, Arora B, et al., (2010) *Prospective evaluation of radiotherapy with concurrent and adjuvant temozolomide in children with newly diagnosed diffuse intrinsic pontine glioma.* Int J. Radiation Oncology Biol Phys 77: 113-118.

13) Sharp JR, Bouffet E, Stempak D, et al., (2010). *A multi-center Canadian pilot study of metronomic temozolomide combined with radiotherapy for newly diagnosed paediatric brainstem glioma.* European Journal of Cancer 46: 3271-3279.

14) Sirachainan N, Pakakasama S, Visudithbhan A, et al., (2008). *Concurrent radiotherapy*

with temozolomide followed by adjuvant temozolomide and cis-retinoic acid in children with diffuse intrinsic pontine glioma. Neuro-Oncology 10: 577-582.

15) Kim CY, Kim SK, Phi JH, et al., (2010). *A prospective study of temozolomide plus thalidomide during and after radiation therapy for pediatric diffuse pontine gliomas: preliminary results of the Korean Society for Pediatric Neuro-Oncology study.* J. Neurooncol 100: 193-198.

16) Kretschmar CS, Tarbell NJ, Barnes PD, Krischer JP, Burger PC, Kun L., (1992). *Pre-irradiation chemotherapy and hyperfractionated radiation therapy 66Gy for children with brain stem tumors.* Cancer 72: 1404-1413.

17) Jennings MT, Sposto R, Boyett JM, et al., (2002). P*reradiation chemotherapy in primary high-risk brainstem tumors: phase II study CCG-9941 of the Children's Cancer Group.* J. Clin Oncol 20: 3431-3437.

18) Doz F, Neuenschwander S, Bouffet E, et al., (2002). *Carboplatin before and during radiation therapy for the treatment of malignant brain stem tumours: a study by the Societe Francaise d'Oncologie Pediatrique.* European Journal of Cancer 38: 815-819.

19) Graham ML, Herndon JE, Casey JR, et al., (1997). *High-dose chemotherapy with autologous stem-cell rescue in patients with recurrent and high-risk pediatric brain tumors.* J. Clin Oncol 15: 1814-1823.

20) Finlay JL, Goldman S, Wong MC, et al., (1996). *Pilot study of high-dose thiotepa and etoposide with autologous bone marrow rescue in children and young adults with recurrent CNS tumors.* J. Clin Oncol 14: 2495-2503.

21) Bouffet E, Raquin M, Doz F, et al., (2000). *Radiotherapy followed by high dose busulfan and thiotepa.* Cancer 88: 685-692.

22) Bouffet E, Khelfasoui F, Philip I, Biron P, Brunat-Mentigny M, Phlip T., (1997). *High-dose carmustine for high-grade gliomas in childhood.* Cancer Chemother Pharmacol 39: 376-379.

23) Jakacki RI, Siffert J, Jamison C, Velasquez L, Allen JC., (1999). *Dose-intensive, time-compressed procarbazine, CCNU, vincristine (PCV) with peripheral blood stem cell support and concurrent radiation in patients with newly diagnosed high-grade gliomas.* J. Neuro-Oncol 44: 77-83.

24) Kedar A, Maria BL, Graham-Pole J, et al., (1994). *High dose chemotherapy with marrow reinfusion and hyperfractionated irradiation for children with high-risk brain tumors.* Med Ped Oncol 23: 428-436.

25) Dunkel IJ, Garvin JH, Goldman S, et al., (1998). *High dose chemotherapy with autologous bone marrow rescue for children with diffuse pontine brain stem tumors.* J. Neuro Oncol 37:67-73.

26) Allen J, Packer R, Bleyer A, et al., (1991). *Recombinant interferon beta: a phase I-II trial in children with recurrent brain tumors.* J. Clin Oncol 9: 783-788.

27) Packer RJ, Prados M, Phillips P, et al., (1996). *Treatment of children with newly diagnosed brain stem gliomas with intravenous recombinant beta-interferon and hyperfractionated radiation therapy.* Cancer 77: 2150-2156.

28) Packer RJ, Krailo M, Mehta M, et al., (2005). *A phase I study of concurrent RMP-7 and carboplatin with radiation therapy for children with newly diagnosed brainstem gliomas.* Cancer 104: 1968-1974.

29) Hall WA, Doolittle ND, Daman M, et al., (2006). *Osmotic blood-brain barrier disruption chemotherapy for diffuse pontine gliomas.* J. Neuro-Oncol 77: 279-284.

30) Greenberg ML, Fisher OG, Freeman C, et al., (2005). *Etoposide, vincristine, and cyclosporine A with standard-dose radiation therapy in newly diagnosed diffuse intrinsic brainstem gliomas: a Pediatric Oncology Group Phase 1 study.* Pediatr Blood Cancer 45: 644-648.

31) Gururangan S, Chi SN, Poussaint TY, et al., (2010). *Lack of efficacy of bevacizumab plus irinotecan in children with recurrent malignant glioma and diffuse brainstem glioma: a pediatric brain tumor consortium study.* J. Clin Oncol 28: 3069-3075.

32) Gilbertson RJ, Hill DA, Hernan R, et al., (2003). *ERBB1 is amplified and overexpressed in high-grade diffusely infiltrative pediatric brain stem glioma.* Clin Can Res 9: 3620-3624.

33) Bode U, Buchen S, Janssen G, et al., (2006). *Results of a phase II trial of h-R3 monoclonal antibody (nimotuzumab) in the treatment of resistant or relapsed high-grade gliomas in children and adolescents.* ASCO Meeting Abstracts: 1522

34) Geoerger B, Hargrave D, Thomas F, et al., (2011). *Innovative therapies for children with cancer pediatric phase I study of erlotinib in brainstem glioma and relapsing/refractory brain tumors.* Neuro-Oncology 13: 109-118.

35) Michalski A, Bouffet E, Taylor RE, et al., (2010). *The addition of high-dose tamoxifen to standard radiotherapy does not improve the survival of patients with diffuse intrinsic pontine glioma.* J. Neuro-Oncol 100: 81-88.

36) Burzynski SR, Janicki TJ, Weaver RA, Burzynski B., (2006). *Targeted therapy with antineoplastons A10 and AS2-1 of high-grade, recurrent, and progressive brainstem glioma.* Integrative Cancer Therapies 5: 40-47.

References from Chapter 10, The Use of Steroids in Patients with DIPG

1) Ryan J., (Jan. 2000). *Radiation somnolence syndrome.* J. Pediatr Oncol Nurs 17(1): 50-53.

2) Dietrich J, Rao K, Pastorino S, Kesari S., (Mar 2011). *Corticosteroids in brain cancer patients: benefits and pitfalls.* Expert Rev Clin Pharmacol 4(2): 233-242.

3) Moliterno JA, Henry E, Pannullo SC., (Sept 2009). *Corticorelin acetate injections for the treatment of peritumoral brain edema.* Expert Opin Investig Drugs 18(9): 1413-1419.

4) Liu AK, Macy ME, Foreman NK., (Nov 2009). *Bevacizumab as therapy for radiation necrosis in four children with pontine gliomas.* Int J. Radiat Oncol Biol Phys 75(4):1148-1154.

References from Chapter 11, Caring for Your Child at Home

1) Aging with Dignity, (2010). *Five Wishes.* Retrieved from Aging with Dignity: *http://www.agingwithdignity.org/five-wishes.php.*

2) Aging wth Dignity, (2010). *My Wishes.* Retrieved from Aging with Dignity: h*ttp://www.agingwithdignity.org/catalog/product_info.php?products_id=85.*

3) Coda Alliance, (2011). *Go Wish - Go Wish Interactive.* Retrieved from The Go Wish Game: *http://www.gowish.org/staticpages/index.php/thegame.*

4) Ethier, A, Rollins, J & Stewert, J. (Eds)., (2010). *Pediatric Oncology Palliative and End-of-life Care Resource.* Glenview, IL, Association of Pediatric Oncology Nurses.

5) Kuttner, L., (1996). *A Child in Pain: How to Help and What to Do.* Point Roberts, WA, Hartley & Marks.

6) Orloff, S., & Huff, S. M. (Eds.). (2003). *Home Care for Seriously Ill Children: A Manual for Parents.* 3rd ed., Alexandria, Virginia, Children's Hospice International.

References from Chapter 14, Future of Genomics and Proteomics in DIPG

1) Albright AL, Packer RJ, Zimmerman R, Rorke LB, Boyett J, Hammond GD, (1993). *Magnetic resonance scans should replace biopsies for the diagnosis of diffuse brain stem gliomas: A report from the Children's Cancer Group.* Neurosurgery 33(6): 1026-1029; discussion 1029-1030.

2) Angelini P, Hawkins C, Laperriere N, Bouffet E, Bartels U, (2010). *Post mortem examinations in diffuse intrinsic pontine glioma: challenges and chances.* J. Neurooncol 101(1): 75-81.

3) Badhe PB, Chauhan PP, Mehta NK, (2004). *Brainstem gliomas: A clinicopathological study of 45 cases with p53 immunohistochemistry.* Indian J. Cancer 41(4): 170-174.

4) Barrow J, Adamowicz-Brice M, Cartmill M, Macarthur D, Lowe J, Robson K, Brundler MA, Walker DA, Coyle B, Grundy R, (2010). *Homozygous loss of ADAM3A revealed by genome-wide analysis of pediatric high-grade glioma and diffuse intrinsic pontine gliomas.* Neuro Oncol 13(2): 212-222.

5) Broniscer A, Baker JN, Baker SJ, Chi SN, Geyer JR, Morris EB, Gajjar A, (2010). *Prospective collection of tissue samples at autopsy in children with diffuse intrinsic pontine glioma.* Cancer 116(19): 4632-4637.

6) Caretti V, Zondervan I, Meijer DH, Idema S, Vos W, Hamans B, Bugiani M, Hulleman E, Wesseling P, Vandertop WP, Noske DP, Kaspers G, Molthoff CF, Wurdinger T, (2011). *Monitoring of Tumor Growth and Post-Irradiation Recurrence in a Diffuse Intrinsic Pontine Glioma Mouse Model.* Brain Pathol. 21(4): 441-451.

7) Chico-Ponce de Leon F, Perezpena-Diazconti M, Castro-Sierra E, Guerrero-Jazo FJ, Gordillo-Dominguez LF, Gutierrez-Guerra R, Salamanca T, Sosa-Sainz G, Santana-Montero BL, DeMontesinos-Sampedro A, (2003). *Stereotactically-guided biopsies of brainstem tumors.* Childs Nerv Syst 19(5-6): 305-310.

8) Frazier JL, Lee J, Thomale UW, Noggle JC, Cohen KJ, Jallo GI, (2009). *Treatment of diffuse intrinsic brainstem gliomas: failed approaches and future strategies.* J. Neurosurg Pediatr 3(4): 259-269.

9) Giese H, Hoffmann KT, Winkelmann A, Stockhammer F, Jallo GI, Thomale UW, (2010). *Precision of navigated stereotactic probe implantation into the brainstem.* J. Neurosurg Pediatr 5(4): 350-359.

10) Hashizume R, Ozawa T, Dinca EB, Banerjee A, Prados MD, James CD, Gupta, N, (2010). *A human brainstem glioma xenograft model enabled for bioluminescence imaging.* J. Neurooncol 96(2): 151-159.

11) Jallo GI, Penno M, Sukay L, Liu JY, Tyler B, Lee J, Carson BS, Guarnieri M, (2005). *Experimental models of brainstem tumors: development of a neonatal rat model.* Childs Nerv Syst 21(5): 399-403.

12) Jallo GI, Volkov A, Wong C, Carson BS Sr, Penno MB, (2006). *A novel brainstem tumor model: functional and histopathological characterization.* Childs Nerv Syst 22(12): 1519-1525.

13) Kumar HR, Zhong X, Sandoval JA, Hickey RJ, Malkas LH, (2008). *Applications of emerging molecular technologies in glioblastoma multiforme.* Expert Rev Neurother 8(10): 1497-1506.

14) Kwon JW, Kim IO, Cheon JE, Kim WS, Moon SG, Kim TJ, Chi JG, Wang KC, Chung JK, Yeon KM, (2006). *Paediatric brain-stem gliomas: MRI, FDG-PET and histological grading correlation.* Pediatr Radiol 36(9): 959-964.

15) Laprie A, Pirzkall A, Haas-Kogan DA, Cha S, Banerjee A, Le TP, Lu Y, Nelson S, McKnight TR, (2005). *Longitudinal multivoxel MR spectroscopy study of pediatric diffuse brainstem gliomas treated with radiotherapy.* Int J. Radiat Oncol Biol Phys 62(1): 20-31.

16) Leach PA, Estlin EJ, Coope DJ, Thorne JA, Kamaly-Asl ID, (2008). *Diffuse brainstem gliomas in children: should we or shouldn't we biopsy?* Br J Neurosurg 22(5): 619-624.

17) Lee J, Jallo GI, Guarnieri M, Carson BS Sr, Penno MB, (2005). *A novel brainstem tumor model: guide screw technology with functional, radiological, and histopathological characterization.* Neurosurg Focus 18(6A): E11.

18) Lonser RR, Warren KE, Butman JA, Quezado Z, Robison RA, Walbridge S, Schiffman R, Merrill M, Walker ML, Park DM, Croteau D, Brady RO, Oldfield EH, (2007). *Real-time image-guided direct convective perfusion of intrinsic brainstem lesions.* Technical note. J. Neurosurg 107(1): 190-197.

19) Mursch K, Halatsch ME, Markakis E, Behnke-Mursch J, (2005). *Intrinsic brainstem tumours in adults: results of microneurosurgical treatment of 16 consecutive patients.* Br J. Neurosurg 19(2): 128-136.

20) Paugh BS, Qu C, Jones C, Liu Z, Adamowicz-Brice M, Zhang J, Bax DA, Coyle B, Barrow J, Hargrave D, Lowe, J, Gajjar A, Zhao W, Broniscer A, Ellison DW, Grundy RG, Baker SJ, (2010). *Integrated molecular genetic profiling of pediatric high-grade gliomas reveals key differences with the adult disease.* J. Clin Oncol 28(18): 3061-3068.

21) Perez-Gomez JL, Rodriguez-Alvarez CA, Marhx-Bracho A, Rueda-Franco F, (2010). *Stereotactic biopsy for brainstem tumors in pediatric patients.* Childs Nerv Syst 26(1): 29-34.

22) Pichler R, Pichler J, Mustafa H, Nussbaumer K, Zaunmuller T, Topakian R, (2007). *Somatostatin-receptor positive brain stem glioma visualized by octreoscan.* Neuro Endocrinol Lett 28(3): 250-251.

23) Roujeau T, Machado G, Garnett MR, Miquel C, Puget S, Geoerger B, Grill J, Boddaert N, Di Rocco F, Zerah M, Sainte-Rose C, (2007). *Stereotactic biopsy of diffuse pontine lesions in children.* J. Neurosurg 107(1 Suppl): 1-4.

24) Sho A, Kondo S, Kamitani H, Otake H, Watanabe T, (2007). *Establishment of experimental glioma models at the intrinsic brainstem region of the rats.* Neurol Res 29(1): 36-42.

25) Siu IM, Tyler BM, Chen JX, Eberhart CG, Thomale UW, Olivi A, Jallo GI, Riggins GJ, Gallia GL, (2010). *Establishment of a human glioblastoma stemlike brainstem rodent tumor model.* J. Neurosurg Pediatr 6(1): 92-97.

26) Thomale UW, Tyler B, Renard V, Dorfman B, Chacko VP, Carson BS, Haberl EJ, Jallo GI, (2009). *Neurological grading, survival, MR imaging, and histological evaluation in the rat brainstem glioma model.* Childs Nerv Syst 25(4): 433-441.

27) Whittle IR, Short DM, Deighton RF, Kerr LE, Smith C, McCulloch J, (2007). *Proteomic analysis of gliomas.* Br J. Neurosurg 21(6): 576-582.

28) Zarghooni M, Bartels U, Lee E, Buczkowicz P, Morrison A, Huang A, Bouffet E, Hawkins C, (2010). *Whole-genome profiling of pediatric diffuse intrinsic pontine gliomas highlights platelet-derived growth factor receptor alpha and poly (ADP-ribose) polymerase as potential therapeutic targets.* J. Clin Oncol 28(8): 1337-1344.

29) Zhang S, Feng X, Koga H, Ichikawa T, Abe S, Kumanishi T, (1993). *p53 gene mutations in pontine gliomas of juvenile onset.* Biochem Biophys Res Commun 196(2): 851-857.

References from Chapter 15, Animal Models for DIPG

1) Barth RF, Kaur B, (2009). *Rat brain tumor models in experimental neuro-oncology: the C6, 9L, T9, RG2, F98, BT4C, RT-2 and CNS-1 gliomas.* J. Neurooncol 94(3): 299-312.

2) Becher OJ, Hambardzumyan D, Fomchenko EI, Momota H, Mainwaring L, Bleau AM, et al., (2008). *Gli activity correlates with tumor grade in platelet-derived growth factor-induced gliomas.* Cancer Res 68(7): 2241-2249.

3) Becher OJ, Hambardzumyan D, Walker TR, Helmy K, Nazarian J, Albrecht S, Hiner RL, Gall S, Huse JT, Jabado N, MacDonald TJ, Holland EC, (2010 in press). *Preclinical evaluation of radiation and perifosine in a genetically and histologically accurate model of brainstem glioma.* Cancer Res

4) Brennan C, Momota H, Hambardzumyan D, Ozawa T, Tandon A, Pedraza A, et al., (2009). *Glioblastoma subclasses can be defined by activity among signal transduction pathways and associated genomic alterations.* PLoS One 4(11):e7752.

5) Hashizume R, Ozawa T, Dinca EB, Banerjee A, Prados MD, James CD, et al., (2010). *A human brainstem glioma xenograft model enabled for bioluminescence imaging.* J. Neurooncol 96(2): 151-159.

6) Holland EC, Celestino J, Dai C, Schaefer L, Sawaya RE, Fuller GN., (2000). *Combined activation of Ras and Akt in neural progenitors induces glioblastoma formation in mice.* Nat Genet 25(1): 55-57.

7) Jallo GI, Penno M, Sukay L, Liu JY, Tyler B, Lee J, et al., (2005). *Experimental models of brainstem tumors: development of a neonatal rat model.* Childs Nerv Syst 21(5): 399-403.

8) Jallo GI, Volkov A, Wong C, Carson BS, Sr., Penno MB, (2006). *A novel brainstem tumor model: functional and histopathological characterization.* Childs Nerv Syst 22(12): 1519-1525.

9) Kondo A, Goldman S, Vanin EF, Sredni ST, Rajaram V, Soares MB, et al., (2009). *An experimental brainstem tumor model using in vivo bioluminescence imaging in rat.* Childs Nerv Syst 25(5): 527-533.

10) Kwon CH, Zhao D, Chen J, Alcantara S, Li Y, Burns DK, et al., (2008). *Pten haploinsufficiency accelerates formation of high-grade astrocytomas.* Cancer Res 68(9): 3286-3294.

11) Lee J, Jallo GI, Guarnieri M, Carson BS, Sr., Penno MB, (2005). *A novel brainstem tumor model: guide screw technology with functional, radiological, and histopathological characterization.* Neurosurg Focus 18(6A): E11.

12) Lee J, Kotliarova S, Kotliarov Y, Li A, Su Q, Donin NM, et al., (2006). *Tumor stem cells derived from glioblastomas cultured in bFGF and EGF more closely mirror the phenotype and genotype of primary tumors than do serum-cultured cell lines.* Cancer Cell 9(5): 391-403.

13) Liu Q, Liu R, Kashyap MV, Agarwal R, Shi X, Wang CC, et al., (2008). *Brainstem glioma progression in juvenile and adult rats.* J Neurosurg 109(5): 849-855.

14) Sho A, Kondo S, Kamitani H, Otake M, Watanabe T, (2007). *Establishment of experimental glioma models at the intrinsic brainstem region of the rats.* Neurol Res 29(1): 36-42.

References from Chapter 17, Convection-Enhanced Delivery in DIPG

1) Bobo RH, et al., (1994). *Convection-enhanced delivery of macromolecules in the brain.* Proc Natl Acad Sci U S A, 91(6): 2076-2080.

2) Chen MY, et al., (2005). *Surface properties, more than size, limiting convective distribution of virus-sized particles and viruses in the central nervous system.* J. Neurosurg 103(2): 311-319.

3) Saito R, et al., (2006). *Tissue affinity of the infusate affects the distribution volume during convection-enhanced delivery into rodent brains: implications for local drug delivery.* J. Neurosci Methods 154(1-2): 225-232.

4) Nguyen JB, et al., (2001). *Convection-enhanced delivery of AAV-2 combined with heparin increases TK gene transfer in the rat brain.* Neuroreport 12(9): 1961-1964.

5) Cunningham J, et al., (2000). *Distribution of AAV-TK following intracranial convection-enhanced delivery into rats.* Cell Transplant 9(5): 585-594.

6) Saito R, et al., (2004). *Distribution of liposomes into brain and rat brain tumor models by convection-enhanced delivery monitored with magnetic resonance imaging.* Cancer Res 64(7): 2572-2579.

7) Perlstein B, et al., (2008). *Convection-enhanced delivery of maghemite nanoparticles: Increased efficacy and MRI monitoring.* Neuro Oncol 10(2): 153-161.

8) Mardor Y, et al., (2005). *Convection-enhanced drug delivery: increased efficacy and magnetic resonance image monitoring.* Cancer Res 65(15): 6858-6863.

9) Varenika V, et al., (2008). *Detection of infusate leakage in the brain using real-time imaging of convection-enhanced delivery.* J. Neurosurg 109(5): 874-880.

10) Raghavan R, et al., (2006). *Convection-enhanced delivery of therapeutics for brain disease, and its optimization.* Neurosurg Focus 20(4): E12.

11) Oh S, et al., (2007). *Improved distribution of small molecules and viral vectors in the murine brain using a hollow fiber catheter.* J. Neurosurg 107(3): 568-577.

12) Sampson JH, et al., (2008). *Intracerebral infusion of an EGFR-targeted toxin in recurrent malignant brain tumors.* Neuro Oncol 10(3): 320-329.

13) Sampson JH, et al., (2010). *Poor drug distribution as a possible explanation for the results of the PRECISE trial.* J. Neurosurg 113(2): 301-309.

14) Sampson JH, et al., (2007). *Induction of hyperintense signal on T2-weighted MR images correlates with infusion distribution from intracerebral convection-enhanced delivery of a tumor-targeted cytotoxin.* AJR Am J Roentgenol 188(3): 703-709.

15) Sampson JH, et al., (2006). *Comparison of intratumoral bolus injection and convection-enhanced delivery of radiolabeled antitenascin monoclonal antibodies.* Neurosurg Focus 20(4): E14.

16) Sampson JH, et al., (2007). *Intracerebral infusate distribution by convection-enhanced delivery in humans with malignant gliomas: descriptive effects of target anatomy and catheter positioning.* Neurosurgery 60(2 Suppl 1): ONS89-98; discussion ONS98-99.

17) Lonser RR, et al., (2007). *Real-time image-guided direct convective perfusion of intrinsic brainstem lesions.* Technical note. J. Neurosurg 107(1): 190-197.

18) Heiss JD, et al., (2010). *Image-guided convection-enhanced delivery of muscimol to the primate brain.* J. Neurosurg 112(4): 790-795.

19) Croteau D, et al., (2005). *Real-time in vivo imaging of the convective distribution of a low-molecular-weight tracer.* J. Neurosurg 102(1): 90-97.

20) Lonser RR, et al., (2002). *Successful and safe perfusion of the primate brainstem: in vivo magnetic resonance imaging of macromolecular distribution during infusion.* Neurosurg

97(4): 905-913.

21) Sampson JH, et al., (2007). *Clinical utility of a patient-specific algorithm for simulating intracerebral drug infusions.* Neuro Oncol 9(3): 343-353.

22) Sandberg DI, Edgar MA, Souweidane MM, (2002). *Convection-enhanced delivery into the rat brainstem.* J. Neurosurg 96(5): 885-891.

23) Occhiogrosso G, et al., (2003). P*rolonged convection-enhanced delivery into the rat brainstem.* Neurosurgery 52(2): 388-393; discussion 393-394.

24) Souweidane MM, et al., (2004). *Interstitial infusion of IL13-PE38QQR in the rat brain stem.* J. Neurooncol 67(3): 287-293.

25) Souweidane MM, et al., (2004). *Interstitial infusion of carmustine in the rat brain stem with systemic administration of O6-benzylguanine.* J. Neurooncol 67(3): 319-326.

26) Luther N, et al., (2008). *Intraparenchymal and intratumoral interstitial infusion of anti-glioma monoclonal antibody 8H9.* Neurosurgery 63(6): 1166-1174; discussion 1174.

27) Luther N, et al., (2010). *Interstitial infusion of glioma-targeted recombinant immunotoxin 8H9scFv-PE38.* Mol Cancer Ther 9(4): 1039-1046.

28) Giese H, et al., (2010). *Precision of navigated stereotactic probe implantation into the brainstem.* J. Neurosurg Pediatr 5(4): 350-359.

29) Pincus DW, et al., (2006). *Brainstem stereotactic biopsy sampling in children.* J. Neurosurg 104(2 Suppl): 108-114.

30) Roujeau T, et al., (2007). *Stereotactic biopsy of diffuse pontine lesions in children.* J. Neurosurg 107(1 Suppl): 1-4.

31) Weber F, et al., (2003). *Safety, tolerability, and tumor response of IL4-Pseudomonas exotoxin (NBI-3001) in patients with recurrent malignant glioma.* J. Neurooncol 64(1-2): 125-137.

32) Lidar Z, et al., (2004). *Convection-enhanced delivery of paclitaxel for the treatment of recurrent malignant glioma: a phase I/II clinical study.* J. Neurosurg 100(3): 472-479.

33) Krauze MT, et al., (2007). *Convection-enhanced delivery of nanoliposomal CPT-11 (irinotecan) and PEGylated liposomal doxorubicin (Doxil) in rodent intracranial brain tumor xenografts.* Neuro Oncol 9(4): 393-403.

34) Debinski W, et al., (1999). *Receptor for interleukin 13 is a marker and therapeutic target for human high-grade gliomas.* Clin Cancer Res 5(5): 985-990.

35) Debinski W, et al., (1999). *Receptor for interleukin 13 is abundantly and specifically over-expressed in patients with glioblastoma multiforme.* Int J. Oncol 15(3): 481-486.

36) Johnson VG, et al., (1988). *The role of the diphtheria toxin receptor in cytosol translocation.* J. Biol Chem 263(3): 1295-1300.

37) Weaver M, Laske DW, (2003). *Transferrin receptor ligand-targeted toxin conjugate (Tf-CRM107) for therapy of malignant gliomas.* J. Neurooncol 65(1): 3-13.

38) Torp SH, et al., (1991). *Epidermal growth factor receptor expression in human gliomas.* Cancer Immunol Immunother 33(1): 61-64.

39) Debinski W, et al., (1995). *A novel chimeric protein composed of interleukin 13 and Pseudomonas exotoxin is highly cytotoxic to human carcinoma cells expressing receptors for interleukin 13 and interleukin 4.* J. Biol Chem 270(28): 16775-16780.

40) Kunwar S, et al., (2007). *Direct intracerebral delivery of cintredekin besudotox*

(IL13-PE38QQR) in recurrent malignant glioma: a report by the Cintredekin Besudotox Intraparenchymal Study Group. J. Clin Oncol 25(7): 837-844.

41) Liu H, et al., (2000). *Interleukin-13 sensitivity and receptor phenotypes of human glial cell lines: non-neoplastic glia and low-grade astrocytoma differ from malignant glioma.* Cancer Immunol Immunother 49(6): 319-324.

42) Joshi BH, Plautz GE, Puri RK, (2000). *Interleukin-13 receptor alpha chain: a novel tumor-associated transmembrane protein in primary explants of human malignant gliomas.* Cancer Res 60(5): 1168-1172.

43) Madhankumar AB, Mintz A, Debinski W, (2004). *Interleukin 13 mutants of enhanced avidity toward the glioma-associated receptor, IL13Ralpha2.* Neoplasia 6(1): 15-22.

44) Patel SJ, et al., (2005). *Safety and feasibility of convection-enhanced delivery of Cotara for the treatment of malignant glioma: initial experience in 51 patients.* Neurosurgery 56(6): 1243-1252; discussion 1252-1253.

45) Verel I, Visser GW, van Dongen GA, (2005). *The promise of immuno-PET in radioimmunotherapy.* J. Nucl Med 46 Suppl 1: 164S-167IS.

46) Becher OJ, et al., (2010). *Preclinical evaluation of radiation and perifosine in a genetically and histologically accurate model of brainstem glioma.* Cancer Res 70(6): 2548-2557.

47) Zarghooni M, et al., (2010). *Whole-genome profiling of pediatric diffuse intrinsic pontine gliomas highlights platelet-derived growth factor receptor alpha and poly (ADP-ribose) polymerase as potential therapeutic targets.* J. Clin Oncol 28(8): 1337-1344.

48) Paugh BS, et al., (2010). *Integrated molecular genetic profiling of pediatric high-grade gliomas reveals key differences with the adult disease.* J. Clin Oncol 28(18): 3061-3068.

49) Gilbertson RJ, et al., (2003). *ERBB1 is amplified and overexpressed in high-grade diffusely infiltrative pediatric brain stem glioma.* Clin Cancer Res 9(10 Pt 1): 3620-3624.

50) Joshi BH, et al., (2008). *Identification of interleukin-13 receptor alpha2 chain overexpression in situ in high-grade diffusely infiltrative pediatric brainstem glioma.* Neuro Oncol 10(3): 265-274.

51) Parsons DW, et al., (2008). *An integrated genomic analysis of human glioblastoma multiforme.* Science 321(5897): 1807-1812.

References from Chapter 19, DIPG and Tissue Donation

1) Albright AL, Packer RJ, Zimmerman R, Rorke LB, Boyett J, Hammond GD., (Dec 1993). *Magnetic resonance scans should replace biopsies for the diagnosis of diffuse brain stem gliomas: a report from the Children's Cancer Group.* Neurosurgery 33(6): 1026-1029; discussion 1029-1030.

2) Broniscer A, Baker JN, Baker SJ, Chi SN, Geyer JR, Morris EB, Gajjar A., (Oct 2010). *Prospective collection of tissue samples at autopsy in children with diffuse intrinsic pontine glioma.* Cancer 116(19): 4632-4637.

3) Angelini P, Hawkins C, Laperriere N, Bouffet E, Bartels U., (Jan 2011). *Post mortem examinations in diffuse intrinsic pontine glioma: challenges and chances.* J. Neurooncol 101(1): 75-81

4) Zarghooni M, Bartels U, Lee E, Buczkowicz P, Morrison A, Huang A, Bouffet E, Hawkins C., (Mar 10, 2010). *Whole-genome profiling of pediatric diffuse intrinsic pontine gliomas highlights platelet-derived growth factor receptor alpha and poly (ADP-ribose) polymerase as potential therapeutic targets.* J. Clin Oncol 28(8): 1337-1344.

5) Paugh BS, Broniscer A, Qu C, Miller CP, Zhang J, Tatevossian RG, Olson JM, Geyer JR, Chi SN, da Silva NS, Onar-Thomas A, Baker JN, Gajjar A, Ellison DW, Baker SJ., (Oct 20, 2011). *Genome-wide analyses identify recurrent amplifications of receptor tyrosine kinases and cell-cycle regulatory genes in diffuse intrinsic pontine glioma.* J. Clin Oncol 29(30): 3999-4006.

6) Puget S, Philippe C, Bax DA, Job B, Varlet P, Junier MP, Andreiuolo F, Carvalho D, Reis R, Guerrini-Rousseau L, Roujeau T, Dessen P, Richon C, Lazar V, Le Teuff G, Sainte-Rose C, Geoerger B, Vassal G, Jones C, Grill J., (2012). *Mesenchymal transition and PDGFRA amplification/mutation are key distinct oncogenic events in pediatric diffuse intrinsic pontine gliomas.* PLoS One 7(2): 303-313.

7) Roujeau T, Machado G, Garnett MR, Miquel C, Puget S, Geoerger B, Grill J, Boddaert N, Di Rocco F, Zerah M, Sainte-Rose C., (Jul 2007). *Stereotactic biopsy of diffuse pontine lesions in children.* J. Neurosurg 107(1 Suppl): 1-4.

References from Chapter 20, Organ and Tissue Donation

1) Armanios A, Grossman S, Yang S, et al. (2004). *Transmission of glioblastoma multiforme following bilateral lung transplantation from an affected donor: Case study and review of the literature.* Neuro-oncology 6(3): 259-263.

2) Berger M, Baumeister B, Geyer J, Milstein J, Kaney P, LeRoux P, (1991). *The risks of metastases from shunting in children with primary central nervous system tumors.* J. Neurosurgery 74: 872-877.

3) Buell J, Trofe J, Sethuraman G, et al. (2003). *Donors with central nervous system malignancies: Are they truly safe?* Transplantation 76(2): 340-343.

4) Buell J, Grossa T, Allowaya RR, Trofea J, Woodle ES, (2005). *Central nervous system tumors in donors: Misdiagnosis carries a high morbidity and mortality.* Transplantation Proceedings 37(2): 583-584.

5) Campbell A, Chan H, Becker L, Daneman A, Park T, Hoffman H, (1984). *Extracranial metastases in childhood primary intracranial tumors: A report of 21 Cases and review of the Literature.* Cancer 53: 974-981.

6) Cavaliere R, Schiff D, (2004). *Donor transmission of primary brain tumors: A neurooncologic perspective.* Transplantation Review 18(4): 204-213.

7) Chui AK, Herbertt K, Wang LS, et al., (1999). *Risk of tumor transmission in transplantation from donors with primary brain tumors: An Australian and New Zealand registry report.* Transplantation Proceedings 31: 1266-1267.

8) Collignon FP, Holland EC, Feng S, (2004). *Organ donors with malignant gliomas: an update.* Am J.Transplantation 4: 15-21.

9) Colquhoun SD, Rober ME, Shaked A, (1994). *Transmission of CNS malignancy by organ transplantation.* Transplantation 57: 970-974.

10) Council of Europe, (1997). *International Consensus Document: Select committee of experts on the organizational aspects of co-operation in organ transplantation. Standardization of organ donor screening to prevent transmission of neoplastic disease.* Transplant Newsletter 2: 4-10.

11) Halpern SD, Shaked A, Hasz RD, Caplan AL, (2008). *Informing candidates for solid-organ transplantation about donor risk factors.* New Eng J.Med 358: 2832-2837.

12) Hoffman H, Duffner P, (1985). *Extraneural metastases of central nervous system tumors.* Cancer 56: 1778-1782

13) Hornick L, Tenderich G, Wlost S, Zittermann A, Minami K, Koerfer R, (2004).

Organs from donors with primary brain malignancy: The fate of cardiac allograft recipients. Transplantation Proceedings 36: 3133-3137.

14) Jonas S, Bechstein WO, Lemmens H-P, et al., (1996). *Liver graft-transmitted glioblastoma multiforme. A case report and experience with 13 multiorgan donors suffering from primary cerebral neoplasia.* Transplantation International 9: 426-429.

15) Kashyap R, Ryan C, Sharma R, et al., (2009). *Liver grafts from donors with central nervous system tumors: A single-centre perspective.* Liver Transplantation 15: 1204-1208.

16) Kauffman H, McBride M, Cherikh W, Spain P, Marks W, Roza A, (2002). *Transplant tumor registry: Donor related malignancies.* Transplantation 74: 358-362.

17) Kauffman HM, (2005). *The United Network for Organ Sharing position on using donors with primary central nervous system malignancies.* Transplantation 79: 622-623.

18) Kauffman HM, Cherikh WS, McBride MA, Cheng Y, Hanto DW, (2007). *Deceased donors with a past history of malignancy: An Organ Procurement and Transplantation* Network/ United Network for Organ Sharing update. Transplantation 84: 272-274.

19) Kleinman G, Hochberg F, Richardson E, (1981). *Systemic metastases from medulloblastoma.* Cancer 48: 2296-2309.

20) Newton HB, Henson J, Walker RW, (1992). *Extraneural metastases in ependymoma.* J. Neuro Onc 14: 135-142.

21) OPTN Organ Procurement and Transplantation Network Annual Report, (2009). Accessed Jun 1, 2011: *http://optn.transplant.hrsa.gov/ar2009/default.htm.*

22) Pasquier B, Pasquier D, N'Golet A, (1980). *Extraneural metastases of astrocytomas and glioblastomas: Clinicopathological study of two cases and review of literature.* Cancer 45: 112-125.

23) Penn I, (1997). *Transmission of cancer from organ donors.* Annals of Transplantation 2: 7-12.

24) Pokorna E, Vitko S, (2001). *The fate of recipients of organs from donors with diagnosis of primary brain tumor.* Transplant Int 14: 346-347.

25) Punnett AS, McCarthy L, Dirks P, Hawkins C, Bouffet E, (2004). *Patients with primary brain tumors as organ donors: Case report and review of the literature.* Pediatric Blood & Cancer 43(1):73-77.

26) Schweitzer T, Vince GH, Herbold C, Roosen K, Tonn JC, (2001). *Extraneural metastases of primary brain tumors.* J. Neuro-Oncology 53: 107-114.

27) Subramanian A, Harris A, Piggott K, Schiff C, Bradford R, (2002). *Metastasis to and from the central nervous system--the 'relatively protected site.'* Lancet Oncology 3: 498-507.

28) Watson CJE, Roberts R, Wright KA, (2010). *How safe is it to transplant organs from deceased donors with primary intracranial malignancy? An analysis of UK registry data.* Am J. Transplantation 10: 1437-1444.

References from Chapter 22, Journey of Sadness and Hopes

1) Feudtner C., (Dec 10 2009). *The breadth of hopes.* New Eng J. Med. 361(24): 2306-2307.

2) Feudtner C., (2005). *Hope and the prospects of healing at the end of life.* J. Altern Complement Med. 11 Suppl 1: S23-30.

3) Hinds PS, Oakes LL, Hicks J, et al., (Dec 10 2009). *"Trying to be a good parent" as*

defined by interviews with parents who made phase I, terminal care, and resuscitation decisions for their children. J. Clin Oncol. 27(35): 5979-5985.

4) Duggleby W, Holtslander L, Steeves M, Duggleby-Wenzel S, Cunningham S., (Sep 2010). *Discursive meaning of hope for older persons with advanced cancer and their caregivers.* Can J. Aging. 29(3): 361-367.

5) Mack JW, Hilden JM, Watterson J, et al., (Dec 20 2005). *Parent and physician perspectives on quality of care at the end of life in children with cancer.* J. Clin Oncol. 23(36): 9155-9161.

6) Mack JW, Weeks JC, Wright AA, Block SD, Prigerson HG., (Mar 1 2010). *End-of-life discussions, goal attainment, and distress at the end of life: predictors and outcomes of receipt of care consistent with preferences.* J. Clin Oncol. 28(7): 1203-1208.

7) Meyer EC, Ritholz MD, Burns JP, Truog RD., (Mar 2006). *Improving the quality of end-of-life care in the pediatric intensive care unit: parents' priorities and recommendations.* Pediatrics. 117(3): 649-657.